Praise for *Young Elizabeth*

"Sparkling, pacey and page-turning, Nicola Tallis's brilliant new study of the early life of Elizabeth I is an outstanding achievement. Combining new research with an engaging style, it ticks every box. Highly recommended!"
—**ALISON WEIR**, AUTHOR OF *THE LADY IN THE TOWER*

"Elizabeth I is one of the most popular figures in history, but this stunning portrayal gives us vivid and compelling new insight into the real woman behind the public image. Told with all of the author's characteristic verve and eye for fascinating period detail, the story of the Virgin Queen's turbulent path to the throne is at once surprising, revealing and utterly irresistible. This is Elizabeth I as you have never seen her before."
—**TRACY BORMAN**, AUTHOR OF *ANNE BOLEYN AND ELIZABETH I*

"The key to the legend of Elizabeth I lies in the violence, tragedy and heady danger of her first twenty-five years. She lost her parents, siblings, freedom and innocence far too soon, but emerged as one of the most iconic rulers in English history. Nicola Tallis charts this extraordinary story with sensitivity, scholarship and compassion, shedding light not only on Elizabeth's apprentice years, but also her complete character."
—**JESSIE CHILDS**, AUTHOR OF *THE SIEGE OF LOYALTY HOUSE*

"Empathetic, thoughtful, and well-written, in this story of the Virgin Queen's rise to power, Tallis has proved again why she is fast emerging as one of Britain's most popular historians."
—**GARETH RUSSELL**, AUTHOR OF *THE PALACE*

"A remarkable achievement – Tallis brings to life the glowing girl behind the iconic mask of the later Virgin Queen. With a wealth of detail unfamiliar even to Elizabethan scholars, it represents a vital contribution to our understanding of the woman and her age. Fresh, vibrant and scholarly, this is history at its very best."
—**SARAH GRISTWOOD**, AUTHOR OF *THE TUDORS IN LOVE*

"This sparkling study ... will delight readers who think they know Elizabeth and those who have yet to become acquainted with her perilous path to the throne."
—LINDA PORTER, AUTHOR OF *KATHERINE THE QUEEN: THE REMARKABLE LIFE OF KATHERINE PARR*

"A beautifully crafted account. Tallis brings the young Elizabeth to life with insight and empathy."
—MICHAEL JONES, AUTHOR OF *THE KING'S MOTHER*

"Tallis has all the skill of a Tudor portrait painter, imbuing her study with immense detail, striking realism and vibrant colour. Her Elizabeth is so perfectly captured, she peers out from the pages at you with steely dark eyes ... Taken as a whole, it is a comprehensive and captivating picture of Gloriana's upbringing."
—JOANNE PAUL, AUTHOR OF *THE HOUSE OF DUDLEY*

"In *Young Elizabeth*, Nicola Tallis takes a forensic view of the Princess's difficult early life, using her considerable expertise as an historian to paint a dramatic and believable portrait of a girl whose future never seemed certain ... Brings to life the girl who would later become England's most iconic ruler."
—ELIZABETH NORTON, AUTHOR OF *THE LIVES OF TUDOR WOMEN*

"A mesmerizing and immersive game-changer. Thick with detail and sharp in analysis, Tallis has expertly woven the most complete and compelling picture of Elizabeth's tumultuous youth to date. A welcome corrective to earlier studies, this is scholarly, popular history at its very finest."
—DR OWEN EMMERSON, CO-AUTHOR OF *THE BOLEYNS OF HEVER CASTLE*

"You cannot fully comprehend Elizabeth I, the Queen, without understanding her hardship and struggles before rising to power. Nicola Tallis's *Young Elizabeth* is the biography we needed on these years before Elizabeth was crowned Queen. Compelling, well-researched, and illuminating, this is a must-read for any Tudor lovers."
—ESTELLE PARANQUE, AUTHOR OF *BLOOD, FIRE AND GOLD*

YOUNG ELIZABETH

Elizabeth I and Her Perilous Path to the Crown

NICOLA TALLIS

PEGASUS BOOKS

NEW YORK LONDON

YOUNG ELIZABETH

Pegasus Books, Ltd.
148 West 37th Street, 13th Floor
New York, NY 10018

First Pegasus Books cloth edition February 2024

ISBN: 978-1-63936-584-5

10 9 8 7 6 5 4 3 2 1

Printed in the United States of America
Distributed by Simon & Schuster
www.pegasusbooks.com

For the love of my life: my wonderful husband, Matthew.

'From the very first moment I saw you
That's when I knew
All the dreams I held in my heart
Had suddenly come true.'

CONTENTS

LIST OF ILLUSTRATIONS

Page 1: Museo Nacional Thyssen-Bornemisza, Madrid / Ian Dagnall Computing / Alamy (top left); © National Portrait Gallery, London (top right); DeAgostini / Getty Images (bottom).

Page 2: Magdalena Mayo / Alamy (top); *Dessins D'Ornements de Hans Holbein*, Boussod, Valadon & Cie, 1886 / Penta Springs Limited / Alamy (bottom).

Page 3: © National Portrait Gallery, London (top left); Royal Collection Trust / © His Majesty King Charles III 2023 (top right); Andrew W. Mellon Collection / National Gallery of Art, Washington, D. C. (bottom).

Pages 4-5: Royal Collection Trust / © His Majesty King Charles III 2023.

Page 6: © British Library / Bridgeman Images.

Page 7: © British Library / Bridgeman Images.

Page 8: Chequers Estate / Album / Alamy (top); www.tudorplace.com (bottom left); National Gallery of Ireland / The Picture Art Collection / Alamy (bottom right).

Page 9: Royal Collection / Pictorial Press Ltd. / Alamy.

Page 10: Private collection. Photo © Sotheby's (top left); National Maritime Museum, Greenwich, London / History and Art Collection / Alamy (top right); Antiqua Print Gallery / Alamy (bottom).

THE HOUSE OF TUDOR

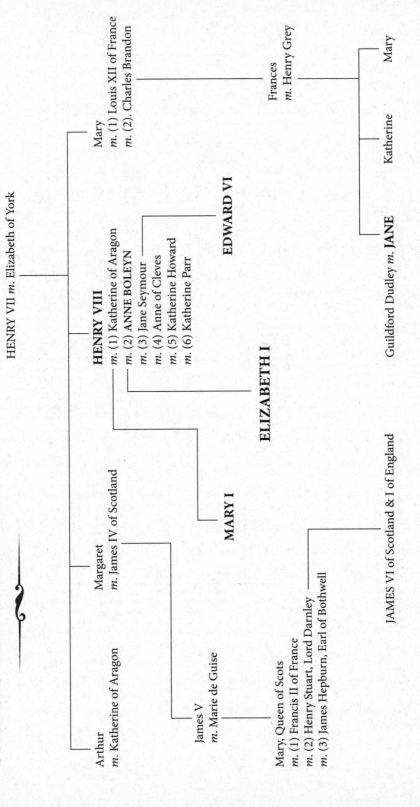

HENRY VII *m.* Elizabeth of York

Arthur
m. Katherine of Aragon

Margaret
m. James IV of Scotland

Mary
m. (1) Louis XII of France
m. (2). Charles Brandon

HENRY VIII
m. (1) Katherine of Aragon
m. (2) **ANNE BOLEYN**
m. (3) Jane Seymour
m. (4) Anne of Cleves
m. (5) Katherine Howard
m. (6) Katherine Parr

James V
m. Marie de Guise

Mary, Queen of Scots
m. (1) Francis II of France
m. (2) Henry Stuart, Lord Darnley
m. (3) James Hepburn, Earl of Bothwell

JAMES VI of Scotland & I of England

MARY I

ELIZABETH I

EDWARD VI

Frances
m. Henry Grey

Guildford Dudley *m.* **JANE**

Katherine

Mary

THE BOLEYN FAMILY

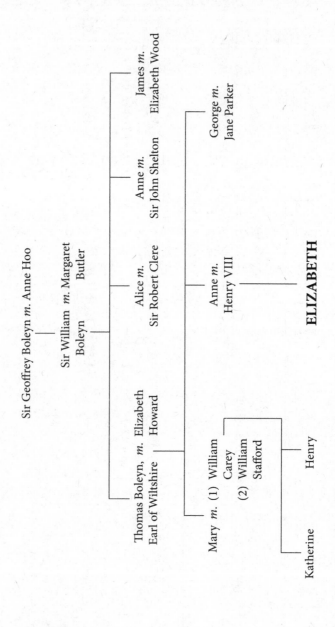

Sir Geoffrey Boleyn *m.* Anne Hoo

Sir William *m.* Margaret
Boleyn   Butler

Thomas Boleyn, *m.* Elizabeth
Earl of Wiltshire   Howard

Alice *m.*
Sir Robert Clere

Anne *m.*
Sir John Shelton

James *m.*
Elizabeth Wood

Mary *m.* (1) William
Carey
(2) William
Stafford

Anne *m.*
Henry VIII

George *m.*
Jane Parker

Katherine

Henry

ELIZABETH

NOTE: For the purposes of clarity I have simplified this family tree and included only those who feature in *Young Elizabeth*.

THROUGHOUT HER YOUTH Elizabeth met, encountered, knew, and engaged with countless people, some of whom had a greater impact on shaping her life than others. To acquaint the reader with these extraordinary personalities, I give below a short biographical sketch of those who played a key part in Elizabeth's story.

Anne of Cleves (1515–57)

Henry VIII's fourth wife was born in Düsseldorf, the daughter of John, Duke of Cleves, and his wife Maria. Little is known about her youth, but she was not particularly well educated. She married Henry VIII on 6 January 1540 at Greenwich, but on 9 July the marriage was dissolved. Anne remained in England for the rest of her life, and seemingly had some involvement in the Wyatt Rebellion. She died at Chelsea on 16 July 1557.

Ascham, Roger (*c.* 1515–68)

The renowned scholar Roger Ascham was born in Yorkshire, but was fortunate enough to have been educated at St John's College, Cambridge. He was part of a circle who were closely associated with Elizabeth, and in 1548 he assumed the post of her tutor at her personal insistence. Ascham was impressed with Elizabeth and the two got along extremely well. In 1550 he left her household under a cloud, in circumstances that are unclear, but by 1555 the two were once more on good terms. Ascham also served as Latin secretary to Mary I.

Astley, Katherine (*c.* 1502–65)

Elizabeth's beloved lady mistress arrived in her household in 1536, and she would remain with her charge for the rest of her life. Better known as

Kate, she was responsible for Elizabeth's earliest lessons, and was devoted to her charge. Arrested several times during the reigns of Edward VI and Mary I, Kate survived her experiences and went on to become first Lady of the Bedchamber when Elizabeth became Queen. She wielded huge influence over Elizabeth, who was left devastated at her death.

Bedingfield, Sir Henry (1505–83)

The man charged with Elizabeth's custody in the spring of 1554 until the following year, Sir Henry Bedingfield was the son of Sir Edmund Bedingfield and his wife Grace. Bedingfield held office under Edward VI but was particularly favoured by Mary I, whose claim to the throne he had supported during the summer coup of 1553. Following Elizabeth's accession, Bedingfield withdrew from public life and spent the remainder of his life in Norfolk.

Boleyn, Anne (*c.* 1501–36)

Elizabeth's mother was the daughter of Sir Thomas Boleyn and Elizabeth Howard. She spent part of her youth in the courts of Europe, and served Katherine of Aragon upon her return to England. After Anne caught Henry VIII's eye in the mid-1520s, he pursued her relentlessly, showering her with gifts. In January 1533 the two were secretly married, by which time Anne was already pregnant. On 7 September she gave birth to Elizabeth at Greenwich Palace. A string of subsequent failed pregnancies meant that Elizabeth was to be her only child, and Anne doted on her. In the spring of 1536, however, almost certainly under the auspices of Thomas Cromwell, Anne was arrested on charges including treason, adultery and incest. Having been tried and condemned, she was executed on 19 May.

Brooke, Elisabeth, Marchioness of Northampton (1526–65)

Elisabeth Brooke was the daughter of George Brooke, ninth Baron Cobham, and his wife Anne, who served several of Henry VIII's wives including Anne Boleyn. Elisabeth joined the household of Katherine Parr, and it was here that she probably met young Elizabeth for the first time. The two became friends, a friendship that would endure for the rest of Elisabeth's life. She became embroiled in an affair with Katherine Parr's brother William, and after a long and complex legal case involving his first wife, he and Elisabeth were eventually married. Sadly, Elisabeth died of breast cancer on 2 April 1565.

Bryan, Lady Margaret (*c.* 1468–*c.* 1551/2)

Elizabeth's first lady mistress was born Margaret Bourchier, and would serve her siblings Mary and Edward in the same capacity. She also served in the household of Katherine of Aragon. Married three times, it was through her second marriage to Sir Thomas Bryan that Margaret became Lady Bryan. She appears to have been very fond of Elizabeth, but transferred to the household of Prince Edward upon the latter's birth in 1537. Little is known of the end of her life.

Cecil, William (1520–98)

Elizabeth was to form a close, lifelong working partnership with Lincolnshire-born William Cecil, the son of Sir Richard Cecil and his wife Jane. Having been educated at St John's College, Cambridge, William later served Edward Seymour, the Lord Protector. He then earned the favour of John Dudley, and in 1550 became one of two secretaries of state to Edward VI. Cecil also managed Elizabeth's estates for her, providing her with much wise advice. Upon Elizabeth's accession he became her chief advisor, and he held other offices throughout her reign. In 1571 he was ennobled as Baron Burghley. The grand Burghley House in Stamford, Lincolnshire, was built for him.

Charles V, Holy Roman Emperor (1500–1558)

The nephew of Katherine of Aragon and cousin of Mary I, Charles V was the son of Philip of Castile and his wife Juana. Charles was the ruler of the vast Habsburg dominions, but despite this he took an active interest in affairs in England and Mary I relied on his advice. He married Isabella of Portugal, but she died in 1539 leaving her husband grief-stricken. Charles never remarried, and having abdicated in 1556, he retired to Spain. He died at the Monastery of Yuste.

Courtenay, Edward, first Earl of Devon (*c.* 1527–56)

During the reign of Mary I, Courtenay's name was to become closely linked with that of Elizabeth, and there were plots for the two of them to be married. A great-grandson of Edward IV, by reason of his blood Courtenay spent most of his youth imprisoned in the Tower of London following the Exeter Conspiracy, which led to the execution of his father. He was released by Mary in 1553 and proposed as a possible marriage candidate for the Queen, although she never considered him to be an option. Courtenay became embroiled in the Wyatt Rebellion in 1554, which saw him returned to the Tower. He was removed to Fotheringhay Castle in the spring, but was released the following year and sent into foreign exile. He died in Padua.

Dormer, Jane (1538–1612)

One of the sources for Elizabeth's life, Jane Dormer was the daughter of Sir William Dormer and Mary Sidney. Jane was a playmate to Elizabeth's brother Edward, but would become a close friend and servant to her sister Mary, to whom she was wholeheartedly loyal. After Mary's death Jane married Philip's envoy Count de Feria, and the couple had two sons. In 1559 they moved to Spain, and in 1567 Jane became a duchess when Philip II made her husband Duke de Feria. She remained in Spain for the rest of her life.

Dudley, John, Duke of Northumberland (1504–53)

Following the execution of his father in 1510, John Dudley – the eldest son of Edmund Dudley and Elizabeth Grey – soon became the ward of

Sir Edward Guildford. Raised in Guildford's household, John married his daughter Jane in 1525 and, together, the couple would have thirteen children. John rose in Henry VIII's favour throughout the King's reign, but it was under Edward VI that he really came to prominence. Created Duke of Northumberland in October 1551, by then he was the most powerful man in the land. In the aftermath of the failed coup to place his daughter-in-law Lady Jane Grey on the throne in 1553, however – which John had fully endorsed and supported – he was arrested. Despite his pleas for mercy, he was executed on the orders of Mary I on 22 August 1553.

Edward VI (1537–53)

Elizabeth's brother was born at Hampton Court on 12 October 1537, Henry VIII's only child with Jane Seymour. He and Elizabeth spent much of their childhoods together and were very close. Following Edward's accession to the throne in 1547 at the age of nine, the siblings were rarely together, and Edward died on 6 July 1553 aged fifteen. He was buried in Westminster Abbey.

FitzGerald, Elizabeth (1527–90)

One of Elizabeth's close friends, Elizabeth FitzGerald was the daughter of Gerald FitzGerald, Earl of Kildare, and Elizabeth Grey. She was born in Ireland, but primarily raised at the English court where she appears to have joined Elizabeth's household at a young age. The two were very close, and remained so for the rest of their lives. In 1543 Elizabeth was married to Sir Anthony Browne, and the couple had two children, though sadly they both died young. Elizabeth's husband died in 1548, and in 1552 she married for a second time. Her second husband was the widowed Edward Clinton (later first Earl of Lincoln). Elizabeth died in 1590, and is buried in St George's Chapel, Windsor.

Gardiner, Stephen (1483–1555)

Gardiner hailed from Suffolk and was educated at Cambridge. He served Cardinal Wolsey, and in assisting efforts to procure the Pope's agreement to the annulment of the King's marriage to Katherine of Aragon, played a role in Henry VIII's 'Great Matter'. In 1531 he was given the bishopric of Winchester, and in 1535 he served as English ambassador at the French court for three years. Gardiner's career was far less successful under Edward VI, however, and he was imprisoned following his opposition to the King's religious reforms. He was released when Mary I came to the throne and she created him Lord Chancellor. Gardiner died on 12 November 1555, and was buried in Westminster Abbey.

Grey, Lady Jane (1536?–54)

The daughter of Henry Grey, third Marquess of Dorset and later Duke of Suffolk by his wife Frances Brandon, Jane was the granddaughter of Mary Tudor, Henry VIII's younger sister. An exceptionally academically gifted young lady, Jane became the ward of Sir Thomas Seymour and spent some time with Katherine Parr – and possibly also Elizabeth. In 1553 Edward VI nominated Jane to succeed him, but after a reign of just thirteen days she was deposed in favour of Mary I. On 12 February 1554, Jane was executed for treason following her father's complicity in the Wyatt Rebellion.

Henry VIII (1491–1547)

Elizabeth's father was born at Greenwich Palace on 28 June 1491, the second son of Henry VII and Elizabeth of York. His elder brother Arthur having predeceased their father, Henry succeeded to the throne following the death of Henry VII on 21 April 1509, and was crowned in Westminster Abbey on 24 June. He would marry six times, his second wife being Anne Boleyn, Elizabeth's mother. He also had several known mistresses, and one acknowledged illegitimate child. Henry died on 28 January 1547, and was buried beside Jane Seymour in St George's Chapel, Windsor Castle.

Howard, Katherine (1522/3–42)

Katherine Howard, Henry VIII's fifth wife, was a cousin of Anne Boleyn
and thus tied to Elizabeth by blood. She had spent much of her youth
in the household of her step-grandmother, Agnes Tilney, Dowager
Duchess of Norfolk, where she had relationships with Henry Manox and
Francis Dereham. Katherine served in the household of Anne of Cleves,
where she caught the King's eye. She and Henry were married on 28
July 1540, and the King was utterly infatuated with his young wife. After
Katherine's past indiscretions were discovered, however, together with
those she had committed with Thomas Culpeper, she was executed on
13 February 1542.

Katherine of Aragon (1485–1536)

The youngest daughter of Ferdinand of Aragon and Isabella of Castile
arrived in England in 1501 for her marriage to Henry VII's eldest son,
Prince Arthur. Following Arthur's death in 1502, Katherine remained
in England, marrying Henry VIII in 1509. The couple had one surviving child, the future Mary I. In 1527 Henry began proceedings to have
his marriage to Katherine annulled, much to Katherine's distress. The
proceedings dragged on for many years, and as they did, Katherine's
health declined. She died on 7 January 1536.

Mary I (1516–58)

The only surviving child of Henry VIII and Katherine of Aragon was
born on 18 February 1516 at Greenwich Palace. Mary enjoyed a happy
childhood until her parents separated and she was forced to join the
household of her baby sister, Elizabeth. Although she was reconciled with
her father after Anne Boleyn's execution, Mary's scars from this traumatic
time never healed. She became Queen following the successful deposition
of her cousin, Lady Jane Grey, in the summer of 1553. On 25 July 1554
Mary married her second cousin, Philip of Spain, although to her great

sorrow they never had any children. Mary died on 17 November 1558 at St James's Palace. She is buried with Elizabeth in Westminster Abbey.

Parr, Katherine (1512–48)

Henry VIII's sixth wife was born in 1512, the daughter of Sir Thomas Parr and Maud Green. An exceptionally intelligent woman, by the time Katherine married the King in 1543 she had been widowed twice. She was a devoted stepmother who doted on Elizabeth and her siblings, with whom she shared academic interests. Following the death of Henry VIII in 1547, Katherine remarried again, this time to Sir Thomas Seymour. She died at Sudeley Castle on 5 September 1548 of puerperal fever, six days after giving birth to her only child.

Parry, Thomas (c. 1515–60)

Parry hailed from a family of Welsh origin, and later joined the household of Elizabeth as her cofferer (treasurer). He was married to Anne, the widowed Lady Fortescue, by whom he had four children. In 1549 Parry was sent to the Tower and questioned over his involvement in the Seymour scandal, but he was later released and allowed to re-join Elizabeth's household. He remained in her service for the rest of his life, and was buried in Westminster Abbey when he died.

Philip of Spain (1527–98)

Elizabeth's brother-in-law was the son of the Holy Roman Emperor Charles V and Isabella of Portugal. He was married four times, with Mary I being his second wife. A devout Catholic, Philip became King of Naples and Sicily in 1554, King of Spain in 1556, and King of Portugal in 1580. In 1588 he famously sent his Armada to invade England, but his fleet was defeated, as were subsequent invasion attempts. He died near Madrid on 13 September 1598, and was succeeded by his son, Philip III.

Renard, Simon (1513–73)

An enemy to Elizabeth, Simon Renard served as the Imperial ambassador at the English court during the reign of Mary I. Mary relied on Renard's advice, and he in turn helped to negotiate her marriage to Philip of Spain. In 1555 he was recalled from England, although he retained an interest in English affairs.

Seymour, Edward, Duke of Somerset (1500–1552)

The elder brother of Queen Jane Seymour, Edward Seymour became Duke of Somerset and Lord Protector in 1547 during the minority of his nephew, Edward VI. He was toppled from power in 1549, and though he was briefly restored to his place on the King's Council the following year, in the autumn of 1551 he was sent to the Tower. On 22 January 1552 Somerset was executed on charges of felony.

Seymour, Jane (1509–37)

The first of Elizabeth's stepmothers was the daughter of Sir John Seymour and Margery Wentworth. Jane served both Katherine of Aragon and Anne Boleyn before her own marriage to Henry VIII on 30 May 1536. On 12 October 1537 Jane gave birth to Edward, Henry's only legitimate son. Tragically, she died twelve days later on 24 October. She is buried with her husband in St George's Chapel, Windsor Castle.

Seymour, Thomas, Lord High Admiral (c. 1508–49)

The brother of both Jane and Edward Seymour, Thomas also had a role to play at the Tudor court. Though he was never as highly favoured as his brother Edward, Henry VIII did entrust him with several diplomatic missions throughout his reign. Following Henry's death Thomas secretly married the King's widow, Katherine Parr, and moved in with her and Elizabeth at Chelsea. When Katherine died days after giving birth to their only child in September 1548, Thomas's behaviour grew increasingly erratic, and he was arrested in January 1549. On 20 March he was executed for treason.

Troy, Lady Blanche Herbert of (14?–*c.* 1557)

Blanche Milborne, Lady Herbert of Troy, was Elizabeth's one-time lady mistress. She was married twice, and was also the aunt of Blanche Parry, one of Elizabeth's closest ladies. Little is known of her relationship with her charge, but given that she received a pension after she left Elizabeth's service, it appears that it was reasonably close. Lady Troy seems to have retired to Troy House in Monmouthshire, and it was probably here that she died. Her date of death is unknown, but it was certainly before Elizabeth's accession and probably in 1557.

Tyrwhit, Sir Robert (*c.* 1504–72)

The man who acted as Elizabeth's custodian at Hatfield while the Seymour scandal played out in 1549 had been Katherine Parr's Master of Horse. Tyrwhit made his home at Leighton Bromswold in Cambridgeshire, and it was here that he died in 1572.

Wyatt, Sir Thomas (1521–54)

The son of the poet and namesake Thomas Wyatt who had once engaged in the game of courtly love with Anne Boleyn, Wyatt hailed from Allington Castle in Kent. He married Jane Haute, by whom he had numerous children, but he placed his family life in jeopardy when he rebelled against Mary I at the beginning of 1554. The Wyatt Rebellion to which he gave his name ended in failure, and Thomas was executed on 11 April.

TIMELINE

28 June 1491	Future Henry VIII born at Greenwich Palace
c. 1501	Probable year of Anne Boleyn's birth
21 April 1509	Accession of Henry VIII
18 February 1516	Princess Mary born at Greenwich Palace
1527	Henry VIII begins proceedings to have his marriage to Katherine of Aragon annulled
January 1533	Henry VIII and Anne Boleyn are secretly married
7 September 1533	Princess Elizabeth born at Greenwich Palace
23 March 1534	First Act of Succession passed by Parliament
7 January 1536	Katherine of Aragon dies at Kimbolton Castle
2 May 1536	Anne Boleyn taken to the Tower of London
19 May 1536	Execution of Anne Boleyn
30 May 1536	Henry VIII marries Jane Seymour
8 June 1536	Second Act of Succession passed by Parliament
12 October 1537	Prince Edward born at Hampton Court
24 October 1537	Jane Seymour dies at Hampton Court
6 January 1540	Henry VIII marries Anne of Cleves
9 July 1540	Marriage of Henry VIII and Anne of Cleves dissolved
28 July 1540	Henry VIII marries Katherine Howard
13 February 1542	Execution of Katherine Howard
12 July 1543	Henry VIII marries Katherine Parr
7 February 1544	Third Act of Succession passed by Parliament
30 December 1546	Henry VIII makes his final will
28 January 1547	Henry VIII dies at the Palace of Whitehall
16 February 1547	Funeral of Henry VIII
20 February 1547	Coronation of Edward VI

May 1548	Elizabeth leaves Katherine Parr's household
5 September 1548	Katherine Parr dies at Sudeley Castle
January 1549	Sir Robert Tyrwhit begins questioning Elizabeth
20 March 1549	Execution of Sir Thomas Seymour
Christmas 1550	Elizabeth joins Edward VI's court
March 1552	Elizabeth visits Edward VI
6 July 1553	Edward VI dies at Greenwich Palace
10 July 1553	Lady Jane Grey publicly proclaimed Queen at the Tower
19 July 1553	Jane deposed, Mary I proclaimed Queen
3 August 1553	Elizabeth joins Mary's ceremonial entry into London
1 October 1553	Coronation of Mary I
12 January 1554	Marriage treaty of Mary I and Philip of Spain signed
25 January 1554	Sir Thomas Wyatt raises his standard at Maidstone
7 February 1554	Sir Thomas Wyatt surrenders
12 February 1554	Elizabeth leaves Ashridge for London
12 February 1554	Execution of Lady Jane Grey
23 February 1554	Elizabeth arrives at the Palace of Whitehall
18 March 1554	Elizabeth taken to the Tower
11 April 1554	Execution of Sir Thomas Wyatt
19 May 1554	Elizabeth taken from the Tower to Richmond
20 May 1554	Elizabeth leaves Richmond for Woodstock
23 May 1554	Elizabeth arrives at Woodstock Palace
25 July 1554	Marriage of Mary and Philip in Winchester Cathedral
4 February 1555	First burning of Mary I's reign takes place
17 April 1555	Elizabeth summoned to Hampton Court
March 1556	Dudley Conspiracy discovered
January 1558	England loses Calais, its last French possession
25 February 1558	Elizabeth arrives in London to visit Mary for the final time
17 November 1558	Mary I dies, Elizabeth I succeeds to the throne
15 January 1559	Coronation of Elizabeth I

AUTHOR'S NOTE

IT HAS BEEN a great delight to have had the opportunity to read many of Elizabeth's original letters, and I am most grateful to her for having had both a very beautiful – and for the purposes of my job – clear hand. The same cannot be said for many of her contemporaries! It has nevertheless given me four years of immense pleasure reading and transcribing the materials that often so vividly paint the picture of Elizabeth's youth, both in her own words and in the words of those who shared her world. Though the original sixteenth-century spellings undoubtedly add to the charm of the period, as always, I have modernized all spelling and punctuation from contemporary sources to allow for a clearer narrative.

Elizabeth had two half-siblings, Mary and Edward, both of whom were also half-siblings of each other. She herself, however, primarily referred to them as her 'sister' and 'brother', and thus to avoid jarring the narrative I have chosen to do the same.

All monetary values have been presented with the contemporary amount, followed by the modern-day equivalent in parentheses. All conversions were done according to the National Archives Currency Convertor (www.nationalarchives.gov.uk/currency-converter) and are approximate values. Please be aware that they may be subject to change.

For clarity, all dates have been calculated using the Gregorian calendar, under which the year turns on 1 January.

THE SOURCES FOR Elizabeth's life are abundant, and though they are less plentiful in places when it comes to her youth, enough survive to paint a vivid and revealing picture of the youngster who would become one of England's most famous queens. We must be grateful for the fact that a number of Elizabeth's own letters survive, distributed between archives, which include the British Library and the National Archives, and written to several recipients. Some of these concern matters of business that reveal the way in which she managed her affairs, while others, written to her stepmother Katherine Parr and her brother Edward VI, for example, show a more personal side of her character and the relationships she shared with members of her family. Many of these letters were also written in her own hand, providing us with the opportunity to witness the beautiful italic handwriting that she was taught in her youth, signed with the beginnings of the elaborate signature for which she would become famed.

Some letters were also written in times of distress, such as the flurry sent to Edward Seymour, Duke of Somerset, when Elizabeth faced interrogation as the Seymour scandal unfolded. These provide an insight into her troubled state of mind as she sought desperately to extricate both herself and her servants from the taint of treason. Most emotive is the famous 'Tide Letter' that Elizabeth wrote on the eve of being sent to the Tower of London, where she faced questioning for her complicity in the Wyatt Rebellion. The letter is truly remarkable, and such survivals provide us with tangible glimpses into her emotions at the most vulnerable times in her life.

Charming details of Elizabeth's childhood come from the letters of her first lady mistress, Lady Margaret Bryan, who wrote to Thomas Cromwell regarding key decisions in the royal infant's life. These provide unique glimpses into how Elizabeth was raised, and the protocol behind how such decisions were made. Likewise, the small snapshots that were provided by

Henry VIII's courtiers give us an insight into how she was developing and her relationship with her father. The evidence regarding her short relationship with her mother is fragmentary, but nevertheless revealing in places.

We also have Elizabeth's household accounts from October 1551 to September 1552, which reveal much about her lifestyle, the relationships she shared, and how she spent her money. These add a splash of colour to the period of her life when she was concentrating on rehabilitating her image in the aftermath of the Seymour scandal and living as a wealthy landowner and mistress of her own household.

Accounts survive from some of those who knew her, most notably Jane Dormer, later Duchess of Feria. Though Jane witnessed some of the events of Elizabeth's youth first-hand, her affinity to Elizabeth's sister Mary made her naturally hostile to Elizabeth when the relationship between the two sisters deteriorated. This becomes apparent when reading Jane's account: in one instance she refers to a great lady who knew Elizabeth 'very well, being a girl of twelve or thirteen, [who] told me that she was proud and disdainful, and related to me some particulars of her scornful behaviour, which much blemished the handsomeness and beauty of her person'. Some of Elizabeth's known behaviour suggests that there is a degree of truth in this, but there is no escaping Jane's obvious dislike of Elizabeth. The same is true of the ambassador's reports of Eustace Chapuys and Simon Renard, both of whom, though well informed in certain respects, were no friends to Elizabeth thanks to their loathing of her mother and proximity to Mary.

Others were more flattering, perhaps too much so. The chronicler William Camden, for example, wrote his account of Elizabeth's life at the suggestion of William Cecil. Although Camden did not begin the work until 1607, several years after Elizabeth's death, it is an extremely complimentary work. Some of his sources are uncertain, for although he had access to many who would have known Elizabeth, he only refers specifically to two. By the same token, *The Miraculous Preservation of the Lady Elizabeth, now Queen of England*, by the martyrologist John Foxe, is also heavily biased in Elizabeth's favour. It was published in 1563 as part of his *Acts and Monuments* (better known as the Book of Martyrs), and was highly critical of the sufferings Protestants had been forced to endure. It was a hugely influential text that served to blacken the reputation – unfairly, in many respects – of Mary I, but in terms of the narrative concerning Elizabeth and her treatment, much of it seems to be accurate and can be partially corroborated by other sources. Foxe was evidently well informed and obviously had a source who was well placed to know the truth of Elizabeth's experiences during Mary's reign. David Starkey has surmised that it was Dorothy Stafford, the second wife of Elizabeth's uncle by marriage, William Stafford, who supplied Foxe with most of the details for the *Miraculous Preservation*, and that is certainly a possibility although she had not been present herself at any of the events documented.[1] Dorothy and her family were living in Geneva, but she would later be greatly favoured by Elizabeth and may be the same Mrs Stafford who is referenced in her 1551–2 accounts.[2]

Documentary sources are extremely effective when it comes to piecing together the complex jigsaw of Elizabeth's youth, but they are not all we have to go on. We are also fortunate to have several portraits of young Elizabeth, most notably the stunning example in the Royal Collection. She appears too in *The Family of Henry VIII* and another, smaller version of a family portrait in the collection of the Duke of Buccleuch and Queensberry, which is a copy of a work that was probably painted during the reign of Edward VI. A further portrait of her can be found at Hever Castle, all of these together serving as evidence of Elizabeth's appearance and confirming her status and value as a member of the royal family.[3] In addition, there are several surviving pieces of material culture that we can link to Elizabeth, including two of the beautifully embroidered New Year's gifts that she gave to her stepmother, Katherine Parr. Not only do these showcase her handwriting, but they also reveal her talent when it came to needlework. Another surviving object from later in her life is the Chequers ring, discussed in Chapter Three. The ring, now at Chequers, the Buckinghamshire residence of the Prime Minister, is a stunning example of a jewel that was owned by Elizabeth. Given its size and the fact that the two tiny portraits within it would only have been visible when Elizabeth chose to view them, it is possible that it served as a personal reminder to her of the mother she had barely known.

Westminster Abbey, 15 January 1559

AGAINST THE BACKDROP of the High Altar in Westminster Abbey, twenty-five-year-old Elizabeth sat enthroned in the ancient, gilded St Edward's Chair that had been used for the anointing of monarchs since the fourteenth century.[1] The majesty of the moment was perfectly enhanced by the splendid thirteenth-century Cosmati pavement on which Elizabeth's throne stood. Crafted by workmen from Rome on the orders of Henry III, the beautifully coloured mosaics contained more than thirty thousand pieces of stone and glass, as well as three inscriptions in brass that referred to the end of the world.[2] Coupled with the young Queen's opulent jewels, these created a scene gleaming with colour.

Her surroundings on this most significant of days were truly magnificent, for the historic Westminster Abbey had been beautifully decorated with the most luxurious tapestries that had once been owned by her father. Featuring scenes from the biblical books of Genesis and the Acts of the Apostles, the tapestries had been woven from a design by the great Italian artist Raphael, and there were others in the Abbey that illustrated the stories of Caesar and Pompey.[3] Resplendent in her sumptuous coronation robes that had formerly been worn by her sister Mary, Elizabeth listened as those in the Abbey were asked if they wished her to be their crowned Queen. The answer was a resounding 'yes', and as the organs, trumpets and drums began to play and the bells rang, 'it seemed as if the world were come to an end'.[4] She then sat serenely as the Bishop of Carlisle placed the sacred St Edward's Crown ceremoniously on her head. Glittering with precious gemstones, the crown had been worn not only by Elizabeth's royal predecessors at the moment of their anointing but also by her mother, Anne Boleyn, at her coronation a quarter of a century earlier. In the final, tangible demonstrations of her power, Elizabeth was presented with the sceptre and the rod as signifiers of royal justice and command.[5]

With Elizabeth having been anointed and crowned, her position was consolidated and reaffirmed: she was Queen of England. The triumphant moment is captured beautifully in a portrait of the young Queen dating from forty years later but probably based on a lost original.[6] Her rich locks of red hair, inherited from her father, hang loose beneath her crown in a sign of virginity, while the dark eyes, which resembled her mother's, stare confidently ahead. Her left hand rests on the orb, while in her right she holds the sceptre, both symbols of her sovereign authority. Her coronation marked a hugely poignant moment for Elizabeth; a moment that had once seemed an impossibility.

INTRODUCTION

'SHE WAS OF admirable beauty, and well deserving a crown, of a modest gravity, excellent wit, royal soul, happy memory, and indefatigably given to the study of learning.'[1] These admiring words, full of honeyed praise, were those of William Camden, first biographer of Elizabeth I in the early seventeenth century. Though Camden may have been the first, he will not be the last to write such a glowing appraisal of the Tudor Queen whose fame has echoed down the passages of time and who continues to inspire endless fascination. I have written about extraordinary women before, but Elizabeth goes beyond the extraordinary. It is little wonder that to writers, historians, novelists and the like, the lure of Elizabeth is irresistible, and I am no exception.

In many ways it is surprising that my attempt to untangle part of her story has taken so long, for thanks to my mother's careful history lessons during childhood, I have been captivated by her – and surrounded by her – since I was very young. Upon a visit to Hatfield House my interest was piqued by the gorgeous silk stockings, hat and gloves once traditionally thought to have been owned by the Tudor Queen, which were all on proud display in the Long Gallery. Such tangible mementoes only reinforced my curiosity, and before long Elizabeth's image, decked in the costly jewels and fine fabrics that she adored, could be found among the posters of my childhood bedroom. I was intrigued by the woman who gazed out from the canvas, who gave no hint of the trauma and uncertainty that had shaped her early life. On my fourteenth birthday my mother painstakingly created the most beautiful Elizabeth cake, hand-painting the Queen's image as she appears in the awe-inspiring Ditchley portrait (much to the astonishment of my friends!). Likewise, as I type in my study, I am surrounded by Elizabeth souvenirs that I have collected from historical sites over the course of many years: candles, postcards, jigsaws, figurines and key rings to name but a few.

While researching and writing *Elizabeth's Rival* in 2016 and 2017, a biography of Elizabeth's kinswoman Lettice Knollys, I was given an opportunity to become acquainted with Elizabeth once more. However, the Elizabeth who I came to see was not the Gloriana that is often conjured to mind when one thinks of the famous Queen. Instead, I felt I was getting to know Elizabeth the woman, and it was not always a pretty sight. A woman who could be jealous of her female contemporaries, was capable of throwing tantrums and prone to being fiercely competitive, this Elizabeth is hard to imagine as we view the steady gaze and serenity of the iconic Queen who looks out at us from her resplendent portraits.

Often, when we think of Elizabeth, it is indeed the image of her as she appears on canvas that springs to mind: a Queen who many revere and who altered perceptions about female monarchy. Yet, aside from the first couple of years of her life when she was her father's official heir, Elizabeth's prospects of ruling the country in which she was born into the royal family were, at one time, all but zero. The stigma of illegitimacy, cast upon her by her own father, meant that she was cut out of the line of succession before her third birthday. When she was officially restored in 1544 by Act of Parliament, her chances of queenship were still only slender and she remained illegitimate. It was not until the reign of her sister, Mary, that what was once a remote possibility became an increasing certainty.

Elizabeth's path to the throne was far from smooth. Besides her enduring the humiliation of being declared illegitimate, she also had to cope with the horror of her mother's decapitation within the confines of the Tower of London at the hands of an expert French swordsman. For two decades of her life, she was forced to play a supporting role of daughter and sister as her father and siblings wore England's crown, not knowing what her own future might hold. This brought with it trials and tribulations, for under their rules Elizabeth was faced with accusations of intrigue, plotting and treason – allegations that once, on her sister Mary's orders, saw her incarcerated in the very same fortress where her mother had lost her life.

Elizabeth, however, was not destined to meet her end within those walls and would eventually be freed from the Tower, though she would never be welcomed back into her sister's court – or her heart – again.

Her relationship with Mary, though once warm, had in many ways been doomed to failure from the outset, through no fault of either woman; the circumstances of Elizabeth's birth were the cause of Mary's torment, and neither could ever fully disentangle themselves from the past. The success of Elizabeth's mother Anne Boleyn in capturing the heart of her father, Henry VIII, resulting in the downfall of Mary's mother, Katherine of Aragon, was a bitter pill that Mary would never be able to swallow. Following her release from the Tower, Elizabeth would spend the remainder of Mary's reign under a cloud of suspicion, but as the 1550s progressed one thing became ever more apparent: with no children to succeed her, Mary had made Elizabeth's path to the throne inevitable. Her failure to produce an heir would pave the way for her sister's triumph.

Henry VIII's younger daughter experienced instability and upheaval from her earliest childhood, enduring grief, suspicion and imprisonment, all resulting in fear, anxiety and a guarded reserve. As Queen, she would craft her name as one of England's most famous monarchs, whose memory has been both celebrated and reviled. But now we must ask how she got there. How did Elizabeth's youth shape her as a person, both in personal terms and when reflecting on the events that led to her accession in 1558? This resilient and pragmatic young woman is the Elizabeth I wanted to find, if I could.

The young Elizabeth has, though, proved at times to be something of an elusive character. Her mother, Anne Boleyn, is the most controversial woman ever to have worn the English crown, yet there is no evidence, for example, that documents how or when Elizabeth learned of her brutal death in May 1536. Such gaps are, of course, frustrating, and in their place the best we can offer are potential theories as to how this event might have impacted on Anne's two-and-a-half-year-old daughter.

Many of Elizabeth's letters, written prior to her accession, survive – some more interesting in content than others.[2] Several were written in her own hand, others were written by a scribe following her dictation but are nevertheless fascinating and revealing in terms of Elizabeth as an individual, a landowner and a friend. One, written to her sister in 1554, is traumatic, giving us an all-too-clear insight into Elizabeth's frame of mind at the most terrifying time of her life, when she faced imprisonment and feared death in the Tower of London, the vision of her mother's head being severed from her body no doubt central in her mind. These are the sources that allow us to witness the 'real' Elizabeth and her vulnerability as a youth in the backbiting, sinister world of Tudor politics.

As Elizabeth's contemporary, Jane Dormer, remembered, 'To write all that might be said of her would fill many volumes.'[3] Elizabeth was a complex figure of many layers, which became ever more apparent over the course of her sixty-nine years of life. This is part of the reason why she is so captivating to scholars and biographers today, and the events of her reign, her relationships, and other areas of her life continue to form the subject of many books, articles, television programmes and the like – a fascination that will surely continue for years to come. Yet the last substantial account of her youth was written more than two decades ago, and thus the time for a fresh appraisal is long overdue.[4]

In writing this book, the Elizabeth to whom I introduce my readers in the first twenty-five years of her life is not the famous Queen. She is instead both a girl and a young woman whose place in the world is uncertain, and whose voice can often be heard through her own words, in her letters and the conversations we know she had. An Elizabeth who is human – a real person who experienced trauma and loss, elation, moments of happiness, astonishing uncertainty and insecurity, fear and, ultimately, success. She endured such emotions on a scale few of us in the twenty-first century will ever be able to fully comprehend. As we will see, she is one whose experience and suffering in childhood tested her endurance and strength of character – and eventually drove her to accede to the throne. That is the Elizabeth whose story this book aims to tell: the infant, the child, the teenager and the young adult who successfully navigated unchartered waters on her unexpected journey from disinherited princess to Queen of England.

Part One

1533–46

'For default of such issue the said Imperial crown and other the premises shall be to the Lady Elizabeth, the King's second daughter, and to the heirs of the body of the said Lady Elizabeth lawfully begotten.'

THIRD ACT OF SUCCESSION, 1544

CHAPTER 1

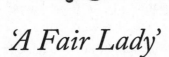

'A Fair Lady'

'The King holding it certain by the report of his physicians and astrologers that the Lady would bear a son, has determined to hold rejoicings and solemn jousts.'

EUSTACE CHAPUYS, 3 SEPTEMBER 1533

W ITH FINE BAY windows, beautifully laid-out gardens and a plethora of fruit orchards, the sprawling red-brick Greenwich Palace was magnificent. Situated on the banks of the River Thames around eight miles downriver from Westminster, the original house, named Bella Court, had been built in the fifteenth century by Humphrey, Duke of Gloucester, uncle and regent to Henry VI. Following Gloucester's disgrace as a result of a scandal that saw his wife tried and convicted for necromancy, and his death amid rumours of poison in 1447, his home had become the property of Henry's Queen, Margaret of Anjou, who renamed it Placentia, meaning 'pleasant place'.[1] It had been a favoured royal residence ever since, and Henry VII spent vast sums transforming Greenwich into a palace fit for the monarch and his court. His son and successor Henry VIII cherished a particular fondness for Greenwich, for he had been born there on 28 June 1491 and often used the Palace for the lavish entertainments that were a regular feature at his court. In the early autumn of 1533, as he waited there for the result of Queen Anne Boleyn's first pregnancy, he was busy planning another celebration – one intended to mark the arrival of the most highly anticipated child in English history: a legitimate male heir.

3

At the time they were preparing to welcome their first child together, Henry and Anne had been married for just a matter of months. They had, though, already endured more obstacles than many faced in a lifetime, the course of their relationship far from smooth. The couple had first met more than ten years earlier while Anne was serving in the household of Henry's first wife, Katherine of Aragon. It was some time before Anne attracted his attention, but in 1526 Henry declared himself to have been 'stricken with the dart of love'.[2] Before long, he had fallen deeply, passionately in love with her. Henry had turned thirty-five that summer, and with his imposing height of 6 feet 2 inches and his athletic physique, coupled with his red-gold locks, he was in his prime. Indeed, just a few years earlier, in 1519, he had been described as 'much handsomer than any other Sovereign in Christendom'.[3] The second son of Henry VII – founding monarch of the Tudor dynasty established a little under half a century earlier – and Elizabeth of York, Henry had been born and raised as the 'spare' rather than the heir.[4] This afforded him a vastly different childhood from his elder brother, Prince Arthur, who had been installed in the stronghold of Ludlow Castle in the Welsh Marches to learn the art of kingship from a young age.[5]

By contrast, Henry had been primarily raised in the nursery palace of Eltham, to the south-east of London, with his sisters Margaret, Elizabeth (who died aged three in 1495) and Mary as his playmates. For a short time a younger brother, Edmund, joined the nursery too, but he tragically died on 19 June 1500, when he was little more than a year old.[6] In spite of the loss of two younger siblings, Henry's childhood was extremely happy and he received the benefit of an excellent education, which is likely to have been supervised by his mother.[7] In 1519, it was said that he was 'very accomplished and a good musician; composed well; was a capital horseman, and a fine jouster; spoke good French, Latin, and Spanish; was very religious; heard three masses daily when he hunted, and sometimes five on other days'.[8] He had also met the philosopher Desiderius Erasmus, who paid a visit to the royal nursery at Eltham in 1499. Henry would continue his scholarly pursuits for the rest of his life, later giving him a shared interest with his youngest daughter.

In April 1502, when Henry was just ten years old, his life changed, and his position was transformed overnight by an unexpected tragedy. Just five months after his splendid wedding to the Spanish Infanta Katherine of Aragon – the most celebrated event of Henry VII's reign – fifteen-year-old Prince Arthur died, possibly of tuberculosis.[9] As his father's sole surviving son, it was on young Henry – now heir to the throne – that all hopes for the future of the Tudor dynasty rested. The following years were marked by further devastation and unhappiness: on 11 February 1503, Elizabeth of York died on her thirty-seventh birthday, within days of giving birth to a princess, Katherine, who also perished.[10] The young Prince Henry was left heartbroken by the loss of his mother and suffered a further blow later that same year when his elder sister, Margaret, left England to marry James IV of Scotland.[11] Henry's close family now consisted of his grieving father, his paternal grandmother Margaret Beaufort, who doted on him and showered him with gifts, and his younger sister Mary, who would grow to become a renowned beauty and of whom he was extremely fond.

In February 1504, this twelve-year-old boy was created Prince of Wales, but Henry VII had learned some valuable lessons from Arthur's death. Paranoid over the safety of his only male heir, the King decided that Henry would remain at court, where he would be able to keep a close eye on him, rather than establish his own household at Ludlow. In August, the Spanish envoy Hernán Duque de Estrada gushed that it was 'quite wonderful how much the King likes the Prince of Wales. He has good reason to do so, for the Prince deserves all love.' There was more to their relationship, though, for Henry was determined to prepare his son for the challenges of kingship that lay ahead. In the view of the same envoy, 'there could be no better school in the world than the society of such a father as Henry VII. He is so wise and so attentive to everything; nothing escapes his attention. There is no doubt the Prince has an excellent governor and steward in his father.'[12]

In the years that followed, Henry was frequently in his father's company, which placed an understandable strain on their relationship as the teenage Prince yearned for greater freedoms. If the Spanish ambassador Gutierre Gómez de Fuensalida is to be believed, young Henry was forced to eat alone and was only allowed to leave his father's palaces for exercise, although this account may have been exaggerated.[13] As he matured, the youngster cut a fine figure and many contemporaries noted the physical resemblance he bore to his maternal grandfather, Edward IV. Writing in October 1507, the Spanish ambassador Dr Roderigo de Puebla determined, 'There is no finer a youth in the world than the Prince of Wales. He is already taller than his father, and his limbs are of a gigantic size.'[14] It was to this striking Tudor Prince that Henry VII's subjects looked as their hope for the future.

The moment came on 21 April 1509, when Henry's father died at Richmond Palace. The man who had established the Tudor dynasty was given a lavish funeral and buried in the Lady Chapel of his own creation in Westminster Abbey next to his wife, as the people turned towards his successor. The new King of England was just a couple of months shy of his eighteenth birthday, and his accession was greeted with popular rejoicing. Henry VIII was 'liberal and handsome', and he wasted no time in taking full advantage of his recently acquired position.[15] Freed from his father's restraining grasp, a glittering world of revelry and opportunity opened before him. Soon, the King's court became renowned for its lavish entertainments and the rich treasures that were displayed throughout the royal palaces.[16] It was not long before Henry made the decision to share his newfound status with a wife, and his gaze fell firmly on one candidate. On 11 June, he married his brother's widow, Katherine of Aragon, who had remained in England following the death of her first husband.[17] It was a popular move, and thirteen days later the couple were crowned in a joint ceremony at Westminster Abbey. Henry adored his new wife, who was six years his senior, but though the marriage began in the manner of courtly love, it would end in bitterness and disappointment.[18]

Fifteen years later, in 1524, marital relations between the royal couple had ceased and a string of pregnancies had produced just one surviving child: Mary, born at Greenwich on 18 February 1516.[19] In 1519, the Venetian ambassador Sebastian Giustinian had described Katherine as 'not handsome, though she had a very beautiful complexion', but just a few years later her physical charms had faded, and years of childbearing had taken its toll on her figure.[20] Indeed, as early as 1519 the French King François I had contradicted the tactful description offered by the Venetian ambassador the same year, distastefully referring to Katherine as Henry's 'old deformed wife'.[21] Henry, for his part, had long since ignored the advice offered by his tutor, John Skelton, to 'choose a wife for yourself and always love her only'.[22] He had not been a faithful husband and throughout the course of his marriage had indulged in several affairs. Heartbreakingly for Katherine, Henry's liaison with one of her ladies, Bessie Blount, had resulted in the birth of the King's acknowledged – albeit illegitimate – son, Henry Fitzroy, later Duke of Richmond.[23] It is possible that Henry also fathered more unacknowledged illegitimate children including a daughter by another of Katherine's ladies, Mary Boleyn.[24] Yet neither of these women succeeded in maintaining Henry's interest for long. With Mary's sister Anne, though, it was an entirely different story. The result of their courtship would have momentous consequences for Henry's country – and his dynasty.

Born in around 1501, Anne, the daughter of Sir Thomas Boleyn, had little to boast of in terms of lineage on one side of her family, at least.[25] Her paternal great-grandfather, Sir Geoffrey Boleyn, 'a sincere honest man', had once served as Lord Mayor of London, but aside from this the Norfolk family from which her father hailed was of rather humble stock.[26] Thomas, however, had the good fortune to marry into one of the greatest families in England: the Howards. His bride Elizabeth was the daughter of Thomas Howard, Earl of Surrey (later second Duke of Norfolk), and heiress Elizabeth Tilney, and their union was likely arranged at a time when the Howards were recovering their position having backed the wrong side at the Battle of Bosworth in 1485. The marriage would, though, bring Thomas prestige more than financial benefit. Married in around 1499, together the couple would have at least five children, three of whom – Mary, Anne and George – survived to adulthood.[27] They were all raised primarily at Hever Castle in Kent, which had been purchased by Geoffrey Boleyn in the mid-fifteenth century.[28] Soon after his wedding, Thomas found that doors at court began to open, and he became a participant in some of the most important events of Henry VII's reign: attending the wedding of Prince Arthur and Katherine of Aragon in 1501; joining the escort of Princess Margaret to Scotland in 1503; and in 1509 taking part in Henry VII's funeral procession. Thomas's luck continued into the reign of Henry VIII, who created him a Knight of the Bath on the eve of his coronation. Before long, Thomas had grown close to the young King and he was soon a regular competitor in the tournaments that were just one of the physical pursuits of which Henry was so fond. By the same token, his wife served in the household of Katherine of Aragon, which ensured they both had close and regular access to the royal couple.

Like Henry, Thomas had also enjoyed the privilege of an excellent education, and his experience meant he was not only well versed in the qualities required of a successful courtier but excelled in them. He had a particular flair for languages – something later inherited by his grand-daughter: his understanding of Latin was good; his French was impeccable. His skills did not go unnoticed, and it was probably these that convinced the King to engage Thomas in his diplomatic service. It was a wise decision, for this was a role in which Thomas shone, demonstrated when he travelled to the court of Margaret of Austria in 1512. A brilliant example of female leadership almost fifty years before Elizabeth's reign, Margaret, for the past five years, had been governing the Low Countries on behalf of her thirteen-year-old nephew, Charles (the future Holy Roman Emperor, Charles V).[29] She immediately struck up a rapport with the new English envoy. So good was it, in fact, that Thomas successfully obtained a highly sought-after place in Margaret's household for Anne, the youngest of his two daughters.[30]

Anne was around twelve years old when she left the idyllic Kent countryside to take up residence at Mechelen near Brussels, where Margaret's court was based, probably in the summer of 1513. She would have been awestruck when she arrived, for Margaret's was one of the most sophisticated courts in Europe and a far cry from Hever Castle, which was tiny by comparison. It was a rare and brilliant opportunity for the impressionable youngster, who quickly became fully immersed in the rich wealth of culture that was to be found there. Margaret was a prolific patron of the arts, and as Anne learned fashionable dances, admired sophisticated art and listened to fine music, her tastes began to take shape.

While at Mechelen, Anne could count as companions not only the rest of Margaret's ladies, but also three girls who would all grow up to become queens and who were to be instrumental in shaping European history: Margaret's nieces Eleanor, Isabella and Mary.[31] It was an extraordinary atmosphere in which to be raised, and through Margaret's example young Anne witnessed the effects of a woman bearing power and influence. It was not lost on her.

Anne quickly settled into her new home, where she won the admiration of her mistress. 'I find her so bright and pleasant for her young age,' a delighted Margaret wrote to Anne's father, 'that I am more beholden to you for sending her to me than you are to me.'[32] Thomas had high hopes that Anne's placement in Margaret's household would prime her to follow in his footsteps and enjoy a career as a courtier, so he must have been thrilled with this report. Learning the appropriate manners and behaviour was one thing, but to become a truly seasoned courtier an excellent command of French was imperative. A tutor, Symonnet, had been appointed to assist Anne in this task, and before long she was reaping the rewards of her lessons within this school of refinement.[33] Later in the summer, a letter to her father from Margaret's summer residence at La Vure – the first to be written independently of her tutor, although perhaps under his watchful eye – confirmed that she was not yet fluent in the language but had made good progress. Anne professed to be excited at the prospect of conversing with the Queen when she was presented at court, which 'will make me all the keener to persevere in speaking French well, and also especially because you have told me to, and have advised me for my own part to work at it as much as I can'. The letter also corroborated Thomas's hope that 'you desire me to be a woman of good reputation when I come to court'.[34]

Anne's time in the household of the power-wielding Margaret was a significant honour for the Boleyn family, but it was destined to be of relatively short duration. After a stay of no more than a year, in August 1514 Thomas reluctantly called for his daughter's removal from Margaret's care.[35] It was necessary, however, for Anne's presence had been requested elsewhere: rather than returning to England, she was instead to travel to

France to join the household of Henry VIII's younger sister, eighteen-year-old Mary, who would wed the ageing Louis XII that autumn – this may have been the queen to whom she had referred in her letter to her father.[36] It is unclear exactly when Anne arrived in France, perhaps not until early 1515 having possibly travelled directly from Margaret's court at Mechelen.[37] Any time she spent with the new Queen of France, who had also taken Anne's sister Mary into her service, was, however, cut short. After just three months of marriage, on 1 January 1515 Louis XII died, leaving his young wife a widow before her nineteenth birthday.[38] Within a matter of weeks Queen Mary had taken her future into her own hands, spurning protocol and secretly marrying her brother's close friend Charles Brandon, Duke of Suffolk, who had been sent by Henry to escort her back to England.[39] Though initially outraged, Henry, after the newly-weds agreed to pay an eye-watering fine, welcomed them back to England, where they arrived in May.[40]

Though Mary Boleyn returned home with the new Duke and Duchess of Suffolk, Anne did not. Instead, she remained in France, where she joined the household of Queen Claude, consort of the newly crowned French King, François I.[41] Here she would remain for almost seven years, largely in the idyllic palaces of Blois and Amboise in the Loire Valley, where Claude spent much of her time.[42] Like Anne, Claude was just a teenager, yet she had been lame from birth and would be frequently pregnant.[43] Moreover, although the French Queen was 'universally loved', she imposed strict moral standards on her household, and thus life with her was to prove a dull contrast to the colourful court life Anne had formerly enjoyed in Mechelen.[44] Despite this, Anne's time in France had a profound impact on her as she continued to absorb the sophistication, fashions and cultures of the French court, and it was later said that 'no one would ever have taken her to be English by her manners, but a native-born Frenchwoman'.[45]

After an absence of eight years, at the end of 1521 Anne was finally summoned home in the belief that she would marry her cousin James Butler, a match her father had been negotiating, with the support of the King's chief advisor Cardinal Wolsey, since the previous spring. It was hoped that this marriage would settle a dispute both parties had been fighting over the earldom of Ormonde, to which Thomas Boleyn believed he was entitled.[46] When his daughter arrived, Thomas was gratified with her development, for Anne now had poise and character and spoke French fluently. She oozed sophistication, with a grace and elegance the likes of which only one who had spent time in the courts of Europe could boast. Later in the sixteenth century even the Catholic recusant Nicholas Sander, who never saw Anne yet was hostile to her on account of the religious differences that divided him from Elizabeth, would write of her that 'she was always well dressed, and every day made some change in the fashion of her garments'.[47]

Anne's marriage to Butler never transpired, but through her father's auspices she was offered a place in Katherine of Aragon's household alongside her sister Mary, now Lady Carey.[48] Anne's time was now spent fulfilling many of the duties she had once performed for Queen Claude: practising music, reading, providing companionship, and sewing, a skill at which she had become very adept. According to George Cavendish, a gentleman-usher in the household of Cardinal Wolsey, for 'her excellent gesture and behaviour, she did excel all other' among Katherine's ladies.[49] Anne was also an expert dancer, and on Shrove Tuesday, 4 March 1522, she made her debut in an elaborate court pageant, *Château Vert*, at York Place, later the Palace of Whitehall. Clad in a sumptuous white satin gown, Anne joined the King's sister Mary, Duchess of Suffolk, and several other ladies as they assumed the roles of damsels in distress and danced amid an elaborately constructed castle. The lead role of Beauty was played by the King's sister, while Mary Boleyn was given the part of Kindness, and Anne was Perseverance. The damsels were rescued by errant knights, one of whom was the King, dressed in crimson satin in the guise of Ardent Desire.[50] At this time, however, Henry showed no interest in Anne. Yet she was not short of potential suitors, and it was probably in 1523 that she began a courtship of her own.

The man who had piqued Anne's interest was Henry Percy, heir of the powerful Earl of Northumberland, whom she had met during his visits to the Queen's chamber.[51] George Cavendish, who wrote as an eyewitness, believed that soon 'there grew such a secret love between them that at length they were engaged together, intending to marry'.[52] However, Cavendish, who is the main source for this episode in Anne's life, tells us that the engagement was dissolved by Cardinal Wolsey at the King's instigation.[53] As the late Eric Ives demonstrated in his excellent biography of Anne, this is unlikely to have been the case, given that Henry was at this time fully immersed in his affair with Anne's sister, Mary. The impetus probably came from Wolsey, who was still hopeful of achieving Anne's marriage with James Butler.[54] Percy was instead betrothed – unhappily – to the daughter of the Earl of Shrewsbury, Mary Talbot, whom he would later marry.[55]

Cavendish relates that Anne held 'a secret indignation against the Cardinal' for breaking her attachment to Percy, and whether this was true or not she would later be afforded an opportunity to revenge herself upon him when he fell from the King's graces.[56] For the time being, though, she once again flourished 'in great estimation and favour' and would shortly gain the admiration of another suitor, Thomas Wyatt.[57] Although he had been married since 1520, Wyatt later separated from his wife on account of her adultery, and most historians agree that he was attracted to Anne.[58] By 1526, though, all thoughts of other admirers were forgotten when a more prestigious suitor presented himself, a suitor to whom Wyatt himself ceded defeat in the manner of courtly love, as evidenced in his poetry about Anne:

> Who list her hunt, I put him out of doubt,
> As well as I may spend his time in vain.
> And graven with diamonds in letters plain,
> There is written her fair neck round about:
> Noli me tangere [do not touch me], for Caesar's I am
> And wild for to hold, though I seem tame.[59]

The rival suitor was the King.

It is unclear exactly when Henry VIII first became attracted to Anne, but it is unlikely to have been earlier than 1525. Many of her contemporaries could not understand the appeal she held for Henry, for she was no great beauty. Writing in 1532, the Venetian diplomat Francesco Sanuto declared, 'Madam Anne is not one of the handsomest women in the world.' She was 'of middling stature, swarthy complexion, long neck, wide mouth, bosom not much raised, and in fact has nothing but the English King's great appetite, and her eyes, which are black and beautiful'.[60] Though Henry was enchanted by her elegant grace, initially he fully expected Anne to submit to his charms and become his mistress. But Anne was different: she had seen the way in which Henry had conducted his affair with her sister before casting her aside when he grew bored, and she was determined not to go the same way. Much to Henry's surprise, she repelled his advances and refused to submit herself to him sexually. Rather than causing him to abandon his prey, Anne's display of womanly virtue intrigued Henry and heightened his desire for her, and he began pursuing her with greater alacrity. Thus began a notorious game of cat and mouse, with seventeen of Henry's impassioned letters to Anne in the Vatican Archives serving as testimony to his growing ardour for her. Written 'by the hand of him who is and always will be yours', Henry implored Anne 'to give up yourself body and heart to me'.[61] Unfortunately, Anne's responses have not survived, but though she kept him at a physical distance, she offered him enough encouragement to convince him to take the relationship to another level.

In 1527, Henry had grown so besotted with Anne that he promised her marriage. He already had a wife, yet it seems he had been harbouring doubts to such an extent that he had probably by this time considered separating from her.[62] Now spurred on by his passion for Anne, Henry began proceedings to have his marriage to Katherine of Aragon annulled on the grounds of her first marriage to his brother, Arthur. Though the Pope had granted Henry and Katherine a dispensation that allowed them to wed, Henry was convinced that his failure to have a son by Katherine was God's judgement on their union, citing Leviticus 20:21 whereby, 'If a man takes his brother's wife, it is an unclean thing: he has uncovered his brother's nakedness: they shall be without children.'[63] Instead, Henry planned to wed Anne, who he was convinced would provide him with the male heir that, in his eyes, Katherine had crucially failed to produce. But it was by no means to be a straightforward path.

The story of Henry VIII's 'Great Matter' as he fought to free himself of Katherine has been detailed many times, and thus there is little need to repeat it here in full.[64] Much to his fury, Henry was met with great resistance from Katherine, who steadfastly denied that her marriage to Arthur had ever been consummated. She refused to accept that her marriage to Henry was invalid, a belief that was echoed by the couple's daughter, Mary. The Queen's protests were to no avail, and Henry became increasingly frustrated with Katherine's refusal to comply with his demands. In 1531, he finally banished her to a series of houses that were a far cry from the luxurious palaces to which she had become accustomed – and she would never see Henry again. She was also forbidden from seeing her daughter, who, much to Katherine and Mary's distress, became estranged from the King. Nevertheless, Katherine had a great deal of support both at home and abroad, including from Henry's own sister, Mary, who loathed Anne on account of her attempts to oust Katherine – to whom she was close – and establish herself in her former mistress's place.[65]

Having looked to the Pope to provide their desired annulment, Henry and Anne were furious when he refused to comply. It was time, Henry decided, to take matters into his own hands. In a remarkable step, he began the process of separating England from the jurisdiction of the Pope in Rome and the Roman Catholic Church, establishing in its place the Church of England with himself at its head. Though from a religious perspective Henry never deviated from Catholicism itself, only from the Pope's authority, his was still a move that would cause a huge, irreparable split within his realm – one with far-reaching consequences, both personal and political, for his successors.

ANNE'S FAMILY ROSE high in the King's favour alongside her, and in 1529 her father was created Earl of Wiltshire, while her brother, George, received the title of Viscount Rochford. But Anne's climb to queenship was slow. Finally, in 1532, after years of stress and continual disappointments, it seemed as though the end goal of marriage was at last within Anne's reach. In September, she was created Marquess of Pembroke in her own right in an elaborate ceremony at Windsor Castle, and so strong was Henry's ardour for her that the disapproving Imperial ambassador Eustace Chapuys noted, 'The King cannot be one hour away from her.'[66] The following month she accompanied Henry to Calais, where he met with François I. Having obtained the French King's support for the marriage, which Henry had expected following the signing of a mutual alliance with François that united them against the Holy Roman Emperor Charles V, by this point it was only a matter of time before Anne became Queen. It was with this in mind that, after years of holding him at arm's length, Anne finally decided to surrender herself physically to Henry.[67] Much to the couple's delight, she was pregnant by Christmas, and thus the matter of officially ending Henry's marriage to Katherine of Aragon became one of urgency.

In spite of his ongoing marriage to Katherine, in January 1533 Henry and Anne were secretly married, but it was only a matter of time before the news became public.[68] On the eve of Easter Anne made her first public appearance as Queen. Attending mass 'in royal state', she was 'loaded with jewels' and attended by as many as sixty ladies, according to Chapuys. One of Anne's greatest enemies, it was he who remarked on her transition from marquess to Queen, saying, 'All the world is astonished at it for it looks like a dream, and even those who take her part know not whether to laugh or to cry.'[69]

In May Anne's pregnancy was formally announced, but for those at court this was a mere confirmation of what many had already known for several months. The same month, Archbishop Thomas Cranmer, a Boleyn supporter who 'turned as the King pleased, flattered and followed him in all his demands', officially declared Henry's marriage to Katherine to be null and void, rendering their daughter Mary illegitimate.[70] It came as no surprise when Katherine refused to accept this judgement, but she was paying a high price for her honour. At the end of July, she was moved to Buckden in Cambridgeshire, where her health quickly began to deteriorate because of the damp, and she was forbidden from receiving visitors. Anne's marriage to the King was avowed to be good and valid, and the couple began looking towards their future. There remained just one further thing to cement Anne's queenship until her baby arrived: her coronation.

On 1 June, the now visibly pregnant Anne was crowned in a ceremony of pure magnificence at Westminster Abbey. In a hugely symbolic gesture intended to highlight her exalted status, she was crowned using St Edward's Crown, usually reserved for the coronation of male monarchs, before receiving the rod and sceptre.[71] Thus, as Eric Ives underlined, 'the mystique of monarchy now belonged to Anne Boleyn'.[72] The accompanying celebrations had been meticulously planned and were staged over the course of four days.[73] Not everyone was in a joyous mood, however. Anne was not popular with her new subjects, and the admittedly biased Chapuys, a friend and supporter of Katherine of Aragon on account of his service to her nephew, the Emperor Charles V of the Habsburg dynasty, declared that she was 'hated by all the world'.[74] Many felt great sympathy for the plight of Katherine and her daughter and refused to accept the validity of Anne's marriage. Anne had many enemies, and they would continue to rear their heads in the coming years.

With the conclusion of her coronation celebrations, Anne began to adjust to her role as Queen. Given her pregnancy, this naturally included preparing for the arrival of her child, and in a move that caused outrage and distress, at the end of July she asked her husband to make a request of his former Queen. The object of Anne's desire was 'a very rich triumphal cloth which she [Katherine] brought from Spain to wrap up her children with at baptism'.[75] Katherine was appalled and flatly refused to hand over the same cloth with which her own children had been christened. As it had been her own personal property prior to her marriage, much to Anne's annoyance she found that Henry was unwilling to press the matter. It would not be long, though, before she had more distressing issues to contend with.

By the summer, it had become apparent that marriage had changed the nature of Anne and Henry's relationship. As Anne's pregnancy progressed and she grew bigger, in keeping with the belief that to engage in sex with a pregnant woman would cause harm to the unborn baby, her husband began to look elsewhere for sexual pleasure. For years Anne had grown accustomed to Henry's endless declarations of love, so she was incensed when she discovered that he had been unfaithful. In an unbecoming scene that proved her inability to adapt to the change from mistress to Queen, she angrily confronted him. Henry was shocked at being reprimanded, for once they were married, he had fully expected Anne to display the same meek and discerning behaviour as her predecessor, turning a blind eye to his infidelities. He had no intention of changing his ways. In a stinging reference to the forbearance shown by Katherine, Henry declared in no uncertain terms that Anne 'must shut her eyes, and endure as well as more worthy persons'. To reinforce the message he added that 'she ought to know that it was in his power to humble her again in a moment more than he had exalted her'.[76] The fiery Anne did not react well to her husband's words, and an air of bad feeling lingered between the couple. This was the uncomfortable situation Anne was faced with in the final months of her pregnancy.

By the time the court reached Windsor Castle in mid-August, tensions between the royal couple had been smoothed out, and they were reported to be 'merry'.[77] They had good reason to be, for, as Chapuys wrote to his master, the Emperor Charles V, the King had been assured 'by the report of his physicians and astrologers that the Lady would bear a son'.[78] Confidence was high, and letters were prepared in readiness to announce the arrival of a prince. Henry was convinced that Anne would shortly provide him with what he desperately craved: a male heir. A son was almost always preferable to a daughter, but in this instance there was a heightened sense of expectation. It was with this in mind that Henry began making plans for a celebratory joust to mark the arrival of his son: a son who would be named either Henry or Edward.

On 26 August, Anne had bidden both her husband and her court farewell, as she took to her gorgeously appointed chamber in Greenwich to await the arrival of her child. No expense had been spared, and the Queen's rooms had been prepared with meticulous attention to detail. Luxurious carpets were laid out and costly tapestries telling the story of

St Ursula – the legendary leader of eleven thousand virgins and reputedly martyred – hung from the walls. The choice of St Ursula would, unbeknown to Anne, prove remarkably fitting to the child she would shortly bear. The centrepiece, though, was 'one of the richest and most triumphant beds', which had formed part of the ransom of John, Count of Angoulême, in the previous century. Childbirth was a process overseen exclusively by women, and as the Queen awaited her baby's arrival she had the company of her ladies, attendants and midwives. Those who had been chosen to care for the royal baby eagerly stood by. They did not have long to wait.

Between three and four o'clock in the afternoon on 7 September, Anne gave birth to her child. The baby was healthy, but it was not the longed-for son Henry had been convinced Anne would bear. Instead, she had borne a 'fair lady'.[79] It was little wonder, therefore, that according to Chapuys their daughter's sex caused both the King and Queen 'great regret'.[80] Whatever disappointment she may have felt, Anne was determined to put a brave face on it, and on the day of her daughter's birth she wrote proudly to the courtier Lord Cobham to inform him of the baby's arrival.[81] Her failure to produce a son nevertheless weakened her position in the eyes of her contemporaries, both at home and abroad – had she had a boy, she would have been untouchable.[82] As it was, though Anne had the King's love, elsewhere she was vulnerable.

Although the good health of his daughter left him with every reason to hope sons would soon follow, Henry was in no mood to celebrate. *Te Deum* was sung at St Paul's the day after the baby's birth, but the jousts the King had planned were cancelled. The letters that had been prepared, confidently announcing the arrival of a prince to the great rulers of Europe, were altered to announce the birth of a princess.[83] The physicians and astrologers who had assuredly predicted a son were met with great reproach, while Anne's enemies rejoiced at the baby's sex.[84]

Chapuys had been told that the infant Princess was to be called Mary, but he quickly learned that this was wrong.[85] The baby, now Henry VIII's sole legitimate heir to the throne, was named Elizabeth as a compliment to the King's much-loved late mother, Elizabeth of York. By happy coincidence, it was a name also shared by the baby's maternal grandmother. The Tudor family had gained another member, but Elizabeth's gender left her father with a greater expectation of her mother. Though she was Henry's heir, the life of his infant daughter began with the hope that a brother would soon follow. Little did he know that Elizabeth would, in time, become his greatest legacy.

CHAPTER 2

'Princess of England'

'That is a title which belongs to me by right, and to no one else.'

LADY MARY VIA EUSTACE CHAPUYS, 16 DECEMBER 1533

T HE DOWAGER DUCHESS of Norfolk, who was in her mid-fifties, walked carefully towards the church, conscious of the precious bundle she carried. In her arms lay the three-day-old Princess Elizabeth, her step-great-granddaughter, wrapped in a cloak of rich purple velvet, the colour reserved for royalty.[1] The mantle's long train was jointly carried by members of Elizabeth's maternal family, including her grandfather, Thomas Boleyn, Earl of Wiltshire, and a canopy was borne over her head by her uncle, Lord Rochford, and members of the Howard clan. The Princess and her party of Anne's relatives were followed by a number of ladies and gentlewomen, all of whom were to bear witness to the splendour of the day's event.

Preparations for Elizabeth's christening gathered pace from the moment of her birth. Though she was not the son her father craved, she was both his heir and a royal child, and royal children could expect the full honours of a suitably magnificent occasion. Henry himself had been christened in the fifteenth-century church of the Observant Friars that lay next to Greenwich Palace, and the same arrangement was put in place for Elizabeth.[2] Greenwich was a hive of hurried activity in the run-up to the event, and numerous labourers had been employed to assist with the preparations: 18lb of candles had been purchased to allow the carpenters to work through the night, such was the urgency.[3] The results were majestic.

On the afternoon of 10 September, Sir Stephen Peacock, the Mayor of London, and forty chief citizens were rowed to Greenwich. Dressed in scarlet and wearing their splendid livery collars, they watched as the tiny Princess and her party processed from the Palace to the church, and it was said that all the 'walls between the King's place and the Friars were hanged with arras [elaborate tapestry], and the way strewed with rushes'. The church was decorated in the same way, and the silver font that stood in the middle of the church was particularly ornate, being 'covered with a fine cloth, and surrounded by gentlemen with aprons and towels about their necks, that no filth should come into it. Over it hung a crimson satin canopy fringed with gold.'[4]

Custom dictated that the King and Queen did not attend their daughter's christening, but all those who had been summoned stepped forward when the Princess arrived, straining to catch a glimpse of their sovereign's newborn heir. Many of the leading nobility of the realm had been afforded a role in the day's ceremonial, the Earl of Essex carrying covered gilt basins, the Marquess of Dorset bearing the salt used as part of the rite of baptism, and the Duke of Norfolk's daughter carrying the chrism 'of pearl and stone'.[5] Two godmothers had been chosen for Elizabeth, one of whom was the Dowager Duchess of Norfolk, in whose arms she lay. The official account begins by telling us that the other was Margaret Wootton, the old Marchioness of Dorset, although she may have been confused with the Marchioness of Exeter, who was named later in the same document.[6] Chapuys was of the opinion that it was the latter who filled this role – much to her distaste, for she was a firm friend and supporter of Katherine of Aragon.[7] The trusted Thomas Cranmer stood as Elizabeth's godfather.

Meeting the Princess at the church door, John Stokesley, Bishop of London, conducted the ceremony, after which Chapuys reported that 'a herald in front of the church door proclaimed her Princess of England'.[8] The trumpets sounded, and in keeping with tradition, gifts were offered for the child, 'after which wafers, comfits, and hippocras [a spiced and sweetened wine] were brought in'. With her christening gifts carried before her by Sir John Dudley and three others, Elizabeth was conveyed from the church to the Queen's chamber in great state. It was a magnificent occasion fully befitting of the King's heir – yet Chapuys, though he had not attended and was naturally hostile, could not resist noting that the christening had been like 'her mother's coronation, very cold and disagreeable'.[9] Though it was his view that many were of the same opinion, the following day 'there was fires made in London, and at every fire a vessel of wine for people to drink for the said solemnity', a gesture much appreciated by the King's subjects.[10]

On 13 December, three months after her elaborate christening, Princess Elizabeth left her first home and her parents behind. Braving the winter weather under the attentive eyes of the nursery staff who had been appointed to care for her, the baby Princess set out on the first stage of her journey to the Palace of Hatfield, just over twenty miles north of London.[11] It was here that Elizabeth's nursery household, separate to that of her parents, was to be established, in an arrangement that was commonplace for royal children.[12] The decision had only been made on 2 December, when the King's Council gathered to discuss business and found the matter of the Princess's household on their agenda. Given that London was frequently a haven of pestilence and disease, there was good reason to remove the King's heir from its centre without delay, and so just eleven days later the Princess and her entourage departed.

Elizabeth's removal from her mother's care came as a great wrench to Queen Anne, who, though she had certainly shown no signs of maternal warmth to her stepdaughter Mary, was from the first extremely protective of her daughter. So keen had her interest in Elizabeth been that, according to the seventeenth-century account of Gregorio Leti, she caused shock when she declared her wish to breastfeed the infant, a request that was categorically denied. Leti is, however, a largely unreliable source and this tale is unsubstantiated elsewhere: it was out of the question that a Queen should suckle her own child.[13] Instead, Elizabeth was immediately given into the care of a wet-nurse named Mrs Pendred, a woman who was probably chosen by the King.[14] Though she was unable to bond with her baby in this way, for the first months of Elizabeth's life Anne was determined to keep her daughter close. So close that the unreliable author of the Spanish Chronicle related that Princess Elizabeth could often be seen lying on a rich cushion beneath the royal canopy, next to her mother's throne.[15]

As her status demanded, Elizabeth travelled to Hatfield in great state, carried in a costly litter with a suitably grand escort. An unimpressed Chapuys noted that the Princess, whom he would disparagingly refer to either as 'the bastard' or 'the little bastard' in his despatches, was 'solemnly accompanied by two dukes [these were Suffolk and Norfolk] and several lords and gentlemen'.[16] He was equally disapproving of the fact Henry had refrained from sending his daughter to Hatfield via a shorter, more direct route. Instead, 'for greater solemnity, and to insinuate to the people that she is the true Princess', Elizabeth travelled through the capital amid great pomp.[17] It was a splendid introduction to public life, and Henry took full advantage of the opportunity to present Elizabeth to his subjects as his legitimate heir.

The King had recently appropriated Elizabeth's new home at Hatfield, which had been built by Cardinal John Morton in 1497.[18] Lady Margaret Beaufort, Elizabeth's formidable paternal great-grandmother, had also used Hatfield as an occasional residence and it was an ideal space in which to raise a royal child. Made up of four wings around a central courtyard and set in a large park well stocked with deer, Hatfield boasted an impressive Great Hall with a timber-beam roof, domestic quarters that included a bakehouse, and fine apartments overlooking an orchard and gardens. The old church of St Etheldreda stood nearby, and Elizabeth and members of her household would have come to know it well.[19] Though Hatfield was located at a safe enough distance from the capital to prevent sickness and virulence from spreading there, it was also close enough to provide easy access to the palaces of Henry's court. Elizabeth was perfectly placed for her parents to visit and send for regular news of her health and antics.

The household at Hatfield came under the overall charge of Sir John Shelton, whose wife, Anne, was the Queen's paternal aunt. She and her sister, Alice Clere, joined Sir John at Hatfield, but though these members of the Queen's family were the most senior in the household, they were not the central figures in Elizabeth's life.[20] That position was reserved for Lady Margaret Bryan, who was responsible for the care of the infant Princess.[21]

Though in her sixties in 1533 and therefore relatively old for the role, Elizabeth's 'lady mistress' was a solid choice with an impeccable record, for she had once fulfilled the same role for the Princess's elder sister.[22]

Lady Margaret was the sister of Anne Boleyn's mother, and thus, like the Sheltons, also had blood ties to Elizabeth.[23] She had once served in the household of Katherine of Aragon but was nevertheless on excellent terms with Elizabeth's mother. Lady Bryan had several children of her own, including the one-eyed courtier Sir Francis Bryan, 'a notorious favourite of the King', and this, coupled with her experience caring for Mary, made her a reliable candidate when it came to the rearing of Elizabeth.[24] From Queen Anne's perspective this meant that though she herself would be separated from her daughter, Elizabeth – from her earliest days – would still be surrounded by those with whom she shared the bonds of blood. This was a practice that Elizabeth would, through her own choice, continue for the rest of her life, keeping her mother's relatives close to her.

Little is known of the relationship that Elizabeth shared with her first lady mistress, but given the high regard in which Lady Bryan was held by the King and Queen, there is every reason to believe that it was warm. As Tracy Borman states, Lady Bryan was 'effectively an extension of Anne' and she would later relay to Thomas Cromwell her belief that she had been 'a mother' to the King's children.[25] Her surviving letters show not only that she took her role extremely seriously but also that she cared deeply about Elizabeth's welfare. While Lady Bryan was in charge, she would always do her best for the young Princess.

Lady Bryan assumed primary responsibility for Elizabeth, but she did not perform her task alone. In accordance with her status, from the moment of her birth Elizabeth was assigned a plethora of staff who ensured that her every need was attended to. Few details of those who made up Elizabeth's nursery in 1533 are known, but it seems likely that it closely paralleled that of her sister at the time of her birth. Mary had been allocated a laundress, a gentlewoman, and a chaplain who also served as her secretary, and these roles can all be found on the earliest surviving list of Elizabeth's staff, which probably dates from 1536. Some may have been with her since birth.[26] It is probable that Blanche Milborne, Lady Herbert of Troy, was one of Elizabeth's household, for she had links with Queen Anne, whom she may have known quite well, and was definitely there later in 1536.[27] We know for sure that in 1533, aside from Mrs Pendred the wet-nurse, Elizabeth's household also consisted of 'rockers', who were tasked with rocking the Princess in her cradle. Mary had had four rockers, and Elizabeth would have enjoyed the same arrangement.[28] Among them was one Blanche Parry, a young lady of Herefordshire origin who was devoted to Elizabeth, 'whose cradle saw I rocked', and would remain in her service until her death in 1590.[29] Blanche was the niece of Lady Troy, who was almost certainly responsible for her appointment.[30] Blanche, and other women the Princess had known since childhood, would prove to be of the utmost importance to her, and Elizabeth would later recite Saint Gregory, who observed that, 'We are more bound to them that bringeth us up well than to our parents, for our parents do that which is natural for them, that is bringeth us into this world; but our bringers up are a cause to make us live well.'[31] Clearly, those who surrounded Elizabeth even at such a young age made a deep impression on her.

Although she was just a baby, Elizabeth was the central and most important figure at Hatfield, and all aspects of life there revolved around her care. As the King's acknowledged, legitimate heir, the Princess was raised surrounded by the full trappings of royalty. A surviving bill shows that for one year alone, from December 1534 to December 1535, her household expenses totalled £111 19s 8d (almost £50,000 today), an eye-watering sum for the needs of an infant.[32] Soon after her birth, various items had been purchased for her nursery at Greenwich, including a table to 'roll the princess's clothes upon', while a 1535 clothes bill shows that Queen Anne had bought seven yards of damask russet for covering Elizabeth's bed.[33] Such luxury embellishments would also have been in use at Elizabeth's Hatfield nursery.

Shortly after Elizabeth's installation there, a new arrival joined the Hatfield household: her seventeen-year-old sister. Mary was 'low rather than of middling stature', and in later years the Venetian ambassador Giovanni Michiel would say that in her youth she had been 'not merely tolerably handsome, but of beauty exceeding mediocrity'.[34] Like her mother Katherine of Aragon, Mary had been forced to endure much trauma and unhappiness at the hands of both her father and Anne Boleyn. As a result of her continued refusal to acknowledge the invalidity of her parents' marriage and her own illegitimacy, she had incurred the fury of her father and earned the enmity of Elizabeth's mother. Their relationship had not improved upon Elizabeth's birth but had in fact worsened, so that Michiel would subsequently recall, 'Few other women in the world of her rank ever lived more wretchedly.'[35] On the same day that Elizabeth was born, Chapuys – Katherine and Mary's champion – had been appalled to discover that 'it was ordered that the true princess should not be so called', while all of Mary's servants were stripped of their livery bearing her device.[36] Sure enough, on 1 October Henry informed Mary that she was no longer entitled to style herself 'princess' and should instead be addressed as 'lady', prompting an emotional reaction. Chapuys had heard rumours that Mary's household would be diminished, and to his dismay, in early November the situation had taken a further turn:

'The King, not satisfied with having taken away the name and title of Princess, has just given out that, in order to subdue the spirit of the Princess [Mary], he will deprive her of all her people, because they put notions into her head, and stop her from obeying him, and that she should come and live as lady's maid with this new bastard [Elizabeth].'[37]

Through no fault of their own but because of the circumstances into which Elizabeth had been born, the foundations of the sisters' relationship were built on bitterness and hostility before they had even met. These were emotions that, on Mary's side at least, never truly disappeared.

True to his word, it was on the King's orders that Mary arrived at Hatfield in December accompanied by just two servants. The Duke of Norfolk, the Queen's uncle and one of Henry's leading councillors, was waiting to greet her, asking 'whether she would not go and pay her respects to the princess'. Mary resolutely replied that 'she knew no other princess in England except herself, and that the daughter of Madame de Pembroke [Anne Boleyn, referring to her position as marquess] had no such title'. She did, however, concede that 'it was true that since the King her father acknowledged her [Elizabeth] to be his, she might call her "sister"'.[38] Mary's insolence did nothing to soften her father's attitude towards her, and as a result she passed a miserable Christmas at Hatfield, where she had 'only one chamber-woman with her, and is in the worst lodging of the house'.[39] Little wonder she spent much of her time weeping in her chamber.

After a month's separation, in the middle of January 1534 the King arrived at Hatfield to visit his baby daughter for the first time. The visit served a dual purpose, for Chapuys believed that Henry had also come to 'persuade or force the Princess [Mary] to renounce her title'. Worried that if Henry saw his eldest daughter his resolve might crumble, the Queen sent Thomas Cromwell and others after her husband to 'prevent him from seeing or speaking with her'. Anne got her way, and 'before arriving at the house he sent orders that she should not come to him'.[40]

But Henry was still determined to bring Mary to heel. While in four-month-old Elizabeth's chamber, he dispatched Cromwell, now his chief advisor, to urge Mary to abandon her claim to her title.[41] Mary replied that 'she had already given a decided answer, it was labour wasted to press her, and they were deceived if they thought that bad treatment or rudeness, or even the chance of death, would make her change her determination'. She nevertheless attempted to win back her father's favour, and while Henry played with baby Elizabeth, Mary begged permission to come and kiss his hand. Her request was refused. Determined not to give up, she tried a different tactic. After Henry had bidden farewell to his infant daughter, he prepared to mount his horse to leave. Mary, meanwhile, had made her way to a terrace at the top of the house, sinking to her knees and joining her hands on sight of her father. When Henry saw her thus, he immediately softened. He 'bowed to her and put his hand to his hat' in response, a gesture that apparently led those present to rejoice and salute Mary 'reverently with signs of good will and compassion'.[42] But it was not enough to repair the relationship between father and daughter.

Mary's hostility to Anne Boleyn and estrangement from her father ensured there was no question of her living in the same kind of luxury as Elizabeth, and her supporters constantly complained about her treatment. Neither did the fraught situation help her to build a bond with her baby sister. Instead, Mary endeavoured to make life as difficult as possible, refusing to attend on Elizabeth or yield precedence. Much to her disappointment, she was supervised not by her former lady mistress Lady Bryan but by Elizabeth's two great-aunts, Lady Shelton and Lady Clere. In light of her perceived disobedience, this was not a comfortable experience for any of them, and Chapuys was told that should Mary continue to use her title of 'princess', Queen Anne had encouraged Lady Shelton to 'box her ears as a cursed bastard'.[43]

Lady Shelton seems to have taken little heed of these orders, leading to a reprimand from both the Queen's brother and her uncle Norfolk for showing Mary 'too much respect and kindness, saying that she ought only to be treated as a bastard'. But Lady Shelton hit back, retorting that 'even if the Princess were only the bastard of a poor gentleman, she deserved honor and good treatment for her goodness and virtues'.[44] There were also rumours that Anne intended to have Mary poisoned, and though there is no evidence to support this, the fact that such rumours were circulating is indicative of the toxic nature of their relationship. Anne's cruel treatment of her stepdaughter was in stark contrast to the warmth and love that she displayed towards her own child and only served to intensify Mary's unhappiness.

At the beginning of March, Anne visited Elizabeth at Hatfield for the first time. She may have been delayed because she was pregnant once more with a child she had conceived soon after Elizabeth's birth, and was thus hopeful of providing her daughter with a younger brother. Lasting for two days, the visit gave Anne the perfect opportunity to spend some time with her infant daughter and to check on her progress. She had not forgotten about her stepdaughter though, and decided to make an attempt to build bridges. Sending a message in which she urged Mary 'to visit her and honor her as Queen', she hoped that Mary would obey. Should she conform, Anne herself would intercede with the King on Mary's behalf and she 'should be as well or better treated than ever'. Mary's response was predictable. She stubbornly replied that 'she knew no Queen in England except her mother', though should Anne be prepared to speak favourably to her father she would be much obliged.[45] Exasperated, Anne tried again but became so frustrated by Mary's intransigence that she resorted to threats. Much to Anne's annoyance, these also proved ineffective. By way of punishment for the unhappy teenager, the Duke of Norfolk took away 'not only her principal jewels and ornaments, but all the others as well', telling Mary that she was not a princess and 'her pomp and pride must be abated'.[46] Elizabeth's infancy rendered her oblivious to the tension and anxiety that played out in these distressing scenes, but they would have pertinent, long-term consequences for her relationship with her sister, for 'thus were sown the seeds of bitterness that grew to maturity more than twenty years later'.[47] Indeed, we can only imagine the depth of resentment Mary felt towards Anne during this time, as her grudge against her stepmother rooted itself deep enough to manifest in Elizabeth's direction almost two decades after Anne's death.

On 23 March 1534, the First Succession Act was passed in Parliament. The Act reinforced Elizabeth's status as the King's heir and formally proclaimed Mary to be a bastard. Further than that, if Henry were to die before Anne, the Act declared that 'she shall be regent and absolute governor of her children and the kingdom, and that applying the title of queen or princess to anyone except the said Anne or her daughter shall be considered high treason'.[48] Elizabeth's mother was to be given full control over her daughter and her realm if her husband predeceased her: a sign of Henry's faith in Anne's abilities and his response to her latest pregnancy. But there was more to the Act than this, for it also stated that, if commanded, the King's subjects must swear an oath acknowledging not only the Act's validity but also the King's supremacy as Head of the Church of England. Many of Henry's friends and courtiers had been opposed to his separation from Katherine of Aragon, but the Oath of Supremacy was one step too far. Among those who found themselves unwilling to take it were Henry's former Lord Chancellor Sir Thomas More and John Fisher, Bishop of Rochester.[49] More had enjoyed a close friendship with his royal master, and the King had been determined to obtain his support for the annulment of his marriage to Katherine of Aragon. It would not be forthcoming, and despite his former friendship with Henry, More was not spared. He and Fisher would eventually pay the heaviest price for their principles, for the Treasons Act, passed the previous November, made the penalty for those who refused to accept the King's supremacy death. This was not enough to convince either More or Fisher, and as a result of their defiance both men met their ends on the executioner's block in the summer of 1535.[50]

At the end of March, the household of six-month-old Elizabeth moved to Eltham Palace, her father's childhood home. Like Hatfield, Eltham was considered to enjoy clean air and was surrounded by three parks, which provided ample hunting.[51] The Palace, one of only six that were large enough to house the entire Tudor court, boasted a spectacular Great Hall with a hammer-beam oak roof that had been constructed by Edward IV in the 1470s.[52] Henry had spent a considerable sum on the Palace, adding a chapel in the 1520s that was gorgeously decorated with gilt leaves.[53] Baby Elizabeth's suite of rooms was elaborate, consisting of a great chamber, a dining chamber, a raying chamber (in which to dress), a bedchamber and even a gallery.[54] As Elizabeth arrived, preparations were underway at Eltham 'against the coming of the prince'.[55]

Mary joined her baby sister, but as she had initially refused to do so it had been a testing journey. The result was that she was 'put by force by certain gentlemen into a litter' and was 'thus compelled to make court to the said Bastard [Elizabeth]'.[56] It came as no surprise then when orders were issued commanding Mary to keep to her chamber when the King and Queen arrived at Eltham to visit Elizabeth. The couple were eager to spend time with their little daughter, who with her mop of red hair was unmistakeably a Tudor, and who would go on to display character-istics from both her mother and her father. Among those who joined the royal couple was Sir William Kingston, the Constable of the Tower, who was also a favoured courtier and noted delightedly that Elizabeth was 'as goodly a child as hath been seen ... her grace is much in the King's favour as goodly child should be, God save her'.[57] This touching report was bolstered by the fact that both Henry and Anne were in excellent spirits, for they were optimistic – once again – that the child Anne now carried was a son. They were not the only ones: 'The Queen hath a goodly belly, praying our Lord to send us a prince', her receiver-general George Taylor wrote.[58] Sadly, their hopes were to prove short-lived.

The King was back with his baby daughter at Eltham in July, but on this occasion his joyous mood had vanished. Much to his dismay, the Queen had lost her baby at full term that summer. To make matters worse, the child had probably been a boy.[59] The loss of their child caused both Henry and Anne great anguish, but it hit Anne particularly hard. To add to her torment, she was aware that her husband's passion for her – once so fervent – was fading fast, and her failure to provide him with a son had only exacerbated this. She was distressed when, not for the first time, Henry 'renewed and increased the love he formerly had for a very beautiful damsel of the court'. A jealous Anne had done her best to have this unidentified woman removed, provoking an angry response from the King. She had, Henry said, 'good reason to be content with what he had done for her, which he would not do now if the thing were to begin'.[60]

Meanwhile, Mary had continued to fight for precedence over her younger sister. When the household stopped at Greenwich en route to Hunsdon at the end of August, Mary took the opportunity to drive her horse forward before Elizabeth's litter, arriving 'about an hour before the Bastard'.[61] Likewise, when taking her place in the royal barge, Mary 'took care to secure the most honorable place'.[62] How much – if any – direct interaction Mary had with Elizabeth at this time is unknown, but what is more certain is that the treatment meted out to the older sibling had become increasingly harsh. In the spring, the sympathy once shown by the Queen's aunt had faded, for Lady Shelton now told Mary that 'if she were in the King's place, she would kick her out of the King's house for disobedience', and such treatment may have contributed to the bouts of ill health Mary suffered throughout her life.[63] In another sign of the mirroring of the sisters' lives, Elizabeth too would be plagued with health problems as she grew, exacerbated in times of stress (see Appendix 1). Back in 1534 though, already feeling unwell shortly after their arrival at Hunsdon, Mary took to her bed with 'her old disease', said to be 'in her head and stomach' as diagnosed by the King's physician William Butts.[64]

The following month, Mary may have been cheered to learn of a conversation that Chapuys had shared with Cromwell, during the course of which the latter had supposedly told the ambassador that 'the said King loved the Princess [Mary] more than the last-born [Elizabeth], and that he would not be long in giving clear evidence of it to the world'.[65] Chapuys admitted that he would have been sceptical of this had it not been for the fact that the King seemed to be softening towards his eldest daughter and had recently given orders that Mary should be treated well. It is unclear what prompted this – perhaps news of Mary's illness – but at the end of October, Mary, having recovered from her malady, was preparing to travel with Elizabeth to Richmond Palace. Before they left, Mary was 'visited by nearly all the gentlemen and ladies of the court', to the Queen's 'great annoyance'.[66] In a further sign that her father was looking upon her more favourably, Mary was provided with a velvet-covered litter that matched Elizabeth's in which to make the journey, a sign that 'the King's severity was abating'.[67] It would prove to be of short duration, however, and the following month Chapuys was irritated to learn that Mary was once more the victim of ill treatment at the hand of the Queen's aunt.[68]

When Elizabeth reached Richmond with its pepper-pot chimneys and fashionable octagonal towers, the masterpiece of her grandfather Henry VII, she received a visit from her mother, who was accompanied by some of her ladies and the Dukes of Norfolk and Suffolk.[69] In order to avoid Anne, Mary 'refused to leave her chamber' until she left, which suggests that she was lodged near to Elizabeth.[70] Anne took great comfort in these visits to her baby daughter, now a year old, especially as the King kept a new unnamed mistress who was sympathetic to Mary.[71] He had not forgotten about his baby daughter, though, and at the beginning of 1535 he began a negotiation in which Elizabeth was to be of vital importance.

Elizabeth had been spending Easter at Eltham in 1534 when some important visitors arrived. Not even a year old at that time, the King's daughter was already being used as a diplomatic tool in the European marriage market – with Anne's encouragement. The Princess was presented to two of the visiting French ambassadors, 'shown to them first in very rich apparel, in state and triumph as a princess, and afterwards they saw her quite naked'.[72] Displaying royal children was not unusual in the complex system of matrimonial negotiations, and the ambassadors reported favourably to their master, François I.[73] It was with this in mind that in February 1535, the first talks of Elizabeth's marriage began as her father and the French King opened negotiations. The proposed groom was François's third son, Charles, Duke of Angoulême, who at thirteen was twelve years Elizabeth's senior.[74] François hoped that, having given Elizabeth the title of 'princess', Henry would 'treat her as his only heiress, so that the Crown of England may come to her on his death'.[75] Henry, of course, still hoped for a son to succeed him. The negotiations quickly ran into difficulties, with Henry refusing to give up the yearly French pension he had been receiving since signing the Treaty of the More in 1525, whereby he had agreed to relinquish some of England's territorial claims in France.[76] François, meanwhile, rejected the suggestion that his son ought to be educated in England. Though the negotiations continued for several months, they would come to nothing. This must have come as a bitter disappointment to Anne Boleyn, whose 'frequent importunities' to the French ambassadors to visit her daughter show that she was very much in favour of the match.[77]

Throughout 1535, Elizabeth moved between the royal residences of Hertfordshire, Surrey and London with her sister, receiving regular visits from her parents. Baby rattles had long been in use, often with a grid containing a ball that was then attached to a handle, and it is plausible that the young Elizabeth may have been given one to play with.[78] She may also have enjoyed playing with a cup and ball, and perhaps also a hobby horse as she grew a bit older. On a more practical level, her first steps could have been taken with the help of a wooden-framed baby walker, to the delight of those that witnessed them.[79]

In the early part of the year, she spent five weeks at court, where she was joined by 'divers of her servants'.[80] Many of Elizabeth's belongings travelled with her, including a splendid new cradle lined in crimson satin with a crimson silk fringe that was made especially for her and also came with its own leather travelling case.[81] Although Hatfield was her main residence, Elizabeth also had the use of Eltham and Hunsdon, close to the Essex border. The King had acquired Hunsdon from the Duke of Norfolk in 1525 and spent lavishly on improvements to the house, which boasted a 'great gallery'.[82] Apartments were likewise set aside for the Princess in the palaces where the court was in residence, in readiness for her visits to her parents. Early in the year she had, for example, been at Greenwich with them.

Anne, renowned for her sophisticated style with a preference for French fashions, lavished her daughter with costly gifts and took great care and expense to ensure Elizabeth was clothed in the richest garments made of the finest materials, as befitted her status. A clothes bill dating from the opening months of 1535 shows not only the Queen's expensive tastes but also the way in which she dressed Elizabeth.[83] The baby's wardrobe was certainly colourful and included an orange gown made of velvet, which must have complemented the red hair she had inherited from her father perfectly; fine black velvet and black satin for partlets (decorative garments covering the neck and upper chest, worn for modesty or warmth); velvet of russet brown for lining a velvet kirtle (part of a gown) of the same colour; and material in crimson, purple and white for lining her costly sleeves.[84] There was also yellow velvet and satin, and the same in green, as well as black velvet for mufflers (a kind of scarf).[85] Elizabeth was modelled as a smaller version of her fashionable mother, and Henry was likewise extremely fond of finery, so it is little wonder that in later life Elizabeth would show a penchant for splendid clothes.

It is possible that Anne also commissioned the artist Hans Holbein to design an elaborate new piece of jewellery for Elizabeth, perhaps with her infant daughter's French matrimonial negotiations in mind. Two versions of the same jewel were sketched by the artist, one with the addition of three pearls.[86] Shaped like a scroll and featuring precious stones, the jewel bore the inscription 'Mi Ladi Prinsis' (My Lady Princess). It has been suggested that Holbein may have designed this piece with Mary in mind, but that seems unlikely.[87] His associations with Anne were far stronger, for he had designed other items for her including a majestic fountain that she gifted to the King.[88] Anne was very fond of personalized jewels, evidenced by the initial items in her own collection – some of which Holbein may have designed – and while there is nothing to suggest that the scroll jewel was ever made, it is plausible that she might have wished her daughter to possess something similar.[89] She was, after all, eager to underline Elizabeth's royal status, and as a luxury item the jewel provided a tangible means of doing so. It may also be no coincidence that Mary had once been depicted wearing a comparable jewel, inscribed with 'The Emperor', at a time when her father had hoped to arrange her marriage to the Emperor Charles V.[90]

Elizabeth was growing quickly. By the time she reached her second birthday in September 1535, Lady Bryan felt the time had come for the Princess to be weaned. This was very much in keeping with contemporary attitudes towards the weaning of girls, who could expect to go through this process as much as a year before boys.[91] Lady Bryan expressed her opinion in a letter to Cromwell, which may have been sent while the King and Queen were on progress in the West Country that summer. In October, the court was on the final leg of that tour when the King sent word from Salisbury that his daughter 'shall be weaned with all diligence'.[92] Although the impetus was very much Henry's, Anne too wrote to Lady Bryan, undoubtedly conveying her own views on the subject.

Before long though, Anne's thoughts would have been occupied elsewhere, for in October she was in the early stages of another pregnancy. Just a few months earlier her third pregnancy had resulted in the birth of a stillborn child, and thus there was greater emphasis than ever on this fourth one.[93] She was fully aware that her husband no longer had the same ardour for her; despite Henry having once been utterly enthralled by Anne, her volatile temper, arrogance and hauteur had long since started to repel him, and in the summer of 1535 the Venetian ambassador reported that 'the King is already tired to satiety of this new Queen'.[94] In turn, Anne was tormented with jealousy over Henry's infidelities. In personal terms their marriage had begun to deteriorate, and dynastically Anne was seen to have failed in her duty thus far. It was little wonder, therefore, that she was full of anxiety over the outcome of her latest pregnancy. The stakes could not have been higher.

CHAPTER 3

'Declared Bastard'

'On the day upon which the Queen was beheaded, at sunrise,
between two and three o'clock, there was revealed to me
(whether I was asleep or awake I know not) the Queen's neck,
after her head had been cut off, and this so plainly that I could
count the nerves, the veins, and the arteries.'

ALEXANDER ALES TO ELIZABETH I, 1 SEPTEMBER 1559

A T THE BEGINNING of 1536, two-year-old Elizabeth was visiting her parents at Greenwich when they received some important news. 'God be praised that we are free from all suspicion of war' was Chapuys' memory of Henry's reaction as he was told that his first wife, Katherine of Aragon, had died at Kimbolton Castle on 7 January 1536.[1] His reference highlighted the concerns he had harboured that the Emperor Charles V, Katherine's nephew, might wage war on the King by reason of his treatment of his aunt. Both Henry and Anne professed themselves to be delighted by Katherine's death, but Anne must have realized that she was vulnerable, for with Katherine gone those who did not acknowledge her marriage to Henry would now consider him a widower.[2] Chapuys was disgusted by the couple's open demonstrations of joy, and this was made even worse because the ambassador knew that Katherine's daughter Mary would be so distraught she 'will die of grief'.[3] When writing his report to the Emperor, he could not hide his distaste: 'You could not conceive the joy that the King and those who favour this concubinage [Anne's family and supporters] have shown at the death of the good Queen, especially the

37

Earl of Wiltshire [Thomas Boleyn] and his son, who said it was a pity the Princess [Mary] did not keep company with her.'[4]

The following day 'the King was clad all over in yellow, from top to toe, except the white feather he had in his bonnet', a bright colour that made an insulting point.[5] This was reinforced when Elizabeth was 'triumphantly taken to church to the sound of trumpets and with great display'.[6] Later that day, 'after dinner, the King went to the hall, where the ladies were dancing, and there made great demonstration of joy, and at last went into his own apartments, took the little bastard [Elizabeth], carried her in his arms, and began to show her first to one, then to another, and did the same on the following days'.[7]

With Katherine's death, Henry perceived that he had been relieved not only from the threat of war with Spain but also from the woman whose obstinacy had triggered his break with the Roman Catholic Church. At this moment of what he saw as triumph, Henry could not resist proudly showcasing Elizabeth – his heir – for all to see. According to Chapuys, there were similar displays on subsequent days, and even a joust. With Katherine dead, Anne made a further attempt to extend the olive branch to her grieving stepdaughter, sending word that if only Mary would submit to her father's will, 'she would be the best friend to her in the world and be like another mother'.[8] Mary refused. Henry and Anne's jubilation would be fleeting, as things were about to go terribly, tragically wrong.

On 24 January, the King was thrown from his horse during a jousting tournament at Greenwich. He 'fell so heavily that everyone thought it a miracle he was not killed', but incredibly he 'sustained no injury'.[9] Five days later, the funeral of Katherine of Aragon took place at the Abbey of Peterborough, and Henry's former wife was laid to rest 'in a grave at the lowest step of the high altar'.[10] In what must have seemed like a cruel twist of fate, that same day Anne miscarried of a foetus 'which seemed to be a male child'.[11] In her distress she was quick to point the finger at her uncle, the Duke of Norfolk, who had delivered the news of Henry's fall, for 'it was said she took a fright, for the King ran that time at the ring and had a fall from his horse', the trauma of which caused her to miscarry.[12] Chapuys had also been told that Anne attempted to blame her husband's infidelity, claiming that, since the love she bore Henry was far greater than that of Katherine of Aragon, 'her heart broke when she saw that he loved others'.[13] Few gave these explanations any credence, and Chapuys believed that some thought the real reason 'was owing to her own incapacity to bear children, others to a fear that the King would treat her like the late Queen'. Whatever the cause, there was no denying that it was a devastating outcome at which Henry showed 'great distress'.[14] In his grief, he could not bring himself to communicate with his wife, except to say that 'he saw clearly that God did not wish to give him male children'.[15]

Anne was distraught at the loss of her child, but she could not afford to wallow. By February she appeared to be confident of becoming pregnant once more, and Chapuys had been told that 'the concubine, after her abortion [miscarriage], consoled her maids who wept, telling them it was for the best, because she would be the sooner with child again, and that the son she bore would not be doubtful like this one, which had been conceived during the life of the Queen; thereby acknowledging a doubt about the bastardy of her daughter'.[16] If Anne did indeed believe this to be the case, it shows that she thought Elizabeth was already feeling the sting of the unprecedented circumstances of her parents' relationship and marriage. Though Henry acknowledged Elizabeth as his legitimate heir, Katherine of Aragon and Mary's faction would always claim that Henry's separation from his first wife had not been lawful and thus that his marriage to Anne had been invalid. Elizabeth therefore provided easy pickings for her mother's enemies, and the stigma of illegitimacy would plague her all her life. This would become ever more apparent as she grew, but in 1536 her youth rendered her oblivious to such concerns over legitimacy.

Anne too had other preoccupations, for despite her optimism at the prospect of a future pregnancy, she suspected that her husband had long since tired of her. By the end of February, the rift between the royal couple was clear for all to see, and several courtiers told Chapuys that 'for more than three months this King has not spoken ten times to the concubine'.[17] Anne had not coped well with the transition from mistress to Queen, and her overbearing and argumentative ways repulsed Henry. He had long since sought comfort elsewhere, but his latest love interest was no passing fancy: indeed, the lady now waiting in the wings would play the same game once so skilfully executed by Anne herself.

JANE SEYMOUR WAS one of the Queen's ladies. The daughter of Sir John Seymour, a Wiltshire knight, Jane had – like her mistress – once served in the household of Katherine of Aragon, for whom she had the utmost admiration. Having been born in around 1509, Jane was Anne's junior by several years, and in both appearance and character they could not have been more different. Where Anne was dark and sallow, Jane was 'of middle stature and no great beauty, so fair that one would call her rather pale than otherwise'.[18] In contrast to Anne's fiery disposition, Jane appeared demure, playing on her virtue and modesty. This seems to have been a very deliberate strategy, masking a steely determination to ensnare the King in the manner Anne once had. It worked. Jane's maidenly behaviour appealed to Henry, and by the time of Anne's latest miscarriage he was giving Jane 'great presents'.[19] Yet Jane made a point of refusing to accept them. In April, for example, the King sent her a letter with a purse full of sovereigns. Rather than opening it, Jane,

> *after kissing the letter, returned it unopened to the messenger, and throwing herself on her knees before him, begged the said messenger that he would pray the King on her part to consider that she was a gentlewoman of good and honorable parents, without reproach, and that she had no greater riches in the world than her honor, which she would not injure for a thousand deaths, and that if he wished to make her some present in money she begged it might be when God enabled her to make some honorable match.[20]*

Henry was enchanted by this virtuous display, and his 'love and desire towards the said lady was wonderfully increased'.[21] The same tactics Anne had once so successfully used to keep Henry enamoured at a distance were now employed by Jane to captivate him once more. On his orders she was installed in apartments at Greenwich that lay close to his own – rooms formerly occupied by Cromwell, who tactfully vacated. To signify that his intentions were honourable, Henry lodged Jane's brother, Edward, and his wife with her, to act as chaperones. Primed by Anne's enemies, Jane had been told that 'she must by no means comply with the King's wishes except by way of marriage; in which she is quite firm'.[22] Chapuys had heard that Jane could be 'proud and haughty', yet her 'great love and reverence' for the Lady Mary, coupled with his loathing for Anne Boleyn, compelled him to support her.[23]

As Henry's ardour for Jane Seymour grew, and with it her influence, so too did the jealousy with which Anne viewed her. During these tense weeks Elizabeth remained at Greenwich with her parents, where her mother was masking her unhappiness by throwing herself into updating her daughter's wardrobe. Already that year Anne had paid for return boat hire from Greenwich to London in order 'to take measure of caps for my Lady Princess, and again to fetch the Princess's purple satin cap to mend it'. Among the other items she had purchased were a 'white satin cap laid with a rich caul of gold' and another of crimson satin.[24] Anne must have taken great pleasure in seeing little Elizabeth so gorgeously bedecked in the latest fashions. Towards the end of April, however, Anne's anxiety grew. Something was afoot, yet she had no idea how deep it ran: unbeknown to her, her former ally Thomas Cromwell was plotting her downfall.

RELATIONS BETWEEN ANNE and Cromwell had long been strained, chiefly on account of their differing views over the dissolution of English monasteries, which had been instigated by Cromwell following Henry's separation from the Roman Catholic Church. Anne had always been in favour of church reform and had encouraged Henry to read the reformist books she owned, but she was against dissolving the monasteries altogether.[25] Instead, she wished to abolish corruption from within them, reform them and use the revenues for charitable causes and education.[26] Cromwell, though also a reformist, pushed for fully dissolving the monasteries, with the funds to be directed into the King's coffers. Foreign policy also played a part in their rift, for while Anne favoured an English alliance with France, Cromwell preferred an Imperial alliance with the Emperor Charles V and had begun to view Anne as a threat. What was more, she had made no secret of the fact that she 'would like to see his head cut off'.[27]

By the spring of 1536 tensions had reached boiling point, and on Passion Sunday, 2 April, Anne's almoner preached a sermon in which he publicly denounced Cromwell and other members of the King's Council, warning that 'a King's councillor ought to take good heed what advice he gave in altering ancient things, and that no people wished to take away the ceremonies of the Church, such as holy water'.[28] Cromwell was furious but bided his time as he prepared to hit back. By 18 April, he had decided that Anne had to go.[29]

On 23 April, St George's Day, the King's Master of Horse Sir Nicholas Carew was admitted to the Order of the Garter, much to the disappointment of Anne's brother, Lord Rochford, 'who was seeking for it, and all the more because the concubine has not had sufficient influence to get it for her brother'.[30] This was not quite true, for though Chapuys intimated that Rochford's failure to win admittance to the Garter was a sign of Anne's lessening power, Eric Ives has shown that this is unlikely to have been the case.[31] As he said, 'Anne did not lightly surrender her husband to Jane Seymour.'[32] Henry may not have been intoxicated by Anne any longer, but she still held some sway, and there is no evidence that he planned to remove her. Indeed, the royal couple were due to travel to Calais in May. Carew, however, was married to Lady Bryan's daughter, Elizabeth, and was a firm member of Jane Seymour's camp; he had become disillusioned with Anne long before 1536 on account of her arrogance and poor treatment of his friends.[33] Once sympathetic to Katherine of Aragon and her daughter, shortly after his election to the Garter, he sent word to the Lady Mary bidding her to be of 'good cheer', for 'the King was already as sick and tired of the concubine as could be'.[34] Carew evidently felt that Anne's star was waning.

It was probably that same day of the Garter election that Cromwell approached the King with some disturbing news about the Queen's

conduct, which he himself would relate in a letter to two of Henry's diplo-
mats serving abroad on 14 May.[35] Anne's living, he told them, was 'so
rank and common that the ladies of her privy chamber could not conceal
it'. In other words, the Queen's morals were being brought into question –
and before long, this gossip had come to 'the ears of some of the Council,
who told his Majesty, although with great fear'.[36] Precisely what Henry
was told during this meeting is unknown, but it was enough for him to
authorize Cromwell to get to the bottom of the matter. Historians are
still divided over Cromwell's involvement in Anne's fall, but the accounts
provided in the surviving sources leave little room to doubt that he was
the prime mover.[37] Indeed, Cromwell himself later admitted to Chapuys
that he had 'planned and brought about the whole affair'.[38]

Forty years later, when Elizabeth herself occupied the English throne,
a lady of the court would observe that the royal household was 'full of
malice and spite', and it was no different in the spring of 1536.[39] Though
she was oblivious to any revelations Cromwell had made to her husband
about her alleged conduct, Queen Anne was becoming increasingly
uneasy in the hostile atmosphere surrounding her. So much so that on
or around 26 April she approached her chaplain, Matthew Parker. Anne
trusted Parker implicitly and implored him to do something for her: if
anything should happen to her, she charged him with keeping a watchful
eye on her child.[40] Elizabeth, Anne's chief jewel and the daughter whom
she adored, was her foremost priority.

Though Anne did not confide her fears, the conversation made a deep
impression on Parker, who would remember in Elizabeth's reign 'the
last words that ever her Majesty's mother spake to me concerning her'.[41]
Parker clearly felt honour-bound by whatever Anne had said to him, for
he later referred to it on several occasions. In 1559, soon after Elizabeth's
accession, he confided to Sir Nicholas Bacon that 'though my heart would
right fain serve my sovereign lady the Queen's majesty, in more respects
than of mine allegiance, not forgetting what words her grace's mother said
to me of her, not six days before her apprehension'.[42] Likewise, in 1572 he
told William Cecil that 'if I had not been so much bound to the mother, I
would not so soon have granted to serve the daughter'.[43] Though Parker

never divulged more on paper, it is tantalizing to consider whether he ever confided to Elizabeth the details of this final conversation with Anne. Perhaps she knew more about her mother's fall than she would ever reveal.

ELSEWHERE, CROMWELL WAS busy putting his case against the Queen into action. According to the account of Scottish theologian Alexander Ales, who later delivered his version of events to Elizabeth (along with a request for financial assistance), intelligence had been gathered that proved Anne had been indulging in illicit affairs with men at court. 'The first accuser' against the Queen was thought to be the Countess of Worcester, one of her ladies who had served at her coronation and to whom she had been close.[44] Ales was ideally placed to recollect how matters played out, for he was at court in Cromwell's entourage. He also knew Archbishop Cranmer, Elizabeth's godfather, well. Ales would later tell Elizabeth that on 30 April, Cromwell and his supporters assured 'the King that the affair is beyond doubt; that they had seen the Queen dancing with the gentlemen of the King's chamber, that they can produce witnesses who will vouch to the Queen having kissed her own brother'.[45]

On that final day of April, as he listened to the evidence that was set out before him, Henry was both furious and seemingly genuinely convinced of his wife's guilt. The accusation of incest with Anne's brother, Lord Rochford, was shocking and sickening, and an additional four men would eventually be charged with having committed adultery with her. One of them, a musician named Mark Smeaton, was 'a player on the spinnet [a small harpsichord] of her chamber' as well as a Groom of the Privy Chamber; he was arrested the same day and taken to Cromwell's house in Stepney for questioning.[46] Such was Henry's anger that it was only a matter of time before the Queen herself was arrested, too.

Later on 30 April, Ales claimed to have witnessed an argument between Elizabeth's parents. Elizabeth herself was also present, although she would never have remembered it. Ales would later report to her, mournfully: 'Never shall I forget the sorrow which I felt when I saw the most serene

Queen, your most religious mother, carrying you, still a little baby, in her arms and entreating the most serene King, your father, in Greenwich Palace, from the open window of which he was looking into the court-yard, when she brought you to him.'[47] By his own admission, 'I did not perfectly understand what had been going on, but the faces and gestures of the speakers plainly showed that the King was angry, although he could conceal his anger wonderfully well.'[48] There is no way of knowing what had prompted the quarrel – perhaps, as her anxiety heightened, Anne had now reached breaking point. Or it may have concerned an unwise conversation that Anne had had with Sir Henry Norris, the King's 'most private and familiar' Groom of the Stool (and one of those who would later be accused of adultery with the Queen), of which Henry may have been made aware.[49] Clutching Elizabeth as they argued may have been Anne's way of attempting to soften Henry's anger towards her by appeal-ing to his love for his daughter – but the love Henry once felt for Anne had by now vanished. Sadly for Elizabeth, the moments spent in her mother's arms were about to come to an abrupt end.

On 1 May, the court was enjoying the usual May Day jousting revel-ries at Greenwich. Elizabeth's uncle, Lord Rochford, led the challengers, while Norris led the defenders. Though the King and Queen were sitting together, Henry was barely on speaking terms with his wife, and when he received a message halfway through, he suddenly left the tournament – and Anne – behind. Alison Weir has surmised that Henry had just been informed that Mark Smeaton had confessed his guilt and incrim-inated others, and this seems highly plausible.[50] Of all the men accused of adultery with Anne, Smeaton was the only one who would ever confess, perhaps as a result of torture or the threat of it, or at the very least the promise of a pardon.[51] A bewildered Anne, now more anxious than ever, must have wondered why Henry had left so suddenly. She would never see him again.

Once the jousting had concluded, Henry's former favourite, Sir Henry Norris, was arrested on the King's orders. Henry questioned him person-ally, accusing him of adultery with Anne but promising him mercy if he confessed.[52] A horrified Norris refused, and he was conveyed to the

Tower the following day.[53] The Queen's brother Lord Rochford, who – unbeknown to him – had been accused of incest with Anne, was likewise arrested on 2 May and sent to the Tower.

Elsewhere, in Greenwich Palace on 2 May, Anne received a summons from the Privy Council. She had no idea of the events that had been taking place around her, yet for some time she had been filled with an increasing sense of foreboding. When she arrived in the Council chamber she found her uncle, the Duke of Norfolk, Sir William FitzWilliam and Sir William Paulet waiting for her. There was no time for niceties, and to her horror she found herself accused of adultery with Smeaton, Norris and one other man who was not named. She would later claim that she had been 'cruelly handled' by the Council, and particularly by the Duke of Norfolk.[54] Anne denied the charges, but it was not enough. That afternoon, with no time to bid farewell to her daughter, she was arrested and taken 'in full daylight' to the Tower by barge.[55] Escorted by the Duke of Norfolk, Cromwell and five others, Anne arrived at the fortress via the ancient Byward Tower, the thundering cannons signalling her arrival.[56] She was given over into the custody of Sir William Kingston, the Constable of the Tower, who had accompanied her from Greenwich and had once observed the happiness of the royal family when the King and Queen visited Elizabeth at Eltham – happiness that now lay shattered. Kingston was tasked with the unprecedented role of jailer to the Queen of England. Anne's composure was fast deserting her, and she asked Kingston woefully: 'Shall I go into a dungeon?' 'No, Madam,' he replied, 'you shall go into the lodging you lay in at your coronation.' These were the Queen's apartments, which had been redecorated just three years earlier to mark that most magnificent of occasions.[57] Anne's reply was extraordinary. 'It is too good for me,' she said; 'Jesu have mercy on me', before kneeling and 'weeping a good pace, and in the same sorrow fell into a great laughing, as she has done many times since'.[58]

Four ladies had been appointed to wait on Anne in the Tower, all of whom were unsympathetic to her plight. She was distressed at having 'such about me as I never loved', yet, Kingston assured her, the King took them to be 'honest and good women'.[59] Two of these were Anne's own aunts, Lady Boleyn, wife of her father's brother Sir James, and Lady Shelton, whose role overseeing life in Elizabeth's household makes it plausible that she reported to Anne about her daughter at this time. Clearly relations between the latter and her niece had soured at some point, for reasons unknown.[60] Mrs Margaret Coffin, the wife of Anne's Master of Horse, and Kingston's own wife, Mary, accounted for the other two ladies. As one who had once served Katherine of Aragon and was extremely fond of the Lady Mary, Lady Kingston certainly had no reason to love Anne.[61] There were also two chamberers (female attendants). Kingston gave orders that none of the women were to communicate with Anne unless his wife were present.

By the end of her first evening in the Tower, Anne was aware that both Norris and Smeaton were there too. Her distress was palpable, and her thoughts turned to her family. 'Oh, my mother, thou wilt die with sorrow,' she lamented. Her thoughts turning darker, Anne proceeded to ask the Constable: 'Mr Kingston, shall I die without justice?' He replied, 'The poorest subject the King hath, hath justice,' at which she laughed.[62] She must have known that her enemies were working for her downfall and would not rest until she had been removed. Though Anne would make several references to members of her family over the course of the coming days, there is no known mention of her little daughter. It is impossible to think that Elizabeth would not have been on Anne's mind, but perhaps she felt it safer to avoid mentioning her daughter at this dangerous and febrile time.

Over the next few days, the details of the accusations laid against Anne became clearer: adultery, incest and treason by conspiring to cause the King's death. The latter was the most sinister, for it would be alleged that Anne had spoken of this with her supposed lovers, telling them that 'she had never loved the King in her heart, and had said to every one of them by themselves that she loved them more than the others'.[63] Her situation would also worsen on account of the dangerous conversation, referred to above, that she had shared shortly before her arrest with Sir Henry Norris, whose position as Groom of the Stool was one of great favour and trust, for it was he who attended Henry as he performed his most intimate human functions. After she asked Norris why he did not go through with his marriage to her cousin Madge Shelton, Norris had replied that he would wait for a time. Anne's answer was shocking: 'You look for dead men's shoes, for if aught came to the King but good, you would look to have me.' Anne recalled that a stunned Norris retorted, 'If he should have any such thought he would his head were off.'[64] Such talk was treasonous, and Anne had panicked when she realized the conversation had been overheard. So much so that in an attempt to save her virtue she had sent Norris to her almoner to swear that 'she was a good woman'.[65] But it was too late: the conversation was reported to Cromwell and would later be used as evidence against Anne. Aside from Anne's brother Lord Rochford, Sir Henry Norris and Mark Smeaton, four other men were also arrested: Sir Francis Weston, William Brereton, Sir Richard Page and Anne's former admirer Sir Thomas Wyatt. Only the latter two would be released without charge.[66]

Thanks to Kingston's detailed reports, the days that followed are some of the best documented of Anne's life, for everything that she said and did was reported to the King's Council. The reports show that she struggled to adapt to her drastic change in circumstances, and her behaviour became increasingly erratic. As Kingston reported, 'One hour she is determined to die and the next hour much contrary to that.'[67] She frequently spoke indiscreetly and was troubled by conversations she had shared with some of the men with whom she was accused, most especially the one with Norris. But she was adamant that she was innocent of the charges she faced. One of the women appointed to wait on her would later tell Chapuys that Anne, 'before and after receiving the sacrament, affirmed to her, on the damnation of her soul, that she had never been unfaithful to the King'.[68] Anne's fall has been the subject of much recent scholarship, but not many truly believe her to have been guilty of the crimes of which she stood accused. The late George Bernard, however, was among the few to suggest that there may have been some truth in the accusations, although he did not agree with them in their entirety.[69] Bernard is, though, among the minority, for most modern historians believe that the charges against Anne were constructed as part of a deliberate plot to engineer her downfall, and indeed many of them can be proven false based on sheer logistics. The first charge of adultery, for example, was said to have taken place at Westminster with Norris on 6 and 12 October 1533, just a month after the birth of Elizabeth and while Anne was still at Greenwich.[70]

A few days after Anne's arrest, Elizabeth travelled to Hunsdon with her sister Mary. There she would remain while the events of Anne's fall played out, oblivious to the fact that she would never see her mother again, and was, indeed, unlikely to remember her. It had been decided that the Queen and the men accused with her would stand trial, and on 12 May Norris, Weston, Brereton and Smeaton were all taken to Westminster Hall for this purpose. Among the commissioners appointed to sit in judgement on the accused was Anne's uncle, the Duke of Norfolk, who had been appointed Lord High Steward of England and would later refer to the 'malice borne me' by both his nieces who had married the King (the other being Henry's fifth wife, Katherine Howard).[71] Anne's father, Thomas Boleyn, had also been summoned to attend and, perhaps in an attempt to cling on to his position – he was still Lord Privy Seal, although this post would be taken from him in June – he was reportedly ready to aid proceedings.[72] As the trials began, all four men were accused of adultery with the Queen. Norris, Weston and Brereton submitted pleas of not guilty; Smeaton alone 'pleaded guilty of violation and carnal knowledge of the Queen'.[73] Though there was nothing substantial in the way of evidence, all four were found guilty and condemned to the hanging, drawing and quartering that constituted a traitor's death. Even Chapuys admitted that the men had been condemned 'upon presumption and certain indications, without valid proof or confession'.[74] It was Anne's turn next.

Never before had a Queen of England been put on trial, and thus nobody quite knew what the protocol for such an event should be. However, many believed that the verdict was a foregone conclusion – including Cromwell, who wrote to two of his colleagues that Anne and her brother 'will undoubtedly go the same way' as those already condemned.[75] It was decided that both Anne and Lord Rochford would be tried in the thirteenth-century Great Hall at the Tower – better known as the King's Hall – and it was there that, on the morning of 15 May, the officials gathered for what was to be a public occasion.[76] Once again the Duke of Norfolk oversaw proceedings, joined by more than two dozen peers of the realm, including Anne's former suitor, Henry Percy, now Earl of Northumberland.[77] Chapuys had also heard that Anne's own father was 'quite as ready to assist at the judgment' as he had been at the trials of the condemned men, but it is uncertain whether he attended Anne's trial. In total, however, Chapuys believed that over two thousand people were present.[78]

Anne was escorted into the hall by Sir William Kingston and attended by her ladies. Wearing a black velvet gown over a scarlet petticoat, the Queen appeared calm and collected, in contrast to the earlier consternation she had shown.[79] Each of the charges, encompassing adultery, incest and plotting the King's death, were read out, and among the accusations levelled were that she and her brother had 'laughed at the King and his dress, and that she showed in various ways she did not love the King but was tired of him'.[80] Anne ably defended herself against her accusers, giving plausible answers and pleading not guilty to each charge. Yet her efforts to absolve herself were in vain. Even though her earliest biographer, William Camden, would later claim that 'the multitude that stood by judged her to be innocent, and merely circumvented', Anne listened in dismay as each of the peers who sat in judgement upon her declared her guilty in turn.[81] With a unanimous guilty verdict, there could only be one outcome. It was left to the Queen's uncle, Norfolk, to pronounce the sentence upon his niece. 'Because thou hast offended against our sovereign the King's Grace in committing treason against his person,' Norfolk began, 'the law of the realm is this, that thou shalt be burnt here within the Tower of London on the Green, else to have thy head smitten off.'[82] The Queen of England was condemned to be burned or beheaded at the King's pleasure, and though she 'preserved her composure' as she heard her sentence, she declared 'what she regretted most' was that the men who were charged with her, 'who were innocent and loyal to the King [were] to die for her'.[83] She must, however, have been desolate at the thought of leaving her baby daughter motherless and would have understood all too well that Elizabeth would be unlikely to remember her.

Later that day, Anne's brother Lord Rochford was tried separately. The charges were similar to those levelled at the Queen, but significantly for Elizabeth one of them was that he had 'spread reports which called in question whether his sister's daughter was the King's child'.[84] It was an accusation to which Rochford did not respond, although he defended himself admirably on many of the other charges laid against him. As with his sister before him, Rochford's words were not enough to save him, and he too was condemned to a traitor's death. Once his sentence had been pronounced, he said that since he had been judged to die, 'he would no longer maintain his innocence, but confessed that he had deserved death'.[85]

The following day, Archbishop Cranmer visited the condemned Queen Anne at the Tower. Though he had once been one of her chief supporters, and he had 'never better opinion of woman', Cranmer was now tasked by the King with obtaining Anne's consent to the annulment of her marriage.[86] She would have recognized that such assent would render Elizabeth illegitimate, but Anne appears to have believed that if she agreed then she would be granted mercy and her life spared. Even Kingston wrote that at dinner that day Anne had spoken of going to a nunnery and was 'in hope of life'.[87] Perhaps it was fear of death that persuaded Anne to give her consent, but she must also have been aware that in so doing she was agreeing to brand her daughter a bastard.

On the morning of 17 May, Cromwell, the Duke of Suffolk and several other lords and members of the King's Council joined Cranmer at Lambeth Palace. There, the Archbishop officially annulled Henry and Anne's marriage on the grounds of 'the King having had connection with her sister'.[88] In other words, Henry's earlier affair with Mary Boleyn was now used as a means of dissolving his marriage to Anne. This was to have significant consequences for Elizabeth, for no longer was she to be styled 'princess' but, similarly to her sister, she was to be addressed as the Lady Elizabeth. She was now 'declared bastard'. What was more, there were whispers circulating that she was not even the King's child; Chapuys had been told that while annulling the marriage, Cranmer 'declared by sentence that the concubine's daughter was the bastard of Mr Norris, and not the King's daughter'.[89] There is no evidence that Henry ever questioned that Elizabeth was his; indeed, according to Ales, 'your father always acknowledged you as legitimate' and nothing could 'persuade the illustrious King that you were not his daughter'.[90] But his daughter Mary would later remark that 'she had the face and countenance of Mark Smeaton, who was a very handsome man'.[91] Elizabeth became aware of such reports, and the stigma of illegitimacy – which had been circulating since the moment of her birth – and murmurings about her parentage would haunt her for the rest of her life.

Later that same morning, the five condemned men were led out of the Tower to nearby Tower Hill and executed. Chapuys claimed that Anne witnessed the executions from the Tower, 'to aggravate her grief', but it is unlikely that she would have been able to do so from where her apartments were situated.[92] Despite their having been found guilty, she knew them to be innocent of the charges of adultery and incest, and she 'asked about the patience shown by her brother and the others'.[93] In a show of clemency, the King had commuted their sentences to decapitation, and it was Elizabeth's uncle, Lord Rochford, who died first. After the axe fell finally on the neck of Mark Smeaton, the remains of the executed men were returned to the Tower for burial; Rochford was buried in the Chapel of St Peter ad Vincula, while the other four men were interred in the adjoining churchyard.

In a final act of mercy to the woman he had once loved so passionately, Henry also commuted Anne's sentence to beheading and even sent to Calais for an expert French swordsman to perform the act – a rarity in England.[94] Much to Anne's distress though, the executioner was delayed, and thus so too was her end, originally scheduled for the morning of 18 May. Kingston's reports show that her state of mind became agitated once more, and he did his best to reassure her that she would feel no pain. 'I heard say the executioner was very good,' Anne said, 'and I have a little neck.' At this, she 'put her hand about it, laughing heartily'. Kingston was amazed: 'I have seen many men and also women executed, and all they have been in great sorrow, and to my knowledge this lady has much joy and pleasure in death.'[95]

As dawn broke on the morning of 19 May, after a sleepless night Anne's time had come. Accompanied by four ladies to the scaffold that had been erected close to the White Tower within the stronghold's precincts, 'she went to the place of execution with an untroubled countenance'.[96] Though she was to be given the privilege of a private execution away from London's crowds, 'a great number of the King's subjects' had still gathered to see her die – as many as a thousand people according to one contemporary.[97] Among them were Cromwell and Elizabeth's illegitimate brother, Henry Fitzroy, Duke of Richmond. Having mounted the scaffold, which was covered with black cloth, Anne was confronted with the headsman who would shortly be tasked with taking her life. A Portuguese witness noted that by this point she was 'very much exhausted and amazed'. Addressing Sir William Kingston, she 'begged leave to speak to the people, promising to say nothing but what was good'.[98] Permission granted, she addressed the gathered crowd in a short speech. 'Good Christian people, I have not come here to preach a sermon; I have come here to die,' she began.

> *For according to the law and by the law I am judged to die, and therefore I will speak nothing against it. I am come hither to accuse no man, nor to speak of that whereof I am accused and condemned to die, but I pray God save the King and send him long to reign over you, for a gentler nor a more merciful prince was there never, and to me he was ever a good, a gentle, and sovereign lord. And if any person will meddle of my cause, I require them to judge the best. And thus I take my leave of the world and of you all, and I heartily desire you all to pray for me.*[99]

Her final words spoken, Anne prepared to meet her maker. We will never know if her thoughts turned to Elizabeth, but given her love for her daughter it is difficult to believe that they did not. Having removed her ermine mantle and English hood, one of Anne's ladies gave her a linen cap with which to cover her hair. There being no block on which to lay her head, she knelt in the straw, arranging her skirts around her feet, and a blindfold was tied about her eyes.[100] According to Ales, Anne herself then 'commanded the executioner to strike'.[101] Moments later, Anne's head was removed with a single swift stroke from the French swordsman.

Her head, having been covered in a white cloth, was taken away by one of her ladies, and this, together with her bodily remains, was interred in the Chapel of St Peter ad Vincula within the Tower. No memorial was ever raised to her, and the only sign of her presence is a marble memorial stone that was installed on the orders of Queen Victoria almost three hundred and fifty years later.[102]

Elizabeth was at Hunsdon when her mother lost her life. Shortly after Anne's execution, Lady Kingston was dispatched to inform the Lady Mary of her stepmother's death, but it is unknown how or when Elizabeth learned of Anne's fate, or whether she understood that it had been her father who was responsible.[103] Given that she was yet to reach her third birthday, it is unlikely she was told then and there that the mother of whom she would likely have no memory was dead, yet later in Elizabeth's life the knowledge of what had happened within the Tower's walls would haunt her, and she would forever harbour a deep loathing of the fortress.[104] Most modern historians believe that Anne Boleyn was the victim of a plot – but, most importantly, what did Elizabeth come to believe? Alexander Ales would later attest to 'the false accusations laid to the charge of that most holy Queen, your most pious mother', and he was probably not the only one who shared such opinions with Elizabeth.[105]

On account of her age and the large periods of time they spent apart, it seems highly unlikely that the infant Elizabeth shared a strongly developed emotional bond with Anne in life, but this is not to say that she did not feel her loss. Her eventual sense of bereavement may also have had some bearing on her health and development, for, as mentioned earlier, we know that she suffered from a variety of ailments in her youth and continued to be troubled into adulthood (see Appendix 1). It is true that once Elizabeth became Queen she made no attempt to remove her mother's remains from the Tower to a more fitting place of burial, neither did she try to revoke the same legislation that rendered her illegitimate, and though there were sound reasons for letting sleeping dogs lie, taken at face value both of these could be seen as evidence of a disregard for Anne.[106] But there are other clues as to her attitude towards her late mother, many of which have been highlighted by Tracy Borman in her fascinating study of Elizabeth and Anne.[107] She would, for example, adopt Anne's motto of *Semper Eadem* ('Always the same') on becoming Queen, as well as Anne's falcon badge, which was used on some of her books – one example appears in St John's College, Cambridge.[108] A virginal probably owned by Elizabeth and now in the Victoria and Albert Museum also displays the falcon badge.[109]

Elizabeth came to share a warm relationship with many of her Boleyn relatives, including Anne's niece, Katherine Carey. Katherine was the daughter of Elizabeth's aunt Mary Boleyn and, on the surface at least, her first husband, William Carey. There is evidence to suggest that Katherine was actually a result of her mother's affair with the King, but if this was the case then it was certainly never openly spoken of or acknowledged at court.[110] Prior to Elizabeth's accession she and Katherine developed a very close relationship, and it is possible that the latter, who was several years older than Elizabeth, was sent to join her household from a young age.[111] Although her name does not appear on the surviving lists of members of Elizabeth's household, it is a possibility and would explain the closeness shared by the two. By the same token, Elizabeth would also become close to Katherine's brother, Henry, who had once been her mother's ward.[112] Elizabeth later promoted not only Katherine and Henry but others among her mother's relatives to positions of great favour, thereby keeping them close to her. These relationships were of the utmost importance to her and provided a way to keep the tenuous memory of her mother alive in her mind.

Two other women who were close to Elizabeth, Mary Cheke (née Hill) and Elisabeth Brooke, came to own and inscribe the Book of Hours that had once been Anne's and in which she had written, 'Remember me when you do pray, that hope doth lead from day to day.'[113] It is possible that Elizabeth would have seen this. Then there is the famous Chequers ring, a beautiful mother-of-pearl band set with gold and rubies, and the monogram 'ER' in diamonds and enamel. The ring features a locket containing two exquisitely painted tiny miniatures. One of these was Elizabeth, while the other is a woman who seems likely to have been Anne. Elizabeth owned this ring during her queenship, although how and when it came into her possession is unknown. It could have been a gift from one of her courtiers; Susan Doran has suggested it may have been given to her by Edward Seymour, later Duke of Somerset.[114] Elizabeth kept it until the end of her life, confirming that it was a treasured piece.

Some of Anne's belongings also found their way into Elizabeth's possession, including one of her famous initial jewels.[115] It seems unlikely that the former Princess would have had much else to remind her of her mother, for in the aftermath of her death her father ordered all traces of Anne to be eradicated. Her portraits were taken down, and most of her badges were removed from the royal palaces.[116] Items of plate featuring Anne's cipher and initial nevertheless remained in use, but there were few signs left of the woman for whom Elizabeth's father had once been prepared to move Heaven and Earth to make her his.[117] Elizabeth, now declared illegitimate and facing an uncertain future, would be forced to live with the effects of Anne's fall for the rest of her life.

CHAPTER 4

'The Late Princess, Lady Elizabeth'

'Then commandment was that she should be called Lady Princess, and the other Lady Princess.'

HMC RUTLAND, I

IN THE AFTERMATH of her mother's death, Elizabeth found herself in the same unfortunate circumstances as her sister Mary, now the closest female relative she had: motherless and illegitimate. Elizabeth's youth ensured she was shielded from the immediate impact of the consequences of her mother's fall, but this would only be temporary. It would not be long before the precocious youngster recognized that she was no longer the most important royal child in the country.

Anne Boleyn had been dead for just eleven days when Henry VIII married Jane Seymour in the Queen's Closet at the Palace of Whitehall (formerly York Place) on 30 May. Shortly afterwards the newlyweds travelled to Greenwich, where Jane was fully honoured as Queen by the courtiers over whom she now presided. There were many who approved of Henry's choice of third wife, among them the courtier Sir John Russell, who wrote to assure the King's uncle Lord Lisle that Jane was 'as gentle a lady as ever I knew, and as fair a Queen as any in Christendom'. Russell was not as complimentary about Elizabeth's mother, of whom he had never been fond, affirming that the King 'hath come out of hell into heaven for the gentleness in this and the cursedness and the unhappiness in the other'.[1] There were few, it seemed, who mourned Anne's passing, and her remaining family largely retired into the shadows. Elizabeth, yet to reach her third birthday, was too young to write to her new stepmother, or indeed to have any true understanding that she had one. Mary's circumstances, however, were completely different, and having obtained permission to write to their father she wasted no time in sending her congratulations from Hunsdon.[2] Mary felt sure that with the death of 'that woman', whom 'I pray our Lord of His great mercy to forgive', her troubles would be at an end and she would soon be reconciled with her father.[3] She was mistaken.

It was probably with the encouragement of Lady Kingston that, just a week after Anne's execution, Mary had written to Cromwell, imploring him to speak to the King and obtain his permission for her to write.[4] Cromwell responded quickly, and on 30 May, the same day as her father's wedding, Mary thanked Henry's chief advisor for 'the great pain and labour' he had taken on her behalf.[5] The following day she wrote to Henry herself, 'humbly beseeching your Highness to consider that I am but a woman, and your child, who hath committed her soul only to God, and her body to be ordered in this world as it shall stand with your pleasure'.[6] Great pressure was now brought to bear on her to accept Henry's supremacy as Head of the Church of England, thereby acknowledging her own illegitimacy. Cromwell, who told her that he thought her 'the most obstinate woman that ever was', urged Mary to comply and warned her against defying her father further.[7]

When a party led by the Duke of Norfolk and the Earl of Sussex arrived at Hunsdon to convince Mary to yield, so vigorous were they in their admonitions that they threatened: 'If she was their daughter, they would beat her and knock her head so violently against the wall that they would make it as soft as baked apples.'[8] Worn down and exhausted, suffering from 'the pain in my head and teeth' and craving her father's love, after years of steadfast defiance Mary finally capitulated.[9] Fearful of the consequences if she continued to refuse, she signed the articles that were placed before her, admitting with the stroke of a pen that her mother's marriage had been 'by God's law and man's law incestuous and unlawful', and that she herself was a bastard.[10] She would never forgive herself for what she believed to be the ultimate betrayal of her mother's memory.

Elizabeth is unlikely to have been fully aware of the emotional torment Mary faced that summer, or that Thomas Wriothesley, a gentleman in Cromwell's service, had apparently been sent to speak with Mary about her younger sister.[11] Mary referenced the conversation in a letter to Cromwell on 23 June, acknowledging that she had previously offended her father by her refusal to address Elizabeth as 'princess'. In a statement that made it clear that she now fully recognized and accepted that both she and her sister were of equal status, Mary declared, 'I shall never call her by other name than sister.'[12] But Mary had more pressing matters on her mind: chiefly, her restoration to royal favour. The benefits of her submission had been immediate, and it was expected that she would shortly be received at court. It was perhaps for this reason that a list not only of Mary's household staff but also of Elizabeth's may have been compiled. The list is undated but was probably collated some time in 1536, and it shows that around the time of her third birthday Elizabeth had acquired a whole host of staff to attend to her every need.

The list provides an intriguing insight into those who surrounded Elizabeth during her early years. Many of these people would have been like family to Elizabeth, and she would forge close and long-lasting relationships with many of them, displaying love and loyalty towards them for the rest of her life. Although Lady Bryan still had overall charge of Elizabeth, her name does not appear on the list. However, we learn that she was supported in her role by five 'ladies and gentlewomen': Lady Troy, Katherine Champernowne, the Countess of Kildare, Elizabeth Cavendish and Mary Norris.[13] It is the mention of Katherine Champernowne, a woman who would become an integral part of Elizabeth's story, that allows us to tentatively date the list, for in October 1536 comes the first dated reference to Katherine being at Hunsdon. At that time, she wrote a letter to Cromwell thanking him for her appointment, which suggests she had only recently arrived in the household.[14]

Lady Troy had once served the Countess of Worcester, one of Anne Boleyn's ladies and, crucially, one of those who had almost certainly testified against the late Queen.[15] Lady Troy had long enjoyed a close connection with the royal household, and as previously noted she may have been in Elizabeth's household from the beginning. In an elegy composed about her, it was claimed that Lady Troy was 'in charge of Queens', for 'a governess she was in her youth'.[16] The elegy was written during the reign of Mary I, and therefore Elizabeth was not one of the 'Queens' mentioned – perhaps this refers to Lady Troy's placement in both Anne Boleyn's household, and Mary's too.[17] Lady Troy did serve Mary, for the elegy explained that 'she gave service all her life, to the one who is Queen today' – Mary I, at the time of its composition.[18] It has been suggested that she may have been put in charge of Mary's household in 1531, when Mary was separated from Katherine of Aragon; this is certainly a possibility.[19] Yet her proximity to Elizabeth as well as Mary is beyond doubt, for the elegy also stated that Lady Troy was the guardian of 'Henry VIII's household and his children yonder'.[20] She would later take over from Lady Bryan and would sleep in Elizabeth's bedchamber with her.[21]

The identity of Elizabeth Cavendish is unknown, but she could have been a relative of George Cavendish, the Gentleman Usher who had once served Cardinal Wolsey.[22] Elizabeth, Countess of Kildare, referred to as Lady Garrett on the household list, meanwhile, had arrived at the English court in 1533 – her husband, Gerald FitzGerald, would die in the Tower the following year having been accused of several crimes, includ-ing corruption.[23] The Countess's young daughter, also called Elizabeth, accompanied her mother and would later become a part of Elizabeth's household and a close friend.

The mention of Mary Norris on the household list probably refers to the daughter of the executed Sir Henry Norris who was implicated in the fall of Elizabeth's mother. Mary was around ten years old in 1536 and was orphaned by the death of her father, since her mother had died when she was younger. It is possible she was placed in Elizabeth's household as a way of providing for her in the aftermath of her father's beheading, while her elder brother, Henry, was given over into the care of their uncle, Sir John Norris.[24] Henry would later be well favoured by Elizabeth and brought into her inner circle, so it seems plausible that the same was true of his sister. Mary only remained with Elizabeth for a short time, however, for in 1537 her name can be found among those who attended the funeral of Jane Seymour, and she was given gifts of jewels after the Queen's death, indicating that she was by then a member of Jane's household.[25]

Following on from the ladies and gentlewomen were two chamberers, Alice Huntercombe and Jane Bradbelt, both of whose names also appear on a later, undated list of household staff.[26] These women would have attended to domestic duties within Elizabeth's chamber, as well as waited on the youngster herself if required. The roles of Gentlemen Ushers, who were responsible for overseeing the lesser servants, were filled by Robert Porter or Power, Richard Sands (both of whom are also present on the later list) and Thomas Torrell. There were also Grooms of the Chamber, who were in charge of the cleanliness of Elizabeth's rooms and of setting the table for meals; two yeomen; and a woodbearer, who oversaw the fires.[27] Her laundry was taken care of by Agnes or Anne Hilton, while in a sign that Elizabeth's spiritual welfare was a strong consideration from the start, a Sir Ralph Taylor was listed as her chaplain. All of the thirty-two people listed would have been responsible for ensuring the youngster's household was run smoothly, and many of them remained with Elizabeth for years.[28]

Mary's household was larger than Elizabeth's, as one might expect given that she was in high favour, was considerably older and thus had different needs and requirements, but many of the roles within the two households matched, in keeping with the sisters' status.[29] The attentions of their new stepmother, however, were largely devoted to Mary. Jane had long been sympathetic to Mary's plight and was determined to restore warm relations between her husband and the eldest of her two new stepdaughters. At the end of June, she wrote a friendly letter to Mary, to which she received an enthusiastic response. Mary was delighted when Cromwell sent a fine horse to Hunsdon to carry her to London, and she left her younger sister behind in early July as she set out for a short trip to the capital. It was at a house in Hackney that, on 6 July, she was privately reconciled with her father, who regretted that 'he had been so long separated from her'.[30] The King made much of her, and Mary was introduced to 'my good mother' Queen Jane, who gave her 'a beautiful diamond' as a gesture of the new familial relationship between them.[31] It symbolized the beginning of a new chapter for Mary, and she returned to Hunsdon following the reunion happier than she had been in years.

Elizabeth was not included in Jane's first meeting with Mary, but she was not forgotten. Her status had now undergone an official change, for on 8 June the Second Act of Succession was passed through Parliament. The Act was to have dire consequences for Elizabeth, as now nobody was left in any doubt of her position. On 5 July, Cromwell wrote to inform Stephen Gardiner, England's ambassador in France, that 'the late Princess, Lady Elizabeth, is by Parliament pronounced also illegitimate'.[32] Officially stripped of the title of 'princess' in the same manner as Mary had been, Elizabeth was her father's heir no longer. Chapuys had his own view of it, informing the Emperor that Elizabeth had been disinherited, 'not as being the daughter of Master Norris, as might have been more honorably said' but instead because the King's marriage to Anne was invalid as 'the King had carnally known the said concubine's sister'.[33] According to one account, it was not long before the sharp young Elizabeth noticed her change in status, enquiring of Sir John Shelton: 'How haps it yesterday Lady Princess and today but Lady Elizabeth?'[34] There is no record of Sir John's response. The Act meant that Henry now had no legitimate child to succeed him, and instead gave him the power to nominate his own heir should he die without issue. This left affairs in the realm in an unusual state, for there was no clear heir. Even Henry's illegitimate son, Henry Fitzroy, would succumb to illness and die on 23 July.[35]

Since her mother's fall, Elizabeth's place in the world seemed uncertain, but it brought about a positive change in her relationship with Mary, which quickly began to thaw. Despite the cruel treatment the late Queen had inflicted on Mary, with Anne's influence removed Mary found herself growing fonder of her younger sister. After all, the child was now motherless through no fault of her own and oblivious to the circumstances in which her mother had been taken from her. It is to Mary's credit that she did not let her hatred of Anne influence her attitude towards Elizabeth at this time, although she would never be fully reconciled with the memory of the woman who had caused her so much pain. As we will see, Mary's behaviour towards Elizabeth was changeable throughout her life, reflective of the fact that the scars caused by Anne never healed. In later years, Mary's hostility to Anne would once more rear its head, directing itself towards Elizabeth: she would subscribe to the rumours surrounding Anne's infidelities and express doubts as to Elizabeth's paternity. But none of this manifested itself now, and it may have been thanks to the encouragement of Lady Bryan and Lady Troy, who had shared relationships with both the royal girls, that Mary began to bond with Elizabeth.

Perhaps Mary did not need a great deal of persuasion to open herself up to her younger sibling, for she was naturally warm in character and had strong maternal instincts. She took the time to play with Elizabeth, lavishing the little girl with affection. What was more, when she wrote to her father from Hunsdon on 21 July, she made sure to mention Elizabeth, taking care to refer to her as 'sister' when relating the child's good health to him. She believed that Henry would be proud of his youngest daughter, for Elizabeth was 'such a child toward, as I doubt not but your Highness shall have cause to rejoice of in time coming'.[36] Mary's accounts, which sadly do not survive prior to December 1536, also provide touching glimpses into the developing relationship between the two sisters. She bought Elizabeth gifts, in December 1537 paying for 'silver [thread] to embroider a box' for her, while in April 1540 Elizabeth was given twenty shillings 'to play her with at' – money with which to play card games that the six-year-old had been taught, perhaps by Mary herself.[37] Even members of Elizabeth's household grew closer to Mary, which was inevitable, given that the sisters were sharing the same space.[38] On one occasion, for example, Mary gave twenty shillings to Elizabeth's Gentleman Usher Robert Porter, the first of several times she would reward her sister's staff with money.[39] There is no record of how Elizabeth responded to Mary's attentiveness, but as a child with no understanding of the politics and pain that had encased her since birth, there is no reason to believe she accepted Mary's kindness with anything other than a childish warmth and good grace. After all, they were family.

With Mary restored to her father's favour, Henry's 'affection for her increases daily'.[40] At the end of July, Chapuys noted that the King planned to present her with a beautiful ring made on Cromwell's orders, with a

Latin inscription stressing the importance of obedience to one's parents. It was undoubtedly intended to serve as a subtle reminder not to cross him again.[41] At this time, preparations were being made for Mary's household in anticipation of her arrival at court, and it was believed that 'she will be magnificently provided for'.[42] Yet, unsurprisingly given that she had no ambassador or foreign allies championing her in the same way as Mary, there is no mention of Elizabeth in relation to her father's affection or that of her stepmother. Moreover, if Lady Bryan is to be believed, the removal of Anne Boleyn had caused many of Elizabeth's needs to be at best forgotten, at worst neglected.

When Anne had been overseeing her daughter's care, Elizabeth had wanted for nothing. The former Queen had taken great pleasure in assembling and maintaining her daughter's wardrobe, providing Elizabeth with costly clothes and accessories befitting her royal status. By the beginning of August though, less than three months after Anne's execution, an exasperated Lady Bryan wrote a frustrated and beseeching letter to Cromwell. Already grieving as a result of the death of her husband, 'my most comfort in this world', Lady Bryan had clearly not been informed of the changes in Elizabeth's status and the implications this might have.[43] As such, Lady Bryan began her letter by seeking clarification:

Now, as my Lady Elizabeth is put from that degree she was in, and what degree she is at now I know not but by hearsay, I know not how to order her or myself, or her women or grooms.

Elizabeth's circumstances were not Lady Bryan's only concern, and she implored,

I beg you to be good lord to her and hers, and that she may have raiment, for she has neither gown nor kirtle nor petticoat, nor linen for smocks, nor kerchiefs, sleeves, rails, bodystichets [bodices], handkerchiefs, mufflers, nor begens [or biggins, a child's cap]. All this her Grace's mistake I have driven off as long as I can, that, be my troth, I cannot drive it no longer.[44]

Elizabeth's apparent lack of clothing could perhaps have been a sign of the child's growth, rather than evidence of deliberate neglect.[45] It may indeed have been the King's newfound attention to Mary that prompted this panicked letter to ensure Elizabeth was not forgotten. But there were other matters worrying the lady mistress too, chiefly about the way in which the household was run. Lady Bryan had clashed with Sir John Shelton, and she sought Cromwell's intervention to 'see this house honorably ordered'. In a swipe at Sir John, she added that if he knew 'what honor meaneth it will be the better ordered'.[46] Highly critical of Sir John's opinions, Lady Bryan claimed that he 'would have my Lady Elizabeth to dine and sup every day at the board of estate' – in other words, to preside over the rest of the household at daily meals as opposed to eating privately in her apartments. This was probably out of a sense of grandeur on Sir John's part, but in Lady Bryan's opinion it was highly inappropriate, for

> *it is not meet for a child of her age to keep such rule. If she do, I dare not take it upon me to keep her Grace in health; for she will see divers meats, fruits, and wine, that it will be hard for me to refrain her from. Ye know, my lord, there is no place of correction there; and she is too young to correct greatly.*

This image of a young child reaching for food and wine that she was not yet old enough to eat and drink is charming to the modern eye, but Lady Bryan was frustrated by Sir John's lack of understanding. She felt that for Elizabeth to eat in such a way would be to allow her to over-indulge on rich, unsuitable foods that would prove detrimental to the youngster's health. To avoid this, she came up with an alternative suggestion, whereby Elizabeth should eat solely with members of her own household:

> *I beg she may have a good mess of meat to her own lodging, with a good dish or two meet for her to eat of; and the reversion of the mess shall satisfy her women, a gentleman usher, and a groom; which been eleven persons on her side. This will also be more economical.*[47]

Lady Bryan's concern for her charge may have been partially motivated by the 'great pain' Elizabeth was experiencing with her teeth, 'which come very slowly'. Elizabeth's teething was challenging for both the toddler and her lady mistress, for Lady Bryan admitted that so great was the pain that it 'makes me give her her own way more than I would'. This indicates that Elizabeth was being spoilt. Even so, perhaps in an attempt to ensure that Elizabeth remained in the forefront of her father's memory, Lady Bryan trusted that 'the King's Grace shall have great comfort in her Grace. For she is as toward a child and as gentle of conditions as ever I knew any in my life, Jesu preserve her Grace.'[48] Henry valued Lady Bryan's opinion and, in a sign that he agreed with her views on how his daughter was raised, sent word to Hunsdon that Elizabeth should indeed take her meals in her chamber from now on, much to Sir John Shelton's chagrin.[49]

AFTER A SUMMER spent at Hunsdon, by the autumn Mary at least, if not Elizabeth too, had moved the short distance to Hertford Castle, which lay in between Hunsdon and Hatfield, and by late October both Elizabeth and Mary had joined the court at Windsor.[50] Significantly, this seems to have been the first occasion on which Elizabeth officially met her stepmother. Although sources regarding her relationship with Jane Seymour are either frustratingly vague or lacking altogether, there is no evidence for the claim that Elizabeth was overlooked by her father and stepmother. On at least one occasion Jane purchased clothes for her – perhaps in response to Lady Bryan's pleas – ordering materials for a 'Scottish hood', as well as a pair of sleeves.[51] Given, though, that the elder of her stepdaughters was just seven years her junior and that Jane had long harboured a fondness for Katherine of Aragon, Mary was a more natural companion for the Queen.

Although being at court with her family may have been pleasant for Elizabeth, who had reached her third birthday the previous month, her father had a more practical reason for ordering the visit. At the beginning of October, a rebellion had broken out in the town of Louth in Lincolnshire, headed by a lawyer named Robert Aske.[52] Before long it had spread into England's northern counties, with a greater number of men flocking to join each day, all marching under a banner of the Five Wounds of Christ. In what became known as the Pilgrimage of Grace, Aske and his supporters were protesting against the dissolution of England's religious houses, whose wealth had then wound its way into the King's coffers and those of members of Henry's court. The rebels even succeeded in taking Lady Eleanor Clifford, the King's niece, hostage at Bolton Abbey, and they soon began to march south to lay their grievances before the King.[53]

The rebels seem to have earned some sympathy from Queen Jane, who 'threw herself on her knees before the King and begged him to restore the abbeys'. Henry was far from impressed and told her, 'prudently enough, to get up, and he had often told her not to meddle with his affairs, referring to the late Queen, which was enough to frighten a woman who is not very secure'.[54] Jane heeded the warning. It was probably to ensure their safety that Henry ordered his daughters to court, but he also seems to have enjoyed the opportunity of spending time with them. Mary was afforded the status of second-ranking lady after the Queen and 'sits at table opposite her, a little lower down, after having first given the napkin for washing to the King and Queen'. Elizabeth was deemed too young to eat with the adults, but in a note written to the French diplomat Cardinal du Bellay, it was said that 'the King is very affectionate to her. It is said he loves her much.'[55] Such glimpses of the father–daughter bond that the pair shared are rare, but there were no signs that her mother's downfall had impacted on Elizabeth's relationship with Henry.

Elsewhere, having been sent north to suppress the rebellion, the Duke of Norfolk successfully managed to disband the rebels with several false promises made on the King's behalf. Robert Aske was granted a formal pardon and was even invited to join the King for Christmas. However, this seemingly peaceful conclusion did not last for long, and Aske would eventually be executed in York in July 1537.

Meanwhile, although Mary was certainly present when the court cele-brated that Christmas of 1536, there is no mention of whether Elizabeth joined her family. It was, though, to be her last Christmas as the baby of the family, for at the beginning of 1537 Queen Jane learned that she was pregnant. Jane must have felt great relief, for rumours speculating that she was unlikely to bear a child had been circulating.[56] The King was elated, and once more the hope and expectation of a male heir was as high as it had been prior to Elizabeth's birth in 1533.

We see only the occasional glimpse of Elizabeth in the spring and summer of 1537, although it is likely that she and Mary were mostly together when the latter was not at court. When the sisters visited court they were in close proximity to their father, for they both had cham-bers at Greenwich, each of which was located immediately above the King's Privy Chamber.[57] Both Elizabeth and Mary also had a permanent lodging at Hampton Court, in Elizabeth's case complete with her own guard chamber and closet.[58] In the spring, she became a topic of conver-sation as the King's Council discussed affairs of state. Thinking about the ways in which Henry might earn the friendship of foreign nations, Elizabeth's role as a bargaining chip was recognized once more. It was said, 'The King has two daughters, not lawful, yet King's daughters', who could serve an important purpose, for 'as princes commonly conclude amity and things of importance by alliances, it is thought necessary that these two daughters shall be made of some estimation, without which no man will have any great respect to them'. It was clear that there were concerns the illegitimacy of the sisters might make them less valuable in the European marriage market. However, it was Mary who was the Council's foremost concern:

> As one of them is older and more apt to make a present alliance than the other, if it might please the King to declare her according to his laws, which, to her estimation, it is thought will be a great thing; or else to advance her to some certain living decent for such an estate, whereby she may be the better had in reputation; it is thought more acceleration would be made for her.[59]

In other words, at twenty-one Mary was deemed more than old enough for marriage by comparison with Elizabeth, and if their father were either to declare her legitimate or to provide her with handsome provisions, it would dramatically improve her marital prospects.

If matters went well for Mary, then 'a like direction should then be taken for Lady Elizabeth, so that the King by one may provide himself of a present friend, and have the other in store hereafter to get another friend'.[60] The sisters were mooted as a way of helping their father to achieve advantageous unions in Europe, and their futures were perceived to be interlinked; the success of one would lead the other to follow her course. Ultimately, whatever hopes Henry and his Council may have harboured of using the girls in such a way came to nothing – negotiations always fell through, allegiances shifted or minds changed. It would not be the last occasion on which Elizabeth's name was mentioned, but the child's origins were destined to haunt her. In March 1538, when a marriage was suggested with a nephew of Charles V, the Holy Roman Emperor supposedly made little comment, merely noting 'the life and death of her mother'.[61]

THROUGHOUT THE COURSE of Queen Jane's pregnancy, Mary spent an increasing amount of time at court with her stepmother, where she was very much made to feel a part of the royal family. Elizabeth, meanwhile, is likely to have remained with her household at one of her usual residences, being too young to offer Jane the same sort of companionship her elder sister provided. Having returned from a short progress through Kent, at the beginning of September the court moved to Hampton Court. The former Thameside palace of Cardinal Wolsey on the outskirts of the capital was to provide the setting for the birth of the royal baby, due the following month. On 16 September, the Queen took to her lavishly appointed chamber accompanied by her ladies. The wait for her child began.

Henry deemed it important to have both his daughters present at a time when he was hopeful of the arrival of a male heir, and it was probably no later than early October that Elizabeth arrived at Hampton Court to join her family, when Mary's privy purse expenses note another payment of twenty shillings to Robert Porter.[62] She was there when, after a long and difficult labour, at two o'clock in the morning of 12 October, her father's wishes were finally granted: the Queen gave birth to a son 'conceived in lawful matrimony'.[63] That same day, a delighted Jane wrote to inform Cromwell of her triumph.[64] With the arrival of his son, all the King's hopes of nearly three decades culminated into a tangible reality: Henry was now the proud father of a legitimate, male heir. The feelings he had experienced upon the births of his daughters could not match the joy and elation he felt upon hearing of the safe arrival of his prince, and he saw it as a sign that God had blessed his union with Jane. For Jane, too, the feeling was one of jubilation, for she had managed in her first pregnancy to achieve that which, after years of strain and heartache, her predecessors had not. Elizabeth's importance was now superseded not only by an elder sister but more significantly by a brother. In terms of precedence, she was very much at the bottom of the hierarchy.

With the Queen's safe delivery came an eruption of universal and heartfelt rejoicing throughout the kingdom. *Te Deum* was sung in St Paul's Cathedral and other churches across London to celebrate the arrival of the longed-for prince. Additionally, 'great fires [were made] in every street, and goodly banqueting and triumphing cheer with shooting of guns all day and night' could be heard throughout the city.[65] With 'the most joyful news that has come to England these many years' came also word that the baby – born on the eve of St Edward's Day – was to be named Edward in honour of his great-grandfather, Edward IV.[66]

Plans for a splendid christening in the chapel at Hampton Court quickly gathered pace, but fearful of infection that could harm his newborn son, the King gave orders limiting the number of servants the attending nobility could bring.[67] Elizabeth, who had just passed her fourth birthday, was also to play a part in the christening. This was more than just a family occasion: for the first time in her short life, she was to play a role on the public stage in the celebration of the arrival of her father's male heir.

On 15 October, three days after Prince Edward's birth, the christening party gathered. In a similar manner to that which had been observed at Elizabeth's own christening, the attendees formally processed towards the Chapel Royal within the precincts of Hampton Court. The party was led by gentlemen carrying torches, which were not to be lit until the Prince had been christened, followed by 'the children and ministers of the King's chapel, with the dean'. Gentlemen esquires and knights, chaplains, abbots and bishops followed, then members of the King's court, including Cromwell, the Duke of Norfolk, and Thomas Cranmer, Archbishop of Canterbury. Notably, 'a taper of wax' was borne by Elizabeth's maternal grandfather, Thomas Boleyn, 'in a towel about his neck'.[68] Thomas was still a member of Henry's court and would seemingly remain in his favour until his death, but one can only imagine his feelings over the arrival of the royal son he had once fervently hoped his daughter Anne would be the one to provide.

Elizabeth was also afforded her own important role, for 'the chrisom [a robe put on a child as a symbol of cleansing its sins] richly garnished [was] borne by the lady Elizabeth, the King's daughter: the same lady for her tender age was borne by the Viscount Beauchamp', Queen Jane's brother, Edward, who was assisted by Lord Morley.[69] This glimpse into Elizabeth's part in the procession and indication of her youth is touching, and that she was carried by the Queen's brother suggests she had indeed been welcomed into Jane's family. Then came the Prince himself, carried under a canopy by the Marchioness of Exeter, who was assisted by her husband and the Duke of Suffolk. Behind them came the Lady Mary, her train borne by Lady Kingston. Mary had been honoured with the starring role, for she had been chosen as the Prince's godmother, and she duly rewarded the midwife, nurse and rockers who had all ensured Edward's safe arrival and care.[70] The role of the Prince's godfathers was assigned to the Dukes of Norfolk and Suffolk, and Archbishop Cranmer, now god-father to two royal children.

Having lived much of her life away from court, young Elizabeth is unlikely to have recognized many of the faces that gathered in the chapel that day and perhaps did not fully understand the magnitude of the ceremony. Once it had concluded, the Prince's name proclaimed and *Te Deum* sung, attention turned to Edward's sisters. Elizabeth and Mary were offered 'spices, wafers, and wine', with the latter presented to Elizabeth by Lord De La Warr. As the party left the Chapel Royal to the sounding of trumpets, 'Lady Elizabeth went with her sister Lady Mary and Lady Herbert of Troy to bear the train [of the Prince]'.[71] Finally, the baby Prince was taken to his parents, where he was given the blessing 'of God, Our Lady, and St George, and his father and mother', while that same day 'the King gave great largess', bestowing gifts of money.[72] Edward's sumptuous christening was Elizabeth's first experience of public ceremony aside from her own, and as the King's daughter she had played her part. The royal family appeared to be complete.

The celebratory mood, however, quickly dampened when, within days, Queen Jane fell ill. Initially it seemed as though she might rally, but before long she grew worse. The cause of her malady has long been said to have been puerperal fever, a uterine infection following child-birth, and her contemporaries certainly attributed her death to its perils. After consulting with medical experts, however, Alison Weir has offered a credible theory that Jane instead suffered two separate illnesses; fresh analysis of the reports provided by Jane's chaplain and physicians, in which they describe her symptoms, suggests that food poisoning followed by an embolism could have led to heart failure.[73] In despair, the Duke of Norfolk wrote to Cromwell urging him to hurry to Hampton Court 'to comfort our good master, for as for our mistress there is no likelihood of her life, the more pity, and I fear she shall not be alive at the time ye shall read this'.[74] Norfolk was right, and on 24 October, twelve days after Edward's birth, Jane died. 'Divine Providence has mingled my joy with the bitterness of the death of her who brought me this happiness', Henry wrote sadly to François I.[75]

Immediately after the Queen's death, some of her jewels were inven-toried and given to members of her household by way of reward. Elizabeth was given several reminders of her stepmother, including a 'little book of gold with the Salvation of our Lady'.[76] She would also be gifted a brooch of gold the following New Year's Day.[77] Four-year-old Elizabeth is unlikely to have fully understood at the time that her stepmother was now gone, dead – as those around her believed – as a result of the dangers associated with childbirth. But although Elizabeth's memories of Jane would have been few, time would reveal that the way her stepmother met her end was painfully imprinted on her memory: dead, in the line of duty. Like her mother's terrible end beforehand, and even the disfavour with which her sister Mary had been treated by their father, it showcased the dangers and trauma royal women could be faced with as they tried to fulfil their roles. They were fates Elizabeth would never forget.

The following month, Jane was given a funeral befitting her status at St George's Chapel, Windsor, where she was laid to rest.[78] Mary attended as chief mourner, supported by many of the ladies of the court; Elizabeth's absence is easily explained by her youth. She probably left court soon after her brother's christening to resume life on one of her Hertfordshire estates, and it is likely that, having fulfilled her duties at the late Queen's funeral, Mary joined her there soon after. Though Elizabeth was still a young child, she was aware that she was no longer the baby of the family and that, like her, her brother was now motherless. Nevertheless, the arrival of Prince Edward was to have notable consequences, perhaps not all to Elizabeth's liking.

CHAPTER 5

———◦◦∾◦———

'She Will Be an Honour
to Womanhood'

*'Went next to lady Elizabeth, who replied to the King's message
with as great gravity as she had been forty years old.'*

THOMAS WRIOTHESLEY TO THOMAS CROMWELL, 17 DECEMBER 1539

U PON THE BIRTH of Prince Edward, the trusty Lady Bryan was
appointed to oversee his care in the same manner as she had once
done for Mary and, until now, Elizabeth. There is no way of
knowing how Elizabeth, who had so far enjoyed Lady Bryan's full attention for the entirety of her short life, reacted to this potential emotional
wrench. However, as the infant Prince had been sent to join the household of his sisters, Lady Bryan was to remain close by, so perhaps it was
not too difficult. In an arrangement that was typical for noble boys, for
the first six years of his life Edward was, in his own words, brought up
'among the women'.[1] There were further shake-ups within the household,
for Sir John and Lady Shelton were to leave when the young Prince was
just six months old, by March 1538, to be temporarily replaced by Lady
Kingston and then by Sir Edward and Lady Baynton, Sir Edward having
served both Elizabeth's mother and Jane Seymour as Vice-Chamberlain.[2]
A replacement lady mistress for Elizabeth was needed, and the woman
chosen was Lady Troy. Given that she had attended Elizabeth at the
Prince's christening, it seems safe to assume that Lady Troy had begun
her new role by this time, and her previous placement in Elizabeth's
household meant she was already a familiar figure to the little girl.

Lady Troy was perhaps a few years younger than Lady Bryan and was reportedly of 'bright, wise countenance'.[3] Her relationship with Elizabeth has often been overlooked, even though she was part of the youngster's life for over a decade and appears to have shared a warm relationship with her new charge. This is largely accounted for by the fact that there are very few documentary references to Lady Troy in relation to Elizabeth, and it is therefore difficult to offer a full analysis of their time together. We know, though, that Lady Troy continued to receive a pension from Elizabeth long after she left her service, probably at some time in 1547, before her charge reached her fourteenth birthday.[4]

Having previously served Mary, Lady Troy was also close to Elizabeth's sister, and there are various references to her in Mary's accounts. In January 1538, for example, Lady Troy's servant received a reward, probably for delivering a New Year's gift to Mary on the lady mistress's behalf.[5] Blanche Parry's servant was also rewarded, suggesting that Mary had grown close to other members of her sister's household too.[6] That same month, Mary sent gifts in the form of a bonnet and a frontlet to Lady Troy, while thirty days later she rewarded one of Lady Troy's servants for bringing her a bottle of vinegar.[7] This pattern of gift exchange continued for the next several years, and Mary even borrowed money from the woman who had once served her.[8]

By reason of his gender, Prince Edward automatically superseded Elizabeth in precedence, but though this was of note to those who surrounded them, to the two young children this mattered very little in their early lives. The two siblings would spend much of their time together, and having both lost their mothers at a painfully young age they had much in common. It was unsurprising that, occupying the same household and with only four years between them, a strong bond was forged between Elizabeth and Edward, probably nurtured by those who cared for them.

Many of Elizabeth's earliest thoughts were of the brother she adored, who had 'four teeth, three full out and the fourth appearing' by the summer of 1538.[9] She liked giving Edward gifts, such as a 'shirt of cambric of her own working', which she presented to him at New Year 1539 – an extremely personal gift that not only showcased Elizabeth's skill with a needle but also displayed her thoughtfulness.[10] It was typical of her to give gifts worked by her own hand throughout her youth, particularly to members of her family. Such presents always made a good impression and were a demonstration of Elizabeth's consideration and desire to be loved and remembered.[11]

Despite there being only a few details of Elizabeth's life for the remainder of the 1530s, aside from the occasional reference in Mary's accounts, we can surmise that life in her household would have been vibrant and full of colour. Mary's accounts help to paint a vivid picture of this, for they show that she employed the services of 'Jane the Fool', and Elizabeth would have benefited as well from the entertainment offered by Jane's displays – her father also had fools, as had Anne Boleyn, so Elizabeth would have been very familiar with them.[12] Likewise, Mary had pets (which included greyhounds and a parrot), as would several of her stepmothers, and it is possible that Elizabeth too would have enjoyed the pleasure of owning a collection of animals herself.[13] Henry VIII's inventory later listed 'two little babies in a box of wood [dolls], one of them having a gown of crimson satin and the other a gown of white velvet', which had been placed in storage, and it is entirely possible that Elizabeth played with these toys during her youth.[14] She would not have lacked for playmates, for by 1539 the Countess of Kildare's daughter, Elizabeth FitzGerald – a renowned court beauty known as 'Fair Geraldine', about whom Henry Howard, Earl of Surrey, would write poetry – had joined her household.[15] It was later said that 'she was brought up with her [Elizabeth] and is devoted to her', and Elizabeth trusted Elizabeth FitzGerald implicitly.[16] In the late 1530s, however, the King felt his youngest daughter had 'too much youth about her'.[17] Perhaps Henry had once deemed it important to allow Elizabeth to have playmates of a similar age, but as she grew he felt she would benefit more from being surrounded by those with the wisdom to instruct and influence her in the behaviour expected from one of her rank.

Elizabeth visited her father at court infrequently, instead moving with Prince Edward between their Hertfordshire residences. Aside from Hatfield and Hunsdon, there was also The More, which had first been beautified by Cardinal Wolsey; Ashridge, a former monastic property that had come into the King's ownership; and Enfield, where the royal siblings were to spend Christmas together in 1542. It is likely that Elizabeth and Edward were staying at one of these when they received a visit from Chapuys at the beginning of March 1538, although he made no mention of the details. Similarly, Lady Lisle, wife of the King's uncle, made reference to having visited the royal children in November 1538.[18] Though she mentioned Elizabeth by name, there were no further details besides the fact that the visit had proved costly, for 'no one comes there but with great rewards'.[19] It is obvious, then, that Elizabeth was still considered to be very much in her father's favour, and would have received rich presents from his courtiers, such gifts being essential. This is further borne out by Henry's own actions. In January 1539, the King ordered clothes for Elizabeth, which included the furring of two nightgowns and a bonnet, while in September payments were made from the King's great wardrobe for crimson velvet for garnishing the palms of Elizabeth and her siblings for Palm Sunday.[20] Clearly, the youngsters were all living in suitably royal style.

THE KING WAS undoubtedly the driving force when, perhaps in 1539 as she reached her sixth birthday, Elizabeth's first lessons began. Prior to this it is almost certain that she received some grounding in education from Lady Troy, who may have taught Elizabeth her alphabet by means of a prayer.[21] In a move that was highly unusual, though, Elizabeth was not assigned an official tutor, but was instead to receive her lessons from a member of her own household. This same person was to be a pivotal figure in her life: Katherine Champernowne.

Katherine, or Kate as Elizabeth fondly came to refer to her, had entered Elizabeth's household for the first time in 1536.[22] She may have earned her place thanks to the auspices of her brother-in-law, Anthony Denny, who would become one of the King's closest servants, though it was Henry who ultimately made the unprecedented decision to appoint Kate to teach his youngest daughter. He clearly approved of her credentials – and with good reason. Under the auspices of her father, Sir Philip Champernowne, Kate had been fortunate enough to receive an education grounded in humanist principles, the curriculum for scholarship of which was based on lessons from classical texts. Kate would, in time, be praised for her efforts in delivering the same to Elizabeth, and the young royal herself later took care to acknowledge that Kate 'hath taken great labour and pain in bringing of me up in learning and honesty'.[23] However, it was not Kate's role as a teacher that would mark her out in the pages of Elizabeth's history but the relationship they shared. The bond between Kate and Elizabeth would become one of the most important and meaningful of Elizabeth's life.

The seeds of education had been sprinkled in Elizabeth's earliest years, and as Kate began to teach her they soon began to blossom. Elizabeth's sister, Mary, had received her first lessons from her mother, Katherine of Aragon, and her governess, Margaret Pole, Countess of Salisbury, before Katherine had tasked the Spanish humanist Juan Luis Vives with writing a manual, *De institutione feminae christianae*, for Mary's education.[24] But there were no such instructions for Elizabeth, and thus no formula detailing her curriculum. Even so, household management, reading and writing would have been expected of a girl of her status, and under Kate's tutelage Elizabeth excelled. Elizabeth probably learned to write using a silver pen, such as the one she received from the scholar Roger Ascham in 1545, while for the most part, the contents of her lessons are likely to have resembled those enjoyed by her sister Mary, whose grounding had also been in humanism.[25] On an intellectual level, though, it became apparent at an early age that Elizabeth outshone Mary – and indeed many of her male counterparts. In time she would share some of her lessons with her younger brother, but though Edward was also studious and enjoyed learning, Elizabeth surpassed him in terms of her ability. The martyrologist John Foxe would later say she did 'rather excel in all manner of virtue and knowledge of learning', winning the admiration of many who knew her.[26]

In 1566 when Elizabeth was Queen, she would tell Parliament that 'I studied nothing else but divinity till I came to the crown', and there is much evidence to corroborate this.[27] From the start, religion would have been an aspect of Elizabeth's upbringing that was afforded close attention. Nothing is known of Sir Ralph Taylor, listed as Elizabeth's chaplain, or Mr Bingham, referenced in Mary's privy purse expenses in the same way, but it was they who would have been responsible for instilling Christian principles in their charge – something that was reinforced in Elizabeth's learning.[28] We also know that Anne Boleyn's chaplain Matthew Parker preached before Elizabeth at least twice, at Hunsdon in 1535 and Hatfield in 1540.[29] Even following Henry VIII's break from the Roman Catholic Church, or chiefly papal authority, the King's beliefs remained intrinsically Catholic and religion was central to everyday life in Tudor England, as Elizabeth would quickly have become aware. Throughout her life, Elizabeth never demonstrated the same depth of piety shown by some of her contemporaries, including her siblings, but it is nevertheless clear that religion meant a great deal to her, and throughout her life she would compose prayers and refer to it in speeches.[30] Raised, like Edward, in the reformed faith and instructed in its principles, she approached religion, as indeed he did too, in terms of a more personal relationship with God, without the intercession of saints who formed an integral part of Catholic worship. Instead, what would later be termed Protestantism relied on books and the ability to read God's word for oneself from the Bible, rather than being dependent on intermediaries such as priests to interpret it. This had become possible following the passing of the Act of Six Articles in 1539, which authorized an English Bible, based on translations by Miles Coverdale and William Tyndale, to be chained in every parish church.[31] Likewise, while Catholics bowed to the authority of the Pope, reformers did not believe in such a hierarchical structure with one individual at the top, neither did they subscribe to the mysteries and symbolism imbued in the Catholic Church. These were the key factors that set both Elizabeth's education and her beliefs apart from those of Mary, who would be staunchly Catholic all her life. As time would reveal, Mary was appalled by Elizabeth's religious grounding.

It is perhaps little wonder that Elizabeth showed an interest in scholarly pursuits, given that both her parents had enjoyed the privileges of an excellent education and sustained this throughout their lives – her mother had even patronized university scholars.[32] Henry VIII had amassed an impressive library, some of which had been inherited from his father and grandfather, and Anne Boleyn had also been extremely fond of books. Given that most of the royal palaces had libraries, the most notable of which were those at Greenwich, Hampton Court and the Palace of Whitehall, it is easy to imagine Elizabeth perusing their shelves whenever she was in residence.[33] Throughout her reign she also received gifts of books from her courtiers, who evidently knew they would be a popular choice, such as at New Year 1563, when William Cecil gave Elizabeth 'a fair book of prayers and many other things in it, covered with silver enamelled with the Queen's and her Majesty's mother's arms on both sides, of gold garnished and clasped with gold set with garnets and turquoises'.[34] This richly decorated object, coming from someone who, as will later become clear, knew Elizabeth well, was probably not only intended to reflect her love of books but also an acknowledgement of Elizabeth's resonance with the mother she had barely known.

In common with both her parents and her sister, from a young age Elizabeth adored music, and given that it formed a vital part of the backdrop of life at the royal court, it was something from which she could not escape even had she wished to. Though she would undoubtedly have been exposed to the strumming of lutes from the beginning of her life, from at least 1537 she is known to have had minstrels in her employ, when both Mary and the King gave them money by way of reward.[35] She was also taught to play several instruments herself, and her earliest biographer, William Camden, would praise her ability to 'sing sweetly, and play handsomely on the lute'.[36] In later life, she would play the virginals with great skill, and like her father she also took great pleasure in writing her own music.[37]

Elizabeth was taught to dance as well, a pastime in which she revelled all her life and continued to participate in when she was in her sixties. Dancing was not the only physical pursuit she enjoyed; throughout her life she adored the outdoors. Riding was considered not only a necessary accomplishment but a beneficial form of exercise, and, in common with her father and sister, she enjoyed hunting and hawking. As her mother had, Elizabeth would also prove to be a skilled needlewoman, whose talents were later put to good use creating gifts for her family.

Whatever approach was taken to Elizabeth's early learning, Kate could congratulate herself, for many of the young girl's contemporaries were impressed with the results. This became apparent in December 1539, when the King's man Sir Thomas Wriothesley arrived at Hertford Castle, where all three of the royal children were spending Christmas.[38] Having first spoken with the Lady Mary, with whom Wriothesley was on friendly terms, he next called upon six-year-old Elizabeth. The King's servant could not fail to be impressed with his master's youngest daughter, for having delivered a message to her from Henry, presumably containing good wishes for Christmas, Elizabeth responded, so Wriothesley said, 'with as great gravity as she had been forty years old'. Henry would have been gratified to hear that Elizabeth was reaping the benefits of her education, her budding abilities summed up in Wriothesley's opinion that, 'If she be no worse educated than she appears she will be an honour to womanhood.'[39] That Elizabeth, at the age of just six, had succeeded in winning the admiration of her father's messenger, himself an educated man, was not mere flattery; he was genuinely impressed, and his comment was an accurate reflection of Elizabeth's academic progress. It would later become apparent that she thrived on learning. Indeed, it was an enthusiasm she would continue to display – and strive to improve upon – for the rest of her life.

By the time of Wriothesley's visit to Hertford, Elizabeth's father was preparing for his fourth marriage. Just days after the death of Jane Seymour, Cromwell and other members of the Council had urged the King to marry again, 'for the sake of his realm', although Cromwell admitted that in his grief Henry was 'little disposed' to it.[40] Given that there was no obvious candidate, before long the search for a fourth wife had begun, and this time politics were to take precedence. In the quest for an advantageous alliance, several prospective European brides were suggested. In December 1537, the English ambassador to the Low Countries, John Hutton, wrote to Cromwell of the Duchess of Milan, who was reported to be 'a goodly personage and of excellent beauty', and of the daughter of the

Duke of Cleves, of whom 'there is no great praise either of her personage or her beauty'.[41]

Foreign matches rarely presented an opportunity for the intended parties to meet beforehand, but Henry was wary of committing himself to a woman whom he had never seen: in sentiments later echoed by Elizabeth, appearance mattered too.[42] He therefore employed the services of his court painter, the exceptionally talented Hans Holbein, who had captured Jane Seymour's image to perfection, to paint the likenesses of several European princesses, including the widowed Duchess of Milan and the two daughters of the Duke of Cleves, one of whom had been mentioned by Hutton.[43] Henry was impressed with Holbein's canvas of Anne of Cleves, which conveyed both her dignity and her charm, and through Cromwell's auspices a match was negotiated and concluded.[44] Anne duly left Cleves in the autumn of 1539, but having reached Calais in December, bad weather prevented her from making the crossing to England. She was obliged to remain on the other side of the Channel for two weeks until the weather cleared, and it was not until 27 December that she landed at Deal, immensely tired and having suffered from extreme seasickness during the voyage. Still, there was little time for her to recuperate, as she was soon greeted by the Duke and Duchess of Suffolk.[45] Henry had been eagerly anticipating the arrival of his future bride and had ensured an official welcoming party was assembled, consisting of the key members of the nobility. Elizabeth and Mary were initially to form a part of this group, but at some point and for reasons that are unclear, this changed; they would have to wait to meet their new stepmother.[46]

On New Year's Eve, Anne arrived at Rochester Castle. Everyone was keen to catch a glimpse of the new Queen, whom the French ambassador described as looking 'about thirty years of age [she was actually twenty-four], tall and thin, of medium beauty, and of very assured and resolute countenance'.[47] Yet there was none more eager than the King himself, who travelled to Kent incognito to meet his future bride for the first time. When the moment came, however, to his horror he found that he did not like what he saw. Lord Russell would later report that Henry was 'marvellously astonished and abashed', and was 'sore troubled'.[48] Shocked by

what he felt were grossly exaggerated accounts of Anne's beauty, he resolutely declared, 'I like her not.'[49] There is no evidence that Anne's looks
were unpleasant, and indeed contemporary reports suggest the contrary.
Evidently, though, she did not appeal to the King, who now did all he
could to extricate himself from marrying her. He returned to Greenwich
Palace furious with Cromwell, whom he now tasked with breaking off
the match. Legal loopholes in the marriage contract were sought, and a
supposed pre-contract between Anne and the son of the Duke of Lorraine
was investigated, but to no avail. Try as he might, there was no way out
without 'making a ruffle in the world' and a momentous scandal: Henry
would have to marry Anne.[50]

On 6 January 1540, the marriage of Henry and Anne took place at
Greenwich Palace. Elizabeth did not attend her father's wedding, and
neither is she likely to have had any understanding of what was clear to
everyone at court except Anne herself: the King had no taste for his new
wife. Henry could not even bring himself to consummate his marriage,
although outwardly he treated Anne with every mark of respect and
courtesy, and she had no indication that anything was amiss. The King
may not have had any interest in his wife, but the second of Elizabeth's
stepmothers certainly showed an eagerness to meet her stepchildren. In
March, Elizabeth and her siblings were at Richmond when they received
a visit from their father and probably Anne too.[51] Nineteenth-century
English writer Agnes Strickland claimed that Elizabeth 'manifested a very
sincere regard' for Anne, but the evidence for their relationship is sadly
limited.[52] What little we do know, however, indicates a warmth that would
be retained long after Henry VIII's death. Moreover, Anne was also served
by Elizabeth's kinswoman, Katherine Carey, who would marry Francis
Knollys in April. Katherine's presence may have served to strengthen the
bonds between stepmother and stepdaughter.

Elizabeth and her siblings may have remained at Richmond through
to April, and they were certainly together for at least part of the month,
as Mary rewarded the Prince's minstrels for playing for her and Elizabeth
twice.[53] The siblings enjoyed their quality time together as they were
entertained by such music, perhaps also sharing a laugh as they played at

cards. While Elizabeth was delighting in her leisure time with Mary and Edward, she was unaware that her German-born stepmother would not bear the title of Queen for much longer, for Henry was already planning on ridding himself of his fourth wife. What was more, at the same time he was making moves to remove Cromwell, the man who had engineered the fall of Elizabeth's mother. It would not be long before news reached Elizabeth and Mary that, on 10 June, Cromwell had been arrested and sent to the Tower – the same prison in which many of his victims had met their ends.

Shortly after, the King's officials were sent to seek the agreement of Anne of Cleves to the annulment of her marriage. No doubt conscious of the fate of her predecessor Katherine of Aragon, and indeed of the gruesome end of Elizabeth's mother, Anne made no protest and showed herself ready to comply with Henry's wishes. Given his previous experience, this must have come as a great relief to Henry, who resolved to be kind to Anne. On 9 July, the royal marriage was officially dissolved on the grounds of non-consummation and because of the earlier pre-contract between Anne and Francis, Duke of Lorraine. Henry was true to his word, and in return for Anne's cooperation he rewarded her with a generous settlement and, she was reassured to hear, 'the King will take her as his sister'.[54] Anne was allowed to keep all her personal jewels and was granted several manors and palaces, including Richmond and Hever, the childhood home of Elizabeth's mother, which had become Crown property following the death of her grandfather, Thomas Boleyn, the previous year.[55] Anne continued to reside in England, where she lived the life of a wealthy noblewoman. She would still pay the occasional visit to court, exchange gifts with her former husband, and retain contact with her former stepchildren for the rest of her life.

HENRY WASTED NO time in moving on from his failed fourth marriage, for his sights had been set elsewhere for some time. On 28 July, he married for the fifth time in a quiet ceremony at his hunting palace of Oatlands, close to Hampton Court.[56] On the same day, his former advisor Thomas Cromwell was beheaded on Tower Hill, his desperate pleas for mercy ignored. As with those who had been executed before him, Cromwell's example demonstrated all too clearly how dangerous Henry's wrath could be, and the brutality with which he dealt with those who committed so-called treason against the Crown. Those who rose in royal favour could fall just as swiftly: nobody was safe.

Henry's bride was Katherine Howard, a former lady of Anne of Cleves who was perhaps as much as thirty years younger than her forty-nine-year-old husband.[57] As a cousin of Elizabeth's mother, Katherine already had kinship ties with Elizabeth, although it is improbable that the two had ever met properly before, as Katherine had only recently arrived at court. Not only was Katherine young, but the French ambassador also thought her rather short, and graceful rather than beautiful. Be that as it may, Henry was besotted with her personal qualities, being 'so amorous of her that he cannot treat her well enough and caresses her more than he did the others'.[58] Katherine was showered with costly gifts of fine clothes and rich jewels, some of which had belonged to her predecessors.[59] These luxurious trappings, however, do not seem to have been enough to impress the eldest of her stepdaughters, at least.

To all appearances, the new Queen did not share a close relationship with Mary, possibly exacerbated by the fact that Mary is likely to have been some years older than her father's new wife.[60] Katherine's feelings towards eight-year-old Elizabeth were warmer, and she appears to have treated her with kindness. Elizabeth would surely have enjoyed the attention paid to her by her new stepmother, and there was more to come, for Katherine's jewel inventory notes that she made several gifts to the little girl. Elizabeth was presented with a pair of beads and a brooch of gold, 'wherein is set an antique head of agate with six very small rubies, and six very small emeralds'.[61] The brooch was listed as a 'little thing worth', which was perhaps the reason it was given to a girl of Elizabeth's youth – but the fact she was presented with such a token by the Queen hints at either a desire from Katherine to build a good relationship with her young stepdaughter or a sign of affection – or indeed both.[62]

Stepmother and stepdaughter were afforded an opportunity to spend time together the following spring, when in May 1541 Katherine sent her barge, which had been freshly strewn with rushes and rosemary, to collect Elizabeth from Suffolk Place in Southwark.[63] On 5 May, Elizabeth was rowed the short distance to the royal manor of Chelsea, where Katherine joined her the next day.[64] The new Queen plainly enjoyed her young step-daughter's company, for it was not until a few days later that she travelled with the King to visit Prince Edward at Waltham Holy Cross in Essex.

Elizabeth was patently old enough to engage with her stepmother, but their relationship was to be cut tragically short. In the summer of 1541, Henry and Katherine headed north on a progress that took them as far as York. While they were away, news came to light about Katherine's conduct prior to her marriage, and it did not paint a favourable picture. In November, soon after their return south, Katherine was arrested. On 23 November, she was stripped of her title of Queen and sent to the former abbey of Syon. As the days passed and the details of Katherine's past began to trickle out, the story must have begun to resonate with Elizabeth as cruelly reminiscent of her mother's – if indeed she was fully aware of it by now. Katherine was accused of adultery, a charge that, unlike that against Anne Boleyn, had not been wholly falsified. It emerged that, having been abetted by Lady Rochford, the widow of Elizabeth's executed uncle George Boleyn, Katherine had been engaging in secret dalliances with Thomas Culpeper, one of the King's gentlemen. As Katherine's biographer Gareth Russell has convincingly argued, however, it is unlikely that her supposed adultery with Culpeper was ever physical.[65] In addition, prior to her arrival at court there had been some form of relationship with her former music teacher, Henry Manox, and one Francis Dereham, which was far more serious. Modern historians are divided over whether these relationships amounted to child abuse, but they unequivocally differed from Elizabeth's own later experiences with Thomas Seymour.[66] Having been tried and condemned at London's Guildhall, both Culpeper and Dereham were executed in December.

Christmas at court was sombre as the King was in no mood to cele-brate, the betrayal of his fifth wife having sent him spiralling into a deep depression. Katherine remained at Syon, and as the beginning of 1542 dawned it became clear that she would not be forgiven. Though she did not stand trial, on 7 February a Bill of Attainder was passed in Parliament that made it treasonable for a queen not to disclose her sexual history to her husband – and such a crime was punishable by death. Just three days later, a terrified Katherine was taken by river from Syon to the Tower, where she was told that both she and Lady Rochford were to die.

Katherine was distraught, and because she 'weeps, cries, and torments herself miserably, without ceasing', she was given a respite of several days to compose herself.[67] This did not last long, however, and on 13 February both Katherine and Lady Rochford were executed on the same spot where Elizabeth's mother had met her end six years earlier. According to the French ambassador Marillac, Katherine was 'so weak that she could hardly speak, but confessed in few words that she had merited a hundred deaths for so offending the King who had so graciously treated her'.[68] Like Anne, both women were interred in the Chapel of St Peter ad Vincula.

Elizabeth was eight years old when Katherine met her end by the executioner's axe. Thus far, she had gained and lost three stepmothers in less than six years – an extraordinarily short time frame that must have had an agonizing emotional impact on the young child. The circumstances surrounding the conclusion of two of these marriages had been terrible: death in childbed and bloody execution. Given that they were largely absent from her life, Elizabeth would not have known any of these women particularly well, yet she was painfully aware of the fates some of them had met. It was enough to make a deep and lasting impression on her that went further than the trauma their loss may have inflicted on her sense of domestic security. Her father had set a clear precedent concerning the way in which wives could be discarded and replaced, and this in turn would have a profound effect on Elizabeth and her own decision-making. It is little wonder that in 1559, soon after her accession, she responded to the Commons petition that she marry with the telling words, 'I am already bound unto an husband, which is the kingdom of England.'[69] She had no desire for marriage, for her earlier experiences had helped to shape her future.

There is little doubt that Elizabeth was inwardly, and later outwardly, scarred by the way in which her father treated and disposed of his wives, particularly in the cases of her own mother and Katherine Howard. Their examples showed all too clearly how those who displeased the King and were condemned of crimes against him would be forced to face his wrath in the most terrifying way. During the reign of her sister Mary, Elizabeth would have good reason to believe that she would share a similar fate, her fears unquestionably heightened by memories of the brutal deaths of Anne and Katherine.

On a personal level, however, she adored the larger-than-life, imposing figure of her father, despite his having been a largely absent parent. By 1542, Henry was no longer the energetic king who had once been able to ride and hunt for hours and who had bounced Elizabeth on his knee when she was a small child. The pain in his legs had become so bad he was unable to walk, and it would only become worse as time went on. None of this seemed to matter to Elizabeth. During Mary's reign the Venetian ambassador Giovanni Michiel observed that 'she prides herself on her father and glories in him', and she certainly took great care to identify herself with Henry publicly.[70] Physically, she bore a strong resemblance to him, with the red hair that was a Tudor family characteristic, as well as his long nose. In fact, Michiel would remark that while Mary 'is of spare and delicate frame, quite unlike her father, who was tall and stout', everybody thought Elizabeth 'resembles him more than the Queen [Mary] does'.[71] This meant that Henry, therefore, 'always liked her'.[72] Father and daughter also shared similar personality traits, including the famous Tudor temper.

From a human perspective, Elizabeth's fondness for her father is perhaps surprising, given that not only did she spend very little time with him – and even less as just the two of them – but also, in political terms at least, she was deemed the least important of his children. With her brother the Prince afforded the status of the King's heir and her sister being both older and the daughter of the universally loved Katherine of Aragon, Elizabeth must, at some point relatively early in her life, have recognized that her standing was very much below that of her siblings. This also helps to explain why she is mentioned less frequently than her siblings in contemporary documents. Likewise, at some point she would have become aware of her mother's fate, although there is little outward indication of the impact this had on her attitude towards her father. It may, as suggested by her surviving letter to him, have made her more eager to please him and win his love, for certainly as she grew, the fates of those who incurred the monarch's anger – not only his wives but More and Fisher, who had died for their refusal to accept Henry's supremacy, Cromwell and others – would have further exemplified the awful consequences of defying Henry. That Elizabeth felt such reverence towards her father can perhaps be seen as a sign of the love that, as a girl deprived of her mother, she craved. Her memories of Henry were formed by her later experiences of him, mostly as she approached her teens. She would doubtless, therefore, have been delighted when she and Mary dined with their father that September: a rare moment of time spent with him.[73]

In the aftermath of Katherine Howard's execution, Agnes Strickland says Elizabeth resided chiefly with Mary at Havering, a palace on the outskirts of London that had formerly been granted to both of their mothers, as well as to Jane Seymour. They largely shared the same residence, and it seems plausible that, with the lack of a stepmother, they may have been closer than ever before. At New Year 1543, Elizabeth gave Mary 'a little chain' and 'a pair of hosen [stockings] gold and silk', and the sisters apparently spent part of the summer together.[74] The subject of Elizabeth's marriage had once again resurfaced, but hers was not the one preoccupying the minds of those at court. Instead, it had become apparent that her father had further matrimonial aspirations of his own.

CHAPTER 6

'Elizabeth, Her Humble Daughter'

*'Gentle Mrs Astley, would God my wit wist what words would
express the thanks you have deserved of all true English hearts
for that noble imp by your labour and wisdom, so flourishing
in all godly godliness, the fruit whereof doth even now redound
to her grace's high honour and profit.'*

ROGER ASCHAM TO KATE ASTLEY, 1545

T HE QUEEN'S PRIVY Closet at Hampton Court, a small upper
oratory, was crowded and stifling on that summer's day, 12 July, in
1543. As nine-year-old Elizabeth looked around, she would have
recognized most of the faces of the handful who had gathered, for not only
was her sister Mary present but so too was their cousin Margaret Douglas
and several members of her father's Council.[1] They had come together as
the privileged few who had been chosen to witness as the fifty-two-year-
old King took his sixth – and final – set of marriage vows. It was the only
one of her father's weddings that she had ever attended, yet Elizabeth
heartily approved of his choice of bride. The woman who stood next to
him was the twice-widowed Katherine Parr, whose sister and brother-in-
law, Anne and William Herbert, had also been invited to attend the nup-
tials.[2] The couple were met to join in marriage, Stephen Gardiner, Bishop
of Winchester, declared, and if anyone knew of any impediment, he should
declare it. None opposing but 'all applauding', including the King and
Katherine, Henry took his intended by her right hand. Repeating the words
after the bishop, he made his vows. 'I, Henry, take thee, Katherine, to my

wedded wife, to have and to hold from this day forward, for better for worse, for richer for poorer, in sickness and in health, till death us depart, and thereto I plight thee my troth.' Katherine repeated the vow made by her new husband, with the additional promise 'to be bonayr and buxom [good and obedient] in bed and at board'.[3] For the fourth time, Elizabeth had a new stepmother. For the first time, however, the Queen's arrival in the royal family would signify something Elizabeth had yet to experience outside of her household in her short life: stability.

Born in 1512 to Sir Thomas Parr and Maud Green, Katherine had been named after Katherine of Aragon, in whose household her mother had served.[4] Sadly, Sir Thomas, who had been well favoured by Henry VIII and flourished under his rule, died in 1517, when Katherine was only a small child and her brother and sister younger still.[5] The responsibility for their care therefore fell solely to their mother, under whose auspices Katherine had been fortunate enough to receive an excellent education. As a result, she had widespread academic interests and by 1543, it seems, an enthusiasm for religious reform.

In early 1543, Katherine found herself widowed for a second time when her husband John Neville, Lord Latimer, died on 2 March.[6] Though she had been married twice, Katherine had only just reached her thirties and was a comely woman, tall with auburn hair, who took great care of her appearance. She adored clothes and jewels and would come to own a sumptuous wardrobe, containing pieces made of the most luxurious fabrics, including silk, velvet and satin.[7] She was also exceedingly cultured, and her queenship would provide her with both the means and the opportunity to fully indulge this, patronizing artists and musicians among others. There was, therefore, much to be admired in her and much that Elizabeth could learn from her.

Significantly, Katherine was also in love – but not with the King. The object of her desire was the dashing Sir Thomas Seymour, brother to the late Queen Jane. But it was not to be. Katherine would later recall the emotional turmoil she experienced at this time, assuring Thomas: 'For as truly as God is God, my mind was fully bent the other time I was at liberty, to marry you before any man I knew.' Still, she believed herself to be set on a wholly different path, explaining, 'Howbeit, God withstood my will therein most vehemently for a time and, through His grace and goodness, made that possible which seemeth to me most impossible – that was, made me to renounce utterly mine own will, and to follow His will most willingly.'[8] In Katherine's mind, it was God who had decided she should take on a far more momentous role, one she could never possibly have expected: that of Queen of England.

Elizabeth's father had been left distraught by Katherine Howard's indiscretions, but it had not been enough to deter him from women permanently. In the same report in which he referenced the execution of the King's fifth wife, the French ambassador Marillac noted, 'It is not yet said who will be Queen; but the common voice is that this King will not be long without a wife, for the great desire he has to have further issue.'[9] Almost a year later, in January 1543, Chapuys thought there were many at court who believed Henry would soon marry again. He admitted, though, that 'hitherto there is no appearance of it', and certainly there was no obvious candidate.[10] But sometime in the spring this changed, and Henry became enamoured of Katherine Parr. Though it was no great love affair in the same manner the King's relationship with Elizabeth's mother had once been, Katherine's personal qualities made her highly desirable to Henry. His sixth wife would have a monumental impact on the lives of his children, particularly his youngest daughter. In the summer, Elizabeth and her siblings were summoned to court to meet their future stepmother, and by 20 June they had arrived at Greenwich. That same day, both Elizabeth and Mary were reported to be in company with Katherine and her sister, Anne Herbert, and it was a joyous meeting.[11] Elizabeth immediately warmed to Katherine, and Katherine herself, having taken responsibility for her second husband's children John and Margaret Neville, was well used to a stepmotherly role.[12]

Henry's sixth marriage signalled the fourth occasion on which he had chosen to marry for personal, rather than political, reasons. At fifty-two years old and with painful ulcers on his legs that had first developed shortly after his jousting accident in 1536, he was by no means in the best of health, and his weight had ballooned.[13] Even so, he was hopeful that his union with Katherine would bear fruit – after all, in his eyes the future of the Tudor dynasty was balanced on the wellbeing of just one prince. Katherine, an extremely sensual woman, seems to have done her best to be enticing, ordering lozenges with which to sweeten her breath and perfumes for her bedchamber at Hampton Court, bathing regularly in milk, and using luxurious oils and rosewater.[14] But she was also mindful of Henry's existing children. From the beginning Katherine treated her role as stepmother to the royal children with the utmost seriousness, taking a keen interest in all of them and lavishing them with gifts, such as cloth of silver for the girls.[15] They, in turn, welcomed her with open arms.

Elizabeth fully embraced Katherine as a mother figure – evidence of her craving for the normality of family life that she had hitherto been denied. It is thought-provoking to consider how drastically different the first ten years of Elizabeth's childhood were compared to those of her father and even her sister. The latter two had both been fortunate enough to enjoy happy childhoods, until the death of Henry's mother and the separation of Mary's parents, respectively: it was a kind of stability of which Elizabeth would have had no understanding. With the arrival of Katherine Parr, however, that would, to an extent, change. In time, the relationship Elizabeth shared with Katherine would come to be one of the closest and most important of her life.

IN THE IMMEDIATE aftermath of the royal wedding there was no time for Elizabeth to get to know her stepmother, as the King and Queen travelled the short distance to Oatlands to enjoy their honeymoon. Soon, Katherine not only succeeded in making a good impression on her stepchildren but likewise earned the approval of her new subjects. In the opinion of Thomas Wriothesley, she was 'for virtue, wisdom and gentleness, most meet for his Highness; and I am sure his Majesty had never a wife more agreeable to his heart than she is'.[16] Elizabeth and her brother returned to Hatfield, but she did not forget Katherine any more than Katherine forgot Elizabeth.[17] Though we have no surviving letters from this time, it seems that Katherine made efforts to stay in touch with Elizabeth regularly. We know, for example, that she sent her stepdaughter, Margaret Neville, to Ashridge in December 1543, to deliver messages on her behalf.[18] Katherine may also have had a hand in organizing Elizabeth's education, and that of Edward: a task to which she devoted herself with the King's approval.

Though the extent of the role Katherine played in supervising the education of her royal stepchildren cannot be confirmed, there is no doubt that she was a safe pair of hands in this respect. Her own relationship with learning continued throughout her life, and she had many scholarly interests, including languages and reading. She recognized and appreciated the benefits of a good education and, undoubtedly noticing that Elizabeth was academically gifted, was determined to nurture this and to ensure the young girl was afforded the same opportunities as her own mother had put in place for her. Elizabeth's sister Mary had received an excellent education, and it seems probable that at some point Henry had the same in mind for his youngest daughter. He now decided, probably with Katherine's influence, that both she and Edward should have male, Cambridge University-educated tutors. Thus, Elizabeth's lessons with Kate Champernowne came to an end, though Kate remained in the household, as indeed did Lady Troy, and continued to play an important role in Elizabeth's life.

It seems likely that Katherine Parr had some sway in the choice of tutors made for the royal children, and it is notable that all these tutors were reformers.[19] In early 1544, John Cheke of St John's College, Cambridge, was appointed to teach the Prince. Cheke would come to be an influential figure in Edward's life, and Elizabeth would in time know him well too. Elizabeth's first male tutor was William Grindal, a renowned scholar who attended St John's College, Cambridge, the foundation of Elizabeth's great-grandmother, Lady Margaret Beaufort.[20] Elizabeth liked her first tutor, who was probably in his twenties, and the feeling was mutual. The great scholar Roger Ascham, who became Elizabeth's tutor after Grindal's untimely death, would later write to her of 'the great love and respect which he [Grindal] always used to feel towards you', and Elizabeth thrived under his tutelage.[21] Grindal had a particular specialism in Latin and ancient Greek, in which he was 'second to none', and these were languages in which he would instruct Elizabeth.[22] As Elizabeth's biographer Anne Somerset highlighted, the emphasis on Greek was new – Henry VIII himself had never studied it, and neither did Mary have more than a basic understanding.[23] Elizabeth's command of Latin, though, would supersede her Greek; she would come to both speak and write the language fluently.

Grindal also earned the approval of Elizabeth's adored Kate Champernowne, who would become Kate Astley in 1545 after her marriage to John Astley, a man with connections to the Boleyn family who would also serve Elizabeth.[24] As part of a circle of reformers, Grindal and Kate were well known to one another, and it may even have been Kate who was initially responsible for recommending him to the King or Queen Katherine. In turn, Grindal had the utmost respect for Kate, whom he believed had given Elizabeth an excellent grounding in the principles of education.

Under Grindal's tutelage Elizabeth began a new and challenging curriculum, consisting of arithmetic, philosophy, geography, astronomy and history, that last of which she loved. She adored reading, but while there are plenty of references to her reading history, notably there is no record of her indulging in less serious subject matter – even her great-grandmother Margaret Beaufort had been fond of a romance.[25] Aside from Latin and Greek, she was also instructed in other languages, for which she demonstrated a particular flair, excelling in French and Italian. William Camden would later claim that before the age of seventeen Elizabeth 'understood well the Latin, French and Italian tongues, and was indifferently well seen in the Greek'.[26] In her twenties, she would start to learn Spanish, although she never fully mastered the language. The month after her death, the Venetian envoy would report:

> She possessed nine languages so thoroughly that each appeared to be her native tongue; five of these were the languages of peoples governed by her, English, Welsh, Cornish, Scottish, for that part of her possessions where they are still savage, and Irish. All of them are so different, that it is impossible for those who speak the one to

understand any of the others. Besides this, she spoke perfectly Latin,
French, Spanish, and Italian extremely well.[27]

Although Elizabeth's schedule would have been characterized as gruelling by many, it was one in which she revelled, taking great pleasure in
her lessons. She quickly proved herself to be an exceptional student who
outdid most of her contemporaries with only a few exceptions – among
them her cousin Lady Jane Grey, who was also renowned for her scholarship.[28] Learning would become a vital part of Elizabeth's routine for
the rest of her life, and, more than that, it was an indispensable part of
her identity of which she was immensely proud. Her love of studying
automatically gave Elizabeth a common bond with her new stepmother,
whom she was eager to impress.

It was to Katherine that Elizabeth's first surviving letter was addressed,
dated 31 July 1544, a year after Katherine and Henry's marriage.
Written at the red-brick St James's Palace, where the entwined initials
of Elizabeth's parents still adorned the gatehouse, the letter shows just
how much Elizabeth was excelling in her lessons. It was written in Italian,
which Elizabeth later perfected under the tutelage of Giovanni Battista
Castiglione.[29] He, along with Grindal and potentially one John Picton,
who Elizabeth later recalled 'in her youth did teach her divers things', may
also have had a hand in shaping the beautiful italic script she had been
perfecting and for which she would later become famed.[30]

'Inimical Fortune, envious of all good,' she began, 'she who revolves
things human, has deprived me for a whole year of your most illustrious presence, and still not being content with that, has robbed me once
again of the same good: the which would be intolerable to me if I did
not think to enjoy it soon.'[31] Elizabeth implied that she had not seen her
stepmother for a whole year since Katherine's wedding, and had missed
her again more recently. If this was indeed the case then Elizabeth cannot
have missed Katherine by much, for just the previous month, on 29 June,
Katherine and the King had attended the wedding of his niece Lady
Margaret Douglas, which took place at St James's, from where Elizabeth
wrote.[32] Whatever the circumstances, the letter reflects her affection for

her stepmother and her yearning for Katherine's company. She evidently knew Katherine cared for her, as the next lines in her letter make clear:

And in this my exile I know surely that your highness's clemency has had as much care and solicitude for my health as the King's majesty would have had. For which I am not only bound to serve you but also to revere you with daughterly love, since I understand that your most illustrious highness has not forgotten me every time that you have written to the King's majesty, which would have been for me to do.[33]

Plainly, Katherine had been a means of communication between Elizabeth and her father too, for which Elizabeth expressed her gratitude. She continued by begging Katherine to continue with this, noting that

heretofore I have not dared to write to him, for which at present I humbly entreat your most excellent highness that in writing to his majesty you will deign to recommend me to him, entreating ever his sweet benediction and likewise entreating the Lord God to send him best success in gaining victory over his enemies, so that your highness, and I together with you, may rejoice the sooner at his happy return. I entreat nothing else from God but that He may preserve your most illustrious highness, to whose grace, humbly kissing your hands, I offer and commend myself.[34]

Much has been made of Elizabeth's comment that she had 'not dared' to write to her father personally, but it is unwise to read into this any further. As David Starkey has pointed out, this was more an issue of etiquette than anything else, and we see the same pattern with Mary, who had frequently written to Cromwell rather than directly to Henry.[35] The letter is, however, revealing in terms of Elizabeth's relationship with her father and shows how much, in seeking 'his sweet benediction', she was eager to please him. It also served as a means of showcasing her learning and command of Italian, and Katherine must have been gratified to see that her stepdaughter's lessons were bearing fruit. Elizabeth ended by signing herself as Katherine's 'most obedient daughter and most faithful servant'.[36]

By the time Elizabeth wrote her letter, her father had left his realm for France, with the reasons for his departure referenced in the same letter. In 1543, Henry had made an alliance with the Emperor Charles V against France, and the following year he sent his brother-in-law Charles Brandon, Duke of Suffolk, to France with a force of men. Suffolk marched with the King's army to the coastal city of Boulogne, to which he laid siege on 19 July. Back in England, although the King's health had seriously declined since his last journey abroad, which had been undertaken with Elizabeth's mother in 1532, he was determined to have one more taste of military glory. Henry decided he would join Suffolk in France and lead his army himself. However, he was astute enough to recognize that any campaign brought with it some risk, so it was only natural that he would wish to consider the future should he not return. It was with this in mind that on 7 February 1544, the Third Act of Succession was passed by Parliament.

Unsurprisingly, the Act named Elizabeth's brother, Edward, as the King's heir. Should Edward die childless, he was to be succeeded by any children the King might have with Katherine Parr. In the event that neither of these options produced heirs, Henry looked towards his two daughters. In a huge turnaround for the sisters, the Act decreed that Mary and her heirs would be the next in line, followed by Elizabeth and hers. It was a significant moment for the pair of them, each of whom had previously been banned from the line of succession by reason of his separation from their mothers. Rather crucially, however, though both were restored to their place in the succession, Elizabeth and Mary remained legally illegitimate. Henry would never move Parliament to restore his daughters' legitimacy, a permanent blot that in Elizabeth's case later gave rival claimants – notably Mary, Queen of Scots – the opportunity to press their own claim to the throne above hers. Indeed, Henry's actions in restoring his daughters to the succession ought not to be overestimated, for he only did so given his lack of male heirs besides Prince Edward.

The King's departure was scheduled for the summer, and on 26 June he enjoyed a sumptuous five-course meal with Elizabeth, her siblings and 'divers other lords and ladies'.[37] Given the reference in Elizabeth's letter to not having seen Katherine, the Queen clearly did not join them. This was the last time Elizabeth would see her father before he departed for France, and it was by all accounts a merry occasion. On 11 July, the King set out in pursuit of military glory, arriving in France towards the end of the month. During his absence, Henry entrusted the governance of the realm to his wife – the second time during his reign he had done so, having given Katherine of Aragon the same responsibility in 1513.[38] With the support of the Council, Queen Katherine was appointed regent, and thus Elizabeth would be given her first opportunity to witness a woman wielding power. It would provide an important grounding in the lessons of queenship.

Just a few days before the King's departure, he had given orders for six-year-old Prince Edward to be removed to Hampton Court and for the Lord Chancellor and Earl of Hertford, Edward's uncle, to 'discharge all the ladies and gentlewomen out of the house' who had until then been responsible for the Prince's care.[39] This signified a turning point in Edward's life, for he was instead to be raised with an all-male household, with Sir William Sidney, who had been the Prince's chamberlain since he was five months old, advanced to the position of steward. Richard Coxe was to take the position of almoner, and John Cheke was to be 'a supplement to Mr Coxe, both for the better instruction of the prince and the diligent teaching of such children as be appointed to attend upon him'.[40] It was almost certainly because of the Prince's placement there that Queen Katherine spent the beginning of her regency at Hampton Court, and she decided that her two stepdaughters should join them. Elizabeth was the last to arrive, but when she did she was welcomed wholeheartedly.

It must have felt like a happy family reunion, for Elizabeth was delighted to see Katherine and it was rare for the royal family – save the King – all to be together. The opportunity to spend some time with her stepmother was particularly welcome to Elizabeth, who was grateful for the chance to get to know her. Katherine in turn was equally eager for Elizabeth's company. Just a few months earlier, in April, Katherine had published her first book, *Psalms or Prayers*, anonymously, first in Latin and the following week in English, and she had been busy ordering copies for her friends.[41] It is feasible that Elizabeth too received a copy, but at the very least she would have felt inspired by Katherine's example and bonded further with her over their shared love of scholarship. The following year, Katherine would become the first English Queen to publish a book under her own name, when her second book, *Prayers or Meditations*, was also published in English. It would prove extremely popular and later inspired Elizabeth when it came to creating a gift for her father.

During her regency, Katherine's husband was never far from her thoughts, and she even sent him a thoughtful gift of venison.[42] As well as advising him about how affairs stood in his realm, in her regular letters to Henry she often took care to add, 'My lord prince and the rest of your majesty's children are all (thanks be to God) in very good health.'[43] By the same token, when Henry wrote home he asked Katherine to 'give in our name our hearty blessings to all our children'.[44] Still, though she was keen to ensure her stepchildren were included in her remembrances to their father, Katherine's foremost concern was the ruling of the country. Determined to prove her worth, it was a task she took most seriously, and one she relished. During this time the impressionable Elizabeth, nearly eleven years old, was given an opportunity to observe a woman bearing rule first-hand, and indeed there is good reason to believe she was impressed by Katherine's leadership.[45] And it was not only Elizabeth who was given the chance to benefit from such lessons, but Mary too. Katherine was no mere figurehead, instead adopting a hands-on approach to monarchy, evidenced by her attendance at Council meetings, signing of documents and issuing of orders in her husband's absence, all on top of seeing to the running of the royal household.[46] What was more, she was good at it, approaching the task with a cool and level head, demonstrating her wisdom.

Witnessing the way in which her stepmother governed her father's realm, Elizabeth could not help but have the utmost admiration for Katherine. We cannot know how deep an impression Katherine's regency had on her, but it did perhaps help to give her a greater sense of confidence in her own abilities. Likewise, when she herself acceded to the throne fourteen years later, the direct style of rulership adopted by Elizabeth bore similarities to that shown by Katherine in 1544, suggesting the lessons learned during Katherine's regency were not lost on her stepdaughter – particularly when it came to image and the projection of majesty and queenship to those around her.[47]

Katherine's wardrobe provided a vital tool that enabled her to underscore her magnificence, and it was almost certainly around this time and to mark her regency that she sat for her portrait with an artist known only as Master John, the magnificent full-length result of which hangs today at the National Portrait Gallery.[48] It is an extremely powerful image, in which Katherine stands every inch a Queen, bedecked in a sumptuous array of clothes and jewels, some of which are likely to have been created according to her own commission.[49] The opulent crown ouche (a brooch or pendant set with jewels) that she wears, for example, was just one of the pieces in her collection that showed Katherine's awareness of her heightened royal status, and it was worn by Katherine in another of her portraits before it was later owned by Elizabeth herself.[50] These displays of power through jewels certainly left their mark on Elizabeth, and she would use her own gems to her advantage when her time to rule came. In the summer of 1544, however, neither Elizabeth nor Katherine could have known that the day would come when Henry's youngest daughter would be given the opportunity to put her abilities and these valuable lessons to the test.

This was one of, if not the happiest, summers of Elizabeth's childhood, as she revelled in the attention of her stepmother and being at court. Alongside Katherine, she and her siblings spent the whole of August at Hampton Court, but with the summer heat there also came the plague, which was rife in London. Desperate to avoid it, the Queen left Hampton Court for a short progress through the countryside of Surrey and Kent, taking her stepchildren with her. Their first stop at the beginning of September was the splendid Woking Palace, the former home and favoured residence of Elizabeth's great-grandmother, Lady Margaret Beaufort.[51] Worried about the contagion, Katherine issued a proclamation banning anyone who had come into contact with the plague from approaching the court, 'to avoid danger to the Queen, the prince and other the King's children'.[52] She nevertheless took time to indulge in the opportunities for leisure that Woking had to offer, including bowling alleys, beautiful gardens and excellent hunting, in which the royal family took great pleasure. At one point that month, the Queen even paid Francis Cornwallis, one of Elizabeth's Gentleman Ushers, for 'riding at her Grace's commandment to the christening of Mr Cotton's child'.[53] While at Woking, Katherine also made time to visit Mortlake, one of her own properties that had formerly been owned by Cromwell, as well as Byfleet, Guildford and Chobham.[54]

Before long, however, the family were at Henry's former nursery, Eltham Palace, where they enjoyed the popular pastime of hawking. It was here they learned that across the Channel, on 13 September, the French had surrendered Boulogne: the King was triumphant.[55] Katherine was jubilant when she was told that Henry had captured the city 'without effusion of blood', and Elizabeth must have been delighted at her father's good fortune – perhaps Henry's victory and success in warfare helped to reinforce her view of him as a hero.[56] Yet she was not to be reunited with him immediately upon his return, for it was instead agreed that Katherine would first meet Henry for a private reunion at Otford.[57] On 30 September, Henry arrived in England in a buoyant mood and took the opportunity of visiting Leeds Castle with Katherine. Elizabeth did not accompany them, and it is uncertain whether she saw her father when the royal couple travelled to Greenwich and then Whitehall before she herself returned home to Ashridge. Happily, though, she saw Katherine again before the year was out, for in late November the Queen made the journey to Ashridge to spend two days with Elizabeth and Edward.[58]

WITH THE RETURN of the King, Katherine resumed her usual role of Queen Consort and stepmother, thus bringing Elizabeth's unofficial lessons in a woman governing a kingdom to an end. Back at Ashridge, the youngster returned to her usual routine, which may have been unwelcome given the time she had so recently spent with Katherine at the heart of events. With Christmas approaching, however, her thoughts turned to New Year. Perhaps feeling inspired by her summer with Katherine and the progress she had made with her lessons, Elizabeth chose to make her stepmother a personal gift that she knew would appeal to her sense of scholarship and sentimentality – maybe Katherine herself even gave some indication of a preference for such a gift during her visit to Ashridge. So it was that for New Year 1545, Elizabeth presented Katherine with her own translation of Marguerite of Navarre's *Miroir de L'Âme Pécheresse* (*The Mirror of the Sinful Soul*). The choice of text was an interesting one: Marguerite had known Elizabeth's mother during her time at the French court – indeed, in 1533 the Duke of Norfolk believed she had been fond of Anne, and two years later Anne herself would send a message assuring Marguerite that 'her greatest wish, next to having a son, is to see you again'.[59] Aside from the personal links with Elizabeth's mother, as a renowned humanist and patroness of religious reform as well as an author, Marguerite was an inspiring example to many young women, perhaps Elizabeth included. David Starkey has surmised that Elizabeth may have read this text with Katherine during the summer, but it is unclear whether Katherine herself would already have been familiar with Marguerite's work, although she would doubtless have been aware of it.[60] In either scenario, *Miroir* was a religious poem that would have been of great interest to her, which likely prompted Elizabeth's choice.

Addressing her gift 'to our most noble and virtuous Queen Katherine, Elizabeth, her humble daughter, wisheth perpetual felicity and everlasting joy', Elizabeth sat down at Ashridge to write a preface on 31 December.[61] She explained to her stepmother that she had 'translated this little book out of French rhyme into English prose, joining the sentences together as well as the capacity of my simple wit and small learning could extend themselves'.[62] The gift, however, had evidently been composed in somewhat of a rush, evidenced by the date of the preface (which obviously meant it also arrived late) and the fact that as the work progressed, so too did the number of errors. Elizabeth herself recognized that it required some improvement, begging Katherine to 'rub out, polish, and mend' the words, which 'I know in many places to be rude and nothing done as it should be'.[63] Self-conscious, she desperately implored her stepmother not to show her work to anyone else, 'less my faults be known of many'.[64] She ended by wishing Katherine 'a lucky and prosperous year', with the 'continuance of many years in good health and continual joy'.[65] It is a charming and thoughtful example of the young girl's work.

Within twelve months, though, there were few mistakes to be seen, for by the following New Year Elizabeth had progressed with her translations in leaps and bounds, demonstrated in the gifts she made to both Katherine and her father. Translation exercises formed an important part of her learning, and she had been working hard to develop her languages. Elizabeth's great-grandmother, Lady Margaret Beaufort, had also been fond of translating texts from French into English, but Elizabeth took this to a new level.[66] As her gift that year, Katherine was to receive an English translation (it was first published in Latin) of the first chapter of John Calvin's *Institution de la Religion Chrestienne* (*Institutes of the Christian Religion*), beautifully bound in blue and embroidered by Elizabeth's own hand in gold and silver thread.[67] On the front were the intertwined initials of the King, HR (Henricus Rex), and Katherine, KP, coupled with further designs of embroidered flowers.[68] In the dedication, which was written in French at Hertford on 30 December, Elizabeth addressed Katherine as 'the most high, most illustrious and magnanimous Princess Katherine', to whom her stepdaughter 'gives greeting and due obedience'.[69] She had chosen to translate this text, Elizabeth explained, 'assuring myself that your highness will pay more regard to the zeal and the desire that I have of pleasing you than you will to the capacity of my simple ability and knowledge'.[70] As a kind of introduction to the principles of Protestantism, the religious text would undoubtedly have pleased Katherine, as would her stepdaughter's evident confidence in the developments she had made with her translation skills. 'I have presumed and undertaken,' Elizabeth wrote, 'to translate into our mother tongue a little book whose argument or subject, as Saint Paul said, surpasses the capacity of every creature.' Though she wrote humbly of 'my simple ability and knowledge', her improvement was clear.[71] Perhaps more than anything else, Elizabeth's advancement can be accredited to the nurturing care she had been shown by Katherine, enhanced by both Grindal and the support network in her household.

The most impressive and magnificent gift given in December 1545, however, was to her father. To him, Elizabeth proudly presented her own translations of her stepmother's *Prayers or Meditations*, not just in one language but in three: French, Italian and Latin. Such a gift showcased her learning perfectly, as well as her desire to impress Henry with it. The book still survives in the British Library today.[72] As with her gift to Katherine, Elizabeth had taken just as much care with the presentation as with the content. All 117 pages were beautifully presented in a single volume, bound in crimson cloth. To demonstrate her skill with a needle, Elizabeth had painstakingly embroidered the cover with Henry and Katherine's initials in rich gold and silver thread, and Tudor roses also formed a part of the decoration, including the briar rose formerly used by Elizabeth's grandmother and namesake, Elizabeth of York.[73] Elizabeth herself would later adopt this emblem, using it as a symbol of purity.[74] The inclusion of such a symbol was Elizabeth's way of identifying herself with the royal family from which she came, and thereby ensuring that her own place within that family was remembered by her father. Henry would have been left in no doubt that Elizabeth was proud of her heritage – a heritage she had inherited solely by right of her father. The gift was highly personal and would have held a sentimental meaning to Henry, who must have been touched and impressed.

For the King too, Elizabeth took the time to compose a letter to accompany her gift – the only one addressed to her father that survives.[75] Crafted in her beautiful italic hand, the note was written in Latin on the same day as Elizabeth's lines to Katherine. 'To the most illustrious and most mighty King Henry the Eighth,' she began, 'Elizabeth, his majesty's most humble daughter, wishes all happiness, and begs his blessing.'[76] The letter is revealing of Elizabeth's feelings towards her father, who she claimed was of 'such excellence that none or few are to be compared with you in royal and ample marks of honour, and I am bound unto you as lord by the law of royal authority, as lord and father by the law of nature, and as greatest lord and matchless and most benevolent father by the divine law'. In wishing to earn her father's approval and praise, however, Elizabeth was understandably nervous: 'I only fear lest slight and unfinished studies and childish ripeness of mind diminish the praise of this undertaking and the commendation which accomplished talents draw from a most divine subject,' she wrote.[77] Furthermore, she explained that her 'pious' gift was 'most worthy because it was indeed a composition by a queen as a subject for her king', which was in turn 'translated into other languages by me, your daughter'.[78] Ultimately, Elizabeth hoped that 'even if it is worthy of no praise at all, nevertheless if it is well received, it will incite me earnestly so that, however much I grow in years, so much will I grow in knowledge and the fear of God and thus devote myself to Him more religiously and respect your majesty more dutifully'.[79] Whatever Henry thought of his daughter's gift, there seems little doubt that these words would have pleased him immensely. At twelve years old, Elizabeth's scholarly accomplishments alone meant she was a daughter to be proud of.

There is good evidence to suggest that Henry was indeed proud of Elizabeth, and with their love of scholarship and literature father and daughter had much in common.[80] Henry was fond of his younger daughter, considering her to be an important member not only of his family but of his dynasty too. Her image appears in a royal genealogy tree in a manuscript in the British Library, alongside that of both her parents and siblings, highlighting her place within the royal family.[81] Dynasty was certainly the foremost theme in Henry's mind when he commissioned a family portrait from an unknown artist in around 1545. Still to be seen hanging on the walls of the gallery at Hampton Court, the portrait, known as *The Family of Henry VIII*, is a visual statement of the Tudor bloodline, its members and those who had helped to create it.[82]

Many theories surrounding the portrait's production have been suggested: David Starkey has conjectured that it commemorated the dinner Elizabeth and her siblings had enjoyed with their father in June 1544 prior to Henry's departure to France, and thus also Mary and Elizabeth's restoration to the throne, while John Guy has even proposed that the impetus could have come from Katherine.[83] It does seem probable that it was painted in order to mark an occasion, and the settling of the succession is the likeliest scenario. Set in a richly decorated space in the Palace of Whitehall, Henry is the central figure, flanked by his son and heir, Edward. On the other side of the King, however, sits not Katherine Parr but Jane Seymour, the woman who provided Henry with his male successor. On either side of these three figures stand Mary on the left, closest to the King's heir, and to the right is Elizabeth. Behind them, glimpses of the King's decorated heraldic beasts can be seen in his Privy Garden, along with two court figures, one of whom is Will Somers, Henry's fool.

Elizabeth and Mary are both dressed similarly in French hoods and burgundy sleeves and kirtles (outer gowns). Their patterned green gowns are similar to their heavy sleeves, but it is Elizabeth's necklace that is of particular interest. Attached to it is one of the initial jewels that were popular and fashionable in the 1530s and 40s, this one displaying the letter 'A'. It is safe to assume that this was the former property of her mother, Anne Boleyn, but how and when it came into Elizabeth's possession, if indeed she did come to own it, is a mystery. In the aftermath of Anne's death, Mary is known to have been given some of her jewels, and it is possible that it came into Elizabeth's hands by way of Mary's gift – after all, if Mary had owned this piece she would certainly have had no wish to keep hold of it.[84] Equally baffling are the reasons why Elizabeth is shown wearing a jewel that connects her so closely to her mother in a family portrait commissioned by her father. Although it is possible to view the jewel as Elizabeth's way of identifying with Anne, it is inconceivable that she wore the pendant without Henry's notice, or indeed, given her desire to please him, his permission. This raises several intriguing possibilities behind the reasons for its selection. Perhaps the likeliest is that it was Henry who ordered his daughter to wear the pendant, as a way of highlighting Elizabeth's illegitimacy on account of her mother's actions.

The same may also be true of Mary, who wears a cross necklace that might have been inherited from her mother. Mary owned several cross necklaces, as her surviving portraits bear witness, and so too did Katherine of Aragon, through whom it is likely Mary received several pieces.[85] By the time of her death, Katherine had few jewels left to bequeath, but one of the two items she left to Mary in her will was a cross necklace.[86] It is just possible that this was the same as that worn by Mary in the family portrait and that it was chosen for the same reason as the jewel worn by Elizabeth, for while the King was eager to acknowledge the status of his daughters, the jewels provided a way of underlining that they were deemed illegitimate on account of their mothers. It was a reinforcement of the fact that both shared similar circumstances – something that may have bound them more closely.

Although Elizabeth was the King's daughter and had been restored to the line of succession, it was an inheritance Henry had no intention of her fulfilling. In personal terms he was proud of her, but in political terms her association with Anne Boleyn had sealed her future. How did Elizabeth feel as she sat for a family portrait commissioned by her father, wearing this jewel that was so closely associated with her mother? Did it inspire sympathy and a sense of loss, pride or perhaps even embarrassment? Sadly, the answer to such a question is destined to remain a mystery.

It was probably the following year, 1546, that Elizabeth sat for a further portrait, the earliest known individual likeness of her to survive, attributed to William Scrots.[87] This image, housed in the Royal Collection at Windsor Castle, may have been commissioned by Henry, though it is first recorded in the collection of Elizabeth's brother as 'the picture of the Lady Elizabeth her grace with a book in her hand her gown like crimson cloth'.[88] It was one of a pair with Edward, also in the Royal Collection – perhaps the artist even worked on them simultaneously, for research has shown that the panels on which both portraits were painted derived from the same tree.[89] Elizabeth's image is striking and exceedingly fine, and it is by far the most compellingly beautiful portrait of her in her youth to have survived. She was by this time thirteen years old, and the physical characteristics she had inherited from her parents are clear to see. From beneath her fashionable French hood, we can see the auburn red hair, parted in the centre, that came from her father, as did her pale colouring and the shape of her nose and mouth. Yet her slender frame and her eyes are unmistakeably those of her mother. Elizabeth is dressed in a rich costume of crimson silk that matches the French hood, while the undersleeves and part of her skirt are made of cloth-of-silver, richly embroidered. She looks sophisticated and elegant, and there is no doubt this was a royal portrait intended both to impress and to highlight Elizabeth's status. Royals frequently donned their finest clothes when sitting for their portraits, so we can assume this was one of Elizabeth's most costly outfits, perhaps purchased by her father or stepmother.[90]

Like her mother before her, Elizabeth was exceptionally fond of clothes – three years before her death, an inventory of her wardrobe listed almost two thousand items – so it seems probable that this was a trend that started early and that the fashionable Katherine Parr had some influence in developing.[91] She cared greatly about her appearance, which was reflected during her queenship, but her wardrobe also served another, more political purpose. Indeed, later in her teens Elizabeth would use clothes to make a point: for example, showcasing her Protestant maidenhood by wearing black and white.

In the William Scrots portrait Elizabeth is bedecked in several costly pieces of jewellery, with a pearl-and-diamond-studded girdle (belt) forming part of a matching set with her square (border of jewels around the neckline) and *habillement* (border on the French hood). Interestingly, the square is identical to that worn in a contemporary portrait of Katherine Parr, while the girdle is extremely similar, suggesting that Elizabeth's stepmother had perhaps loaned her some of her jewels.[92] The front of Elizabeth's hood boasts a further row of pearls and gold beads, which match those she wears around her neck, and a jewelled pendant from which three pearls are suspended is attached to her necklace. A larger pendant of diamonds in a cross shape is fastened to her dress at her breast, joined to which are three pearls, and it is just possible that this may have been loaned by Katherine Parr, who owned several similar jewels – a smaller piece in a comparable style is just visible at the front of Elizabeth's girdle.[93] She also wears four diamond rings, and an elaborate set of beads shaped like pots are attached to her girdle.

The portrait's high status is reinforced by the Latin inscription: *Elizabetha/(?Filia) Rex/Angliae* – she is Henry's daughter.[94] Other elements of the portrait are revealing in terms of Elizabeth's character, notably the presence of two books. Her finger marks a page in what may be a copy of the New Testament, suggesting that the artist and viewer are causing some interruption to her reading. On the stand behind her is probably a copy of the Old Testament, and taken together these books are indicators both of Elizabeth's scholarly abilities and of her religious devotion.[95] The background apparently underwent alterations before completion; originally painted to reference classical themes, it was changed to reflect a plainer, palace setting, perhaps at the King's own instigation.[96]

By 1546, when this portrait is likely to have been painted, Elizabeth seems to have been spending much of her time in the Queen's company, where, in terms of rank among the women at court, only Katherine and Mary superseded her. In May, she and Mary topped the list of ladies attendant at court, along with their cousins Lady Margaret Lennox (formerly Douglas), Lady Frances Grey, Marchioness of Dorset (mother of Lady Jane Grey), and her sister Lady Eleanor Clifford, Countess of Cumberland.[97] A few months later, the Admiral of France arrived to seek peace with Henry on his master's behalf, in a lavish visit for which Elizabeth was also present. The King was keen to create an impression for the Admiral to take back to François I, and it was observed that 'great preparation is made for him at Hampton Court'.[98] The Palace was to provide the setting for the ten days of revelries that followed, and Henry's display of grandeur extended to the Admiral's welcome, for he was 'magnificently received, being met on his way to Hampton Court by the Prince and more than 800 horsemen, mostly in cloth of gold. He was presented with a sideboard of gold plate and other gifts such as horses, dogs, silver cups etc.' The visit ultimately led to a peace treaty, and 'the signature of the treaty was publicly performed' in the Chapel Royal.[99] Aside from his French guest, none of her father's majesty would have been lost on Elizabeth.

Bedecked in the costly jewels that Henry had ordered for her from French, Flemish and Italian jewellers, Katherine, with her queenly image, continued to impress Elizabeth.[100] The time spent in Katherine's company brought Elizabeth into contact with the Queen's circle of highly educated ladies and gentlemen, including Jane Dudley, whose son Robert would later become one of Elizabeth's closest friends – and suitor.[101] Moreover, several of Katherine's ladies would later serve Elizabeth: Mrs Eglionby would become Elizabeth's Mother of the Maids, and Elizabeth Norwich, the daughter of Katherine's former gentlewoman Susan Norwich, joined Elizabeth's household at some point prior to January 1547.[102] The daughter of Katherine's chamberer Bridget Skipwith was also in Elizabeth's service before 1558.[103]

There was also another who Elizabeth befriended under Katherine's auspices and with whom she would become close. Elisabeth Brooke was the niece of Sir Thomas Wyatt, the poet who had once played the game of courtly love with Elizabeth's mother.[104] It is unclear if Elisabeth arrived at court in 1542 or 1543, as she is sometimes confused with her aunt and niece, but it is certain she was serving in Katherine Parr's household in 1543 and would remain with her for the entirety of Katherine's reign.[105] Around the same time that Katherine married the King, Elisabeth had become involved in an affair with the Queen's brother, William, who had a tumultuous and complicated marital set-up, to say the least. Since 1527 William had been married to Anne Bourchier, sole heiress of the Earl of Essex, in a match that had been arranged by his mother at great expense. It was an extremely unhappy marriage, and by 1541 Anne had eloped with her lover, by whom she bore an illegitimate child. Eventually, in 1543, the vows were annulled by an Act of Parliament at William's request, and he soon turned his attention towards Elisabeth Brooke. Elisabeth, who was beautiful and kind, was well thought of in the Queen's circle, and before long their relationship became well known at court. It was Elisabeth Brooke who would inscribe her name in the Book of Hours owned by Elizabeth's mother, and with her love of music and easy charm it is not difficult to see why her personality appealed to Elizabeth.[106] It seems that the seeds of what would become a close friendship were sown at this time.

As for Elizabeth's own household, there had been some changes. In a household list that was likely composed in 1546, Lady Troy's name no longer appears, though she was probably still in Elizabeth's service, as she was listed among those in the household who received mourning materials at the King's death.[107] Kate Astley topped Elizabeth's list of gentlewomen, and we know that at some time in the 1540s, before Henry VIII's death, she was 'made her mistress by the King'.[108] Kate's name was followed by that of Elizabeth's close friend Elizabeth FitzGerald. Next on the list came Mary Hill, who would also become an important friend. Mary had unsuccessfully attempted to gain a place with Elizabeth in 1539, but she was probably only a year or so older than Elizabeth and thus would nevertheless still have been young when she joined.[109] She was an interesting character whose father had served as Sergeant of the Wine Cellar to the King, a prestigious post that probably earned Mary her place in Elizabeth's household. Like Elizabeth, she had many academic interests and came from a scholarly family: something that would have bound her to Elizabeth further. She would later marry John Cheke, tutor to Elizabeth's brother. The final gentlewoman listed was Blanche Parry, who had been with Elizabeth all her life, adored her and had once been her rocker.

Many of Elizabeth's other staff remained as they had been in 1536, although her household had now grown in keeping with her changing needs.[110] One John Gough, for example, was responsible for the care of her clothes, while the listing of two grooms of the stable, Owen Haye and Thomas Clevet, shows she was now riding and keeping horses.[111] At thirteen years old in September 1546, Elizabeth was a cultured and educated young woman who was enjoying the pursuits and activities one might expect for a youth of her status. She was living a privileged lifestyle as the King's daughter, and though the politics of her father's world were forever changing as councillors rose and fell from grace, Elizabeth's place in it – with the help of Katherine Parr's influence – appeared stable. It would not be long, however, before life took a wholly different turn.

IN THE AUTUMN or winter of 1546, Elizabeth left court for Hertfordshire. By now, her father's failing health had worsened and he was seriously unwell. Though young, Elizabeth was smart enough to recognize that Henry was often in pain, and his health issues were clear for all to see. He was severely overweight and unable to walk unaided, instead being carried between the rooms of the royal palaces. Understandably, Henry's health impacted on his moods, and as the Christmas season approached there were no merriments to be had. The King was alone at Whitehall, where the Imperial ambassador, Van der Delft, reported that he 'keeps himself secluded from all but his councillors and three or four gentlemen of his chamber'.[112] Henry had recently been ill with a fever, and although he assured the ambassador that he was now quite recovered, Van der Delft was sceptical. He was right to be wary, for behind the closed doors of Henry's apartments those who were close to the King saw what was coming: Henry's decline was permanent.

Meanwhile, 'the Queen and Court have gone to Greenwich, although she has never before left him on a solemn occasion'.[113] Mary joined Katherine, but though they attempted to celebrate the season as usual, the King's presence was missed. Even Elizabeth and Edward observed the festivities separately, much to Edward's dismay. Writing to his sister from the manor of Tittenhanger near St Albans on 18 December, he lamented, 'Change of place, in fact, did not vex me so much, dearest sister, as your going from me.'[114] 'Nothing', he said, 'can happen more agreeable to me than a letter from you; and especially as you were the first to send a letter to me, and have challenged me to write. Wherefore I thank you, both for your goodwill and zeal.' Edward was consoled by the fact that 'I hope to visit you shortly (if no accident intervene with either me or you), as my chamberlain has reported to me. Farewell, dearest sister!'[115] Perhaps nine-year-old Edward's hope was borne of a childish ignorance about the reality of their father's health, for one thing was certain: Henry VIII was dying, and with that the dynamics of Edward's relationship with Elizabeth would change forever. She would never see her father again.

Part Two

1547–54

'She was a lady, upon whom nature had bestowed, and well placed, many of her fairest favours; of stature mean, slender, straight, and amiably composed; of such state in her carriage, as every motion of her seemed to bear majesty.'

SIR JOHN HAYWARD, *ANNALS OF THE FIRST FOUR YEARS OF THE REIGN OF QUEEN ELIZABETH*, ED. J. BRUCE, CAMDEN SOCIETY, VII (LONDON, 1840)

CHAPTER 7

'My Lady was Evil Spoken Of'

'As touching my lord's boldness in her chamber, the Lord I take to record I spake so ugly to him – yea, and said that it was complained on to my lords of the Council – but he would swear, "What do I? I would they all saw it!" that I could not make him leave it.'

THE CONFESSION OF KATE ASTLEY, FEBRUARY 1549

I T WAS AROUND midnight when Archbishop Cranmer reached the King's bedchamber at the Palace of Whitehall. Just a few hours earlier, Sir Anthony Denny, the King's trusted Groom of the Stool, had bravely advised his master that he must prepare to meet his maker, for death was swiftly approaching. Henry knew his end was near, yet he dozed for an hour or two before summoning Cranmer. By the time the Archbishop arrived, the dying King's powers of speech had deserted him, and a squeeze of the hand was all he could offer when Cranmer asked for a sign that he put his faith in Christ. After much suffering, at two o'clock on the morning of 28 January 1547 Henry VIII died at the age of fifty-five.

For several days the late King's passing was kept a closely guarded secret, and 'even the usual ceremony of bearing in the royal dishes to the sound of trumpets was continued'.[1] Those around Henry, meanwhile – chiefly Edward Seymour, Earl of Hertford, who was backed by Secretary of State William Paget and Sir Anthony Denny – were busy laying the foundations of the next reign.

Finally, on 31 January, Sir Thomas Wriothesley stood in Parliament with tears in his eyes as he announced the King's death to the House of Commons.[2] Despite the tumult and bloodshed that had occurred throughout Henry's reign, he had been a legend in his own lifetime, and would continue to be remembered as such as the lives of his children played out.[3] Two days later, the late King's leaden coffin was taken to the Chapel Royal at Whitehall, where it lay in state. It was the end of an era, and for Elizabeth, the beginning of a significantly different – more uncertain – one.

Elizabeth had passed the Christmas of 1546 at Enfield with only her household for company, and towards the end of January she was pleased to be reunited with her brother, who had been escorted from Hertford by his uncle Edward Seymour and Henry VIII's former Master of Horse Sir Anthony Browne.[4] The joy the siblings felt at being together once more was to be cruelly shattered, for the news of their father's death was soon delivered – news that would change their lives and their relationship forever. According to Sir John Hayward, who wrote the first account of Edward's reign in 1630, when the youngsters were told that their father had died 'they both broke forth into such unforced and unfained [sic] passions, as it plainly appeared that good nature did work in them'.[5] Henry had been an absent parent and a distant figure to Elizabeth in many ways, yet as her only surviving parent his death came as a crushing blow to the teenager who had idolized him: for the rest of her life Elizabeth would continually identify herself with her father, referring to him in glowing terms.

At the age of thirteen, Elizabeth was an orphan, and even as daughter of the late King and sister to the new, she could very feasibly have wondered what the future held for her. In late 1545 there had again been talks of her marriage, this time to the Prince of Spain, but once more they had come to nothing, apparently by reason of Elizabeth's maternal heritage affecting her '*qualitas*' (quality).[6] Edward's fate held no such uncertainty. In accordance with the terms of their father's will, Elizabeth's nine-year-old brother was soon declared King Edward VI of England. Yet it was by no means an easy inheritance, for the England that Henry VIII had left behind was torn by religious divides, and his court was rife with rival factions vying for power.

Life was about to diverge for the royal siblings, who until now had spent much of their early years together, revelling in one another's company. With Edward's accession, this came to an abrupt end – and so too did their childhoods. Never again would Elizabeth spend so much time with Edward, and neither would they be as close. Instead, as sovereign Edward was to take up immediate residence in the London palaces his father had so recently occupied. There was no time to waste and, soon after informing his royal nephew of his father's death, Edward Seymour hurriedly conveyed him to the Tower, from where he would prepare for his coronation. The reason for his haste would soon become apparent. As Elizabeth bade her brother goodbye, life as she knew it changed permanently: she was left behind.

IN HIS FINAL weeks, Henry VIII had composed his last will, which was signed on 30 December 1546.[7] The dying King recognized that his son's youth rendered him unable to govern his kingdom alone, and he therefore made provisions for the years until Edward reached his majority at the age of eighteen. Refined with the support of his trusted councillors, these stipulations resulted in a regency Council consisting of sixteen members appointed to oversee the governance of the realm until Edward came of age. In a deliberate move, Henry had neglected to appoint any one figure as its head: all were to be equal. However, to one among Henry's Council, such an arrangement was unacceptable, and in the immediate aftermath of the King's death this figure moved swiftly to defy his wishes.

Edward Seymour was the young Edward VI's maternal uncle, who had once carried Elizabeth in his arms at his nephew's christening. Seymour had been well favoured by his brother-in-law Henry, but with his nephew's ascendancy he spied an opportunity for greater rewards. A man of immense ability, Seymour was intelligent, hard-working and popular with the common people. Backed by other supporters within the Council, within days of his nephew's accession Seymour had been created both Duke of Somerset and, on 21 March, Lord Protector, assuming power against the late King's express command. Seymour nevertheless managed successfully to curry the support of some of those who had been closest to Henry VIII in his final years, including Elizabeth's godfather, Archbishop Cranmer, Sir Anthony Denny and Secretary Paget. These men were all familiar to Elizabeth, although it is unlikely she knew any of them well, with the possible exception of Denny, thanks to his links with members of her household.

Not everyone was happy about the appointment of the Lord Protector and the regency Council, however. Elizabeth's stepmother, Katherine Parr, had hoped – not unreasonably, given her success in 1544 – that her late husband would entrust her with the role of regent to the young King, and thus also with the governance of the realm. There is a possibility that this was very much in her mind when a portrait of Katherine that may have been painted in the last year of Henry's life was created, perhaps, like those of Elizabeth and Edward, by William Scrots. The portrait, in which Katherine wears a rich costume of black and a fashionable French hood, shows her wearing many of her finest jewels including those at her cuffs, which bore the Latin inscription *Lavs Devs* ('Praise God'). Feasibly, this was Katherine's attempt to firmly identify herself with the royal family, and establish her queenly authority and place within it.[8] If this was the case, however, then it would prove unsuccessful. Despite her capabilities, ultimately Henry had always been opposed to the idea of female rule unless there was absolutely no alternative, and his views had not changed by the time of his death. Katherine was therefore bitterly disappointed to discover she had been afforded no place in the new regime.

Initially, she was determined to fight back, but before long it became obvious that Katherine would be forced to take a back seat and settle quietly into the role of Queen Dowager that Henry had expected her to take.[9] She certainly had ample means of doing so, for financially her late husband had left her well provided for, with £3,000 (£1,264,000) in jewels, plate and household stuff, an additional £1,000 (£421,357) in cash and full use of all of her lands.[10] Though she had been cast into the background in political terms, Katherine was determined to maintain a good relationship with her stepson, to whom, probably in an attempt to keep herself at the forefront of his mind, she had recently sent a jewel containing portraits of both herself and his father as a New Year's gift.[11] She also continued to write to Edward, who in turn responded, doing his best to comfort Katherine over the loss of 'the greatest and best of beings'.[12]

IN MATERIAL TERMS, as he had for Katherine, Henry had taken care to ensure his daughters were looked after. Both Elizabeth and Mary were treated as equals and were to be given 'money, plate, jewels and household stuff' to the value of £10,000 each (£4,213,600): an extremely generous sum.[13] Additionally, they were each to receive a bountiful £3,000 (£1,264,000) per year until they were married.[14] When they did marry, each was to be given an identical dowry, which would be reduced should either of the girls marry without the consent of the Council – even with her father gone, Elizabeth's status meant she would never be given the freedom to marry without the approval of others. But, should either Elizabeth or Mary choose to wed without the Council's blessing, the consequences would be harsh: they would automatically forfeit their place in the line of succession. Elizabeth's age meant she was too young to obtain her inheritance immediately, but her father's provisions ensured that when she did so, several years later, she would be very wealthy indeed.

The late King's funeral took place on 16 February, 'in a most magnificent manner'.[15] All mourners were provided with black cloth, including Henry's fool, Will Somers.[16] Black velvet was ordered for Elizabeth and her household, although, in keeping with the tradition that women did not join the funerals of kings, she did not attend and had in any case been unwell with 'the pain in my head'.[17] Neither did her siblings, but those who did gathered in the spectacular gothic surroundings of St George's Chapel, Windsor Castle, to pay their final respects. Katherine Parr watched the obsequies – which were led by Stephen Gardiner, Bishop of Winchester – in private from the ornamented wooden closet that had been made for

Katherine of Aragon and that was richly decorated with her pomegranate badge.[18] When the service concluded, Henry was laid to rest alongside his third wife and mother of his son, Jane Seymour. Despite Henry's hopes and plans, no monument was ever erected to his memory.[19]

IN THE DAYS following the royal funeral, the supporters of Edward Seymour, Duke of Somerset, were soon rewarded. John Dudley, Henry VIII's former Lord High Admiral, was made Earl of Warwick, while his position of Lord High Admiral was passed to Somerset's younger brother, Thomas, who was also created Baron Seymour of Sudeley. Already, though, the Imperial ambassador Van der Delft was hinting at some future discord between the Seymour siblings, for 'they are nevertheless widely different in character'.[20] It would soon become apparent that the younger brother craved power and influence on a far greater scale – power that the new Lord Protector was plainly not prepared to offer him, much to Thomas's resentment.

The Seymour brothers and their supporters were prominent among the procession for Edward VI's coronation on 20 February, and Thomas – along with the newly ennobled Earl of Warwick and Katherine Parr's brother, the recently created Marquess of Northampton – was given the honour of carrying the King's train. Neither Elizabeth, Mary, nor their stepmother was present to watch as Archbishop Cranmer crowned the young King in Westminster Abbey, and Somerset was the first to pledge his loyalty to his nephew: it was clear in which direction the tide of power had turned.[21] Elizabeth was nevertheless anxious to retain contact with the brother with whom she had shared much of her childhood, and just days before his coronation she wrote thanking Edward for 'proof of his feelings towards me in my absence by sending a ring'.[22] To her sorrow, though, from now on she would see him only infrequently.

Elizabeth may have been largely overlooked as the new Edwardian regime sought to establish itself, but she remained in her stepmother's thoughts. It had been made clear to Katherine Parr that she was expected to retire into a quiet life on her estates, yet she was keen to ensure that her change in status did not affect the relationships she had taken the time and care to nurture with Henry's children. She was, after all, the closest parental figure any of them had, and there was no reason why that should change. Her bond with Elizabeth had always been especially close – indeed, she had been more of an influence on her life than the girl's biological mother, and by the beginning of March she had invited the orphaned youngster to join her household.[23] Any anxiety Elizabeth harboured over her future in the aftermath of her father's death was to be of short duration, thanks to the offer of a home with her beloved stepmother. She was delighted to receive Katherine's invitation, which provided her with some much-needed security at a time when she was vulnerable, mourning her father and trying to understand her place in the world. Before long, she, Kate Astley and her husband John, Elizabeth's tutor Grindal, her recently appointed cofferer Thomas Parry (described perhaps unfairly by Elizabeth's biographer Anne Somerset as a 'fat, self-important Welshman') and the rest of her household had moved to join Katherine.[24] It was probably at around this time, however, that Lady Troy left. According to the later depositions of four of Elizabeth's gentlewomen, as reported by her interrogator Sir Robert Tyrwhit, she was forced out by a jealous Kate Astley, who 'could abide nobody there [sleeping in Elizabeth's chamber] but herself'.[25]

The royal manor house at Chelsea was a charming red-brick building that benefited from piped water from a nearby spring. It had wonderful gardens with a blend of fragrant herbs such as bay and rosemary, and an orchard in which grew peach and cherry trees.[26] The scent of roses and lavender filled the air, and it was to this beautiful setting that Katherine chose to remove in the aftermath of her royal husband's death. Having spent time there with Katherine Howard in 1541, Elizabeth was already familiar with Chelsea and was pleased to have the opportunity to make it her new home with Katherine Parr. She quickly settled into life at her stepmother's manor, continuing her lessons with Grindal under Katherine's supervision. For the first time, Elizabeth found herself in daily contact with her stepmother, a circumstance she revelled in as she enjoyed

Katherine's company and the attention that was paid to her. It also seems she was given a relative degree of freedom, for the Duchess of Somerset, the new Lord Protector's wife, would later scold Kate Astley 'for my Lady Elizabeth's going at night in a barge upon the Thames, and for other light parts'. The Duchess had been so incensed by this that she made it clear to Kate she was 'not worthy to have the governance of a King's daughter'.[27]

Elizabeth also encountered Katherine's household once more, including her friend Elisabeth Brooke, who had remained with the Queen Dowager – by the end of the following January, Elisabeth would be married to Katherine's brother, apparently with the encouragement of both Katherine herself and her close friend Katherine Willoughby, Duchess of Suffolk.[28] Thanks to the provisions Henry VIII had made for his widow, Katherine continued to live in the lavish style to which she had become accustomed during her queenship. Indeed, her cousin, Sir Nicholas Throckmorton, would write,

> Her house was term'd a second court of right,
> Because there flocked still nobility.[29]

Not only was life at Chelsea regal and magnificent, but Elizabeth and Katherine probably took the opportunity to indulge in practising their linguistic skills and sharing conversations about books and religion – Katherine's third book, *The Lamentations of a Sinner*, was published during this time, in November 1547. Notably, *Lamentations* expressed some of the radical religious views Katherine had kept under wraps during the reign of her more religiously conservative late husband, and it is wholly possible she wielded some influence over Elizabeth in this sphere.[30] In 1550, the scholar Roger Ascham, who had taught Elizabeth while she was in Katherine's household, would inform a correspondent that Elizabeth's 'study of true religion and learning is most energetic', and Katherine was at least partially responsible for shaping and nurturing this.[31] At some time after March 1548 the reformer Miles Coverdale, who had translated the Bible into English, joined Katherine's household as her almoner.[32] Coverdale had been living abroad, and it is unclear whether he arrived while Elizabeth was still in residence, but she was certainly exposed to and owned his work.

THOUGH ELIZABETH WAS happily settled in the female-led household at Chelsea, enjoying Katherine's company, it soon became apparent that on the Queen Dowager's side, something was lacking. Elizabeth's was not, it transpired, the only presence she craved. Thomas Seymour, the younger of the new King's uncles, was approaching forty. His surviving portraits show him to have been a man of handsome dark looks, with a long nose and a beard. A fourth son, Thomas was 'fierce in courage, courtly in fashion, in personage stately', could sing and write poetry, and thrived on action and adventure.[33] Charismatic and capable of exuding exceptional charm, it is little wonder Thomas was extremely popular among his contemporaries – far more so than his brother – on account of 'his liberality and splendour'; he had the kind of overpowering magnetism that drew people to him.[34] Yet he was also arrogant, reckless and excessively ambitious, driven by a thirst for power. Under Henry VIII, Thomas had enjoyed tastes of both diplomacy and the military, but he had never fully earned the late King's trust or admiration. He was appointed to the Privy Council just days before Henry's death and seemingly without the King's consent – it was later reported that while on his deathbed, hearing Thomas's name called out, the dying King had cried, 'No, no,' through failing breath.[35] The onset of his nephew's reign signified a fresh start, though, and Thomas's fortunes seemed set to rise. Not only did his elevation to a peerage and his appointment as Lord High Admiral bring him prestige, but the revenues generated by the grant of a multitude of lands boosted his income considerably. Likewise, through an enticing combination of a cash loan and grand promises to arrange a marriage between her and the young King, in early 1547 he had also acquired the wardship of Elizabeth's cousin, Lady Jane Grey, who came to live at his London residence, Seymour Place. But none of this was enough. A jealous man, Thomas resented the power and influence wielded by his elder brother, the Protector, and sought to obtain more for himself.

Katherine Parr was either blind to Thomas's less desirable qualities, or chose to overlook them, for to her Thomas's allure proved irresistible. Having been in love with him prior to her royal marriage, her passion for Thomas had not faded. Though she was still in mourning for Henry, soon after his death she and Thomas began an affair. For the first time in her life, Katherine was free to follow her heart, and she was completely besotted with Thomas. He, in turn, reciprocated her feelings and began pursuing her with alacrity, albeit in secret because of Katherine's status as the King's widow. With the connivance of a trusted servant and having made his way through the fields surrounding the house, Thomas was regularly ushered quietly into Chelsea for trysts with Katherine, although she was at pains to urge that he must 'come early in the morning, that ye may be gone again by seven o'clock, and so I suppose ye may come without suspect'.[36] Katherine's sister Anne Herbert, though not part of the household, soon recognized what was happening, so there seems to be at least a possibility that Elizabeth, living under the same roof, had some idea of what was going on.[37] Before long, though, Katherine and Thomas's relationship had become serious, and in June the Imperial ambassador, Van der Delft, was reporting rumours that the couple would marry.[38] Little did he know, the wedding had already taken place.

Unbeknown to Katherine, she was seemingly not Thomas's first choice, and initially he probably harboured hopes of a marriage with either Elizabeth or Mary. Indeed, Elizabeth herself would later confess that, after Thomas's marriage to Katherine, she had learned from Kate Astley that: 'If my Lord might have had his own will, he would have had me [Elizabeth], afore the Queen.'[39] Such knowledge, Kate Astley claimed, had been told her 'both by himself and by others'.[40] In a similar vein, Van der Delft would later inform his master that Thomas had asked his brother's permission to marry Mary. The Protector was 'displeased and reproved him, saying that neither of them was born to be King, nor to marry King's daughters'.[41] Thomas realized that, for whatever fanciful hopes he may have had, neither the Protector nor the Council would ever consent to a match with Mary or

Elizabeth, thereby making it impossible for him to achieve his goal without thwarting the inheritance promised to the sisters by their late father's will. Katherine, however, was an altogether different prospect. This was borne out by a conversation Kate Astley later recalled having with Thomas when she came across him in St James's Park. On telling him that she had heard he wished to marry Elizabeth, Thomas refuted the claim. 'Nay,' he said. 'I have not to lose my life for a wife. For it has been spoken, but that cannot be. But I will prove to have the Queen.' Listening carefully as he spoke these words, Kate replied, 'I hear you are married already.'[42]

The details of Katherine's fourth wedding are unknown; her biographer Susan James suggests it may have taken place at Baynard's Castle, the home of Katherine's sister where she was a frequent guest, perhaps some time in May.[43] Coming within a matter of months of Henry's death, the marriage was a bold move on Katherine's part, which explains why it was conducted in secret, yet from her perspective it was also the culmination of all her personal hopes. No longer was she compelled to marry for duty; she had instead chosen to follow her heart. We do not know how or when Elizabeth learned of her stepmother's marriage, but by July the news had become public.

Understandably, Katherine was particularly anxious to obtain the good opinion of her stepson, Edward, who had learned of the marriage by June. To her immense relief, the young King professed himself to be delighted, congratulating the 'honourable and entirely beloved mother' he adored and promising Katherine: 'I will so provide for you both.'[44] Edward, after all, had always been fond of his uncle Thomas, assuring Katherine that he 'being mine uncle, is of so good a nature that he will not be troublesome any means unto you'.[45] Others, however, greeted news of the marriage with outrage. Both the Lord Protector and his wife, whom Katherine detested, having once written acidly to Thomas that 'it is her custom to promise many comings to her friends, and to perform none', were furious, not least because the couple had failed to obtain the permission of the King's Council.[46] Closer to home, others were also unhappy.

Thomas had approached Elizabeth's sister, Mary, for her help in furthering the match, but she had firmly declined to be 'a meddler in the matter, considering whose wife her grace was of late', which tells us precisely how she felt about it.[47] Mary showed herself to be utterly horrified by what she perceived as a complete lack of respect to the memory of her late father, who had, after all, only been dead for a short time. Her relationship with Katherine, which had always been warm, immediately cooled. What was more, Mary wasted no time in urging her teenage sister to think of her reputation and disassociate herself from the stepmother who had put her personal desires before duty, instead asking Elizabeth to join her and make her home on one of Mary's estates. In the aftermath of her father's death Mary had been living quietly on her properties away from court, where the Council – fearful that her strong fervour for Catholicism put her at odds with the new regime and made her a figurehead for discontent – hoped she would remain. Elizabeth, meanwhile, was happily settled at Chelsea and had no wish to leave – in fact, it would soon become clear that she did not share Mary's feelings of distaste.[48] The elder sister was shocked, and the episode may have placed a strain on the relationship between them. For Mary, who had a strong sense of morality, Elizabeth's decision must have reminded her of Anne Boleyn, whose moral values had been considerably scrutinized just a decade earlier. If this was indeed the case, it would not be the last time Mary would unfavourably compare her sister with her scandalous mother.

With news of their marriage now public and the King's approval won, Thomas wasted no time in moving to Chelsea to join Katherine and Elizabeth. His ward, Jane Grey, appears to have remained largely at Seymour Place, and it is improbable Elizabeth saw much of her – the cousins were not close. The Admiral immediately assumed the role not only of head of the household, but also of stepfather and guardian to Elizabeth, winning the affection of the key members of her household as well as her own: Kate Astley and Thomas Parry. Kate was particularly infatuated by the new master of the house, falling for his charms and intent in her belief that he would have made a very suitable husband for her mistress. However, it was not long before Thomas, partially entrusted with Elizabeth's care, took advantage of the teenager's proximity, and his relationship with his new charge took a highly inappropriate turn.

Thomas was a newly married man in a match made primarily for personal reasons, yet it quickly became obvious that his wife was not the only object of his desire. His feelings towards Elizabeth were far from purely platonic. Thanks to the later confession of Elizabeth's devoted Kate Astley, we know that very soon after the Admiral arrived at Chelsea, he 'would come many mornings' into Elizabeth's chamber, sometimes before she had risen.[49] On the occasions when he found her up, he would bid her good morning and 'strike her upon the back or on the buttocks familiarly, and so go forth through his lodgings; and some time go through to the maidens [Elizabeth's ladies] and play with them, and so go forth'.[50] If Elizabeth were still in bed, though, 'he would put open the curtains, and bid her good morrow, and make as though he would come at her'. In response, she 'would go further in the bed, so that he could not come at her'.[51]

Elizabeth, who would turn fourteen in September, was highly impressionable, but she must have realized that, coming from such an unacceptable source as her stepmother's husband, Thomas's behaviour went well beyond the bounds of propriety. Nevertheless, she was also intrigued by the handsome older man who showed her such attention, and she appears to have been genuinely attracted to him – the equivalent of a teenage crush, although she would never openly acknowledge as much. Even so, her fascination with Thomas seemed clear enough during the regular entertainments that Katherine staged at Chelsea. Dancing was a popular pastime in the household, and Elizabeth looked on as Thomas danced with Katherine's close friend Katherine Willoughby, Duchess of Suffolk. Always eager for an opportunity to participate in the amusement she adored, when it was Elizabeth's turn to choose a partner, 'she hath chosen my Lord Admiral', and 'she would laugh and pale at it' in a light-hearted manner.[52] Thomas was gratified, and continued in his attentiveness to her. For Elizabeth, it was the first time in her life she had been paid such intimate flattery and initially she found it impossible not to respond to the Admiral's flirtatious behaviour.

The morning visits continued, and as Thomas entered Elizabeth's chamber one morning, in what had become his usual habit, he found that his wife's stepdaughter was still in bed. Unfazed by the presence of

Kate Astley, Thomas seized upon Elizabeth's vulnerability as she roused herself from sleep, and boldly 'strove to have kissed her in her bed'.[53] Even for Kate Astley this was too much and, horrified, she 'bade him go away for shame'.[54] Yet the morning calls carried on. Before long, however, Elizabeth herself recognized that the Admiral had gone too far. She began to feel alarmed and desperately tried to avoid his advances. Given that he held a key to every room in the house, this became increasingly challenging. Hearing the lock turn in her door one morning and knowing that Thomas was about to enter, an anxious Elizabeth 'ran out of her bed to her maidens, and then went behind the curtain of the bed'.[55] Rather than leaving when he saw that she had gone, though, a determined Thomas waited for Elizabeth to come out.

By now, those around Elizabeth were fully aware of the Admiral's behaviour and speaking of it among themselves. Kate Astley, who had not witnessed this latest incident, heard of it from Elizabeth's Gentleman Usher, Robert Porter.[56] Perhaps recognizing that she had not done enough to protect her young charge and realizing that Thomas was putting Elizabeth's reputation at risk, Kate decided to take matters into her own hands and confront him. Approaching him in the gallery, Elizabeth's lady mistress warned Thomas that 'these things were complained of' and 'my Lady was evil spoken of'. Rather than listening to Kate's grievances, however, Thomas exploded in a fit of rage. 'God's precious soul!' he cried; he would tell his brother the Protector how he had been slandered.[57] Furious at being rebuked by a member of Elizabeth's household, 'he would not leave it', he retorted, 'for he meant no evil'.[58] He had no intention of curbing his conduct.

It is difficult not to judge Thomas's behaviour through modern eyes, which given his age and position of power, would consider it child abuse. But in the sixteenth century, though such actions would have been deemed highly inappropriate, popular judgement would not have labelled them in the same way. Concepts of maturity and ideals of behaviour were different five hundred years ago, and of greater concern was the potential damage Thomas could inflict upon Elizabeth's reputation: she was, after all, the King's sister and the daughter of the great King Henry VIII. In royal circles, unmarried women were expected to be both modest and chaste, beyond all reproach. Any hint of scandal could ruin a woman's good name and with it all prospects of an advantageous marriage.

The Admiral's conduct inevitably provoked gossip within the household, and his early-morning visits to Elizabeth's chamber were soon common knowledge. As a mature and experienced man, Thomas was fully aware of the vulnerable position in which he was placing his teenage charge. He was also putting his relationship with his own wife at risk, but such was his arrogance that he disregarded both Katherine's feelings and any consideration for Elizabeth's position. His selfish nature was all too clear to see. If the household was aware of what was going on, surely Katherine must also have heard the whispers. She assuredly knew of them by the time the household moved to Hanworth in the summer heat of July.

Lying on the outskirts of London, Hanworth was a moated manor house that had once belonged to Elizabeth's mother. Here, there were reminders of Anne Boleyn all around, for the ill-fated Queen had taken great care to bedeck her manor with the most lavish and fashionable furnishings, which all came at great expense. Upon the arrival of Katherine's household in 1547, archery butts were immediately set up in the gardens for the ladies to enjoy in the summer weather.[59] Even at Hanworth, Thomas's morning visits showed no signs of abating, though Elizabeth did her best to avoid them, taking care to ensure she was always up by the time he reached her chamber. There were only two occasions Kate Astley could recall when Elizabeth had not yet risen, and on both of these Thomas was accompanied by Katherine. Kate would later claim she had told the Queen of the Admiral's behaviour, but Katherine 'made a small matter of it to me'.[60] Nevertheless, whether because of this conversation, her own aroused suspicions or to satisfy herself that her husband's behaviour towards her stepdaughter was nothing more than innocent fun, Katherine decided she would join Thomas during his regular visits to Elizabeth's chamber. Inwardly, at least, she must have recognized that her husband's conduct was improper, but, as Elizabeth Norton has highlighted, upon marrying him she had also vowed to obey him and ceased to act independently.

Thomas had full control of Katherine's assets, and she was aware of how volatile he could be.[61] This was borne out by Thomas Parry's later statement in which he claimed to have heard that the Admiral was an 'oppressor', and 'how cruelly, how dishonourably, and how jealously' he had used Katherine.[62] Not only was she therefore in a terrible predicament, but Katherine was also deeply in love with Thomas. Whatever misgivings she may have had about the situation, she was apparently prepared to turn a blind eye – even to join in.

The specifics of these romps would later come to light in great detail when Thomas fell from royal favour and the Council was seeking evidence against him, much to Elizabeth's distress. Kate Astley remembered that once, when Thomas and Katherine arrived for a joint visit to Elizabeth's chamber, the pair 'tickled my Lady Elizabeth in the bed'.[63] Kate anxiously confided in the Admiral's servant John Harington that 'my Lord and the Queen came divers times to my Lady Elizabeth's chamber, which was well taken of by everybody; but my Lord came some time, without the Queen, which of some was misliked'.[64] In other words, the visits were deemed acceptable with Katherine's presence, but when Thomas came alone eyebrows were, unsurprisingly, raised.

Coming so early in Elizabeth's adolescence, her experiences with Thomas – and indeed Katherine too – may have left her feeling confused. We do not know how much she understood about sex, but she had certainly never had any experience of men in a sensual or romantic context. What is more, the very people who were responsible for her care were now putting her at risk and exposing her to behaviour that, if made public, could ruin her. It would not be the last occasion on which Elizabeth's reputation came under threat, but in this instance it served to reinforce her vulnerability and her changing place in the world. Thomas would not have dared to exhibit such behaviour during the lifetime of Elizabeth's father. Her brother the King and his Council, preoccupied with matters of state, were unlikely to be giving much thought to Elizabeth – she was on her own.

Now that Katherine was involved, however, there was no reason for Thomas to restrict his antics solely to morning chamber visits. He took full advantage of this. One day that summer, Elizabeth and Katherine were enjoying a walk through Hanworth's fragrant gardens, famous for their strawberries, and also boasting an aviary from which birdsong could be heard and an orchard.[65] The pleasant stroll took a more serious turn when Thomas appeared and 'cut her gown in an hundred pieces'. Mortified when she saw the state of Elizabeth's shredded dress, Kate Astley did not refrain from chiding her charge. It was not her fault, a despondent Elizabeth replied, for 'she could not do with all, for the Queen held her, while the Lord Admiral cut it'.[66] 'Well,' Kate replied, 'I would my Lord would show more reverence to you, although he be homely with the Queen.'[67] Once again, Katherine was seemingly making allowances for exploits she knew would be frowned upon if they were known elsewhere. Her motivation for doing so can only be explained by her subordination to Thomas in what was very much a patriarchal society, coupled with feelings of intimidation. Her love for him was also a key factor, so intense that it led her to abandon her usual good sense and decorum. In so doing, however, she placed her stepdaughter in a position that was at best precarious and at worst dangerous.

Though she may not have admitted as much in public, Katherine's suspicions about the relationship between her husband and stepdaughter were becoming progressively stronger. Thomas Parry would later admit that 'the Queen was jealous of her and him', which Kate Astley believed prompted Katherine to tell an extraordinary story.[68] During a conversation at Hanworth, said Kate, the Queen – in what Astley felt was Katherine's attempt to warn the lady mistress to 'take more heed' – had informed her that the Admiral had 'looked in at the gallery window' and, to his shock, saw 'my Lady Elizabeth cast her arms about a man's neck'.[69] Horrified at what she took to be a genuine tale, Kate Astley immediately hurried to question Elizabeth about the mystery encounter. Through tears the teenager denied that such a thing had ever taken place. Kate could ask her ladies if it were true or not, Elizabeth said. 'They all denied it', and it dawned on Kate that such an incident was impossible, 'for there came no man but Grindal', Elizabeth's tutor.[70] She suspected that the story had, in fact, been fabricated by Katherine because of her jealousies over her stepdaughter's relationship with Thomas, and this does seem to be a genuine possibility. After all, if Katherine had really been made aware of any such scenario that threatened Elizabeth's honour, why did she not confront her stepdaughter directly, rather than leaving Kate Astley to deal with it? The only credible answer is that Katherine recognized it was a fiction, whether her own or Thomas's. The warning flag had been raised, but on the Admiral's part it would soon become evident that it was not heeded.

CHAPTER 8

————— ❧ —————

'Truly I was Replete
with Sorrow'

'Elizabeth, there sojourning a time,
Gave fruitful hope through blossoms' bloom in prime.'

SIR NICHOLAS THROCKMORTON, AFTER 1571

I N THE FINAL days of January 1548, Elizabeth received a letter. 'I can easily estimate, most illustrious lady,' the great scholar Roger Ascham began as he sat down at Cambridge to compose his thoughts, 'your grief at the death of our friend Grindal.'[1] Earlier that month, Elizabeth had been left equally devastated and terrified by the death of her tutor, William Grindal, who had succumbed to the plague. Fortunately, the highly contagious disease that killed this brilliant young mind did not spread to the rest of the household, or indeed to Grindal's royal pupil, but it did cut short what had been a successful and fond working relationship. Ascham attempted to divert Elizabeth's mind from the death of her tutor, although he recognized that both the support of Kate Astley and Elizabeth's own 'prudence' would help to relieve the 'bitterness' that grief brought with it; at fourteen, Elizabeth's strength of mind was already noted by those around her.[2] Ascham urged Elizabeth that the best way to honour her tutor would be 'to bring to maturity that excellent learning of which you have had the seeds laid by Grindal'.[3] He also reminded her: 'I shall think it my greatest happiness, if the time ever comes when my services can be of use to you.'[4] Elizabeth would take him at his word.

135

By the time Elizabeth received Ascham's letter, she had spent Christmas apart from Katherine and Thomas, who had journeyed to Seymour Place for the festive season. The distance gave Elizabeth a welcome break from the Admiral's advances, but Grindal's death also left her with much to ponder. A replacement tutor would clearly be needed, and though they were apart, Elizabeth and Katherine exchanged messages on the subject. Katherine was eager for her employee Francis Goldsmith, who served as her solicitor and a gentleman of her Privy Chamber, to accept the post, but Elizabeth had an altogether different candidate in mind.[5] Shortly after sending his letter of condolence, Roger Ascham paid Elizabeth a visit, and in a note written soon afterwards to John Cheke, Ascham admitted, 'That illustrious lady is thinking of having me in the place of Grindal.'[6] Honoured at having being singled out personally, Ascham at once 'declared that I was ready to obey her orders'.[7] He was amply qualified for the post, for, like Grindal, he hailed from St John's College, Cambridge, where he had successfully obtained a fellowship. However, he recognized that there was competition for the role of tutor to Elizabeth, for she herself had told him: 'The Queen and the Lord Admiral had laboured in favour of Goldsmith.'[8] Perhaps reluctantly, Ascham 'advised her to comply', and 'I praised Goldsmith to her, and exhorted her, as much as I could, to follow their judgment in such a matter.'[9] After all, the most important thing, Ascham counselled her, was that her learning ought to be nurtured. He was already impressed with Elizabeth's understanding of Latin and Greek, gushing to Cheke that 'it cannot be believed' what level she would accomplish if she continued in this way.[10]

Having agreed to discuss potential tutors further when next they met, soon after Ascham's visit Elizabeth joined Katherine and Thomas in London. When she arrived, she found Thomas in a state of agitation because of growing tensions between himself and the Protector – feelings that Katherine shared, partially on account of the Protector's refusal to return her royal jewels, as well as her antipathy towards his duchess.[11] Katherine, however, had other preoccupations, for at the age of thirty-five she had recently learned that she was pregnant for the first time. By contemporary standards, she was considered old to be bearing her first child, but despite her age both expectant parents were overjoyed and cherished high hopes that the baby would be a 'little knave'.[12] The household would be gaining another member, and one who would demand a great deal of Katherine's love and attention. Elizabeth probably deemed that she would not be one of Katherine's primary focuses for much longer.

Delighted though she likely was for Katherine, Elizabeth had her own matters to consider and wasted no time informing her stepmother of her preference for Ascham to assume the position of tutor. Even at fourteen, she was remarkably headstrong with a mind of her own, and it was Katherine who ended up backing down. Her decision to do so is significant and shows her willingness to allow Elizabeth independence to make her own choices about her future. She did, of course, have prior knowledge of Ascham's abilities, and would probably also have been assured by those who knew him, chiefly John Cheke, to whom Katherine was close, that he would be a suitable candidate.[13] Whatever the circumstances, Elizabeth was elated, and before long Ascham had joined the household and assumed his new post.

Elizabeth continued to flourish under the guidance of her new tutor, and Ascham claimed that his young student 'favours me wonderfully'.[14] William Camden, always praising of Elizabeth, would later enthuse that 'she was a kind of miracle and admiration for her learning amongst the princes of her time' – in other words, she stood out and was noticed next to her royal contemporaries.[15] She quickly settled into a routine, starting her morning with the study of the New Testament in Greek. In the afternoons, her attentions turned to classical authors such as Isocrates and Sophocles, works that Ascham felt were useful for his pupil to 'gain purity of style, and her mind derive instruction that would be of value to her to meet every contingency of life'.[16] Before long, he had added further texts to Elizabeth's curriculum, including *Commonplaces*, a religious text by German reformer Philip Melanchthon, which Ascham hoped would 'teach her the foundations of religion, together with elegant language and sound doctrine'.[17] Together, the pair also absorbed most of the great classical Cicero, and much of Titus Livius's *History of Rome*: texts that greatly aided Elizabeth's understanding of Latin.[18] However, 'Whatever she reads she at once perceives any word that has a doubtful or curious meaning.' She enjoyed 'a style that grows out of the subject; chaste because it is suitable, and beautiful because it is clear'. She also liked 'modest metaphors', and ultimately 'her judgement is so good, that in all Greek, Latin, and English composition, there is nothing so loose on the one hand or so concise on the other, which she does not immediately attend to, and either reject with disgust or receive with pleasure'.[19]

Ascham believed that when teaching, 'love is better than fear, gentleness better than beating, to bring up a child rightly in learning', and these were the methods he employed while working with Elizabeth and subsequently published in *The Schoolmaster*, the third volume of which he dedicated to his talented pupil.[20] They were clearly effective, for in 1550 he would write: 'Her mind has no womanly weakness, her perseverance is equal to that of a man, and her memory long keeps what it quickly picks up.'[21] Such a scholarly youngster was a joy to teach, and Ascham was honoured to have been given such an opportunity.

Elizabeth may have been excelling in her lessons, but her arrival at Seymour Place quickly reignited the stress she had suffered at Chelsea and Hanworth. She, and Katherine too, may have hoped that with Thomas's initial departure for London, a line had been firmly drawn under the antics of the past. But it was not to be. Upon her arrival in his home, his territory, the Admiral immediately slipped back into his old ways, trying a slightly different tactic with his house guest. Kate Astley recalled that Thomas would come to Elizabeth's chamber each morning 'in his night gown, barelegged in his slippers'. To his evident disappointment, though, Elizabeth was by now well and truly wise to his behaviour and the vulnerable position in which it placed her. She made sure she was up and reading her book each morning – perhaps her Greek New Testament – so that when the Admiral would 'look in at the gallery door', there was nothing for him to do but 'bid my Lady Elizabeth good morrow, and so go his way'. Mindful of the Queen's admonishment of her at Hanworth the previous year, Kate reached a point where, in the hopes of protecting Elizabeth, she once again attempted to confront Thomas, telling him 'it was an unseemly sight to come so bare legged to a maidens chamber'.

Predictably, the Admiral was 'angry' at being berated once again but said nothing further.[22] Thanks to his conduct, however, Elizabeth's relationship with her stepmother was about to take a devastating turn.

Katherine's unborn child 'stirred apace' and the pregnancy was progressing well, although she was experiencing troublesome morning sickness.[23] As spring arrived, the Dowager Queen was happy to leave the capital behind and return to the pretty gardens at Hanworth, accompanied by her husband and her stepdaughter. But though she was pleased to have been reunited with Elizabeth, she was growing ever more suspicious of her husband's attentions towards her. Conscious that Thomas had a temper, she chose not to broach the subject with him; nevertheless, 'suspecting the often access' he had to Elizabeth, she determined to keep a close eye on him.[24] In so doing, she would receive an unwelcome shock.

Elizabeth's cofferer, Thomas Parry, would later recall that while seeking out her husband and stepdaughter, Katherine 'came suddenly upon them, where they were all alone, (he having her in his arms)'.[25] Katherine was horrified at the betrayal of 'my sweetheart and loving husband' and the girl she had treated like a daughter, and was overwhelmed by her emotions.[26] Predictably, 'the Queen fell out, both with the Lord Admiral, and with her Grace also'.[27] We will never know exactly what happened or how Elizabeth came to find herself in such a compromising position – after all, for some months she had done her best to avoid Thomas's advances. Elizabeth Norton has surmised that while Elizabeth was attracted to the Admiral, she did not know how to handle either the situation or his attentions.[28] Given her youth and inexperience, this is both highly plausible and understandable, and it is more than probable that it was Thomas who instigated the embrace. What angry and woeful words passed between the trio are likewise destined to remain unknown, but Parry believed that a devastated Katherine summoned Kate Astley and 'told her fancy in that matter; and of this was much displeasure'.[29] The Queen was furious that the lady mistress had failed to heed her warning and keep a closer eye on her charge. There could be no question of Katherine looking the other way this time; matters had already gone too far, and she was forced to confront the situation in which Thomas had selfishly placed her.

Katherine was greatly preoccupied with plans for her confinement, and arrangements for her to travel to Sudeley Castle, Thomas's Gloucestershire seat, were already well underway. The last thing she needed was to reconsider Elizabeth's future, but it was clear that her stepdaughter could no longer remain under the same roof and alternative domestic arrangements would have to be made. Parry was unsure precisely how events played out, or at least he pleaded ignorance, but he was adamant that 'this was the cause why she [Elizabeth] was sent from the Queen; or else that her Grace parted from the Queen'.[30] Elizabeth would no longer remain in Katherine's household.

The breakdown in her relationship with Katherine was difficult for Elizabeth, who had relied on the security offered by her stepmother for the past five years. She had already lost both her parents, and recent events now left her in danger of losing another who had filled that role. It remained to be seen whether her damaged connection with Katherine could ever be repaired.

AS ELIZABETH SET out on the first stage of her journey from Hanworth the week after Whitsun, she was reassured in some part by 'the manifold kindness' she received from her stepmother upon her departure.[31] Nevertheless, 'truly I was replete with sorrow to depart from your highness'.[32] Unbeknown to Elizabeth, she would never see Katherine again. Prior to Elizabeth's leaving, Katherine had been unwell, exacerbated by the stress she had experienced as a result of her husband's relentlessly inappropriate behaviour towards Elizabeth. But it had not been long before the relationship she shared with her stepdaughter had begun to heal, so much so that Katherine felt comfortable enough for Thomas to accompany Elizabeth for at least part of her journey, chatting to Kate Astley along the way.[33] Elizabeth was destined for Cheshunt, the Hertfordshire moated manor house that was home to Sir Anthony Denny, Henry VIII's former Groom of the Stool and a man whom the Imperial ambassador described as 'the most confidential of any of the gentlemen of the chamber'.[34]

Elizabeth had known Denny all her life, and he was also Kate Astley's brother-in-law, for since 1525 he had been married to her sister, Joan, with whom he shared twelve children.[35] It was probably this familial relationship that made Cheshunt the ideal choice of refuge for Elizabeth, for it prevented too many questions being asked over her departure from Katherine's household. Joan Denny was also on friendly terms with Katherine, but it seems unlikely that the Dennys were aware of the real reason for the arrival of their house guest. After all, Sir Anthony was close to the Lord Protector. If he did know, then he and his wife were discreet enough to keep quiet.

With lots of young children, the household at Cheshunt was bustling and full of noise, with very little room for privacy. Such an environment would have kept Elizabeth occupied, but shortly after her arrival, probably in June, her thoughts were elsewhere. She was busily exchanging letters with her stepmother, and with Thomas too, who kept her informed of Katherine's pregnancy.[36] Indeed, matters appear to have been resolved and no ill feelings harboured, for Elizabeth assured Thomas: 'I am a friend not won with trifles, nor lost with the like.'[37] There had been great concerns that the flirtation would prove damaging to Elizabeth's honour, and this was something she and Katherine discussed prior to her leaving. Though, by her own admission, Elizabeth had not had much to say at the time, the distance between them gave her an opportunity to reflect on Katherine's words. She referenced them when she wrote to her stepmother soon after her arrival at Cheshunt:

And albeit I answered little, I weighed it more deeper when you said you would warn me of all evils that you should hear of me: for if your grace had not a good opinion of me, you would not have offered friendship to me that way that all men judge the contrary. But what may I more say than thank God for providing such friends to me, desiring God to enrich me with their long life, and me grace to be in heart no less thankful to receive it than I now am glad in writing to show it. And although I have plenty of matter, here I will stay for I know you are not quiet to read. From Cheston [Cheshunt] this present Saturday. Your highness' humble daughter, Elizabeth.[38]

Elizabeth, probably from a sense of guilt, had been unwilling, or perhaps unable, to offer much by way of response to whatever words Katherine had spoken during their final meeting. Evidently, there was uneasiness that rumours of the goings-on at Chelsea and Hanworth may begin to circulate – hardly surprising, given that most of the household were aware of Thomas's visits to Elizabeth's chamber. How much they knew of her sudden departure cannot be gauged, but surely it would have been a cause for gossip. The letter confirms that Katherine had offered to warn Elizabeth should she hear of any such talk, for which Elizabeth expressed her gratitude. The teenager's subsequent words suggest that Katherine had now forgiven her stepdaughter, leaving Elizabeth humbled. Her experience with Thomas had been dangerous, but she was truly sorry for the pain it had caused the stepmother she genuinely loved and cared for, who in turn had done so much to love and nurture her. This episode in Elizabeth's life highlighted her vulnerability and her own response to that, making a deep and lasting impression on her.

While Elizabeth adapted to life in the Denny household, in mid-June Thomas and a now heavily pregnant Katherine left Hanworth, and the bad memories it contained, behind. There was every reason to avoid London and its surroundings that summer, for the plague was rife, and the King and his court had fled to avoid 'the danger of the prevalent sickness in London'.[39] Katherine and Thomas travelled to Sudeley Castle, where Katherine would spend the remainder of her pregnancy. To accommodate his royal wife and her retinue, the Admiral had spent the sum of £1,000 (£421,000) on improvements to the castle, preparing a nursery and ensuring that Katherine was housed in the style to which she had become accustomed.[40] Katherine found that she relished life in the country, enjoying walks in the park and relaxing in the company of Thomas's ward Lady Jane Grey, as well as members of her household.[41] She had also been reconciled with her eldest stepdaughter, Mary, who wrote to Katherine that summer trusting 'to hear good success of your Grace's great belly'.[42] Katherine missed Elizabeth, though, and continued to write to her, their relationship thawing further as all past matters were seemingly forgiven, if not forgotten.

Elizabeth, in turn, appreciated Katherine's remembrances and took the time to tell her so. On 31 July, though she had 'very little leisure' (perhaps the Denny children were keeping her busy!), she sat down to pen what was probably her last letter to her stepmother.[43] In her clear and beautiful hand, she thanked Katherine for her letters, which 'be most joyful to me in absence'. They meant even more 'considering what pain it is to you to write, your grace being so great with child and so sickly', because of which 'your commendation were enough in my lord's letter'.[44] Plainly Thomas, with Katherine's knowledge and approval, had also been writing to Elizabeth. She continued,

I much rejoice at your health with the well liking of the country, with my humble thanks that your grace wished me with you till I were weary of that country. Your highness were like to be cumbered [encumbered] if I should not depart till I were weary being with you, although it were in the worst soil in the world, your presence would make it pleasant.[45]

Elizabeth also referred to Katherine's 'busy child', joking that 'if I were at his birth no doubt I would see him beaten for the trouble he has put you to'. She assured her stepmother: 'Master Denny and my lady with humble thanks prayeth most entirely for your grace, praying the almighty God to send you a most lucky deliverance.' Likewise, 'my mistress [Kate Astley] wisheth no less, giving your highness most humble thanks for her commendations'.[46] With the example of Jane Seymour before her, Elizabeth would have been only too aware of the dangers Katherine faced as she approached childbirth. Everyone hoped for a safe and positive outcome.

By the time Katherine read Elizabeth's letter, she would have taken to her chamber at Sudeley. All the preparations for her baby's arrival had been made, and it was here, within the peaceful surroundings of her husband's country seat, that on 30 August she gave birth not to the son whom she and Thomas had confidently believed she was carrying, but to a baby girl. The infant was named Mary in honour of the elder of Katherine's two stepdaughters, and her proud father wasted no time in writing to his brother the Protector to announce her arrival. He responded immediately, congratulating the new parents on their 'happy hour' with the birth of 'so pretty a daughter'.[47] However, though initially it seemed Katherine had been successful in 'escaping all danger' following her delivery, her health soon took a turn for the worst. As she lay in her chamber, she began to descend into delirium – puerperal fever had set in. Despite the comforting words of her faithful friend Lady Tyrwhit, who assured her that she 'saw no likelihood of death in her', Katherine knew her end was approaching.[48]

As her life began to ebb away, the memory of her husband with Elizabeth returned to haunt Katherine, and she could not help but berate him. An anxious Thomas had remained by his wife's side as she grew increasingly sick and was clutching her hand when Katherine turned her head to Lady Tyrwhit, who was standing nearby. 'My Lady Tyrwhit,' she began. 'I am not well handled, for those that be about me careth not for me, but standeth laughing at my grief; and the more good I will to them, the less good that they will to me.' Realizing that she was referring to him, a stunned Thomas responded, 'Why sweetheart I would you no hurt.' But Katherine was not soothed by these words, replying, 'No, my Lord, I think so.' Sensing that what she said next should be delivered with more privacy, she spoke into his ear: 'But, my Lord, you have given me many shrewd taunts.'[49] Was this a reference to Thomas's reaction when Katherine had berated him over his behaviour towards Elizabeth? Or distress over something more general that Katherine had previously been forced to suppress? Lady Tyrwhit believed these words were spoken with good memory, and 'very sharply and earnestly, for her mind was unquieted'.[50] Aware that Lady Tyrwhit had heard the conversation, the Admiral called her to one side and asked her what his wife had said. Lady Tyrwhit had little time for Thomas, 'and I declared it plainly to him'.[51] Returning to his wife, in his continued efforts to calm Katherine, Thomas lay down on the bed next to her but was unable to soothe her troubled thoughts. Lady Tyrwhit, perceiving 'her trouble to be so great that my heart would serve me to hear no more', removed herself.[52] Katherine's suffering would soon be at an end.

On 5 September, two days before Elizabeth's fifteenth birthday,

Katherine died at the age of thirty-six. The stepmother who had cared for the teenager as if she were her own child, and whom Elizabeth had adored in return, was gone. Two days after she had breathed her last, Katherine's funeral was conducted at St Mary's Church within the grounds of Sudeley Castle. The young Lady Jane Grey assumed the role of chief mourner, and the service was performed by Katherine's almoner, Miles Coverdale, according to Protestant rites.[53] Following the ceremony, the late Queen was laid to rest within the church, the only Queen of England to be buried on a private estate.[54]

How and when Elizabeth received the news of Katherine's death is unknown, as is her reaction. Soon afterwards, though, Katherine's chaplain John Parkhurst composed an epitaph that contained the emotive lines:

For the departed, we her household flow with watery tears;
Damp is the British earth from moistened cheeks.[55]

Given the close bond she and Katherine had once shared, it is easy to imagine that Elizabeth would have felt the same. She had lost not only a mother figure once more, but someone who had championed her, loved her and consistently encouraged her. Perhaps she also felt a sense of guilt over her apparent betrayal of Katherine and the circumstances in which she had left her household. Katherine's death is likely to have struck a further chord because it provided a reminder of the perilous process of childbirth. For Elizabeth, this afforded more tangible evidence of the uncertainties faced by women in marriage – royal or not. Thus far she had witnessed how vulnerable marriage could make a woman, not just in Katherine's case but as shown by the example of all of her father's wives, leaving them with no control over their ultimate fate. It was a memory that she carried with her when it came to considering her own future. Katherine was gone, but the imprint she had made on Elizabeth's life remained, and by her she would never be forgotten.

'Incontinent [immediately] after the death of the Queen,' Elizabeth fell ill, and we can assume that whatever symptoms she was experiencing were probably intensified by grief.[56] Still, her history of sickness did not prevent the spread of gossip. More than half a century later, King Edward's child-hood playmate Jane Dormer related a story. There was a rumour, she said, of 'a child born and miserably destroyed', although nobody knew to whom the infant belonged. Though she did not know the details, Jane had heard that the midwife who delivered it had been brought blindfolded to a house and 'saw nothing in the house while she was there' but candlelight. The midwife had said, though, that it was 'the child of a very fair young lady'.[57] Jane also reported that 'there was a muttering of the Admiral [Thomas Seymour] and this lady, who was then between fifteen and sixteen years of age'.[58]

Despite depictions in modern popular culture, there is no evidence whatsoever that Elizabeth ever consummated her relationship with Thomas, let alone became pregnant and had a child by him. It is highly improbable, and there is no conclusive evidence that she was ever anything other than 'the Virgin Queen' she later claimed to be. As a fervent Catholic who was close to Elizabeth's sister Mary, Jane Dormer had her own reasons to be hostile to Elizabeth. If the story was true, she continued, 'it was the judgement of God upon the Admiral; and upon her, to make her ever after incapable of children'.[59] It would not be the last occasion on which Elizabeth was reported to have had a child out of wedlock, throwing her chastity into question.

Pregnancy was not the cause of Elizabeth's malady, and though her symptoms on this occasion are unknown it is telling that this would not be the first time she fell ill at a time when she had experienced trauma or was placed under strain. There are numerous instances where there is evidence of her surroundings or her emotional wellbeing impacting on her in a physical capacity, and it seems no coincidence that the aftermath of Katherine's death was one of them. Throughout her life, Elizabeth would be plagued by bouts of poor health, and on this occasion there was enough concern for her welfare for the Lord Protector to send her both a kind letter and the royal physician, Doctor Bill, who had once served Henry VIII.[60]

In a letter that perhaps dates from around September, Elizabeth wrote to thank the Protector, assuring him that Doctor Bill's *diligence and pain has been a great part of my recovery. For whom I do most heartily thank your grace, desiring you to give him thanks for me, who can ascertain you of my state of health, wherefore I will not write it.*[61]

Elizabeth's polite note suggests that, though well enough to write, she was not yet fully recovered. Neither was she the only one who had been suffering since Katherine's death.

Thomas Seymour had been 'so amazed' by grief at the loss of his wife that 'I had small regard either to myself or to my doings'.[62] Despite his treatment of Katherine, Thomas genuinely mourned her. In his initial shock, he decided to break up Katherine's household, which included his own ward Lady Jane Grey, whom he sent home to her parents at Bradgate Park in Leicestershire.[63] However, it was not long before he realized this was a mistake and attempted to re-establish the household and regain Jane's custody. Thomas perceived the high value of a royal ward, and recognized that if he could achieve her marriage to his young nephew the King, his own position would be strengthened. Her parents, the Marquess and Marchioness of Dorset, were initially reluctant to comply, but after some financial persuasion and the further promise of an attempt to wed her to the young King, they eventually 'could not resist him'.[64] Meanwhile, Kate Astley later admitted to having been told by Lady Tyrwhit that, 'Men did think that my Lord Admiral kept the Queen's maidens together to wait upon the Lady Elizabeth, whom he intended to marry shortly.'[65] Kate did not forget this conversation, and true it was that, having regained his ward, Thomas now turned his attentions elsewhere.

CHAPTER 9

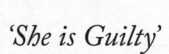

'She is Guilty'

'Master Tyrwhit and others have told me that there goeth rumours abroad which be greatly both against mine honour and honesty, which above all other things I esteem.'

ELIZABETH TO THE LORD PROTECTOR, 28 JANUARY 1549

LIZABETH WOULD LATER confess that, shortly after Katherine's death, while she herself lay sick at Cheshunt, Kate Astley urged her to write to Thomas, 'to have comforted him of his sorrow' in a gesture he would doubtless appreciate, 'because he had been my friend in the Queen's time'.[1] Elizabeth had just passed her fifteenth birthday and, though young, was learning from her past encounters; she was wise enough to ignore Kate's counsel, telling her that she believed such a letter to be unnecessary. In that case, Kate herself would write, she told Elizabeth, in a letter that she appears to have shown her mistress, who later claimed to have no recollection of its contents.[2] In Katherine's lifetime, although Kate had not taken enough action to keep her charge safe, she had been anxious to protect Elizabeth's reputation throughout the goings-on at Chelsea and Hanworth. But she herself had fallen victim to Thomas's charms and was more than a little fond of him. So much so that Elizabeth admitted that her lady mistress had 'spoken to me of him many times'. Now Kate perceived an opportunity for Elizabeth, telling her: 'He that would fain have had you, before he married the Queen, will come now to woo you.'[3]

Though Elizabeth agreed that 'he himself would peradventure have me', she knew full well that 'the Council will not consent to it'.[4] That was the salient point. Conversations of this kind were dangerous, for both Elizabeth and her lady mistress knew that, given her royal status, the Council's consent was essential to any marriage she made, and it was certainly never going to be granted to Thomas. Kate later confessed that her husband 'hath divers times' warned her 'to take heed', for he had heard that Elizabeth did 'bear some affection' for Thomas and 'sometimes she would blush when he were spoken of', but Kate did not listen.[5] Likewise, though Elizabeth had previously done her best to distance herself from him, her entanglement with Thomas would soon become infinitely worse.

While Elizabeth now found herself talking with Kate about Thomas's intentions, he too, having returned to London in the aftermath of Katherine's death, had been busy engaging with those who were close to her. His court agent, William Wightman, later claimed that his master had had 'divers conferences' with Elizabeth's lady, Mary Hill.[6] Mary had apparently been sent by the Duchess of Somerset to 'comfort' Thomas, but the two also spoke about Elizabeth. Mary, after all, had known her royal mistress well since childhood, remaining in Elizabeth's household until her marriage in May 1547 to the King's tutor, John Cheke.[7] All this became clear in Kate Astley's later confession, when she admitted that shortly before Christmas 1548, Mary Hill (now Cheke) had told her that Thomas planned to visit Elizabeth, 'but he feared it would be said, that he came a wooing'. He was also concerned, for 'there was a saying, that he did not use my Lady Elizabeth well, when she was in his house'. As Elizabeth had feared, rumours were spreading.[8]

Using Wightman as a messenger, Thomas approached another of Elizabeth's close friends, Elizabeth FitzGerald, now the widowed Lady Browne.[9] The Admiral thought well of Elizabeth's childhood companion, to the point of apparently bequeathing money to her in his will.[10] Now, however, he asked Wightman to make a bizarre request of Lady Browne, desiring her to 'break up house, and sojourn with my Lady Elizabeth's grace'.[11] Wightman was unsure of Thomas's reasoning, admitting that the Admiral may have intended to use Lady Browne to help further his suit to Elizabeth, her being 'wise and able to compass matters'.[12] But Lady Browne sagely refused to be drawn into Thomas's plans, showing more circumspection than some. When the Admiral sent a message conveying his wish to speak with her, she excused herself by saying that she was 'verily purposed to go to my Lady Elizabeth's house the next morning very early'.[13]

Having recovered from the illness she had suffered around the time of Katherine's death, in October Elizabeth left the Dennys' hospitality at Cheshunt behind. She remained on good terms with her hosts, and though Sir Anthony would die in September 1549, she kept in touch with Lady Denny.[14] For the first time, the late King's youngest daughter was to set up a household of her own, travelling the short distance to her childhood home of Hatfield. Yet even now, there was no escaping from Thomas, whose servant, Edward, and John Seymour – either Thomas's illegitimate brother or his nephew – were to accompany her on her passage.[15] During the course of the journey, Edward told Kate Astley that his master was 'an heavy man for the Queen', yet Thomas's grief for Katherine seemed somewhat contradicted by John Seymour.[16] Chatting to Kate along the way, he let slip that the Admiral had boldly bade him ask of Elizabeth 'whether her great buttocks were grown any less or no?'[17] With such inappropriate chatter taking place between members of the households, it was little wonder tongues were wagging.

With her return to Hatfield, Elizabeth found herself the mistress of a large household, which, according to her cofferer Thomas Parry, totalled between a hundred and twenty and a hundred and forty people.[18] She could come and go and order as she pleased, but her education also remained a priority. She continued her lessons under Roger Ascham's tutelage, while privately Thomas was still a topic of conversation between herself and Kate Astley. Kate could not help but meddle and was seemingly more eager to speak of Thomas than was her mistress. She told Parry, 'I would wish her his wife of all men living', and also spoke freely with Sir Robert Tyrwhit, Katherine Parr's former Master of Horse, who urged her to 'take heed, for it were but undoing, if it were done without the Council's consent'.[19]

Soon after their arrival at Hatfield, Kate begged Elizabeth's permission to visit London. Knowing this to be unusual, Elizabeth demanded to know the cause, to which Kate replied that 'she would speak with my Lord Admiral'.[20] Though only fifteen, Elizabeth was shrewder than her lady mistress and refused the request, warning that people would say she had sent Kate on her behalf (Kate did later travel to London but would maintain that she had no contact with Thomas).[21] This did not prevent Elizabeth from writing to Thomas about business affairs though, requesting his favour to her new chaplain, Edmund Allen, who carried the letter.[22] She must have been aware that gossip was reaching the ears of those at court as to the nature of her involvement with the Admiral, but she chose to ignore it.

In December, however, circumstances became truly dangerous. Around two weeks before Christmas, Thomas Parry travelled to London, where he visited the Admiral at Seymour Place, and before long he too had fallen captive to the charms that had enraptured both his mistress and Kate Astley. Elizabeth had been planning to spend the festive season in London so that she might visit the King, and she had hoped to take up residence at Durham House on the Strand. Much to her chagrin, though, Thomas confirmed via Parry that the Council had commandeered Durham House as a mint, forcing her to seek an alternative. Thomas came to the rescue, telling Parry that he would be happy to lend her Seymour Place instead, 'stuff and all'.[23] It was a generous offer, communicated with 'such kindness and gentleness' and coupled with the suggestion that Thomas would visit Elizabeth.[24] 'I could not deliberate thereof with him,' Parry replied. 'I had no such commission, nor I did not know her grace's pleasure.'[25] He wasted no time in trying to establish Elizabeth's wishes, writing to Kate Astley and relaying Thomas's proposal of Seymour Place, as well as 'how willingly the Lord Admiral would have seen her grace'. Evidently, Parry was aware of the Admiral's interest in his mistress. At Hatfield, meanwhile, Kate Astley read Parry's message and conferred with Elizabeth. Given the gossip in the capital it would be too dangerous for Thomas to visit her, for, Elizabeth later recalled, it was said that 'my Lord Admiral should marry me'. Perhaps prematurely, Elizabeth would dismiss this tittle-tattle as 'London news'.[26]

Back in the capital, Parry spoke with Thomas on several more occasions. The cofferer was flattered at having been taken into the Admiral's confidence and did not therefore find it suspicious when he began to grill him as to the details of Elizabeth's household, lands and finances. By making such enquiries of a prize he would never be granted permission to win, Thomas was playing with fire, but Parry readily supplied him with everything he asked, prompting the Admiral to probe him further. How many people were in Elizabeth's household? What houses did she have? Were the lands good and what state were they in? Parry did not know all the answers, but 'I thought it was such as was appointed by her father's will and testament.'[27] Did she have her Letters Patent, granting her full control of her lands? No, Parry answered. The more Thomas asked, the more certain Parry became that 'there was some matter betwixt them'.[28] Heading back to Hatfield shortly after, where he knew Elizabeth would want to know what had passed between them, Parry boldly decided he would ask his mistress about her relationship with the King's uncle.

Parry arrived at Hatfield before Christmas, and relaying Thomas's offer of Seymour Place to Elizabeth directly he found that she 'seemed to take very gladly, and to accept it very joyfully and thankfully towards him'.[29] Elizabeth's emotions were clearly conflicting, for though she had previously done her best to distance herself from Thomas, this made it obvious that she still harboured some kind of attachment towards him. Thinking of the reports he had heard of an intended marriage between the pair and remembering that whenever Thomas was spoken of his mistress seemed 'very glad to hear of him', Parry felt emboldened to ask her something: if the Council should allow it, Parry queried, would she marry the Admiral? It was an impertinent question for a cofferer to ask his royal employer, and in the non-committal manner for which she would later become famed, Elizabeth replied, 'When that comes to pass, I will do as God shall put my mind.'[30] However, she later recalled – or pretended to recall – the conversation differently, claiming she had demanded of Parry what he meant by asking such a thing of her before dismissing it.[31] Whatever transpired, one thing was clear: Elizabeth knew of Thomas's feelings and intentions towards her and appeared to show an interest in return. With Thomas now a free man, her attitude had changed since the days spent at Chelsea and Hanworth when she had done her best to avoid him, and her head and her heart seemed torn. But in her head, she must have known that marriage could never be a genuine possibility.

ELIZABETH NEVER STAYED at Seymour Place that Christmas, but shortly after the festivities had concluded, Parry was back in London. This time, he was visiting court and took the opportunity of visiting the Admiral in his chamber there. 'How doth her grace?' Thomas asked. She was well, Parry answered. Thomas enquired as to when Elizabeth would be at court, to which Parry responded that he did not know, for 'my Lord Protector's grace was not resolved upon the day'. 'No,' Thomas replied bitterly, recognizing that his brother would have no wish for him to be in Elizabeth's company, 'that shall be when I am gone to Boulogne.' Given that 'Boulogne' was pronounced as 'Boleyn', this prompted him to make a slur on Elizabeth's heritage, and he quipped, 'No words of Boleyn.'[32] The conversation continued, and Parry audaciously told the Admiral that it was the wish of Kate Astley that 'her grace were your wife of any man living'. Here, reality appears to have kicked in, for Thomas responded that 'it will not be', for 'my brother will never agree unto it'.[33] After a few more shared words, during which Parry sensed Thomas was galled, he left. He would never see the Admiral again.

Parry was right to sense Thomas's fury, for the Admiral had long had more than Elizabeth on his mind. In the months since Katherine Parr's death, the rift between the Seymour brothers had grown ever wider as the Admiral grew increasingly resentful of his brother's power – and his own lack of it. With Katherine's calming influence removed, there was nobody to steady him, and he proved to be his own worst enemy. For some time, knowing that their young nephew, the King, objected to the fact that 'my uncle of Somerset dealeth very hardly with me, and keepeth me so straight, that I cannot have money at my will', Thomas had resolved to play 'the good uncle', supplying Edward with pocket money, which was delivered by one John Fowler, a royal servant.[34] The money was gratefully received, and by 'kindness and gifts' Thomas 'succeeded in gaining preference over his brother in the King's affections'.[35] But he expected a return. Fowler was required to speak well of Thomas to the King and deliver information on his behalf, and it seems that he did just that.

Nevertheless, the Admiral's position was growing ever more dangerous and his behaviour alarmingly erratic. As well as his exchanges with Elizabeth's servant, he had been conversing with his brother-in-law the Marquess of Northampton, the Marquess of Dorset and others at court, vehemently criticizing his brother's regime. He was also involved in various schemes in an attempt to raise his own support network, doing all he could to blacken the Protector's name.[36] It seemed he was fully intent on bringing his brother down, and he recognized that in doing so, his best chance of achieving his own route to power lay in securing the King's person.[37] On a January evening in 1549, however, he went too far in the attempt.

The winter evening of 16 January was cold and crisp, and within the Palace of Whitehall all was quiet. The stillness was broken, however, by a sudden noise from the King's apartments: the 'barking of the dog that lies before the King's door'.[38] Awakened by the hound, the gentleman who slept in the King's bedchamber stumbled to see what was amiss. As he hurried to the door, he saw the dead body of the King's dog in a pool of blood – the royal pet had been stabbed. 'Help! Murder!' he cried out in panic as the King's guards came running.[39] Whoever had killed the dog had fled the scene, and when 'everybody rushed in' to the chamber, 'the only thing they found was the lifeless corpse of the dog'.[40] Suspicion immediately landed on Thomas, who had been seen in the Palace that evening and who also had a key to the King's apartments. Indeed, the Imperial ambassador, Van der Delft, who had not been in England but had heard reports of the evening's events, was told that the Admiral had 'attempted to outrage [kidnap] the person of the young King by night'.[41] Yet, having been panicked by the barking dog as he attempted to enter his nephew's rooms, Thomas had vanished into the night. He – either bravely or foolishly – appeared in Parliament the following day, and by eight o'clock that evening he found himself on his way to the Tower.

The Council now set about gathering evidence against the Admiral. Learning that he had been arrested, and in their haste to disassociate themselves from him, his former friends, colleagues and employees were all eager to supply it. Lady Jane Grey's father, the Marquess of Dorset, who had once done his utmost to cultivate Thomas's friendship, now offered to testify against him, as did his servant John Harington. Crucially, so too did William Wightman, who made no effort to conceal the fact that his master had been visited on several occasions by Thomas Parry, cofferer to the Lady Elizabeth. Elizabeth's name was now dragged into Thomas's treason.

Three days after Thomas's arrest, on 20 January there was the sound of horses' hooves on the ground as Elizabeth's former host Sir Anthony Denny and Lord St John rode into Hatfield. Unbeknown to Elizabeth, her lady mistress Kate Astley and her cofferer Thomas Parry were also to be arrested and taken to the Tower for questioning over their involvement with the Admiral. Shortly afterwards, Kate Astley's husband, who was already in London, was taken to the Fleet Prison.[42] Two days later, Elizabeth was bewildered when Sir Robert Tyrwhit and his wife arrived at Hatfield to take charge of the household. The couple were already familiar to Elizabeth, for both had been key members of Katherine Parr's entourage, and they were probably aware – or had at least heard the rumours – of much of what had previously transpired at Chelsea, Hanworth and Seymour Place. It was Lady Tyrwhit who had attended the former Queen and witnessed her torment in her final days, and neither she nor her husband harboured any warm feelings towards Thomas. It seems unlikely, given what transpired, that they were particularly fond of Elizabeth either. The feeling was mutual.

Because of her association with Thomas, to her horror Elizabeth now found herself under suspicion of intriguing with him; Sir Robert had been ordered by the Council to extract a confession from her regarding her dealings with him. She was about to embark on the most treacherous period of her life to date, for if it were shown that she had knowledge and approval of Thomas's plans to marry her without the Council's consent, then she too would be implicated in the treason of which he now stood accused. If such a thing could be proven, the consequences Elizabeth faced could be dire, even fatal.

Elizabeth now knew that Thomas had been arrested, yet she was unaware, until reading a letter forged by Sir Robert to her gentlewoman Blanche Parry in which he pretended to be one of Blanche's friends, that Kate Astley and Thomas Parry had been taken to the Tower. Powerless to protect her servants, Elizabeth was 'marvellous abashed' as she read the terrible news and 'did weep very tenderly a long time' in her distress.[43] Her friend Lady Browne had joined her at Hatfield, whether on the Council's orders or of her own accord, and Elizabeth now demanded to know of her whether her servants had 'confessed anything or not'.[44] Lady Browne immediately reported Elizabeth's reaction to Sir Robert, who was clearly using her to spy on her friend – though it is worth noting it is unlikely Lady Browne did so willingly. Elizabeth's emotional reaction, though, confirmed that she was fully aware Kate and Parry possessed knowledge that could land them all in a great deal of trouble. She sent for Sir Robert, telling him she could not remember much but she would reveal to him everything she knew. In truth, however, she had no intention of doing so. Admitting only that she had written to Thomas to press the suit of her chaplain, Edmund Allen, Elizabeth also told Sir Robert that she had asked Thomas to give full credit to her cofferer, Parry. She had done so, she insisted, only in respect of her hopes of obtaining Durham Place at Christmas. She also admitted she had known that Kate Astley had written to Thomas, telling him not to visit her 'for fear of suspicion'. Elizabeth claimed to be 'much offended' when she learned of the letter but revealed nothing further.[45]

While Sir Robert listened as Elizabeth disclosed these minor details, he found himself growing increasingly frustrated, for he knew this was not the full story. When she had said her piece, Sir Robert implored her to 'consider her honour and the peril that might ensue, for she was but a subject'. He urged her to blame the doings with Thomas on her servants, for her youth would then be considered 'both with the King's Majesty, your grace [the Protector] and the whole Council'. How could a naïve teenage girl, after all, be held accountable for such careless talk? But she 'will not confess any practice by Mistress Astley or the cofferer [Parry]'.[46] Sir Robert sensed that the task of convincing Elizabeth to admit to her full dealings with the Admiral would not be easy, and he was right; on that day, at least, Elizabeth would admit nothing further. Nevertheless, as Sir Robert composed his letter to the Lord Protector the same day, he made his opinion clear: 'I do see it in her face that she is guilty.' Yet, as he also admitted, 'she will abide more storms' before blaming anything on her servants.[47]

Thanks to his 'gentle persuasion', the following day Sir Robert believed Elizabeth's attitude towards him had thawed. She was starting to warm to him, he felt – so much so that he supposed 'a good beginning' had been made, and 'I trust more will follow'. Despite his hope, though, the reality was that he had not gleaned much of further import. He had seemingly underestimated the teenager now in his charge, who he admitted 'hath a very good wit'.[48] Two days later, on 25 January, Sir Robert's optimism had disappeared altogether, as he finally realized no further information would be forthcoming. Some inducement of Elizabeth would be needed, and Sir Robert entreated the Lord Protector to allow Lady Browne, who had now left Hatfield, to return. In Sir Robert's opinion, Lady Browne's help was crucial, for 'there is nobody may do more good to cause her to confess the truth than she'. He believed that Lady Browne was a wise counsellor who had influence with Elizabeth (as indeed she clearly did) and might be able to sway her friend to reveal all she knew. The Protector replied immediately, but there seems to have been no reappearance of Lady Browne. In any case, it would take more than the persuasions of a friend to coax Elizabeth into confessing.

By 28 January, Sir Robert had become exasperated. He had, he wrote to the Protector, tried 'all means and policies' in an attempt to induce her to 'confess more'.[49] Once again, it did not work, and Sir Robert was convinced that Elizabeth must have made a 'secret promise' with Astley and Parry 'never to confess to death'.[50] If this was the case, then in Sir Robert's view the only two who could extract the truth from Elizabeth were the King and the Protector.[51] He was quickly becoming exhausted in the attempt. That same day, Elizabeth herself also wrote to the Protector directly, thanking him for his 'gentleness, and goodwill towards me'.[52] Patently trying to win his good graces, she acknowledged that as 'an earnest friend' he had counselled her to reveal all she knew, which she did willingly.[53] In reality this was very little, for she merely repeated everything she had already told Sir Robert, insisting that in regards to Kate Astley's wish for her to marry Thomas, the lady mistress 'would never have me marry' without the consent of 'the King's Majesty, your grace's, and the Council's'.[54] Playing on her piety, Elizabeth declared that everything she had said had been the truth, 'whereof my conscience beareth me witness, which I would not for all earthly things offend in any thing; for I know I have a soul to save'.[55] If she remembered anything further, she would write or else ask Sir Robert to do so. She was nevertheless horrified to hear from Sir Robert – doubtless in a further attempt to sway her into a confession – that unsavoury rumours were spreading 'that I am in the Tower; and with child by my Lord Admiral'. Elizabeth was always sensitive about her reputation and popularity with the people, and she took this final opportunity to plead with the Lord Protector: 'My Lord these are shameful slanders, for the which, besides the great desire I have to see the King's Majesty, I shall most heartily desire your Lordship that I may come to the court after your first determination; that I may show myself there as I am.'[56] She was desperate to prove her innocence but her pleas fell on deaf ears: Elizabeth remained at Hatfield.

IN THE TOWER, pressure was being brought to bear on Elizabeth's servants, Kate Astley and Thomas Parry. Both were kept in stringent conditions, with Kate complaining that 'it is so cold that I cannot sleep in it and so dark that I cannot in the day see, for I stop the window with straw; there is no glass'.[57] Little wonder, then, that they were both paralysed with fear. It was Parry who cracked first, admitting he had talked with Thomas about Elizabeth and her estates, confessing to the conversations he had shared with Kate Astley and even acknowledging that he had been sworn to secrecy by Kate, to whom he had promised: 'I had rather be pulled with horses' than breathe a word of what they had spoken.[58] Kate Astley, meanwhile, would 'utter nothing'. Yet when, on 2 February, she was brought 'face to face' with Parry, who declared his confession, she was horrified. Though she called him a 'false wretch', berating him for divulging all, she was now left with no alternative but to do the same.[59] She buckled under the pressure during the course of her three examinations, each account being written by the Principal Secretary, Sir Thomas Smith.[60] All of her own dealings and those that Elizabeth had had with Thomas Seymour were revealed: the details of the early-morning romps came spilling out, and Kate admitted that she had spoken to Elizabeth 'divers times' of a marriage between her and Thomas, though she was adamant that she had never wished for such a thing without the consent of the Council.[61] Now that Kate and Parry had revealed all, the only thing that remained was to obtain a confession from Elizabeth herself.

Back at Hatfield, Sir Robert Tyrwhit continued to interrogate Elizabeth but had progressed no further. However, when the confessions of Kate and Parry were delivered into his hands, they provided him with exactly what he needed. As Elizabeth was familiar with both her servants' writing 'with half a sight', when she witnessed their confessions with her own eyes, she knew that 'they have both confessed all they know'.[62] On 5 February, Sir Robert advised the Protector that Elizabeth had been 'much abashed, and half breathless' when reading the confession of her lady mistress.[63] Leaving her to mull over what she had read, Sir Robert managed to extract her promise that the following day, she 'will call all things to her remembrance'.[64] Sure enough, Elizabeth cracked. She set out her confession in which she outlined Kate Astley's indiscreet comments about the Admiral, and Thomas's questioning of Parry in regards to her affairs, begging to be forgiven if she had forgotten anything and assuring the Lord Protector that if she should remember anything more, then 'I will send you word of them, as they come to my mind'.[65] Sir Robert was not fully convinced by the confession, maintaining his belief that there had been some kind of collusion between Elizabeth, Kate and Parry, and he told the Protector so when he forwarded it to him on 7 February. But he recognized that Elizabeth would not admit anything that implicated her servants; 'they all sing one song', he grumbled.[66]

If Elizabeth hoped that, with her own confession and those of Kate and Parry, matters were resolved, then she was sorely mistaken. Though she would no longer face daily interrogations from Sir Robert, much to her dismay he remained at Hatfield, overseeing the running of her household. Matters were made worse when, on 17 February, she received a letter from the Council informing her that Kate Astley would not be returning to her service, having 'showed herself far unmeet to occupy any such place'. Instead, she would be replaced by Lady Tyrwhit, and the Council trusted Elizabeth would 'accept her service thankfully, and also hear and follow her good advice from time to time'.[67] The Council's disapproval of Kate was plain, but Elizabeth was furious and heartbroken: Kate had been with her since the earliest days of her childhood, and thus Elizabeth could probably not remember a time when she had not been there. She was more than a member of her household; she was family.

Lady Tyrwhit's feelings upon acquiring such a post were no warmer than Elizabeth's, and when she advised the teenager that she had been tasked by the Council to see that she was well governed, she was met with a cool response. 'Mistress Astley was her mistress,' Elizabeth replied, and she needed no other.[68] Sir Robert noted that she spent the whole night weeping and was still in low spirits the following day. Her distress was understandable given that Lady Tyrwhit's own husband admitted she was 'half a scripture woman', whose personality must have come as a dull contrast to the lively and vivacious Kate.[69] Sir Robert could only marvel at the 'love yet she beareth' to Kate, whom Elizabeth hoped would return. He had yet to fully understand that Elizabeth would always show herself fiercely loyal to those to whom she was close.[70] By now, she was aware that Thomas's household had been disbanded, and that could only signify one thing: impending doom.

ELIZABETH'S INTERROGATIONS MAY have ceased at this point, and unbeknown to her the worst was over, but Thomas had yet to be dealt with. Upon his arrest, Lady Jane Grey returned home for the final time, while her father the Marquess provided a testimony against Thomas, admitting that the Admiral had told him 'he loved not the Lord Protector, and would not have any Protector'.[71] Even the young King was implored to offer a statement, remembering that his uncle had called him a 'beggarly King', in reference to the fact that the Protector left him short of money.[72] Edward admitted that, in order to remedy this situation, Thomas had personally given him money via his servant Fowler, who told him: 'You must thank my Lord Admiral for gentleness that he showed you.'[73] As for Thomas, he was, unsurprisingly, uncooperative, revealing very little under questioning and making no mention of Elizabeth. He denied attempting 'to remove the King out of my Lord Protector's hands' and divulged little else, instead asserting his right to a public trial.[74] But he did try to make amends with his brother, assuring him in writing on 27 January that 'if I meant either hurt or displeasure to Your Grace, in this or any other thing that I have done, then punish me to extremity'.[75]

Thirty-three charges had been levelled at Thomas, covering everything from his supposed attempts to obtain the King's custody, to the accusation that he had 'plotted to kill the Protector', and 'the most important being that he had planned to marry the Lady Elizabeth without consent of the Council'.[76] On 23 February, the Lord Chancellor, Richard Rich, visited Thomas, where he read out the indictment against him. Though he gave Thomas an opportunity to respond to the charges, the Admiral declined to do so unless put on open trial. But there was to be no trial for him, and thus no chance to defend himself against the allegations of which he stood accused. The Council laid the evidence against him before the King, who agreed that he was guilty and should be attainted. Thus Thomas was condemned by an Act of Attainder, passed through the House of Lords on 25 February and the Commons on 5 March.[77] This was done 'almost unanimously', with few prepared to speak up in his defence.[78] The Imperial ambassador Van der Delft had heard that 'some claimed in Parliament that he ought to be heard personally, but their opinions availed him little', and thus the Admiral was condemned on 'the evidence produced in proof of thirty charges brought against him'.[79] There seemed to be no hope of his life being spared, even by reason of family ties with his royal nephew and the Protector, the latter of whom 'was so heavy and lamentable' when discussing Thomas's fate with the Council.[80] In echoes of his father before him, it was the King who gave the order for his uncle to be put to death, all former fondness for him seemingly forgotten. A warrant was duly drawn up and signed by the Council: the Protector's was the first signature upon it.[81]

With Thomas having left instructions for his and Katherine Parr's little daughter, Mary Seymour, to be entrusted to the reluctant care of Katherine Willoughby, Duchess of Suffolk, all that remained for him was to meet his end.[82] Even as it drew near, though, the Admiral could not help but plot. According to the admittedly hostile account of Hugh Latimer, Bishop of Worcester, who attended him in the Tower, Thomas 'wrote certain papers', two of which were addressed to Elizabeth and Mary. In these he urged the sisters to 'conspire against my Lord Protector's grace'.[83] They were later found, according to Latimer, sewn between 'the soles of a velvet shoe' and thus never reached their intended recipients.[84]

On the morning of 20 March, just six months after the death of Katherine Parr, Thomas mounted a scaffold on Tower Hill. His brother had taken care to remove himself from the capital, probably unable to bear what came next; Elizabeth herself would later write that she heard him say he had cause to regret his brother's fate.[85] It was not a clean death; it took two blows of the axe to sever Thomas's head: a grim-faced Latimer asked, 'Who can tell but that between two strokes he doth repent?'[86] Thus, Thomas died, 'very dangerously, irksomely, horribly'.[87] This figure who had played a prominent, perilous role in Elizabeth's life was destined to be a ghost of the past and was returned to the Tower for burial. He was laid to rest in the Chapel of St Peter ad Vincula, where Anne Boleyn had been buried thirteen years earlier.

It has often been said that Elizabeth responded to the news of Thomas's death with the phrase, 'this day died a man of much wit and very little judgement'.[88] The source for this quotation is dubious, and thus her true reaction cannot be known with certainty. Judging by a letter she later wrote to her sister when her own life was in jeopardy, however, there is good reason to think she believed his death unjust.[89] Hugh Latimer, for his part, left none in any doubt of his feelings, asserting that Thomas 'was a wicked man: the realm is well rid of him'.[90]

Thomas's brutal removal brought the chapter of Elizabeth's life as she had once known it in Katherine Parr's household to a terrifying end. Katherine was gone, Thomas was gone, and Elizabeth's beloved servants, most particularly Kate Astley, had been taken from her. She was fifteen and entirely bereft. The scandal of Elizabeth's association with this dangerous man would not be forgotten. Her involvement with the Admiral had come close to permanently tarnishing her reputation, and she had learned some valuable lessons from it; lessons that would leave her wary in her dealings with men and later reinforce and influence her decisions towards matrimony. Likewise, she would be equally cautious about disclosing her feelings, doing her utmost to mask them and keep her own counsel. Thomas was dead, but Elizabeth never forgot the man by whose charms she had once been captivated; indeed, his end would later return to haunt her, when she was faced with the greatest crisis of her life.[91]

CHAPTER 10

'A Very Great Lady'

'The brightest star is my illustrious Lady Elizabeth, the king's sister.'

ROGER ASCHAM TO JACOB STURM, 4 APRIL 1550

'SHE GOES CLAD in every respect as becomes a young maiden', the scholar John Aylmer wrote admiringly of Elizabeth in December 1551.[1] The tutor of Lady Jane Grey could not fail to be impressed by his pupil's cousin and the sober manner in which she dressed. Elizabeth would always be conscious of her image, but in the aftermath of the Thomas Seymour scandal, as rumours abounded and life resumed a more stable course, it mattered more than ever. The whole affair had not only forced her to grow up quickly but also changed her. She became eager to embrace the image of a Protestant maiden, who 'is elegant rather than showy' with a 'contempt of gold and headdresses' favoured by other court ladies.[2] Instead, Elizabeth dressed plainly in black and white, earning her the approval of many of her fellow Protestant contemporaries. She would never be as demonstrative in her faith as either her brother, Edward, or her cousin Jane Grey, but she was known for her Protestant beliefs and would be the dedicatee of four religious texts during Edward's reign.[3] This was just as well, for as Edward's reign progressed it became apparent there were no lengths to which the young King was not prepared to go in the cause of religion.

Edward VI had been raised among those with radical religious views, and though only young he had always been steadfastly devoted to the Protestant cause (the term Protestant would not, though, be used in England until the 1550s). What was more, he was determined to carry his country with him. The England he had inherited was a country torn in conflicting directions as a result of the Reformation and Henry VIII's split from the Roman Catholic Church, and Edward was eager to be the one to unite it. In January 1549, the Act of Uniformity was passed in Parliament with Edward's full support. The momentous Act confirmed the use of Protestant rites in all churches across the country, and with it too came the introduction of the Book of Common Prayer. Composed in English by Archbishop Cranmer, godfather to both Edward and Elizabeth, the prayer book now became the sole religious text to be used in churches across the land. Cranmer was fully supportive of Edward's intentions in the cause of religion, and champions of religious reform celebrated such bold moves, which had never been seen in England before.

With their religious similarities, Edward would doubtless have been gratified by the New Year's gift Elizabeth made to him on one occasion. Extending her talent for personalized items, she made an offering of a translation from Italian to Latin of Bernardino Ochino's 'Sermon on the Nature of Christ'.[4] Elizabeth's dedicatory letter conveyed her love for Edward, for she wrote that 'So nature decrees, your authority urges and integrity compels me to regard you with respect, since you are my sovereign, and to treat you with deepest affection, since you are my only and most dearly beloved brother.'[5] Yet there was more to her gift than this, for the choice of text gives a greater insight into her religious beliefs. Ochino was an Italian monk who had come to England in 1547 at the invitation of Archbishop Cranmer. Many of his views were not only radical, but controversial, including his belief in Predestination, which put him completely at odds with the Catholic Church. It was little wonder, then, that Ochino had been accused of heresy by the Pope, forcing him to flee Italy for Switzerland.[6] Elizabeth, though, opted to avoid the controversial aspects of Ochino's work when preparing her translation, and instead, as she wrote in her letter, 'the subject is the nature of Christ'. The sermon she had translated urged the reader to love Christ and to have faith.[7] It encouraged a more direct approach to Christ, in keeping with her religious views, and in so doing, as Maria Perry asserted, Elizabeth 'unconsciously stated what was to be her own position amidst the doctrinal issues that were to trouble the Church of England for the next half century'.[8]

As Elizabeth joined her brother at court for Christmas 1549, arriving 'with great pomp and triumph' and being 'continually with the King', it was reported that the Council 'have a higher opinion of her for conforming with the others and observing the new decrees'.[9] Elizabeth's compliance with the new regime was being highlighted to the watching courtiers – yet there were many, including members of her own family, to whom the news of Edward's reforms came as utterly abhorrent. Among them was Elizabeth's sister Mary, who 'remains constant to the Catholic faith' to which she had been devoted all her life.[10] Having been bullied so relentlessly by her father, Mary was not prepared to be so again, and especially not by a brother who was two decades her junior. Back in April, Mary had assured her cousin the Emperor Charles V that 'in life and death I will not forsake the Catholic religion', and she was true to her word.[11] She steadfastly refused to conform to Edward's religious policies and instead made a show of emphasizing her devotion to Catholicism. She deliberately flouted his authority and in a show of defiance ordered the Catholic Mass to be celebrated in her chapel. Though she declared that her body was obedient to the King, her soul, Mary declared, was committed first to God. Matters were to become so bad for Mary that in 1550 she seriously considered fleeing the realm, and plans were put in place for her escape, though they would come to nothing.[12]

Elizabeth, herself still recovering her standing with the King and Council, wisely refrained from any involvement in the troubles between her siblings that saw Edward grow progressively frustrated by Mary's attitude. In the aftermath of Henry VIII's death, the sisters were living separate lives, underscored by Elizabeth's earlier decision to remain with Katherine Parr rather than joining Mary when the news of Katherine's marriage to Thomas Seymour became known. In 1554 the Venetian ambassador Giacomo Soranzo would assert that Mary did not love Elizabeth 'as she had demonstrated by very clear signs, even in the lifetime of King Edward', and though Mary's behaviour in the opening months of her reign contradicts this to some extent, it seems credible that the two were no longer as close as they once had been.[13] It is nevertheless clear that they remained in touch – frequently, for at least some of the time – for in Elizabeth's only letter to her 'Good sister' to survive from Edward's reign, she not only thanked Mary for 'oft sending to me', but told her that 'you may well see by my writing so oft, how pleasant it is to me'.[14] The tone of her letter, though friendly, nevertheless does not contain the same level of warmth as Elizabeth's letters to Edward. What is more, though the sources are silent on Mary's thoughts on the outcome of the Seymour scandal, it is difficult to imagine that she viewed Elizabeth's involvement in it with anything other than distaste. The differences between them would become more apparent still in the coming years, as the sisters came to represent two contrasting sides of the religious spectrum, rent apart by the zealous and fervent rule of their brother.

Elizabeth's efforts for the time being, however, were centred elsewhere – chiefly on reframing her image and regaining her servants. 'I have a request to make unto your grace', she had begun a letter to the Lord Protector on 7 March 1549. Though she worried that 'your lordship and the rest of the Council will think that I favour her evil-doing for whom I shall speak for', she was desperate to be reunited with the woman who had 'been with me a long time and many years': Kate Astley.[15] Despite the urgings of the Council and one man in particular, William Cecil, who thought 'Astley the unmeetest woman to be about such a personage as your grace is', Elizabeth was determined to gain Kate's freedom and her company.[16]

Cecil was of Lincolnshire origin and served the Lord Protector before becoming one of two secretaries of state to Edward VI, yet he would become a good friend to Elizabeth and in time one of the most important men in her life.[17] Indeed, when she obtained her landed inheritance as bequeathed to her by her father, she would employ Cecil to help oversee the running of her estates.[18] She trusted him implicitly, and theirs was to be a strong, lifelong working partnership that began in Elizabeth's youth. Not only was Cecil both wise and sensible, but he also had firm links with many in her circle, for he was close to Elizabeth's tutor Ascham, as well as John Cheke, whose sister Mary was Cecil's first wife.[19] Elizabeth's first known correspondence with Cecil probably dates from the end of 1546, when she had sought a licence from him on behalf of Hugh Goodacre, who was likely one of her chaplains.[20] Goodacre was, so Elizabeth told him, 'of long time known unto us to be as well of honest conversation and sober living, as of sufficient learning and judgement in the scriptures to preach the word of God'.[21] It was standard practice for those who were in privileged positions to seek favours for those who either petitioned them to do so or were members of their own household, and given Cecil's standing with the Lord Protector, Elizabeth recognized that he was well placed to oblige. His advice about Kate Astley was another matter entirely, and she probably did not react well to Cecil urging her to accept Lady Tyrwhit. His feeling was that she needed 'some sober woman about you', and thus he advised her 'to conform yourself to all other things meet for your honour and estate in such sort'.[22] But Elizabeth would not give Kate up.

By the end of the spring of 1549, her hopes appeared to have borne some fruit, when both Kate and Thomas Parry were freed from their imprisonment. By September, they were allowed to return to their mistress at Hatfield, Kate having promised never again to plot on Elizabeth's behalf.[23] It was with this in mind that, on an unknown date, the Tyrwhits also departed. Elizabeth was overjoyed to have her servants back, but all three were marked by their experiences and from now on would take care – for the time being, at least – to exhibit more caution. This became clear when, on 24 September, Elizabeth received a visit from the Venetian ambassador. Though nothing of import was discussed, in her wish to be transparent Elizabeth ordered Parry to write to Cecil on her behalf immediately, knowing that this news would then be passed to the Protector.[24]

Earlier that same month she had reached her sixteenth birthday. Elizabeth's tutor Roger Ascham wrote to his friend John Sturm, that she 'shows such dignity and gentleness as are wonderful at her age and in her rank', and with the milestone birthday came too Elizabeth's majority.[25] The following March she would take legal possession of all the lands and estates her father had granted her in his will, making her a wealthy landowner in her own right. Most of her time was now spent overseeing her household, which divided its time between Enfield, Ashridge and Hatfield, the latter of which became hers following an exchange of lands with the Crown, in which she gave up a Lincolnshire estate.[26] She also inherited Durham Place on the Strand, once taken from her on the Lord Protector's orders and requisitioned as a mint, and it was there that Elizabeth made her London base.[27] During the latter years of the reign of Henry VII, Durham Place had served as home to Katherine of Aragon in the aftermath of Prince Arthur's death and, more pertinently to Elizabeth, her own mother had resided there the year prior to her birth. It was perfectly situated for Elizabeth's visits to the capital, as it was just a stone's throw from both the Palace of Whitehall and St James's Palace. She took the management of these estates very seriously and was interested in acquiring more: when Stephen Gardiner, Bishop of Winchester, was imprisoned in the Tower for his refusal to conform with Edward's religious changes, the Imperial ambassador reported Elizabeth's desire to obtain some of his lands. She was, he said, 'in love with a certain manor, which she is said to be sure of acquiring'.[28] On this occasion, though, she was to be unsuccessful.

Elizabeth had more time for estate management when her formal education ceased, after Roger Ascham had returned to Cambridge in 1550. He had always been seriously impressed with 'my illustrious mistress, the Lady Elizabeth', whose accomplishments were so great that, waxing lyrical, he declared: she 'shines like a star'.[29] Yet the tutor whom Elizabeth had once been desperate to obtain seems to have left somewhat under a cloud, later telling the German reformer Martin Bucer 'how badly I was treated', not by Elizabeth but 'by some of her household'.[30] Precisely what happened and to whom Ascham was referring is unknown, but it apparently caused a rift between the scholar and Elizabeth herself, as Ascham sought Bucer's help 'to replace me in my lady's favour'.[31] The estrangement had certainly been smoothed over by 1555, by which time Ascham was back at court serving as Latin secretary to Queen Mary and informally giving Elizabeth Greek lessons.[32] In the meantime, Elizabeth retained her enjoyment of scholarly pursuits, as she did all her life, spending three hours of each day reading history. Clearly, though, there were many who believed she was mature enough now to manage by herself, including

William Cecil, who wrote to her: 'It hath pleased God to endow you with some gifts of knowledge in learning more than is common to others, you are in that respect at this present sufficiently able to direct yourself.'[33] Her intelligence and ability were visible to her contemporaries, and these traits would serve her well in the years to come when she would be forced to navigate her way through the backbiting atmosphere of the court.

WITHIN HER HOMES Elizabeth was surrounded by luxury, and an inventory of Henry VIII's belongings that was compiled shortly after his death gives us vivid insights into this. Among the items listed in 'the Lady Elizabeth's Garderobe', which she inherited after her father's death, were beautiful pieces of costly tapestry, including four depicting the story of Hercules, all of which had the King's arms stitched into the border.[34] Another six pieces told the story of *The Book of the City of Ladies*, by the Italian poet Christine de Pizan – a work that had gained fame across Europe for its portrayal of a city ruled by women.[35] *The Book*, written at the beginning of the fifteenth century, told the story of a metaphorical city occupied by women whose scholarly achievements and qualities of leadership were celebrated, highlighting wise and courageous female exemplars throughout history. It was highly praising of the French Queen, Isabeau of Bavaria, who became regent on behalf of her son because of the illness of her husband, Charles VI.[36] It is not known whether Elizabeth ever engaged with the text, but certainly the theme of the tapestries – chiefly of highly educated women, and women wielding power – reinforced some important lessons that she had already begun to learn and with which she would resonate. There were also luxurious Turkey carpets, 'two chairs of cloth of gold' made with crimson velvet and fringed with red silk, and two roundels of wood with 'the King's arms with letters in them painted and gilt'.[37] An assortment of splendid cushions was listed, three of cloth of gold with purple velvet and pearls, and many others in a variety of colours.[38] Though the trappings Elizabeth inherited from her father were splendid, they were nothing in comparison to those that surrounded the King in the royal palaces, or, perhaps more pertinently, those in her sister Mary's possession. The items Mary had inherited following their father's death were more numerous, and included both beds and cloths of estate, which would have hung above her chair as a symbol of authority.[39] Though Henry's will had treated both daughters as equals, it seems that when it came to the physical distribution of household items and furnishings, Elizabeth, as she had been during her father's lifetime, remained bottom of the pecking order. Nevertheless, the objects she owned were lavish, and when she became Queen she would always show a fondness for luxury.

The kind of lifestyle Elizabeth was enjoying as mistress of her own household can also be gleaned from a single surviving set of accounts. Covering the period from October 1551 to September 1552 while she was primarily at Hatfield, they were recorded by Thomas Parry and overseen by Walter Buckler, former secretary to Katherine Parr and now serving Elizabeth.[40] She herself signed each page, evidence of her growing interest and care when it came to managing her own affairs. It was a big responsibility for a youngster but one she could assuredly handle, overseeing expenses for the repair of her estates, particularly Hatfield, where 'divers locks' and glazing of the windows were arranged.[41] The accounts also show the money that was outlaid on covering the daily costs of the household, such as the bakehouse and the cellar, as well as that spent on items like fresh fish, veal, lamb, bacon, mutton and salt.[42] Given that the water in England was not considered drinkable, it is no surprise that the household consumed beer and wine in large quantities. Sweet wine and Rhenish was purchased from a Richard Thornton, while spices and wax for candles were also bought.[43] Elizabeth's horses were well provided for, and as well as payments made for shoeing, among the items purchased for the stables were oats and hay.[44]

Elizabeth Ballard was responsible for Elizabeth's washing and laundry, and money was also spent on new clothes.[45] These were ordered largely from 'her grace's tailor', Warren, who provided 'divers' robes for her.[46] Costly materials to make new garments were also purchased, such as velvet, some of which was to be made into a pair of sleeves, and there was enough left over for two French hoods.[47] Meanwhile, Kate Astley and others were reimbursed for money outlaid on Elizabeth's behalf, including that spent on damask and crimson satin.[48] In a reflection of her frequent health complaints, Elizabeth's letters to her brother often refer to her troublesome ailments, such as 'a disease of the head and eyes'.[49] It was therefore no surprise that she employed the services of Dr Huicke, Katherine Parr's former physician, who would serve Elizabeth for many years.[50] As was expected of a woman of her rank, Elizabeth also provided money in alms to impoverished men and women on numerous occasions, as well as to a poor woman from Ireland – perhaps a nod to the roots of her friend, Lady Browne.[51] Rewards were likewise given to those who brought her gifts, which was a fairly regular occurrence. Among various tokens she received, Elizabeth was presented with a cygnet, fruit and pigeons.[52]

Besides her other financial commitments, Elizabeth would not forget her love of learning, and she gave money to the academics of Cambridge, as well as to one penurious scholar at Oxford.[53] Payments were also made for the books Elizabeth cherished, and to her chaplain, Edmund Allen, for a Bible.[54] In a similar vein, thirty shillings were paid to Mr Rouse, the preacher.[55] There were rewards too for the King's drummer and piper, and payments were made towards clothes for the children who had participated in a performance with a company of players.[56] Money was outlaid to a gentleman who played the lute, as well as to More the harper – almost certainly the same William More, the blind harpist, who had once served Elizabeth's father and been imprisoned in the Tower in 1539 for an unknown reason.[57] New lute strings for Elizabeth's own instrument were also purchased from one John Baptist.[58] On another occasion, she even treated herself to a new table made from walnut.[59] Life in the household at Hatfield, as evidenced by such payments, was both vibrant and varied.

Elizabeth's accounts also show that she was in contact with a vast number of people; we can see that in October 1551, for example, she gave a ten-shilling reward to a messenger from the King's Council.[60] They also provide a brief glimpse into some of her relationships. In an interesting link with her mother's family, Edmund Boleyn, 'her grace's kinsman', was given money, as were both 'Mr Carey' – Elizabeth's cousin – and on a separate occasion his wife, 'at her departing from Hatfield' in 1552.[61]

These references confirm that Elizabeth had a strong family network around her in her youth, who were unswervingly loyal to her and would continue to be so throughout her life.

Intriguingly, in December 1551 a payment was made for the christening of 'Mrs Pendred's child'.[62] It seems probable that this was the same Mrs Pendred who had suckled Elizabeth as a baby and with whom she had presumably remained in touch – could Mrs Pendred even have been staying at Hatfield, and could Elizabeth perhaps have stood as godmother to the child her former wet nurse now mothered, thus explaining the payment?[63] It is certainly a possibility. Money had also been outlaid for the christenings of the children of people that Elizabeth had known since childhood, including the child of her cousin, Henry Carey, and given to the poor at the christening of Henry Norris's child – son of the same man who had been executed for adultery with Elizabeth's mother, and whose sister had once been a member of Elizabeth's household. It is likely that Elizabeth was godmother to both of these children, and there were others besides, including the son of her former servant and friend Mary Cheke, to whose child's christening Elizabeth sent her old groom William Russell on her behalf.[64] In 1550 she had also stood as godmother to young Henry, the son of Sir William Cavendish and his wife Bess, better known as Bess of Hardwick.[65] In later years, Elizabeth would become very fond of Bess and particularly her third husband William St Loe, who was a member of Elizabeth's household. The Cavendishes were just one couple among many who cultivated the friendship of the King's sister, and in so doing they helped to expand both Elizabeth's network and her popularity.

Finally, Elizabeth had her wage bill to consider, and with Kate Astley receiving £7 15s (£2,128) for half a year's service, there was no doubt that she was at the top of the hierarchy. By contrast, Blanche Parry, for example, was paid £5 (£1,370) for the same.[66] Notably, five shillings (£68) was also paid to Elizabeth's former lady mistress Lady Troy, by means of a pension. In a sign of its importance, the Knight Marshall's servant (the Knight Marshall was a member of the royal household, a position held by Sir Ralph Hopton) was paid for delivering this.[67]

There were various matters requiring Elizabeth's attention in these years, as both her accounts and her letters of the period bear out. Many survive from this time, demonstrating the seriousness with which she approached business affairs and the running of her estates. One letter was addressed to leading councillor William Paget, in which she sought his assistance against 'one that names himself to be your servant', in a matter of claiming lands that she believed to be hers under the terms of her father's will.[68] In another she petitioned the unknown addressee on behalf of her servant Anthony Wingfield, who sought a position in the royal household. Wingfield was, she affirmed, 'a man for his honesty, sobriety, and virtuous qualities worthy of much commendation'.[69] She wrote in a similar vein to Lord Darcy in the interests of her kinsman Henry Carey, asking if Darcy might 'exercise him in service of the King's Majesty, as you can best'.[70] Thereby, 'you shall not only do me great pleasure, but bind him'.[71] Another letter was addressed to Thomas Cawarden, the King's Master of the Revels, who was responsible for overseeing royal festivities.[72] Elizabeth would reward Cawarden upon her accession with the important post of Lieutenant of the Tower, but the bonds of their relationship were forged earlier, probably in Edward's reign.[73] Through her letters to these men, it is apparent that she was building and consolidating a network of supporters around her, largely consisting of those who were close to the King.

It was not unusual for favours to be sought from those who had close ties to the court, especially as Elizabeth herself was a relatively infrequent guest. When she did visit, however, she was always welcomed by the King, who was joyful at the opportunity to spend time with his much-loved sister. In turn, she once assured Edward in a letter that 'your absence has increased rather than lessened my love for you'.[74] What was more, thanks to a shift in the dynamics of power, by the end of 1549 Elizabeth's position at court had changed.

Many of the policies of the Lord Protector had long been unpopular, and he had been losing supporters among the Council. Even the young King was growing increasingly resentful of his uncle, largely because he was kept continually short of funds. At the beginning of October, having heard that several of his former colleagues were marching to confront him, Somerset fled with his nephew to Windsor Castle 'late in the night'.[75] His efforts to protect himself were in vain, and on 11 October, a dramatic coup d'état was staged that saw the Protector thrown into the Tower. It was a circumstance that both Elizabeth and Mary were informed of by means of a letter from the Council, who were heartily sick of Somerset's 'pride and ambition'.[76] Though he would be released and restored to his place on the Council early the following year, the Protector's rehabilitation was brief. On 22 January 1552, much to the grief of the common people with whom he was so popular, Somerset was executed for felony and buried close to his brother Thomas in the Chapel of St Peter ad Vincula within the Tower. The title of Lord Protector was abolished, never to be revived – at least in Elizabeth's lifetime – again.[77] In Somerset's place emerged another contender for power: one who was ambitious and who, as time would reveal, would stop at nothing to secure his own position.

John Dudley, Earl of Warwick, had been favoured by Elizabeth's father – he had even attended her christening – and was previously one of the Lord Protector's key supporters. He came from a tainted line, however, for his father, Edmund Dudley, though one of Henry VII's key ministers, had been executed for treason in 1510 on the orders of Henry VIII.[78] This did not hinder his son's rise to power, and having been brought up in the household of Sir Edward Guildford, who purchased his wardship and whose daughter he would marry, Dudley was given the opportunity of a career at court. Gradually he rose in Henry VIII's favour, and he would serve as Vice-Admiral and Lord Admiral from 1537 to 1547. Dudley also served the King in a military capacity in Scotland and France in 1544, and joined the Protector at the Battle of Pinkie Cleugh in the first year of Edward VI's reign. Though he had initially supported Somerset and been rewarded with the earldom of Warwick in 1547, Dudley did not scruple when it came to engineering the downfall of his former patron. By March 1550, Dudley was 'absolute master' of the realm.[79] Indeed, by October 1551 he would be created Duke of Northumberland and was the wealthiest and most powerful peer in the kingdom. The chief supporters of this man who 'governs absolutely' were the naïve Henry Grey, formerly Marquess of

Dorset but created Duke of Suffolk at the same time as Northumberland's own elevation, and the charming and affable William Parr, Marquess of Northampton, brother of the deceased Queen Katherine and husband of Elizabeth's friend Elisabeth Brooke.[80] Under Northumberland's direction, these three men were now the most important at court and, like the King, they were all champions of Protestantism. The salient point from Elizabeth's perspective, however, was that Northumberland's attitude towards her was significantly different from that of Somerset. Under the Protector, the allowance allotted to Elizabeth by her father had often been paid irregularly and, frequently, not in full; there was no such delay from Northumberland.[81] By the same token, the King's uncle had never particularly encouraged Elizabeth to visit her brother, whereas Northumberland had no problem with her doing so and always paid reverence to her. Though much of her time was still spent on her Hertfordshire estates, Elizabeth took advantage of opportunities to visit Edward. Not only did she seemingly get along well with Northumberland, but she also had good relationships with members of his family. Northumberland had thirteen children, more than half of whom survived infancy, and many would have become familiar faces to Elizabeth at Edward's court.[82] Some would become lifelong friends, most particularly Robert, who, along with Edward's childhood companion Barnaby Fitzpatrick, was sworn in to the King's Privy Chamber staff as one of six ordinary gentleman on 15 August 1551.[83] Just the previous summer, on 4 June 1550, Robert had married Amy Robsart, in what may have been a love match.[84] This did not, however, prevent him from sharing an especially warm friendship with Elizabeth: one that would, in later years, be the subject of much court gossip and speculation.

HAVING SPENT THE Christmas of 1549 at court with Edward, Elizabeth was delighted to share the festivities of Christmas 1550 with him too. She arrived in considerable state, with 'a great suite of gentlemen and ladies, escorted by one hundred of the King's horse. She was most honourably received by the Council, who acted thus in order to show the people how much glory belongs to her who has embraced the new religion and is become a very great lady.'[85]

Mary had also journeyed to share the occasion with her siblings, but on what was to be the last Christmas all three would spend together there was little joviality between her and Edward. The young King had become more and more frustrated by Mary's refusal to conform to his religious policies, and when he took the opportunity to berate her, his elder sister burst into tears. She explained to the Council that when 'I perceived how the King, whom I love and honour above all other beings, as by nature and duty bound, had been counselled against me, I could not contain myself and exhibited my interior grief'. Edward, though, was so affected by this that his 'good nature could not suffer the sight of my tears, and showed the same himself, filling me with sorrow for having caused him to weep'. He 'benignly requested me to dry my tears, saying he thought no harm of me', but though a line was drawn under the matter during the festive period, it would not last for long.[86]

Elizabeth, by contrast to Mary, was treated with great reverence by the Council, and both the French and Venetian ambassadors were believed to have made their obeisance to her.[87] Given the lack of interest she had received at the hands of the Lord Protector, this must have been very welcome. Edward was overjoyed at having been reunited with his 'Sweet Sister Temperance' for Christmas, though with this in mind it is perhaps surprising that Elizabeth rarely features in the journal kept by the young King.[88]

In a sign of the deepening fractures between the siblings, by New Year Mary had gone, while Elizabeth remained by Edward's side, where the youngsters continued to enjoy the delights of the season. On the Day of Epiphany, the French ambassador dined with Edward and Elizabeth, and 'after dinner the King and the Lady Elizabeth were taken to see some bear-baiting and other sports'.[89] Though cruel and sickening to the modern eye, blood sports were enjoyed by both siblings, and they were probably something in which they jointly participated during their earlier years. Certainly, Elizabeth would show an enthusiasm for them throughout her life, and it served as another common interest that bound her to her brother.

While Elizabeth basked in the favour of the King and Council, Mary stood for something entirely different and was shut out in the cold. Elizabeth must have been aware of the tense exchanges that had taken place between her siblings as they continued to clash over religion, but in January 1551 they grew worse. Edward had far from forgotten the recent scene with Mary, and he was not prepared to let the matter lie. Elizabeth was still at Greenwich on 28 January when he wrote to Mary in plain terms. It seemed clear to him that, 'our nearest sister, in whom by nature we should place reliance and our highest esteem, wish to break our laws and set them aside deliberately and of your own free will; and moreover sustain and encourage others to commit a like offence'.[90]

Edward proceeded to lecture her, insisting that she must comply and forbidding her from hearing mass. Mary replied quickly, saddened by the fact that Edward's words had caused her 'more suffering than any illness even unto death'. She denied the accusations he made against her and professed, 'I will live and die your most humble sister and loyal subject.'[91] With so much tension between them, it must have been with great trepidation that Mary arrived at court on 17 March, by which time Elizabeth had long absented herself. The welcome afforded to her was startingly different to that which Elizabeth had been given, for Mary was 'received very simply'.[92] Though Edward greeted his sister kindly, it was not long before the topic of religion raised its head.

After a strained meeting for which the Council was also present, Edward took to his journal to record his frustration with Mary. He wrote that he had told her 'how long I had suffered her mass in hope of her reconciliation', but he could bear it no longer.[93] Mary answered that 'her soul was God's, and that she would not change her faith, nor hide her opinion through contrary doings'.[94] Though young, Edward too was fervent in his religious faith and unimpressed with his sister's defiance. He realized, however, that there was little he could do to force her to conform. Mary was not alone in her refusal to abandon Catholicism; another who 'remains constant in the ancient religion' was Stephen Gardiner, Bishop of

Winchester, later one of Mary's most enthusiastic supporters.[95] Gardiner had been extremely vocal in his rejection of Edward's religious policies – an intransigence that ultimately landed him in imprisonment in the Tower. Edward might not have been able to act against Mary, but he could move against Gardiner, who was stripped of his bishopric the month before Mary's arrival in London and had many of his lands confiscated. More was to come when, in April, soon after Mary's visit to court and much to her distress, her chaplain, Francis Mallet, was 'seized and thrown into the Tower'.[96] It was clear which way the religious tide had turned.

Elsewhere, unlike Mary, Elizabeth was eager to identify herself with Edward, and after consulting with Cecil she came up with the idea of referring to herself as 'the right excellent Princess the Lady Elizabeth her grace, the King's Majesty's most honourable sister'.[97] Moreover, in 1551 in a gesture of affection, Elizabeth sent the King her portrait together with a letter in which she urged, 'I shall most humbly beseech your majesty that when you shall look on my picture you will witsafe to think that as you have but the outward shadow of the body afore you, so my inward mind wisheth that the body itself were oftener in your presence.'[98]

Such was his love for his sister that Edward had paid a £10 (£2,700) reward to one George Tarling or Teerlinc, who had taken his artist wife to visit Elizabeth in person 'to draw out her picture'.[99] Levina Teerlinc hailed from Bruges, and she and her husband had arrived in England during the reign of Elizabeth's father, when Levina was responsible for painting a miniature of Katherine Parr.[100] She would paint Elizabeth more than once and would continue to serve her after her accession. On one occasion, she gave Elizabeth the beautiful gift of 'the Queen's person and other personages, in a box finely painted'.[101]

Elizabeth's likeness was in demand, for there was much talk of her at court. In the same way as during her father's lifetime, she continued to provide a potential bargaining chip in the European marriage market, but if a match were to be made it was imperative that it should be advantageous to the realm. There had been many whispers of her marriage, and in November 1550 it was even rumoured that Northumberland was about 'to cast off his wife and marry my Lady Elizabeth, daughter of the late King, with whom he is said to have had several secret and intimate personal communications; and by these means he will aspire to the crown'. There is no evidence that the Duke hoped to do any such thing, although, as will soon become clear, his aspirations to the crown were certainly present. He had nevertheless taken an interest in plans to marry Elizabeth off and in March 1551 was reported to be considering a match for her. The candidate he had in mind was the brother of the French Duke of Guise, about whom there was 'secret talk of a marriage' at court. It was apparently for this reason that Elizabeth 'very hastily but with great care had her portrait painted just before the gentlemen left for France, so that they might take the picture with them'. A French match was not the only consideration, though, and the Imperial ambassador believed a potential marriage with the King of Denmark's heir was also on the cards.[102] By November this was thought to be the favoured match, 'because of religion and for other reasons', and indeed, at the close of 1550, Edward had noted in his journal that he had already sent an envoy with 'private instructions' to this end.[103] By the spring of 1553, however, Sir Richard Morison, who was writing from Brussels, reported to the Council that he had been visited by Francisco D'Este, an Italian nobleman. He had asked Morison if he had ever heard any suggestion that his nephew, the Prince of Ferrara, ought to be married to Elizabeth. Morison admitted that he had not, which prompted D'Este to enquire about the seventeen-year-old. Morison's response was that 'if God had made her a poor man's daughter, he did not know that prince that might not think himself happy to be the husband of such a lady'.[104] While D'Este agreed, nothing further came of it, and in 1558 Ferrara would marry Lucrezia de Medici, the first of his three wives. Even so, talk of such matches as these showed that with her status as the King's sister, competition for Elizabeth's hand in marriage was rife.

Elizabeth's rank was reinforced at New Year 1552, when she paid the goldsmith John Crocke for gilt plate, which she distributed widely among the nobility, receiving a flurry of gifts from the cream of them in return.[105] Among them were her friend, Mary Cheke, the Countess of Oxford, the Marquess of Winchester, and the King.[106] It was thus obvious that Elizabeth was not only highly esteemed by the monarch, but those at court were aware of it and seeking her favour too. It would not be long before the siblings were reunited, for in March Elizabeth once more journeyed to court. Durham Place had been readied for her arrival, but Elizabeth was not there long before she 'rode through London unto St James's in the field, the King's place'.[107] Once again, she travelled in style, accompanied by 'a great company of lords and knights and gentlemen, and after her a great number of ladies and gentlewomen'.[108] Elizabeth's rank was clear for all to see, and, that the King allowed his sister the use of St James's Palace was an indication of the high regard in which she was held.[109]

Elizabeth was a courteous guest, and while she was there she took care to reward 'sundry persons', including the King's footman, a groom, the gardener and the keeper of the great park.[110] She was also treated to a performance from Lord Russell's minstrels and received the welcome gift of a book from a Frenchman.[111] The main purpose of her visit was, of course, to see Edward, and two days after her arrival at St James's, Londoners were given another opportunity to see the King's sister. For her ride through St James's Park, Elizabeth was treated very much as the leading lady of the realm, and the path from the park gate to the Palace of Whitehall was strewn with 'sand fine'. Though it was only a short journey, a high level of pomp and ceremony were employed, as Elizabeth was accompanied by 'dukes, lords, and knights, and after ladies and gentlewomen a great company, and so she was received into the court goodly'.[112] Given that the only two dukes in the realm at their liberty were Northumberland and the Duke of Suffolk, father of Lady Jane Grey, for the old Duke of Norfolk was a prisoner in the Tower, it must have been they who accompanied her.

The King's sister 'was very honourably received' at court, although the Imperial ambassador had heard a bizarre rumour about her marriage: 'They say that the Earl of Pembroke, who is a widower, is trying to obtain her in marriage, but she refuses her consent. It is believed that the Duke of Northumberland has something to do with her attitude, for he will not suffer the Earl to make such a marriage, unless for some very good reason.'[113] If this was indeed a topic of conversation then it was not taken seriously, for no further mention of it was made. Indeed, in

Northumberland's eyes Elizabeth was far too important a bargaining chip to be given away to Pembroke.

As we have seen earlier, the seeds of doubt at the prospect of marriage had already been sown in Elizabeth from a young age, and towards the end of the reign of her sister, Mary, in what is the earliest recorded reference in her own words of her aversion to the married estate, Elizabeth was to recollect that, having been offered 'a very honourable marriage or two', she had petitioned Edward in the presence of some of his Council to allow her to remain single.[114] With her father's disastrous example before her and the scandal surrounding Thomas Seymour, Elizabeth's reluctance to wed needed no assistance. Nevertheless, rumours of her marriage and potential candidates for her hand would continue to swirl for several decades – later with her connivance.

By the end of the month, Elizabeth had returned to Hatfield, rewarding the bellringers at Barnet along the way.[115] As she busied herself with ordering flowers and herbs for her home, she could not have known it but never again would she be received with such ceremony and deference at Edward's court.[116] Indeed, as she resumed her life and affairs on her Hertfordshire estates, she would have been blissfully unaware of what lay ahead or that she would soon have need of the network of supporters she had been building.

CHAPTER 11

'Being Illegitimate and
Not Lawfully Begotten'

*'Of my other grief I am not eased, but the best is that
whatsoever other folks will suspect, I intend not to fear your
grace's goodwill, which as I know that I never deserved to
faint, so I trust will stick by me.'*

ELIZABETH TO EDWARD VI, 1553

'LIKE AS A shipman in stormy weather plucks down the sails tarrying for better wind, so did I, most noble King, in my unfortunate chance a Thursday pluck down the high sails of my joy and comfort.'[1] Elizabeth could not hide her disappointment when, having set out to visit Edward in February 1553, she received word that the King was unwell and thus her visit would have to be cancelled. Returning to Hatfield, she nevertheless trusted 'one day that as troublesome waves have repulsed me backward, so a gentle wind will bring me forward to my haven. Two chief occasions moved me much, and grieved me greatly, the one, for that I doubted your Majesty's health, the other, because for all my tarrying I went without that I came for.'[2] She was relieved when she learned that her brother had recovered, yet remained desperate to see him. Ending her letter 'as one desirous to hear of your Majesty's health, though unfortunate to see it, I shall pray God forever to preserve you', she signed herself: 'Your Majesty's humble sister to commandment.'[3] Tragically, Elizabeth would never see Edward again.

The young King had fallen sick of a fever earlier that month, which not only ruined his hoped-for reunion with Elizabeth, but had also prevented him from fully engaging in a visit from his sister Mary, whose reverent reception came as a stark contrast to the treatment she had received during her earlier sojourns at Edward's court. The Imperial ambassador, Jehan Scheyfve, reported: 'When she went to Court, the Duke of Northumberland and the members of the Council went to receive her even to the outer gate of the palace, and did duty and obeisance to her as if she had been Queen of England.'[4] It was almost as if they were preparing for her accession.

This change in attitude must have alerted Mary to the seriousness of Edward's malady, and sure enough, she was alarmed by the poor state of her brother's health. Edward was confined to bed, suffering from a fever as well as shortness of breath. On 17 March, Scheyfve told his master the Emperor Charles V that the King 'has never left his room' since the illness, and the physicians had been tasked with keeping a close eye on him.[5] Edward had been unwell before, such as the previous spring when he had contracted measles and at Christmas when he caught a cold. Such occasions had caused Elizabeth much concern, and on receiving a letter from Edward after his recovery from one such illness, she replied saying 'that a precious jewel at another time could not so well have contented as your letter in this case hath comforted me'.[6] This time, however, Northumberland was obviously concerned enough to keep Mary informed of Edward's condition by letter, an approach of which she was wary given that, though their relationship had once been warm, in recent years it had certainly cooled. At the beginning of April, the weather being warm and bright, Edward had recovered enough to venture outdoors for fresh air, though his physicians were still keeping a close eye on him. He nevertheless appeared to be improving, and he prepared to leave Whitehall for the healthier air of Greenwich. Just over two weeks later, however, the situation had taken a serious and drastic turn.

'I hear from a trustworthy source that the King is undoubtedly becoming weaker as time passes, and wasting away', Scheyfve noted in his letter to the Emperor on 28 April.[7] 'The matter he ejects from his mouth,' he had heard, 'is sometimes coloured a greenish yellow and black, sometimes pink, like the colour of blood.'[8] This contrasted sharply from Scheyfve's last report, where the news of Edward's health had been more optimistic. The teenage King was now dangerously ill, and 'there seems to be no improvement in his condition, and he has only shown himself once, in the gardens, the day after his arrival'.[9] His physicians were at a loss to determine what was wrong, but on one point they were agreed: if the King did not show any improvement soon, his decline would be fatal.

News of Edward's illness must have left Elizabeth seriously shaken, not only in personal terms but also in consideration of her position. For the past few years – since the Thomas Seymour affair – she had prospered, living her life largely as she chose and revelling in the attentions that were paid to her when she visited court. She had once written to Edward that, 'as so much weight rests on the prosperity of princes, your majesty's well-being ought to be desired and wished for by all with the heartiest of prayers'. For 'without it, in fact, the subjects of this kingdom can in no wise be safe and secure'.[10] No subject would be left more vulnerable by the King's death than Elizabeth.

In early May three new physicians, including Northumberland's own, had been appointed to treat the King. By 12 May, they had diagnosed him with a 'suppurating tumour' on the lung, which was causing some terrible symptoms.[11] Scheyfve had heard that Edward was 'beginning to break out in ulcers; he is vexed by a harsh, continuous cough, his body is dry and burning, his belly is swollen, he has a slow fever upon him that never leaves him'.[12] The King was plainly dying, growing weaker by the day. Throughout his illness Northumberland remained by Edward's side, but Elizabeth was probably alarmed and her suspicions raised when word spread that, at the end of April, the Duke had arranged a marriage alliance for his son, Guildford, with her own cousin, Lady Jane Grey.[13] According to some, 'the greatest doer' in the marriage had been Elizabeth's friend, Elisabeth Brooke, but the teenagers had nevertheless been betrothed with 'the consent and approval of the King and his Council'.[14] The chronicler Robert Wingfield believed that Northumberland had bullied Jane's weak father into going along with this plan, and Jane's mother was unequivocally opposed to the marriage, as, indeed, was Jane herself.[15] Besides the obvious advantages it brought the Dudleys of marrying into the royal family, many were suspicious as to Northumberland's motives for such a match, and the timing only added fuel to the fire of conjecture.

On the subject of marriage, at the beginning of May ambassador Scheyfve had heard that Elizabeth herself was shortly expected in the capital, where there was talk of Northumberland's eldest son, John, discarding his wife in order to marry her.[16] Scheyfve conceded, though, that this was unlikely, and there was no evidence of any such plan.[17] Even so, his reports convey the uncertainty and uneasiness that was afoot as everyone – including Elizabeth – waited to see how events would unfold.

On 25 May, in what was to be a triple wedding alongside one of her sisters and one of Northumberland's daughters, Lady Jane Grey was married to Guildford Dudley in a splendid celebration at Durham House.[18] The property that had until recently been Elizabeth's was now Northumberland's London townhouse, and in exchange she had received the fallen Protector's masterpiece, Somerset House. The clothes for the wedding party were generously supplied by the King, who also sent 'presents of rich ornaments and jewels to the bride'.[19] Northumberland had arranged entertainments on a lavish scale, and 'the French ambassador was present, and most of the English nobility'.[20] Though the marriage had Edward's blessing, he was too ill to attend, and just five days after the wedding Scheyfve remarked that he was 'wasting away daily'.[21] The poorly teenager 'cannot rest except by means of medicines and external applications' and 'his body has begun to swell, especially his head and feet'. At the same time, Scheyfve reported that Elizabeth had been asked to stand as godmother to the baby daughter of the Queen of France, with yet another rumour circulating – not for the first time – that there was a possibility of a French marriage for her.[22] His sister's matrimonial arrangements, though, were the last thing on Edward's mind.

At the end of May Elizabeth wrote to the Council on a matter of business concerning pasturage rights at Woburn, but took care to desire them 'to make my humble commendations to the King's majesty, for whose health I pray daily, and daily and evermore shall so do during my life'.[23]

Thanks to her contacts, notably Cecil and her friend Elisabeth Brooke, she was probably aware that Edward's prognosis was not good.[24]

It later emerged that ambassador Scheyfve had advised Elizabeth's sister 'not only to harbour no suspicions of the Duke [Northumberland], but to have confidence in him'.[25] Mary, rightly, had no such trust, and, given his recent political machinations involving Lady Jane Grey, it is unlikely by this point that Elizabeth did either, even though she had previously been on good terms with Northumberland. It was of the King, though, that the sisters ought to have harboured more worries. As the fatality of his illness dawned on him, Edward realized his time was running out and began to consider the future of his realm.

At fifteen years old, Edward was yet unmarried and thus had no children in whom to invest the throne. His father's will had made provisions for such a circumstance, and by its terms the next in line was Mary, whom Henry had rendered illegitimate and who was the sibling with whom Edward had repeatedly clashed over their religious differences. He detested Mary's devotion to Catholicism, a faith she would undoubtedly attempt to restore to the realm should she succeed him. This filled Edward with horror, for he had spent the past six years attempting to secure the Church of England and all that it encompassed. The thought of his efforts being undone was not a price he was prepared to pay: Mary could not be allowed to replace him. Then there was Elizabeth, the sister whom Edward adored and with whom he had shared much of his childhood. Though not as expressive in her faith as either of her siblings and more subtle, Edward knew she shared a similar religious grounding, and she was also fiercely intelligent. She could certainly be entrusted with the future security of the Church of England. Elizabeth's own personal qualities were beyond question, but there was a sticking point, and it was a large one: her mother. The fall of Anne Boleyn and Elizabeth's subsequent illegitimacy had always cast a stain over her, and according to one contemporary chronicler, Edward told his councillors: 'She were a bastard and sprung from an illegitimate bed.'[26]

Elizabeth's, and indeed, Mary's illegitimacy posed a genuine problem, for though Henry VIII had restored both of his daughters to the line of succession, he had done so without ever legitimating them. According to the contemporary chronicler Robert Wingfield, Edward addressed the circumstance of his sisters' illegitimacy with his councillors. Mary, he told them, 'was the daughter of the king by Katherine the Spaniard, who before she was married to my worthy father had been espoused to Arthur, my father's elder brother, and was therefore for this reason alone divorced by my father'. But it was, Edward said, 'the fate of Elizabeth, my other sister, to have Anne Boleyn for a mother; this woman was indeed not only cast off by my father because she was more inclined to couple with a number of courtiers rather than reverencing her husband, so mighty a king, but also paid the penalty with her head'.[27] If Edward were to rule out Mary, so too, on the same grounds, would he have to disinherit Elizabeth. It was with this in mind that he made a decision that placed his responsibility to his realm above all else.

Despite growing progressively unwell, Edward was determined to find the strength to do what he believed to be his duty. In the privacy of his chamber, he took up his quill and began to write a document that would have momentous consequences for both Elizabeth and Mary: 'My Devise for the Succession'.[28] Each word Edward wrote was extraordinary and unprecedented, for he now attempted to overrule the plans for succession put in place by his late father, excluding both his sisters. The Devise made no mention of either Elizabeth or Mary, and thus with the stroke of Edward's pen, unbeknown to Elizabeth she was removed from the place in the succession that her father had restored to her just a decade ago.

Having made the decision to disinherit his sisters, with Northumberland's support Edward declared that in the case of 'lack of issue of my body', the throne ought to be inherited by the heirs Henry VIII had named following the succession of his own progeny. When Henry had made his final will in 1546, he had cut off the Scottish line of his elder sister, Margaret, Queen of Scots, and instead decreed that if none of his children produced heirs of their own, then the crown should go to the heirs of his younger sister, Mary, Duchess of Suffolk.[29] The first of these was Mary's eldest daughter, Frances Grey, Duchess of Suffolk. However, Henry had overlooked her, and though the reason for this was never clarified it is wholly possible that it was on account of the fact that he recognized that power would ultimately be invested in her husband, Henry Grey, of whom the late King had had no high opinion.[30] In any case, like his father, Edward believed that a male heir was always preferable to a female one. Frances, however – who had been summoned to Greenwich by Northumberland to renounce before Edward any claim she may have had to the throne – had three daughters, but at thirty-five she was still young enough to have sons. This was Edward's first thought, and he initially ruled that his successor should be 'the Lady Frances's heirs male', followed by the 'heirs male' of Frances's eldest daughter Jane Grey, and then any sons her younger sisters might produce.[31] However, realizing that time was running out and that he was not going to live long enough for Frances to produce any male heirs, it was probably on 10 June, with Northumberland's encouragement, that Edward amended his Devise. He removed all thought of Lady Frances's male heirs and added two words to 'the Lady Jane's heirs male'. Instead of any sons Jane might have, Edward decreed that his successor ought to be 'the Lady Jane and her heirs male'.[32] The addition of 'and her' changed everything, and the newly married Jane Grey, who had until now been third in line to the throne, became Edward's heir.

The terms of the Devise were kept under wraps, but rumours that Mary and Elizabeth had been excluded were circulating by 12 June.[33] There was no escaping from the fact that the Devise was, however, completely illegal, for with his rapidly declining health there was no time for Edward to pass it through Parliament. He was, therefore, entirely reliant on his councillors to ensure its terms were upheld. Many were dubious, unhappy at seeing the order prescribed by Henry VIII ignored, but Edward was determined that the Devise should be adhered to. At his insistence, on 21 June the Council reluctantly signed a document acknowledging the changes to the succession. According to the chronicler Robert Wingfield, 'fear finally overcame their sense of duty'.[34] It was decided: when Edward died, Jane Grey would be Queen.

With the succession settled on Edward's Protestant cousin, Northumberland became father-in-law to the future Queen. It is unclear precisely how far he may have influenced Edward's decision, but the teenage King undoubtedly had a mind of his own and was not afraid to use it. Evidently, however, Edward's Devise strengthened Northumberland's grip on power should matters go the way he thought – and hoped – they would, and certainly many of his contemporaries believed he had been closely involved. At Hatfield, how much Elizabeth knew of what was afoot remains obscure, but she must have been aware of the rumours. By this time, ambassador Scheyfve recognized that the Duke's 'designs to deprive the Lady Mary of the succession to the crown are only too plain'.[35] Yet nobody quite seemed to know what to do with Elizabeth. As Scheyfve conceded, 'they are not too particular about her, and reasons for excluding her from the succession might easily be found'. Moreover, the ambassador had once again heard it said that

if the Duke of Northumberland felt himself well supported, he would find means to marry his eldest son, the Earl of Warwick, to the Lady Elizabeth, after causing him to divorce his wife, daughter of the late Duke of Somerset [the Lord Protector]; or else that he might find it expedient to get rid of his own wife and marry the said Elizabeth himself, and claim the crown for the house of Warwick as descendants of the House of Lancaster.[36]

It was not the first time similar talk of a marital alliance between Elizabeth and a member of the Dudley family had been rife, but though Northumberland was unquestionably ambitious, at this moment his energies were seemingly focused elsewhere. He was busy doing all he could to secure both French support and the loyalty of as many lords as possible to ensure his daughter-in-law's succession. It is little wonder that Scheyfve claimed 'everyone is murmuring against Northumberland, saying he is a great tyrant, that he has poisoned the King, and wishes to plunge the kingdom into disturbances and hand it over to the French'.[37] The rumours of poison abounded not only in the final weeks of Edward's lifetime, but also long after his death. There is, though, no evidence to substantiate them.[38]

By 24 June, months after he had first fallen ill with this bout of sickness, Edward's death was expected imminently, for 'he has not the strength to

ABOVE: Elizabeth's father, Henry VIII, had once been described as 'much handsomer than any other Sovereign in Christendom'. Elizabeth bore a close physical resemblance to him.

ABOVE: Though Elizabeth's mother, Anne Boleyn, was 'not one of the handsomest women in the world', with her charms and 'her eyes, which are black and beautiful', she succeeded in capturing the King's 'great appetite' for many years.

ABOVE: Greenwich Palace, the palatial setting for Princess Elizabeth's birth on 7 September 1533. Greenwich was a well-favoured royal residence but would later provide the backdrop for the arrest of Elizabeth's mother.

ABOVE: The Old Palace at Hatfield, where Elizabeth spent much of her youth. Hatfield was the setting for some of the most momentous events of her life, and it was here that she learned that she was Queen in 1558.

BELOW: Hans Holbein's 'My Ladi Prinsis' jewel design. The artist may have sketched this with Princess Elizabeth in mind, perhaps at the behest of Anne Boleyn.

ABOVE LEFT: Elizabeth's elder sister, Mary, was the daughter of Katherine of Aragon. Though Mary detested Elizabeth's mother, she acknowledged Elizabeth to be her sister, and was kind to her younger sibling as she grew.

ABOVE: Elizabeth's first solo portrait was painted by William Scrots in around 1546, when she was thirteen. It is a magnificent image in which she is fully bedecked in the trappings of royalty.

LEFT: Elizabeth's younger brother, Edward, on whom she doted. The siblings adored one another, and spent much of their childhoods together.

The Family of Henry VIII was an important piece of Tudor propaganda, which highlighted Elizabeth's place within the royal family.

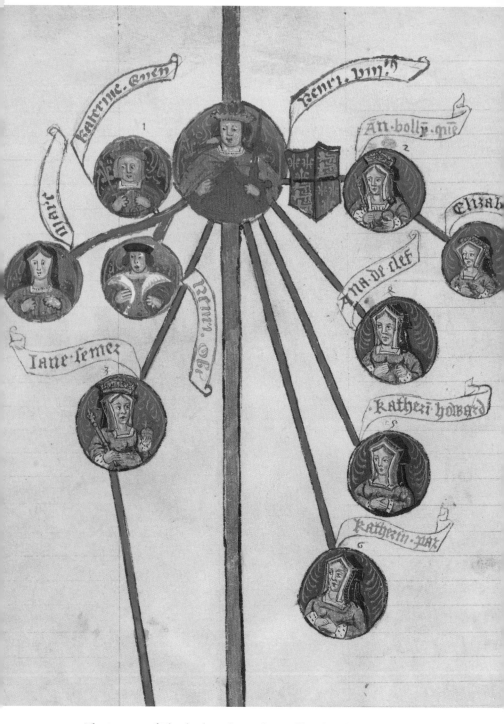

ABOVE: The images of Elizabeth and members of her family as they appear in a royal genealogy tree in a manuscript in the British Library.

RIGHT: The dedication Elizabeth wrote to her father in her New Year's gift to him reveals her pride in being his daughter, as well as her desire to please him.

ILLVSTRISSIMO. AC
potentissimo Regi, Henrico octa
uo, Anglię, Francię, Hibernięq,
regi, fidei defensori, et secundum
christum, ecclesię anglicanę et hi
berni(ę) supremo capiti. Elizabeta
Maiest. S. humillima filia, omnē
foelicitatem precatur, et benedicti
onem suam suplex
petit.

Quemadmodum immortalis
animus immortali corpori prę
stat, ita sapiens quisque iudicat

The Chequers Ring, owned by Elizabeth later in her life. Inside the locket are two exquisitely painted miniatures, one of which is Elizabeth. The other is likely to be Anne Boleyn, and was perhaps a personal reminder to Elizabeth of her mother.

ABOVE: Kate Astley, Elizabeth's devoted Lady Mistress. Kate and Elizabeth formed a lifelong bond and were fiercely loyal to one another.

ABOVE: Elizabeth FitzGerald, Elizabeth's childhood companion. The two became firm friends at a young age and would remain close throughout the testing days of Elizabeth's youth.

stir, and can hardly breathe. His body no longer performs its functions, his nails and hair are dropping off, and all his person is scabby.'[39] Just over a week later, on 2 July, Nicholas Ridley, Bishop of London, led a service at St Paul's. Tellingly, he did not include the prayers that had traditionally been said for Mary and Elizabeth – a clear sign of what was to come. Sure enough, on 4 July Scheyfve was informing the Emperor: 'I hear for a fact that the King of England has made a will, appointing as true heir to the Crown, after his death, Suffolk's eldest daughter [Jane Grey], who has married my Lord Guildford, son of the Duke of Northumberland. The Princess [Mary] has been expressly excluded on religious grounds and because she is asserted to have disobeyed the King and his Council.'[40]

Everyone at court now knew that a plot to disinherit the King's sisters was afoot, and gossip was circulating that Edward was dead already. At Greenwich, however, he still clung to life, but he was in agony. Finally, on the evening of 6 July, his suffering came to an end. 'I am faint; Lord have mercy upon me, and take my spirit' were the final words Edward uttered before he died in the arms of Sir Henry Sidney, his childhood friend and Northumberland's son-in-law.[41]

THROUGHOUT THE EVENTS of spring and summer 1553, Elizabeth's voice is almost completely unheard; all we have is the surviving letter she wrote to the Council on 31 May, concerning the business of her pastural rights at Woburn. We do not know how or when she came to learn of Edward's death, but her grief may be easily imagined. In the space of six years, she had lost her father, her beloved stepmother and now the brother with whom she had shared her childhood. She had partaken in Edward's christening, joined in his lessons, and the siblings had formed a close bond that only changed because of circumstance upon Edward's accession to the throne. Elizabeth was now more alone than she ever had been, in a world where her future was increasingly uncertain.

In the aftermath of Edward's death, the chronicler William Camden related an intriguing tale. He tells us that the 'breath was scarce out' of

Edward's body before Northumberland sent messengers to Elizabeth. They were tasked with asking her to renounce her claim to the throne for 'a sum of money' and 'certain lands to be settled on her'.[42] Elizabeth, so Camden says, replied by saying that Mary needed to answer this proposition first, for as long as her sister lived she was unable to challenge anyone else anyway. It is a fascinating story that highlights Elizabeth's shrewd nature and is in keeping with her character, but it is not corroborated elsewhere. What is certain is that when Elizabeth learned of Edward's death, there was every reason for her to exhibit caution and lie low, waiting to see how events played out – and this is precisely what she did. After all, if Northumberland were to succeed in securing the throne for his daughter-in-law, Lady Jane Grey, Mary would be his chief preoccupation.

In the days preceding Edward's death, Mary had been at Hunsdon, but hearing of the rumours to disinherit her she started making secret preparations to thwart Northumberland. He had sent his son Robert in an attempt to apprehend her, and having heard that the Duke intended to seize her, she had planned her escape before Edward breathed his last, leaving on 4 July and fleeing towards East Anglia. She made 'a difficult and tiresome journey' to part of the realm where she was a great landowner, it being said that 'she is loved in the kingdom, especially in that part'.[43] However, upon consultation with five colleagues who had arrived in London on 6 July – including Simon Renard, the Burgundian diplomat who served the Emperor Charles V, and who would be no friend to Elizabeth – Scheyfve and the other Mary loyalists believed her cause was lost: they felt 'her promotion to the crown so difficult as to be well-nigh impossible in the absence of a force large enough to counterbalance that of her enemies'.[44] They knew Mary intended to fight for her birthright, but with Northumberland in control of the capital the odds were stacked against her. After all, 'He has seized the treasury and money-reserves of the kingdom, has appointed his own men to the command of fortresses, has raised a force of artillery, fitted out warships for service, and has men ready to go on board as soon as he shall issue the order.'[45] The ambassadors were sure Mary would not be able to curry enough support to stand against Northumberland – and he was about to make his next move.

On the afternoon of 10 July, four days after the King's death, crowds gathered at the Tower to witness 'the ceremony of the state entry' as the new Queen, Jane, was proclaimed with 'the accustomed pomp'. Her elaborate train was carried by her mother and she was joined by her family before being escorted inside the walls of the ancient fortress. When it was over, criers at street corners published an order that had been issued in Jane's name, whereby 'the Lady Mary was declared unfitted for the crown, as also the Lady Elizabeth. Both ladies were declared to be bastards.' In an attempt to instil fear among the citizens, it was said that Mary 'might marry a foreigner and thus stir up trouble in the kingdom and introduce a foreign government, and also that as she was of the old religion she might seek to introduce popery'. Yet despite these words, no one present 'showed any sign of rejoicing' and 'no one cried: "Long live the Queen!" except the herald who made the proclamation and a few archers who followed him'.[46] As the daughters of King Henry, Elizabeth and Mary had always been popular with the Londoners, and there were few who wished to see them disinherited, particularly on account of a girl from Leicestershire whom few knew. It was not the start that Northumberland had hoped for, but there was no going back now.

Having had her inheritance taken from her once before by her own father, Mary, meanwhile, was not prepared to give up without a fight. The day before the proclamation she had arrived at her Norfolk base of Kenninghall.[47] It was from there that she received confirmation of Edward's death, and she wasted no time in making her intentions known. Summoning those of her supporters and household who had joined her, before them she now proclaimed herself Queen, much to their elation. She knew, however, that there was much to be done, and: 'She has also written letters to the Council, which they received yesterday, declaring herself Queen. We have been told that when the letters arrived the Council were at table, and were greatly astonished and troubled.'[48] Having obtained this news from Mary's servant, Thomas Hungate, a seething Northumberland now knew that he had a fight on his hands.

From Kenninghall, Mary decamped to Framlingham Castle, 'the strongest castle in Suffolk', which lay just five miles from the coast.[49] She began to muster her troops, and she did so with much success: before long around fifteen thousand men had gathered to lend her their support.[50] She held her nerve as 'things here are in a state of turmoil and war against the Lady Mary'; she knew Northumberland was preparing to send a force against her.[51] On 14 July, he, as 'the best man of war in the realm', left London in her pursuit.[52] The Imperial ambassadors, who had been warned by the Council not to interfere or to come to Mary's aid, were in despair, for they feared that there was no doubt that 'my Lady [Mary] will be in his hands [Northumberland's] in four days' time unless she has a sufficient force to resist; and we may inform your Majesty that the Duke is raising men wherever he can and is strong on land and by sea'.[53] Despite her popularity, Mary found herself in grave danger.

As Mary fought for her throne, at Hatfield Elizabeth continued to keep out of sight. She must have received some information of what was going on around her, yet the Imperial ambassadors' reports in the days that followed Edward's death afforded her barely a mention, and all other sources are frustratingly silent. This in itself is, though, indicative of her caution. The fact that she was one step further removed from the throne than Mary worked in her favour, for it took her away from Northumberland's immediate firing line: it was Mary who was caught in his crosshairs. Despite the physical and possible emotional distance between herself and Mary in recent years, Elizabeth was astute enough to recognize that her own right to the throne rested on Mary's claim first and she cannot have taken kindly to the news that her brother had chosen to unlawfully deprive them both of their inheritance. Jane's instalment as Queen considerably weakened her own position and undermined the provisions put in place by her father, albeit illegally. Though they may have spent a short amount of time together under Katherine Parr's auspices, despite their religious similarities Elizabeth is unlikely to have been close to Jane Grey; her later cruel treatment of Jane's sisters confirms that she was not fond of the family. Perhaps her feelings towards them originated at this time.

In the days after Mary's arrival at Framlingham, 'men from all ranks of life were joining her every day', signalling a dramatic turnaround for her cause.[54] The Council was growing 'anxious, fearing that the people may rise, that my Lady's forces may grow stronger, and that the new Queen may not be accepted by the Commons'. In order to address this, 'a strong guard is being mounted round the Tower, where the Queen and the council are, to protect her from a popular tumult; for they know that my Lady Mary is loved throughout the kingdom, and that the people are aware of their wicked complaisance in allowing the Duke to cheat her of her right'.[55]

Support for Jane was ebbing away at an alarming rate, exacerbated by Northumberland's departure from the Tower. His absence from the capital meant there was no strong figurehead left to bind Jane's supporters, for there were few among the Council who had any respect for the teenage Queen or her father. Thus, there was little she could do to prevent them from fleeing the Tower as they heard which way the tide was turning, leaving her and her family ensconced inside. Moreover, to his dismay Northumberland found that elsewhere in the country support was dwindling too. By the time he arrived in Bury St Edmunds on 17 July, just twenty-four miles from Framlingham, many of his men had deserted. He also feared that Mary's cousin and chief supporter, the Emperor Charles V, 'may take a hand in the game' on Mary's behalf, which caused him to send his kinsman Henry Dudley to the King of France to secure his support.[56] Feeling there was no alternative, Northumberland retreated to Cambridge in the hope of raising further support, but with more and more men declaring for Mary across the country, it seemed clear that his play for power was coming to an end.

On 19 July, two members of the Council, the Earl of Shrewsbury and Sir John Mason, stepfather of Elizabeth's friend Mary Cheke, sought out the Imperial ambassadors at their lodgings.[57] The ambassadors listened as the two men informed them that, together with most of their colleagues, they 'had been persuaded that the Lady Mary was rightful Queen, and had decided to proclaim her as such this very day'. The ambassadors were so amazed at these words that 'they thought they must be dreaming'.[58] Though they were uncertain what had moved the Council to this course, they believed that its members had been influenced by 'the popular rising, the increase of the Lady Mary's force and the fact, reported here this morning, that seven of the best warships had surrendered to her'.[59] Whatever the circumstances, the ambassadors were gratified when, two hours after hearing this news, 'the Lady Mary was proclaimed Queen of England amidst the greatest rejoicing it is possible to imagine: cries of "Long live the Queen!", bonfires lit all over the city, and such a concourse of people as never was seen, who came forth as if they had been waiting to hear that my Lady's right was restored to her'.[60]

While London celebrated the new Queen's success with alacrity, Mary herself learned of her victory the following day when the Earl of Arundel and William Paget arrived at Framlingham to deliver the news and seek her pardon. She willingly gave it. Mary was triumphant, having obtained a 'renowned victory without fighting or shedding much blood'.[61] Meanwhile, after a reign that had lasted just thirteen days – nine of which had been conducted in public, Jane was deposed. She 'has been shut up in the Tower with her husband and the Duke's wife', and as Jane and Guildford 'receive sour treatment', thoughts of what her fate might be loomed.[62]

Who delivered the news of Mary's ultimate success to Elizabeth and when is not certain, but she must have had a good idea of what was coming in the days leading up to Jane's deposition, as support for her cousin faded. She had been silent in the days since Edward's death but wasted no time in ingratiating herself with her sister – now England's Queen. On 22 July, the Imperial ambassadors reported that 'the Lady Elizabeth had written to the Queen to congratulate her on her accession'.[63] She could not have failed to recognize the import of Mary's success for her too, for with the proper order as Henry VIII had willed it restored, she was now next in line to the throne: it was the closest she had been since babyhood, and if it were to remain that way then Elizabeth would have to tread carefully. Anxious to make her obeisances to Mary in person but conscious that their brother had been dead a mere matter of days, Elizabeth begged her sister to 'let her know in what dress she desires to see her when she goes to salute her: whether her garb shall be mourning or not'. Intriguingly, the ambassadors also told the Emperor: 'The Lady Elizabeth will then make further declarations to the Queen by word of mouth.'[64] What these were are destined to be known only to the sisters and those who were privy to the conversation, but if Northumberland had indeed made overtures to Elizabeth about renouncing her claim to the throne, perhaps she chose this moment to disclose the details.

While Elizabeth prepared to meet with Mary, Northumberland, who had been apprehended in Cambridge by the Earl of Arundel, and many of his supporters, including his sons, were rounded up and taken to the Tower. The Imperial ambassadors were of the opinion that 'if he is brought in by daylight the people will not give him leisure to enter his prison at the Tower, but will massacre him, as his crimes deserve'.[65] It came as no surprise to them, then, when on 25 July Northumberland, who had just days before entered the fortress in a display of magnificence at Jane's proclamation, was now 'led like a criminal and dubbed traitor'.[66] For the Duke himself, mercy seemed unlikely, but his wife was released from the Tower on 26 July and immediately rode towards the Palace of Beaulieu in Essex, where the Queen was in residence following her departure from East Anglia to take possession of her kingdom. The Duchess hoped for an audience with Mary 'to move her to compassion towards her children'.[67] The Queen refused to see her.

Elizabeth was soon on her way to the capital, for having been told that mourning clothes would not be required, she left Hatfield to greet the new Queen as Mary made her way towards London. On 29 July, Elizabeth arrived at Somerset House on the Strand, 'that large and goodly house', which she had acquired by exchange earlier that year. She was 'well accompanied with gentlemen, and others', wearing the Tudor colours of green and white.[68] Presumably, she was also joined by Kate Astley and her ladies, who all rested at Somerset House that evening. At seven o'clock the following morning, she made the short journey east through Cheapside towards Aldgate to await Mary, apparently accompanied by a thousand horses of 'gentlemen, knights, ladies, and their servants'.[69] As she rode through the streets, Elizabeth witnessed first-hand the adulation of the people, who were full of joy and elation at Mary's accession. She must have been thrilled to hear that there were also many cheers for her, as she had always been well loved by the London crowd.

On 2 August, both she and Mary reached Wanstead, where they were reunited for what is likely to have been the first time since Christmas 1550. Describing Elizabeth as 'a girl of seemly and elegant appearance with a disposition suited to her beauty', Robert Wingfield says that she came to 'wish the Queen joy as well as to offer her fealty as was fitting'.[70] The Imperial ambassadors, who made it their business to be well informed, observed that Mary 'welcomed [Elizabeth] with great warmth, even to kissing all her ladies'.[71] Though in recent years they may no longer have been as close, all was well between the two sisters, and in an early sign of Mary's generosity, Elizabeth's 'estate has been increased since the Queen's accession'.[72] As Mary began to take control of her realm, she was happy to have her younger sister by her side. With the onset of a new reign, Elizabeth, meanwhile, was probably feeling insecure about both her future and her faith. Thus, for as much as Mary was content to keep her close, Elizabeth, in a bid to remain in her good graces, was more determined than ever to be seen by the Queen's side.

THE FOLLOWING DAY, Queen Mary walked through Aldgate, where 'a great number of streamers [were] hanging about the said gate'.[73] She smiled as the crowds cheered, trumpets sounded and the Earl of Arundel rode before her with the ceremonial sword in his hand. Mary looked majestic in purple velvet embroidered with gold, the Imperial ambassadors reporting that 'her face is more than middling-fair; her equipage was regal', as she was escorted by 'the nobility in great numbers'.[74] Mary basked in the adoration of the crowds, for she was 'so welcome to everyone', and her subjects were overjoyed that she had received her rightful inheritance.[75] Behind her walked Elizabeth, for whom there was no escaping Mary's popularity as the Londoners cheered and cried. They had pulled out all the stops and so numerous were the celebrations that even the Imperial ambassadors decided to 'forbear' on informing their master of the full details.[76]

That same evening, Mary arrived to take up residence at the Tower, 'where all her prisoners were in confinement; and there was such a discharge of ordnance, that the like has not been heard there these many years'.[77] As she entered the fortress, Stephen Gardiner, Bishop of Winchester; Elizabeth's great-uncle, the old Duke of Norfolk, 'an old man with one foot in the grave'; the Duchess of Somerset, wife of the executed Lord Protector; and Edward Courtenay, son of the executed Marquess of Exeter – all of whom were Tower prisoners – presented themselves before Mary 'to ask for her pardon and their full liberty'.[78] They had done nothing, she replied, for which they should sue for mercy, and 'she was sorry that they should have suffered and been detained so long'.[79] They were all set free. It would not be long, though, before – on Elizabeth's account – Mary would have cause to regret Courtenay's release.

Immediately after Mary's rapturous reception, Elizabeth joined her sister's newly established court. Relations between her and the new Queen began amicably, and the martyrologist John Foxe claimed that Mary 'would go no whither, but would have her by the hand, and send for her to dinner and supper'.[80] The atmosphere at court, however, was not pleasant: many were canvassing for the death of Lady Jane Grey. Mary, though, was determined not to begin her reign with bloodshed and instead wanted to show mercy to the cousin who she recognized had not sought to take her throne. Even at this early stage in her reign, she planned to release Jane with a full pardon, although not before taking 'the greatest possible care for the future'.[81] A grateful Jane, in turn, would declare from her prison in the Tower: 'The Queen's Majesty is a merciful princess: I beseech God she may long continue and send his bountiful grace upon her.'[82] The lives of her family and most of Guildford's were to be spared, with the predictable exception of Northumberland. The man condemned as a traitor against the Queen was executed on Tower Hill 'in the presence of over fifty thousand people' on 22 August.[83]

Jane Grey and her faction were not the only ones who had enemies, however; the Imperial ambassadors, most especially Simon Renard, were extremely hostile to Elizabeth. Even at this early stage in Mary's reign, they believed she posed a threat to the Queen, and they expressed their concerns to their master on 16 August. They had been discussing 'the presence at court of the Lady Elizabeth, who might, out of ambition, or being persuaded thereto, conceive some dangerous design and put it to execution, by means which it would be difficult to prevent, as she was clever and sly'.[84] According to Camden, many of those close to Mary were fearful of Elizabeth on account of religion and because they 'perceived all mens [sic] hearts and eyes to incline towards her as towards the rising sun'.[85] Mary, after all, was now thirty-seven years old, unmarried and childless, and thus it was only natural that, given the twenty-year-old Elizabeth was heir to the throne, the Queen's subjects would look towards her when considering the future. There certainly seems to have been some substance to their fears, for at the end of the month the ambassadors were reporting rumours (almost certainly misplaced) that Elizabeth hoped to marry Edward Courtenay, himself in possession of royal blood, for his maternal grandmother was Katherine of York, the sixth daughter of Edward IV.[86] They also harboured other misgivings:

> *Likewise it would appear wise in your Majesty not to be too ready to trust the Lady Elizabeth, and to reflect that she now sees no hope of coming to the throne, and has been unwilling to yield about religion, though it might be expected of her out of respect for your Majesty and gratitude for the kindnesses you have shown her, even if she had only done so to accompany you. Moreover, it will appear that she is only clinging to the new religion out of policy, in order to win over and make use of its adepts in case she decided to plot.*[87]

It was only a matter of time before such views began to affect Mary herself, and in the coming weeks her suspicions of her sister quickly gathered momentum. The new Queen's reign had only just begun, yet beneath the surface tensions soon began to simmer. The cracks that were beginning to show would swiftly grow irretrievably wider.

CHAPTER 12

'The Lady Elizabeth is Greatly to Be Feared'

'The Queen has sent us word that she has half-turned already from the good road upon which she had begun to travel.'

THE IMPERIAL AMBASSADORS TO THE EMPEROR CHARLES V,
19 SEPTEMBER 1553

IN EARLY SEPTEMBER, the Imperial ambassadors were enjoying a meal in the London house of the recently released Stephen Gardiner.[1] Gardiner had only been free for a few short weeks, yet already Queen Mary had made him Lord Chancellor, a significant honour demonstrating her faith in him. As he hosted the ambassadors and revelled in his change in fortune, he left his guests in no doubt of which way the religious wind in the country was blowing: unsurprisingly, it was headed firmly in the direction of restoring the realm to the Catholic faith under the authority of the Pope in Rome. The religious differences between Mary and Elizabeth had always been present, yet now, the Chancellor informed the ambassadors, 'persuasion has been used to try and correct the Lady Elizabeth and induce her to forsake error'. While Gardiner (like the ambassadors) was mistrustful of Elizabeth and her motives, his view was that these efforts had been successful, for he told his guests that Elizabeth 'held out good hopes of amendment, and will bear witness to her change of heart this Feast of the Nativity of the Virgin' on 8 September. The ambassadors were naturally wary of Elizabeth, and more so now, but felt that time would reveal 'whether she is doing so out of deceit, and the better to play the game of which she is suspected'.[2] They were right to harbour doubts about her sincerity.

Mary's accession signified a considerable shift in Elizabeth's relationship with her sister, for queenship gave Mary a power that, had it not been for the premature demise of her brother, she could never have anticipated. She recognized, though, that she had no political experience, and although she was hard-working and determined to succeed, she relied on her councillors for guidance – chiefly Gardiner, but also William Paget and the Imperial ambassador Renard to whom she quickly became close. Even so, Mary's position meant that, for the first time, she wielded authority over Elizabeth. This, in turn, enabled her to bring pressure to bear on her sister in terms of their differing approaches to religion, and that is precisely what she intended to do.

Warned by Pope Julius III to exhibit caution when it came to religion, Mary began with only subtle changes.[3] On 8 August, Edward VI had been laid to rest in Westminster Abbey, his funeral having been conducted according to Protestant rites.[4] Mary, however, was determined to remember her brother in her own way, and so she held a Catholic mass at the Tower in Edward's memory. Elizabeth did not attend either service. She was, nevertheless, all too aware of her vulnerability at this point, particularly in matters of religion. She was alone in a world where she had no place, and there was none save herself to champion her interests. Mary's intentions were made clearer still with a proclamation that month, in which she stated that she

cannot forsake that faith that the whole world knows her to have followed and practised since her birth; she desires rather, by God's grace, to preserve it until the day of her death; and she desires greatly that her subjects may come to embrace the same faith quietly and with charity, whereby she shall receive great happiness. She makes known to her beloved subjects that out of her goodness and clemency she does not desire to compel anyone to do so for the present, or until by common consent a new determination shall be come to.[5]

Mary may have claimed that she had no wish to force her subjects to conform to her faith, but the reference to 'a new determination' was telling – her patience soon faded. Moreover, in the same statement she made it clear that derogatory words such as 'papist' and 'heretic' aimed at insulting Catholics were to be banned, and that none of her people should 'under pretext of sermons or lessons, either in church, publicly or privately, interpret the Scriptures, or teach anything pertaining to religion, except it be in the schools of the university'. She genuinely wanted them all to be able to live 'in peace and Christian charity', but it was not long before it became evident that this would be a challenge.[6] The same month as Mary's proclamation, mass had been sung at St Paul's and other London churches, but although many were joyous at the prospect of England returning to Catholicism, there were also those who were fiercely opposed. Preaching continued, and pamphlets decrying 'hardened and detestable papists' were intercepted, urging that 'the great devil', Stephen Gardiner, in particular, should be 'exorcised and exterminated' lest he be given an opportunity to 'poison the people and wax strong in his religion'.[7] Over the course of the following weeks, many leading Protestant bishops, including John Hooper, Hugh Latimer and Nicholas Ridley, were arrested and imprisoned. On 14 September Archbishop Cranmer was also sent to the Tower for speaking out against the mass.

With religious tensions rife, it was little wonder that, as Gardiner had implied to the Imperial ambassadors, Elizabeth quickly capitulated to the pressure that was brought to bear on her in terms of religion, although she did not do so 'without a certain amount of stir'. She was reported as having cast off 'the errors and convictions in which she had been brought up' because she felt that 'the Queen did not show her as kindly a countenance as she could wish, and judging and supposing that the reason of it was her obstinacy in error, she besought the Queen to grant her a private audience in a place apart'.[8] In other words, before long Elizabeth had sensed a cooling in Mary's attitude towards her, which she felt had her adherence to Protestantism at its heart. In her usual shrewd manner she declared herself ready to conform to Mary's wishes, but Elizabeth knew that she had enemies at court, the Imperial ambassadors and Gardiner chief among them, and, anxious lest they should drip poison into the Queen's ear, she sought to meet with Mary privately in order to address her fears.

Two days later, Mary agreed, and within Richmond Palace the siblings met 'in a certain gallery where there was a door or half-door between the Queen and the Lady Elizabeth, who each went accompanied, the Queen by one of her ladies, the Lady Elizabeth by one of her maids'. Having had some time to consider the best approach, Elizabeth 'knelt down on both knees; weeping, she said she saw only too clearly that the Queen was not well-disposed towards her, and she knew of no other cause except religion; she might be excused in this because she had been brought up in the way she held, and had never been taught the doctrine of the ancient religion'.[9]

This was a clever card for Elizabeth to play, for Mary could not deny that her younger sister had indeed been raised in the reformed faith, with no opportunity for instruction in the old. Aside from their mothers, their religious differences served as a wedge between them: one that seems not to have mattered when Elizabeth was younger, but that had only grown and been reinforced during Edward's reign. With the onset of Mary's queenship, this fracture was becoming more apparent still, as Elizabeth represented the other side of the religious spectrum – a fact Mary's enemies knew all too well. Elizabeth had no desire to convert to Catholicism, but she recognized that in political terms her proximity to Mary's throne and her religious leanings made her the most exposed she had ever been in her life. She also realized that the best way to soften Mary's attitude towards her was to appeal to her piety. Determined to appear compliant, with a willingness to be swayed, 'She besought the Queen to send her books contrary to those she had always read and known hitherto, so that having read them she might know if her conscience would allow her to be persuaded; or that a learned man might be sent to her, to instruct her in the truth.'[10]

Believing Elizabeth to be sincere, Mary was overjoyed to hear these words and was only too happy to grant such a request. Jane Dormer recalled that 'all the reign of Queen Mary, the Lady Elizabeth did hear daily two masses, one for the living, another for the dead, seeming extraordinary devout to our Blessed Lady; and in her troubles being examined about religion, she prayed God, that the earth might open and swallow her up alive, if she were not a Roman Catholic'.[11] Jane's remembrances may have been true, but in reality it was all an act. Elizabeth was doing nothing more than what she believed she must to navigate the dangerous waters in which she now found herself: it was a matter of survival. This would quickly become apparent, as although she was supposedly 'converted and abjured her errors, and went to hear mass on the day of the Nativity of Our Lady' on 8 September, on the way she attempted to swerve: 'She tried to excuse herself, saying she was ill, and complained loudly all the way to church that her stomach ached, wearing a suffering air. We have heard that several of the councillors have had a hand in it, and it is believed that she was told that unless she took up the old religion the Queen would not let her remain at Court.'[12]

It was true that, as previous experiences had shown, Elizabeth suffered from all manner of health complaints that would plague her throughout her life, but on this occasion, few were deceived by her display of sickness. Indeed, suspicions were reinforced when she missed another mass later that month, much to Mary's frustration.[13] The Imperial ambassadors remained mistrustful of Elizabeth's true motives, and Simon Renard felt that there were more than religious considerations to be aware of. 'The Lady Elizabeth is greatly to be feared, for she has a power of enchantment, and I hear that she already has her eye on Courtenay as a possible husband,' he declared warily.[14]

Like Elizabeth, Edward Courtenay was of royal descent, and his parents, the Marquess and Marchioness of Exeter, had been close to Henry VIII and Katherine of Aragon. The Marquess was executed at the end of 1538, accused of involvement in the Exeter Conspiracy, a plot to overthrow Henry VIII with himself as the replacement.[15] The Marchioness and her only son, the teenage Edward, were attainted, leaving them unable to inherit any of the former Marquess's lands and goods. They were imprisoned in the Tower, where Edward remained for the rest of Henry VIII's reign and the entirety of Edward VI's, by reason of his royal blood.[16] During his imprisonment, Courtenay devoted himself to 'all virtuous and praiseworthy studies', with the result that 'he is very proficient, and is also familiar with various instruments of music'. For this reason, 'his prison and confinement have not been grievous to him, but have been converted into liberty by his studiousness and taste for letters and science'.[17] With Mary's accession, though, Courtenay's fortunes changed, and he was released from the Tower after a fifteen-year imprisonment. Mary was extremely close to his mother, who was taken into her confidence, and favours for Courtenay himself quickly followed. Immediately there were rumours that 'he will be married to the Queen as he is of the blood royal', but Mary dismissed all thoughts of this – she would tell Renard that 'she knew no one in England with whom she would wish to ally herself'.[18]

Nevertheless, on 3 September Courtenay was created Earl of Devon. At around twenty-six years old, he was a physically impressive man: handsome, tall, fair, it was said that 'there is in him a civility which must be deemed natural rather than acquired by the habit of society; and his bodily graces are in proportion to those of his mind'.[19] His family was also one of the oldest Catholic families in England. In spite of this, his contemporaries recognized less desirable qualities in him too, and Courtenay's behaviour soon drew comment, for he was 'beginning to give himself airs of importance, and he is courted and followed about by the whole court'.[20] Mary may have decided that she would not wed Courtenay, but that only meant rumours connecting him to Elizabeth would spread: indeed, from now on her name was to become inextricably linked with his.

'Several intrigues are being hatched in her name, with her knowledge and encouragement,' the Imperial ambassadors reported in mid-September, unable to resist laying some allegations at Elizabeth's door.[21] Mary desperately wanted to believe that her sister's shows of deference and willingness to convert to Catholicism were genuine, but, her fears fuelled by Renard, she did not trust Elizabeth. It had not gone unnoticed that Elizabeth was on excellent terms with the French ambassador, Antoine de Noailles, and Renard was convinced that the two were plotting with Courtenay. Mary, though, had been naturally warm-hearted towards her sister for much of their lives, and despite her misgivings she continued to treat Elizabeth with extreme generosity. On 21 September, when the two were at St James's Palace preparing for Mary's coronation, the Queen gifted Elizabeth several costly items of royal jewellery, many of which had once been owned by their stepmothers, most recently Katherine Parr.[22] Other pieces carried different sentimentalities, such as 'a brooch of the history of Pyramus and Thisbe with a fair table diamond garnished with four rubies', which, telling the tale of the ill-fated lovers, had been given to Mary by their father in 1546.[23] Elizabeth also received a pair of white beads trimmed with gold.[24] Such rich presents were characteristic of Mary, who was always generous to those she loved and had always showered her sister with gifts.[25] Even so, Mary was growing ever more suspicious of Elizabeth's religious motives, and it may have been now that she took the opportunity of having a conversation with her younger sibling, which she relayed to the ambassadors. The Queen told them she had spoken to Elizabeth frankly and 'asked her if she firmly believed what the Catholics now believed and had always believed concerning the holy sacrament, telling her plainly that it was said she went to mass in order to dissimulate, out of fear or hypocrisy; and she begged her to speak freely and declare what was in her mind'.[26]

Elizabeth replied carefully, and though she was 'very timid and trembled' when she spoke, she answered that she had considered publicly declaring that she went to mass 'because her own conscience prompted and moved her to it; that she went of her own free will and without fear, hypocrisy or dissimulation'.[27] It was a good answer, but Mary was wary, and the ambassadors too urged her not to trust Elizabeth, particularly given her known friendship with Noailles and the rumours linking her to Courtenay. For the time being, however, Mary, who had more pressing concerns demanding her attention, let the matter lie.

Whatever doubts Mary was harbouring against Elizabeth's sincerity, there was no question of her being omitted from what came next. On 27 September, Elizabeth joined her sister in the royal barge as they travelled by water from Whitehall to the Tower, where, in keeping with tradition, the Queen was to take up residence in the lead-up to her coronation. A 'peal of guns' was sounded before the Queen's arrival, and the sisters were accompanied by 'divers other ladies of name', as well as by the

Council.[28] Aside from the previous month, when she had gone there with Mary during her triumphant entrance into London, there is no record of Elizabeth ever having visited the fortress in which her mother had lost her life, nor would there have been any reason for her to have done so. But thoughts or talk of Anne Boleyn had no place on this occasion. This was Mary's moment – her chance to shine – and Elizabeth was to play a supporting role.

On 30 September, Mary left the Tower in a richly decorated chariot, gorgeously bedecked in 'a gown of blue velvet, furred with powdered ermine'.[29] She was covered in the costly jewels she adored and wore a small crown, looking every inch the Queen. As the Londoners who had gathered to watch her pass cheered, behind the Queen's chariot came another with a canopy of 'cloth of silver all white' and six horses wearing the same, carrying Elizabeth and her former stepmother Anne of Cleves.[30] Anne had remained out of the spotlight since her separation from Elizabeth's father, so this invitation to appear publicly with Elizabeth must have been welcome. Another chariot carried several of Mary's ladies, all of whom were undoubtedly overjoyed at having the opportunity to witness their mistress's triumph. On this day of Mary's glory, the streets of the capital had been hung with costly tapestries and decorated with triumphal arches, and 'the crowd was countless'.[31] The cream of the English nobility was in attendance that day, but it was Elizabeth who caught the eye of many. Indeed, the chronicler Robert Wingfield described her as 'the lovely Princess Elizabeth, the Queen's sister, whose beauty was of no common order'.[32] Perhaps, as she listened to the rapturous reception afforded to Mary, Elizabeth privately considered that one day they could be cheering for her.

The most important moment, however, was to follow. On 1 October, Mary was crowned in Westminster Abbey, with all 'the pomp and ceremonies' that such an occasion entailed.[33] The Lord Chancellor Stephen Gardiner, Bishop of Winchester, conducted the ceremony, for Elizabeth's godfather Archbishop Cranmer, who would normally have done so in his capacity as Archbishop of Canterbury, remained imprisoned in the Tower. Gardiner anointed the Queen twice and she was crowned with three crowns, before he handed her the sceptre and orb, symbols of royal power.[34] Thus, significantly, Mary became the first female regnant sovereign of England to be anointed. Elizabeth and Anne of Cleves bore witness to this consequential moment in England's history, watching as Mary savoured every last second of her glory. Elizabeth also took an oath of loyalty to the Queen, though many would soon doubt her sincerity – they may have been right to do so. At around five o'clock in the afternoon, after the ceremony concluded, Mary was carried in a litter to nearby Westminster Hall, where a sumptuous banquet had been prepared. She sat on the ancient Stone of Scone, which had been covered in brocade, and Elizabeth once more was placed with Anne as they enjoyed the celebrations. This was, though, the last time she would share a joyous occasion with her sister. Trouble was brewing for Elizabeth, for rumours were spreading that, via Henri II's ambassador Noailles, she was in secret communication with the French King. Unbeknown to her, that intelligence had been discovered.

MARY RECOGNIZED SHE had inherited a country that had, under the auspices of Edward VI and his advisors, been turning very firmly towards Protestantism. Despite her August proclamation to allow all men to worship freely, her fervent desire to restore England to the Catholic Church soon took over. On 5 October, the first Parliament of her reign met, and Mary was determined to address the religious issue. The Act of Repeal was immediately passed, undoing all the religious reforms that Edward had striven to enact and suppressing the Book of Common Prayer. Under Edward, the Catholic mass had been banned and he had personally forbidden Mary from attending any, but to her elation it was now to be celebrated openly once more. Parliament would not, however, sanction the restoration of papal authority in England, and thus Mary, as her father and brother had been before her, remained Supreme Head of the Church. In essence, the church settlement now reverted to the form that it had taken in the final years of Henry VIII's reign. Few of her subjects resisted such changes – probably few really understood. For the most part, people were content to live a life in which they worshipped in whichever way the law prescribed. As Mary's reign progressed, however, there were those among her subjects for whom this spelled disaster, and some were not prepared to renounce their beliefs. Many, including Elizabeth's friends and members of her family, prepared to leave England for exile abroad, fearful of what the result might be if they stayed. For Elizabeth, however, flight was not an option.

Mary's first Parliament had important consequences for Elizabeth in another, more personal, regard. Mary had always taken the annulment of her parents' marriage and her subsequent bastardy extremely personally, and it was a wound that had never healed. Parliament immediately revoked the legislation denouncing her as illegitimate, meaning she was now undeniably the rightful claimant to the throne. Now, it was only Elizabeth who remained tainted with the stain of illegitimacy, and Mary and her supporters would ensure that it remained that way. The hostile Simon Renard supposed that Elizabeth might use this as an excuse to stir up trouble; later, in 1557, the Venetian ambassador Giovanni Michiel was of the opinion that she did not 'believe herself less legitimate than her Majesty'.[35] This critical moment in the legal status of both sisters also seems to have marked a turning point in their relationship. Writing the following summer in 1554, the current Venetian ambassador Giacomo Soranzo held the view that 'From that time forth a great change took place in Queen Mary's treatment of her [Elizabeth], for whereas until then she had shown her every mark of honour, especially by always placing her beside her when she appeared in public, so did she now by all her actions show that she held her in small account.'[36] The cause of this change of heart may have been partially linked to the past. For most of their lives the sisters had been deemed of equal status in legal terms. However, Mary's legitimation coupled with her queenship now made her far superior to Elizabeth. Encouraged by the hostile Imperial faction as well as Gardiner, Mary had grown increasingly suspicious of Elizabeth, and the process of her own legitimation also seems to have reawakened some of her memories about the past and the wrongs done to her by Anne Boleyn. Now that

Mary was in a position to do so, she was determined to exclude Anne's daughter Elizabeth from the succession altogether. Instead, the Queen gave precedence to her royal cousin, Lady Margaret Douglas, Countess of Lennox. The two women had much in common, including religion, and Mary hoped that she might be able to alter the succession to allow Margaret to succeed her.

Earlier in October, the Emperor, who was just as distrustful of Elizabeth as his ambassadors were, had urged Renard to warn Mary to beware, for the signs of an understanding between 'the Lady Elizabeth and the French ambassador are open and clear to all'. He gave orders to set spies to watch her, 'so that she shall find no opportunity to intrigue or carry on secret practices with the [French] ambassador or anyone else, to the disadvantage and prejudice of the Queen'. Though far away from Mary physically, the Emperor bore a strong and powerful influence over her and he ultimately believed that she would never be truly safe unless Elizabeth was locked away in the Tower.[37] It did not help that rumours of a possible marriage to Courtenay continued to circulate, though Elizabeth's voice on this subject is silent. Given her distaste for marriage, which would be made clearer still as Mary's reign progressed and further attempts were made to foist suitors upon her, it seems unlikely that this was a possibility she entertained. Whatever the truth from her side, Courtenay himself was now forced to deny that he had ever contemplated such a match. He would rather marry a simple girl than Elizabeth, he declared scornfully, for the latter 'was a heretic, too proud and of too doubtful lineage on her mother's side'.[38] Unsurprisingly, such comments did not go down well with Elizabeth, who was by now preparing to leave court.[39]

She did so at the end of October, although she remained in London and was probably aware that there were spies in her household, reporting on her every move.[40] This probably forced her into being shrewder and more cautious than ever, perhaps exacerbated by what happened next. Though Mary had refused to countenance the executions of Lady Jane Grey and her husband, she was still under pressure to deal with them and in mid-September had at last agreed that some form of justice needed to have appeared to have been done. It was with this in mind that she acknowledged that they should be 'tried and sentenced to receive capital punishment for the crimes they have committed'.[41] Thus, on 13 November, Jane Grey, her husband Guildford Dudley, two of his brothers, and Archbishop Cranmer, who was tried alongside them for his role in the Lady Jane Grey coup, were all found guilty and condemned at Guildhall for treason and sentenced to traitors' deaths. Yet at this stage, their condemnations appeared to be nothing more than a formality, for no further move was made against them and Renard reported his belief that 'Jane will not die'.[42] Despite the verdict, Mary could not bring herself to take the life of her young cousin, whose only crime was her royal blood. Giacomo Soranzo recalled that Mary's 'countenance indicates great benignity and clemency': it was her prerogative as Queen to be merciful, and it was one that, in this instance, she intended to use.[43] The condemned prisoners were all returned to the Tower, where the following month Jane was given the freedom to walk in the Queen's garden and on Tower Hill.[44] Jane's death sentence, albeit not enacted, nevertheless served as a chilling warning to Elizabeth.

For some time the air had been rife with tension, and at court there was much talk of the succession. It was a subject very much on Mary's mind, and in late November she summoned Renard, on whom she had a growing reliance, to discuss it. Her attitude towards Elizabeth in this respect was quickly becoming fixed, and though by the terms of Henry VIII's will Elizabeth was unequivocally her heir, 'the Queen would scruple to allow her to succeed because of her heretical opinions, illegitimacy and characteristics in which she resembled her mother; and as her mother had caused great trouble in the kingdom, the Queen feared that Elizabeth might do the same, and particularly that she would imitate her mother in being a French partisan'.[45]

In the space of just a few short months, all of Mary's former warmth towards her sister had seemingly evaporated, and she could not help but continually associate her with Anne Boleyn and the division that she had caused. Mary was now desperate to ensure Elizabeth did not succeed her, for 'she only went to mass out of hypocrisy, she had not a single servant or maid of honour who was not a heretic, she talked every day with heretics and lent an ear to all their evil designs, and it would be a disgrace to the kingdom to allow a bastard to succeed'.[46]

Mary now bore Elizabeth no goodwill, but her councillor William Paget urged her to abandon her plans to alter the succession, feeling that as 'Parliament had accepted the Lady Elizabeth as proper to succeed, it would be difficult to deprive her of the right she claimed without causing trouble'. However, knowing by now that Mary was leaning towards a foreign marriage for herself – one that would be unpopular in England – Paget suggested that the people might be more accepting of it if Elizabeth were to be married to Courtenay. If this were done then Paget felt that the succession would be settled by allying Elizabeth with a Catholic Englishman: Courtenay would be satisfied and 'Elizabeth turned away from the intrigues and evil disposition that had perhaps been encouraged by the French and heretics'. Even Renard accepted that this alternative would not only be popular with the people but also provide the best way of neutralizing the Queen's sister, for 'if Elizabeth were excluded she would continue to intrigue with the French and heretics and seek out all possible means to cross the Queen's wishes, to such a point that it would become necessary to break with her altogether and imprison her, unless it were decided to dissemble'.[47]

Any consideration Mary may have given to marrying Elizabeth to Courtenay were brought to an end, though, when, on 24 December, the Emperor, whose advice she had sought, provided an answer. In his view, 'if it is possible to avoid this marriage, it will be best to do so. We do not consider that it would be at all in the Queen's interests to have it take place, for it would unite them in the leadership of the faction that opposes her, and give us reason to dread a conspiracy against her life with the object of setting them on the throne.'[48] Mary's mind was made up.

The relationship between Elizabeth and Mary remained fraught, and it was made worse in late November, when the Queen advised Renard that two of Elizabeth's 'principal supporters, on whose advice she had constantly relied down to the present day', had approached Paget and told him that although they had served Elizabeth a long while, their duty to the Queen bound them to speak. The identities of these people are unknown, but they reportedly divulged that for the past month Elizabeth 'had acted in secret, conferring with a priest who was said to be a Frenchman and a preacher at the French church in London'.[49] They did not know what her motives were, but Paget now had good reason to believe the gossip was true: Elizabeth had indeed been intriguing with the French.

MARY'S REIGN WAS still in its infancy and already Elizabeth was under grave suspicion. It was probably little wonder that at the beginning of December, worried by Mary's treatment of her, she asked permission to leave London for Hertfordshire, a request over which Mary dithered. Renard was firm in the opinion that Elizabeth ought to remain in London, where her movements could be watched, but after consultation with her Council the Queen decided to let her sister go. Not without a word of warning, though, and two days before her departure Elizabeth spoke with Paget and the Earl of Arundel, both of whom advised her to avoid colluding with the French. They recognized that the atmosphere was highly charged and that misgivings concerning her were strong: they, at least, had no wish for Elizabeth to land herself in danger. She, in turn, denied any suggestion that she was acting hypocritically regarding religion, insisting that she was doing as her conscience dictated. In order to prove it, she would take priests with her, 'dismiss those of her servants who were suspect, and do all in her power to please the Queen'.[50] She took care to show this when she 'very courteously took leave of the Queen', as she departed to spend Christmas at Ashridge.[51] Mary 'gave her sister a rich coif of sable', but by now she was more distrustful of Elizabeth than ever.[52] Her antipathy was fanned by Renard as well as Gardiner, who were fearful of Elizabeth and what she represented: namely, a younger, Protestant alternative. There was no doubt that just half a year into Mary's reign, the united front of sisterhood had crumbled.

Afraid that in her absence her enemies might attempt to poison the Queen's mind against her – a genuine and likely possibility – Elizabeth wrote to Mary asking her not to believe anyone who tried to do so. But according to Renard, who encouraged but was not responsible for the Queen's hostile feelings, old wounds had once again resurfaced, and Mary was struggling to let go of the past. It was only too plain that 'she still resents the injuries inflicted on Queen Katherine, her lady mother, by the machinations of Anne Boleyn, mother of Elizabeth, and recalls trouble and unpleasantness before and since her accession, unrest and disagreeable occurrences to which Elizabeth has given rise. There is no persuading her that Elizabeth will not bring about some great evil unless she is dealt with.'[53] Renard was probably alluding to Elizabeth's disingenuous approach to religion and the talk of her communications with the French, for it was obvious that he believed Elizabeth was stirring up dissenters to Mary's rule.

It was little wonder Elizabeth felt vulnerable, and in what was likely an attempt to defuse the situation she asked Mary 'for ornaments for her chapel: copes, chasubles, chalices, crosses, patens and other similar objects. The Queen ordered all these things to be sent to her, as it was for God's service and Elizabeth wished to bear witness to the religion she had declared she meant to follow.'[54] Mary was not fooled by her sister's efforts to placate her, but she would soon have greater issues with which to contend. Unbeknown to her, a plot was brewing – a plot in which Elizabeth would become directly implicated and one that would place her in the gravest peril of her life.

CHAPTER 13

'She Has Been the Cause of
All the Trouble'

'When all these heads are off no one will be left in the realm
able to resist the Queen.'

SIMON RENARD TO PRINCE PHILIP, 19 FEBRUARY 1554

'HER FIGURE AND face are very handsome, and such an air of dignified majesty pervades all her actions that no one can fail to suppose she is a Queen', Giacomo Soranzo wrote of Elizabeth in the summer of 1554.[1] She was growing into a young woman who drew much admiration, but she was not a Queen. The ambassador's ponderings nevertheless reflected the thoughts of many, for Elizabeth was extremely popular among the English people. Indeed, by the end of 1553 there were those within the realm who believed Elizabeth should be Queen, and nor was this simply idle talk: plans were afoot that sought to change Elizabeth's position in the world, bringing Mary down in the process.

At the time of her accession, Mary was thirty-seven and was described by Soranzo the following summer as being 'of low stature, with a red and white complexion, and very thin; her eyes are white and large, and her hair reddish; her face is round, with a nose rather low and wide; and were not her age on the decline she might be called handsome rather than the contrary'.[2]

By contemporary standards, Mary was indeed considered old to be unwed, and thus from the moment she became Queen the matter of her marriage was deemed to be of the utmost urgency. Although she was a

Queen regnant in her own right, the idea of ruling without a husband was not an option Mary's councillors had ever considered. Female rule was primarily a new concept in England, the only disastrous precedent having been set by Henry I's daughter, the Empress Matilda, in the twelfth century. Though Matilda had attempted to rule, she had never been crowned and was eventually replaced in favour of her cousin, Stephen of Blois.[3] By contrast, although Mary's rule was accepted and she was deemed to be a hard worker with a strong sense of duty, having a husband to guide and support her in the governance of her kingdom was considered a necessity. From a personal perspective, Mary had no interest in matrimony and confided in Renard that 'she had never felt that which was called love, nor harboured thoughts of voluptuousness, and had never considered marriage until God had been pleased to raise her to the throne, wherefore her own marriage would be against her inclinations'.[4] However, she did recognize that from a political standpoint it was her duty to provide her kingdom with a Catholic heir, thereby also blocking Elizabeth's path to the throne. As Renard put it, if Mary were to produce a child, 'Elizabeth would cease to matter'.[5] Though many of her contemporaries would have considered the possibility of Mary having children slim, it must be remembered that just a few years earlier Katherine Parr had borne her first child at thirty-six.

Though Mary had dismissed it, there were many at court, chiefly Gardiner, who were in favour of the Queen marrying Courtenay. But though Mary was fond of Courtenay's mother, Gertrude, she had never considered the match. Likewise, she was uninterested in the suggestion of her former stepmother, Anne of Cleves, who had spoken to her 'about a marriage with the Archduke [Ferdinand]' – nephew of the Emperor.[6] Her own thoughts were elsewhere. She knew her mother had cherished hopes that she would marry into the country of her own birth, Spain, and she had once been betrothed to her cousin, the Emperor Charles V. Though the Emperor was always her most fervent supporter and she relied on his guidance and advice, Renard had been commanded 'to tell her that, if age and health had permitted, [he] would have desired no other match, but as years and infirmity rendered [his] person a poor thing to be offered to her', such a marriage would not be possible.[7] Charles was a widower, and at fifty-three years old he was exhausted after years of travelling and war. He was also unwell, long crippled by gout, and had largely retired from public life.[8] Having sought the Emperor's advice on suitable prospective husbands, however, Renard informed Mary that his master could think of 'no one dearer to you or better suited than my Lord the Prince', his heir, Philip.[9] At twenty-six, Philip was eleven years Mary's junior, yet he had also been widowed and was in need of a wife.[10] His portrait by the great master Titian, which Mary received in November from his aunt, Mary of Hungary, who believed it to be 'a very good likeness', shows him to have been handsome.[11] Even nearly a decade later, in 1561, the Venetian ambassador would assert that 'although he is small in stature he is so well made, and his limbs so well-proportioned and symmetrical, and he dresses with so much cleanliness and taste, that it is not possible to behold anything more perfect than himself'.[12]

Mary agonized over the decision, unable to sleep and having 'continually wept and prayed God to inspire her with an answer'.[13] The choice she faced, in her mind, was whether to marry Philip or not to marry at all.[14] Finally, on the evening of 28 October, she summoned Renard to her chamber. When he arrived, he found the Queen alone save for Susan Clarencius, her favourite lady.[15] Mary had considered all things, she told him, and consulted with her councillors, the Earl of Arundel, William Paget and Sir William Petre. After much indecision, 'she felt herself inspired by God, who had performed so many miracles in her favour, to give me her promise to marry his Highness there before the Holy Sacrament, and her mind, once made up, would never change, but she would love him perfectly and never give him cause to be jealous'.[16] Renard was elated, and having committed herself, Mary was 'utterly delighted to embrace a Spanish marriage'.[17] Many in her realm, however, would be horrified.

The news of the Queen's intended marriage was not immediately made public, but gossip was rife. Within days of her acceptance of Philip's hand, Mary confided in her Lord Chancellor Gardiner. Having championed Courtenay from the start, the Chancellor's reply was predictable: 'And what will the people say? How will they put up with a foreigner, who will promise things he will not keep once the marriage has been concluded?'[18] Mary had made up her mind and would not be swayed, yet Gardiner's views were echoed by many. It would be a hard task persuading the Queen's subjects to accept a Spanish consort. On 8 November, she summoned her Council to inform them of her decision, and though many had seen it coming they could not hide their shock. Nevertheless, having had time to digest the news and in the face of the Queen's determination, by the following month they had accepted it and 'are unanimous in their support of the alliance'.[19]

Their reaction was as nothing compared to that of the general populace, who were outraged when the news became public. The idea of a foreign consort who might attempt to swallow England into the Habsburg empire, involve the country in foreign wars, coupled with the fact that Philip was a well-known Catholic, was deeply unpopular. Though Mary tried her best to be as sensitive as possible to the fears harboured by her subjects, she was furious when, on 16 November, Sir John Pollard, the Speaker of the House of Commons, accompanied by the Duke of Norfolk, Gardiner and many others, came to ask that she choose a husband from within the realm.[20] The Speaker proceeded to point out 'all the disadvantages, dangers and difficulties that could be imagined or dreamt of in the case of her choosing a foreign husband'. Among other things,

> the people would be displeased because they and the nobility wished the opposite to happen; the foreigners would wish to lord it over the English; the kingdom would be put to expense in entertaining them; if the Queen were to die without issue her husband would try to carry off the money, artillery and everything else he could seize; he would promise and not keep his word; he would wish to take her away from the kingdom out of husbandly tyranny; if he had children and the Queen were to die, he would try to get the Crown for himself.[21]

This tirade naturally caused Mary great offence, but she managed to retain her composure as she answered that 'Parliament was not accustomed to use such language to the Kings of England, nor was it suitable or respectful that it should do so'.[22] Furthermore, Mary had no intention of backing down: she would marry Philip.

The Queen's intended marriage caused great uneasiness among her subjects, though there is little hint as to Elizabeth's feelings. Its effects were not lost on her, though, for several years later, on the brink of her own accession, she referred to the fact that 'the Queen had lost the affection of the people of this realm because she had married a foreigner'.[23] She was not wrong. Gardiner, though admittedly biased because of his desire for Mary to marry Courtenay, had been right when expressing his concerns, for the English had always been suspicious of foreigners and their ways, and many were fearful. This was only heightened by the fact Philip knew nothing of England and spoke no English, which provided a further bone of contention on top of the febrile issue of religion. For one discontented group these fears manifested themselves into the biggest threat of Mary's reign. What was more, it spelled great danger for Elizabeth.

IN LATE NOVEMBER, a clandestine meeting was held in London. Although today there is still no certainty as to quite who was at the head, the individual who gave his name to what came next was Sir Thomas Wyatt, 'a young man disposed to every kind of mischief and an experienced soldier'.[24] Hailing from Allington Castle in Kent, Wyatt was the son of the same Sir Thomas Wyatt who had once admired Elizabeth's mother.[25] Perhaps on account of some of his father's troubled experiences while serving Henry VIII on an embassy to Spain, Wyatt, like many in England, harboured a deep loathing for the Spaniards and now planned a rebellion in an attempt to prevent Mary marrying Philip. Among others, he was joined by Sir Peter Carew, later reported to be on good terms with Elizabeth, Sir James Croft, Sir Nicholas Throckmorton and Sir William Pickering, who had served as ambassador at the French court during the reign of Edward VI, as well as Sir George Harper, whose half-brother Thomas Culpeper had been executed for his involvement with Katherine Howard.[26] Though he was not present for the initial meeting, the conspirators were also joined by the Duke of Suffolk – father of the deposed Jane Grey – and his two younger brothers, Thomas and John.[27] Given that the plot did not involve his daughter in any way, Suffolk's motives for participation have been questioned. Religion could have been a factor, but Renard claimed that in the Duke's confession, which no longer survives, one of his reasons was the low estimation in which the Council held him.[28] Two brothers of Elizabeth's friend Elisabeth Brooke were also involved, and, crucially, so too was Edward Courtenay, his motivation stemming from disappointment at having his suit rejected by the Queen. The French ambassador Noailles also lent the plotters his support on behalf of his master Henri II, and, intriguingly, Mary later referenced the fact that her former stepmother Anne of Cleves had likewise backed the rebels. It was clear that several people of note had become so disillusioned with the Queen's choices – or, in some cases, for reasons of their own – that they now united in a common cause.

The conspirators were all well connected – and they all had contacts within Elizabeth's household. Angry at the prospect of the Queen marrying a Spaniard and driven by religious concerns, the men planned to oppose the match in the strongest possible terms. Knowing how unpopular the marriage was among Mary's subjects, the conspirators were also confident of receiving an outpouring of support. There was more to the plot than this, however, for they wished not only to make a stand against the marriage but to depose Mary in the process. Though the chronicler Robert Wingfield claimed Wyatt 'first gave out that he had taken up arms solely for love of his country, not to harm the Queen, but to hinder this marriage, lest Spaniards, who are arrogant and indeed wanton men, should reduce the English nation to a base slavery, from which they shrink far more than from death', it was clear that Mary did, in fact, feature in the conspirators' plans.[29] The Imperial ambassadors believed that the rebels were using the Spanish marriage as an excuse, and were actually motivated by religion and a desire to set another upon the throne. Given the dismal failure of the coup to set up Jane Grey as Queen, there was no question as to who would replace Mary: Elizabeth.

Elizabeth was outwardly seen to conform to the Queen's religious policies, but the reality is that nobody was fooled, least of all Mary.[30] Given her popularity, she was an ideal replacement for Mary, and the only thing that could heighten this was if she were to marry Courtenay, himself generally well liked. This is what the rebels intended, planning to achieve their ends by launching a four-pronged rising across the country that would ultimately descend on London, depose the Queen and oust her government. Elizabeth provided a natural figurehead for those who were opposed to Mary's regime – as the Queen and her supporters had known and feared from the start.

How much did Elizabeth know of the plans? It is her own artful character that prevents us from truly knowing the full answer, for there was certainly never any solid proof of her involvement and she was too clever to incriminate herself. In October, Renard learned that Elizabeth had spent more than two hours in private conversation with Sir William Pickering, with whom she was friendly.[31] He suspected that they had spoken of the French ambassador Noailles, but to what purpose is unclear. She was also on good terms with Sir James Croft, so at the very least we can assume that she was probably aware of what was afoot and that it was being done in her name. As Anne Somerset has highlighted, Elizabeth herself alluded to her own knowledge of the affair in 1566, telling a parliamentary delegation that she had not named a successor because of her experiences during Mary's reign. There were members then sitting, she recalled, who had hoped to make her an instrument in their treason: 'I had great occasions to hearten to their motions', and 'were it not for my honour, their knavery should be known'.[32] This suggests she neither approved nor was actively involved, but equally that she made no attempt to halt the rebels' plans or to report them. In fact, John Guy believes Kate Astley's husband, John, probably provided a means of communication between Elizabeth and Wyatt, which is reinforced by Astley's flight to Padua with John Cheke in the aftermath of the rebellion.[33]

On 17 December, Mary confided in Renard that 'she had for some days past been ill of melancholy caused by the rumours that were going the rounds among her subjects'. She knew that anti-Spanish feeling was rife but was shocked when 'several people had warned her that attacks, verbal and written, were being made against the Spaniards and the alliance in terms that rang with revolt'. This so distressed Mary that the 'ladies of her chamber, alarmed by the talk they had heard from certain gentlemen, [spoke] to her in such a tone of fear that she had fallen a prey to melancholy and sadness to the point of illness'.[34] As of yet, however, she had no idea about Wyatt, his fellow conspirators and the schemes they were hatching. It would not be long before she found out, and shortly before Christmas plans for the rising appeared to have been finalized. The conspirators agreed that they would march on Palm Sunday, 18 March, but before long events forced them to take speedier action.

The Queen and court celebrated Christmas at Richmond Palace, where, despite the anxiety she had been experiencing, the jollities for the first festive season of Mary's reign were particularly joyous. Elizabeth spent Christmas and New Year at Ashridge, and there was no such merriment there, for she was unwell. Though Mary's mounting dislike of her sister was becoming ever more evident, she was courteous enough to send a message enquiring after her health, together with a gift of plate. She received little by way of thanks.[35] The Queen's mind was elsewhere, however, for on 2 January 1554 an embassy sent by the Emperor arrived in London to conclude the Spanish marriage treaty, whose terms had been roughly agreed upon the previous month.

It was bitterly cold when the Spaniards, headed by Count Egmont, landed at Tower wharf, yet still 'there was great shooting of the guns' in welcome. They were met by Sir Anthony Browne, one of Mary's favoured courtiers, and as the party moved towards Tower Hill they were joined by Courtenay and others.[36] From there, they travelled the short distance to Durham Place on the Strand, where the embassy was to be lodged.[37] None of the Queen's subjects showed any expression of joy at the arrival of the Spaniards, and instead the people, 'nothing rejoicing, held down their heads sorrowfully' while young boys in the streets pelted the party with snowballs.[38] In the days that followed, the Spanish envoys were feasted and entertained in a lavish manner as the terms of the marriage treaty were thrashed out and finalized. It was stated that Philip was to enjoy 'the royal title and style', but, given the fears surrounding his involvement in English affairs, the agreement underlined that he would not be given any power above that of his wife.[39] Instead, Philip would do nothing more than 'assist his consort in the task of government, saving always the kingdom's laws, privileges and customs'.[40] On 12 January, the marriage treaty was 'signed, sealed and delivered', and three days later it was publicly proclaimed.[41] Plans for the wedding, which at Mary's insistence could not take place until after Lent, were now underway.

Elizabeth received the news of the conclusion of Mary's marriage treaty via a personally penned letter from the Queen, and she took her time to reply. Asking the Queen's forgiveness for not writing sooner, Elizabeth explained, 'I have been troubled, since my arrival at my house, with such a cold and headache that I have never felt their like, and especially during the last three weeks I have had no respite because of the pain in my head and also in my arms.' Her body also swelling, Elizabeth's illness was genuine, and she may have been suffering from an inflammatory kidney disease known as nephritis. She acknowledged Mary's letter, though, which the Queen had written 'to tell me of the conclusion of your marriage and of the articles to accompany it. This is a deep and weighty matter, but I have no doubt that it will redound to the glory of God, the repose of your Majesty and the safety and preservation of your kingdoms.' She assured Mary that, 'as I know of no one more bound by duty and inclination to wish your Highness all prosperity, than myself, so no one shall be found, though comparisons be odious, more ready to pray God for you or more desirous of your greatness'.[42] She made no mention of the rebellion, so did she speak truth? Mary would soon have cause to think not.

Meanwhile, word of the intended rising had begun to leak. Although the details were still unknown, by early January Renard was aware of it, but it was not until 18 January that he told the Queen of what he knew. By then, the plotters had resolved to act immediately. At the beginning of the month Sir Peter Carew, who Renard described as 'the greatest heretic and rebel in England', disobeyed a summons to court.[43] His reasoning was that 'he had no horses', and though it is unclear exactly why he was summoned, we can suppose that it was probably because the

Council had heard some word of what was brewing in the south-west. His refusal to come drew suspicion and alerted the Council to danger.[44] Orders were immediately given to seize him and convey him to the Tower, but they came too late. He and his brother slipped away and managed to flee to France.[45]

With the discovery of Carew's treachery, suspicions fell elsewhere, and on 21 January Courtenay, of whom Renard had confided his misgivings to Mary, was questioned by Gardiner at the latter's home in Southwark. This caused the conspirators to panic, for as David Loades asserted, Courtenay was 'a liability rather than an asset', and he certainly could not be trusted not to betray them.[46] Thus it came as no surprise that 'this young fool of a Lord Courtenay' revealed everything, admitting that the possibility of a marriage with Elizabeth had been suggested to him, but 'he would rather go back to the Tower than ally himself to her', professing his loyalty to the Queen and begging her forgiveness.[47] Gardiner, who had long been fond of Courtenay, must have been pleased to hear the latter declaration, for he had previously advised the young lord 'to marry the vilest woman in England rather than Elizabeth'.[48] He now hurried to relay everything to the Queen. Renard was convinced (correctly) of the French King's involvement in the rebellion, his objective being 'that the country may be roused to revolt, [Mary's] marriage prevented, and Courtenay raised to the throne by means of a marriage with the Lady Elizabeth'.[49] Gardiner thought the same and was of the opinion that Elizabeth's friendship with ambassador Noailles made her a party to it. It seems that Elizabeth had indeed had some communication with Henri II, but she was astute enough to recognize that the French King had no real interest in her. Though eager to remove Mary, his real purpose would have been to install in her place his son's betrothed, Mary, Queen of Scots, who had a claim to the English throne through her grandmother Margaret Tudor, thereby bringing England under French control. Neither Renard nor Gardiner was a friend to Elizabeth, and they agreed between themselves that she ought to be confined to the Tower to ensure Mary's safety. Renard assured his master that 'I will do all I can to obtain that result.'[50]

When Wyatt and his fellow conspirators learned of Carew's flight and Courtenay's confession, they realized that in order to stand any chance of success they had no choice but to put their plan into effect immediately. In an attempt to keep Elizabeth out of the reach of the Queen and Council in the coming days, Sir James Croft rode to Ashridge, hoping to convince her to travel to Donnington Castle, a property she owned near Newbury.[51] Wyatt also sent word advising her to move, and according to one story, 'a bracelet was conveyed to her by Sir Thomas Wyatt, wherein all the secrets of that conspiracy lay hid'.[52] Through the auspices of her servant Sir William St Loe, Elizabeth reportedly responded to this message verbally with a non-committal reply. St Loe would later be committed to the Tower accused of involvement in the plot, but came 'with a wonderful stout courage, nothing at all abashed'.[53] He survived his ordeal.

The keeper of Donnington was Sir Thomas Cawarden, who was a friend not only to Elizabeth but also to Wyatt – he had associations as well with Anne of Cleves. The castle itself had many advantages, not least its structure as a medieval fortress, which made it fully defensible from attack.[54] It also linked with the main road to Marlborough, making it easily accessible from London. But Elizabeth remained unwell; she was going nowhere. There was nothing for Croft to do but ride on towards Wales, from where he would rally his forces. Critically, though, Elizabeth did not move – and she made no attempt to inform Mary of what she knew either.

Mary, however, was aware of the hoped-for move to Donnington, 'whither, as we understand, you are minded shortly to remove'.[55] She referenced this in a letter she wrote to Elizabeth on 26 January, in which she urged her sister to come to court for her own safety. Addressing Elizabeth as her 'dear, and entirely beloved sister', she notified her of 'certain evil disposed persons' who 'do travail to induce our good and loving subjects to an unnatural rebellion against God, us, and the tranquillity of our realm'. She advised her to come to court for 'the surety of your person, which might chance to be in some peril'.[56] The reference to Donnington, however, served as a warning to Elizabeth that not only was Mary well aware of the conspirators' desire for her to move, but also that she knew – or at least suspected – that her sister had been in communication with the conspirators.

When Mary was told of the plans of Wyatt and his co-conspirators and the progress of the intended revolt, her initial thought was to send the Duke of Suffolk to deal with the rebels. She was as yet unaware of Suffolk's treachery, and given his familial relationship to Lady Jane Grey may have seen this as an opportunity for him to prove his loyalty. On 25 January, the messenger she had sent carrying his summons rode into the courtyard of the Charterhouse, Suffolk's home in Sheen. There, he found the Duke outside, ready to mount his horse. The Queen had requested his presence, the messenger told him, at which Suffolk – who had no idea of the reason for the summons – managed to retain his composure. 'Marry,' he began. 'I was coming to her grace. Ye may see I am booted and spurred ready to ride; and I will but break my fast, and go.'[57] Yet, despite the Queen's request, Suffolk had no intention of riding to court, for he had instead been on the verge of departing to rally the Midlands. Having rewarded the messenger, who he sent to receive refreshment in the Charterhouse kitchens, the Duke rode away from his home, and from his wife and two younger daughters, for what would be the final time.[58] Departing London, he was intent on rebellion as he fled towards his power base in the Midlands, 'like the proverbial stag running into an arrow'.[59]

That same day, realizing that there was no time to waste, Wyatt raised his standard at Maidstone, just three miles from his family seat at Allington Castle to the north of the town, while his colleague Sir George Harper read a proclamation in which he announced the rebels' grievances in Rochester. Wyatt soon moved to join him there, making Rochester his headquarters for the campaign.[60] Wyatt was an ideal choice of leader for the Kent rising, his origins giving him enough standing in the locality to command respect, and he was 'full of confidence'.[61] In many respects he had every reason to be, for it has been estimated that by 27 January he had around two thousand men under his command at Rochester, as well as smaller forces elsewhere in the county.[62] It was a significant number, but Kent proved to be the only region that showed any realistic sign of posing a threat to Mary and her government. Despite the attempts of Wyatt's colleagues to drum up support elsewhere in the country, they were far from successful.

In Devon, for which region Sir Peter Carew had been responsible, the Welsh Marches under the leadership of Sir James Croft, and the Midlands commanded by the Duke of Suffolk, the rebellion quickly failed due to a lack of popular support; though the idea of the Spanish marriage was loathed, love for and loyalty towards Mary was still high. Mary's supporters were now intent on rounding up the conspirators. Though Carew had already fled abroad, on 2 February Suffolk and his brother were captured by the Earl of Huntingdon on the Duke's estate at Astley in Warwickshire.[63] With the help of Huntingdon's dog, 'the Duke was found in a hollow tree and John [Suffolk's brother] buried under some hay'.[64] Shortly afterwards, Croft was also captured, and all of the men were taken to the Tower. Back in London, Katherine Parr's brother, the Marquess of Northampton, had also been placed in the Tower as a precaution, as it was feared that he favoured the rebels (especially unfortunate for him, as he had only been released following the Lady Jane Grey coup in December).[65] Three-quarters of the planned four-pronged attack had thus been suppressed. In Kent, however, Wyatt and his followers presented a far more grave challenge.

Determined to thwart the rebels before they could march any closer to London, on 28 January the Queen sent the elderly Duke of Norfolk in pursuit. Given that he was eighty years old, Norfolk was a strange choice, but he may have been selected for his Catholic faith and unwavering loyalty to Mary, not to mention the fact that the execution of Northumberland – who had been one of the country's key military men – meant that her choices were very limited.[66] Norfolk had also enjoyed much military success throughout the course of his career and had been trusted by Henry VIII to fulfil similar missions, including commanding the King's forces during the Pilgrimage of Grace. He was supported on this expedition to Kent by Sir Henry Jerningham, captain of the Queen's bodyguard and 'a fine soldier'.[67] Jerningham was the son of the same Lady Kingston who had attended Anne Boleyn in the Tower, and he enjoyed Mary's complete trust.[68] Yet Norfolk and Jerningham's combined skills and experience were not enough to disband Wyatt's forces, and to their dismay they found that as they approached Rochester with 'six or seven hundred men', part of their own army defected to the rebels.[69] Norfolk and his remaining troops were left with no choice but to flee, leaving behind seven pieces of artillery, plate and money that were appropriated by the rebels.[70] This did much to swell Wyatt's spirits, and he felt confident enough to leave Rochester and begin the march towards London. The news of this caused great alarm at court, but it was not necessarily the size of Wyatt's force that created panic; more anxiety over the loyalty of the capital that had so recently cheered for Mary's accession but was now rife with anti-Spanish feeling.[71] Mary, though, was prepared to fight.

ON 29 JANUARY, the Imperial ambassadors expected to hear Elizabeth's reply to the Queen's summons. As ever, highly critical of her, they felt strongly that if she did not come then 'there is no doubt that she has been the cause of all the trouble'.[72] Elizabeth's response evidently arrived soon after, for in the same despatch they noted that she had sent word that she was too ill to travel. Aware that her refusal to come could be interpreted as a sign of her guilt and complicity, she 'begged the Queen to send her own doctor to see whether it was feigned or no'.[73] Spies in her household watched her every move, and suspicions of her were reinforced when the postbag of Noailles, the French ambassador, was seized by Gardiner.

Inside was found a copy of one of Elizabeth's letters to Mary, written 'not three days since', which 'proves that she has an understanding with the King of France'.[74] Given her friendship with Noailles and his known contact with the conspirators, it did not look good, for it seemed to indicate that Elizabeth herself had given the ambassador the letter. Certainly, this was what Mary believed, and she later told Sir Henry Bedingfield that the incident showed Elizabeth had knowledge of the 'unnatural conspiracy' against her.[75] Indeed, the discovery gave the Imperial ambassadors the excuse they needed to urge the Queen to issue orders for her sister's arrest, but no move was made against Elizabeth as she lay on her sickbed.[76] Mary had a more immediate threat to deal with.

As word reached London that Wyatt and his men were marching towards the capital, preparations to defend the city against attack began. The Tower, where Lady Jane Grey still lay incarcerated, was armed, but Mary had very limited resources and no real means of resistance. This naturally made her anxious, and she did not know who she could trust. After many squabbles within the Council as to the best course of action, it was agreed that the Queen would appeal to the loyalty of her people directly. On 1 February, Mary travelled the short distance to London's Guildhall, the administrative and ceremonial seat of the City of London, escorted by the Council, and in her hand she carried her sceptre, 'in token of love and peace'.[77] Addressing those of her subjects who had gathered to see her, the Queen, face to face with those she ruled, attempted to explain her unpopular planned marriage. Yet she told a blatant lie, for she claimed that she had been advised by her Council and 'in no wise adopted in accordance with her own personal desires'.[78] This was patently untrue, as nobody had forced her to look outside the realm for a bridegroom and many had expressed their misgivings. The choice had been Mary's, and hers alone. She then turned her attention to the threat posed by the rebels, imploring her subjects to take up arms against Wyatt and all who followed him. If they did so, 'she was minded to live and die with them'.[79]

Mary had done her best to save her crown, and what was more, it had the desired effect. The Londoners who had shown her such loyalty in the uncertain days before her accession, now did so again. 'So elegant and eloquent was her speech,' Renard apprised the Emperor, 'that all the people cried out loudly that they would live and die in her service, and that Wyatt was a traitor; and they all threw up their caps to show their goodwill.'[80] With Wyatt guilty of treason, the city braced itself for what the populace felt was sure to come.

There was not long to wait. Two days after Mary's rousing speech, on 3 February Wyatt, whose path to London had been unopposed, arrived in Southwark with no more than three thousand troops.[81] He was close to London Bridge, but there were cannon waiting and the rebels were unable to cross the river into the city. Three days later they retreated to Kingston, where they hoped to cross the bridge near Hampton Court. But fortune was against them once more, as the rebels found the bridge had been broken. Wyatt was not deterred, and not only fixed the bridge but, according to Renard, 'seeing the ferry boats lying unguarded in the river, he got all his men across during the night and approached this town, coming up to within six miles of Westminster and St James's'.[82] As the rebels moved ever closer to the city, the Londoners began to panic.

On 6 February, a spy from Wyatt's camp had been hung on a gibbet in St Paul's churchyard, thereby sending a clear message to those who took up arms against their sovereign.[83] However, with Wyatt now marching towards St James's, suddenly the threat posed by the rebels seemed very real. Mary's Council, aware that they did not have the resources to crush them, were so anxious when they heard of the rebels' advance that they disturbed the Queen's slumbers between two and three o'clock in the morning on 7 February, begging her to flee by boat for her own safety. Yet Mary remained calm, instead summoning Renard to consult with him. The ambassador felt strongly that she would lose her kingdom if she fled, for 'if London rose the Tower would be lost, the heretics would throw religious affairs into confusion and kill the priests, Elizabeth would be proclaimed Queen, irremediable harm would be the result'.[84] Mary listened, and upon his advice she refused to go. She instead entrusted her safety to the Earl of Pembroke, 'a nobleman of especial courage and high spirit', and Lord Clinton.[85] These loyal adherents promised the Queen victory and, mustering their forces – by no means comparable in numbers with those of the rebels – waited for Wyatt and his men to arrive.

To his disappointment, as Wyatt approached the city he now found that the citizens did not flock to his banner, and he had underestimated the strength of the Queen's forces. The cavalry of Pembroke and Clinton managed to rout many of the rebels, but Wyatt was able to detach himself with a small force. By now, though, his men were exhausted and ravenous with hunger, not 'in any good order or array', and Wyatt was fast losing control.[86] His numbers were dwindling as men deserted, but he would not give up yet. On 7 February, he and his remaining men marched through

Temple and down Fleet Street, but upon reaching Ludgate he found the gates closed against him. From the other side of the gate, Lord William Howard, Elizabeth's maternal uncle, cried out, 'Avant. Traitor! Thou shalt not come in here.'[87] Realizing that he could advance no further, a dejected Wyatt turned his forces and, though low in spirits, began to march back. He made it as far as Temple before he was cornered by the Earl of Pembroke's cavalry. As the Queen's troops fell on him, Wyatt was left with no choice but to surrender. In a final display of arrogance, he refused to do so unless it were to a man of appropriate status. 'If I shall needs yield,' he declared, 'I will yield me to a gentleman.'[88] Sir Maurice Berkeley stepped forward and arrested him: there was no question as to where he would be taken.

Later that day, Wyatt was conveyed to the Tower by water, 'a worthy and extremely fitting place for his wickedness'.[89] He was escorted by Sir Henry Jerningham, who was elated to see Wyatt finally thwarted. When the prisoner arrived at the fortress, Sir John Brydges, the Lieutenant of the Tower, was waiting for him. Grabbing Wyatt roughly by the collar, Brydges exclaimed, 'Thou villain and unhappy traitor! How could thou find in thine heart to work such detestable treason to the Queen's Majesty?'[90] Wyatt had little to say. In the following days, the Tower saw an influx of prisoners as the leaders, including Suffolk and his brother Thomas, Sir James Croft, the Cobham brothers, Harper and other rebels, were rounded up. Courtenay would also be brought to the Tower. They waited to hear what their fate would be, with little hope for mercy.

The rebellion had been crushed with very little spilling of blood, or, as Renard put it, 'thus was Our Lord pleased to give the Queen the victory with a loss of only two men and three wounded; an evident miracle'.[91] Yet there was no denying that the rebels had posed a serious threat to Mary that placed both her throne and her life at risk. Moreover, she suspected that there were those close to her who had been involved, confiding to Renard: 'The Lady (Anne) of Cleves was of the plot and intrigued with the Duke of Cleves to obtain help for Elizabeth.'[92] The true extent of Anne's involvement in the rebellion can never be fully known, but a further intriguing insight appeared in Renard's report on 8 February, in which he told the

Emperor that the King of France would make war on England partially because he 'has promised the Duke of Cleves, at the Lady Elizabeth's request, thus to revenge himself for Henry VIII's repudiation of his sister, and in order to give the German princes an opportunity of turning their forces against your Majesty's dominions'.[93] This suggests that Elizabeth may have been colluding with Anne, but there is no indication that she was ever questioned about this. Likewise, it seems that Anne was never interrogated, though it is perhaps telling that she did not attend Mary's wedding, and neither is there any evidence of her appearing at court again. Instead, she seems to have remained living quietly on her estates. Nevertheless, when Anne died in July 1557, on the Queen's orders she was buried in Westminster Abbey.[94] Not everyone would be so fortunate.

In the aftermath of the rebellion, Mary's earlier inclination to show mercy faded:

> The Queen says that God has miraculously permitted all this to come out and furnished her with means to put a stop to it by punishing the guilty authors in time, for otherwise heresy would have found its way back to the kingdom, she would have been robbed of her state and England subjected to the will of the French. So she is now absolutely determined to have strict justice done and make herself strong against further eventualities.[95]

Her resolve had hardened, and Wyatt's treachery would have dire consequences for Elizabeth and other members of her family. The day after Wyatt's arrest, the Queen was due to consult with her Council over the fates of Courtenay and her sister, 'who is fortifying herself in her house'. It had been reported, however, that Elizabeth was so ill that 'she now uses in a week the same quantity of victuals that used to last her a month'.[96] Elizabeth's poor health would not be enough to save her from what was to come.

The Wyatt Rebellion left Mary with no choice but to change course. Though she chose to pardon some of the rebels who were brought before her with halters about their necks, that was not the fate of all.[97] More than a hundred people were executed, their remains publicly displayed as a terrible example to every subject who viewed them. In London, 'one sees nothing but gibbets and hanged men', Renard remarked grimly.[98] By the same token, the treachery of those whom the Queen had formerly forgiven, chief among them the Duke of Suffolk, left her 'resolved to let justice have its course, as her clemency has already been abused, and allow their heads to be cut off'.[99] More tragically, Suffolk's daughter, Lady Jane Grey, and his son-in-law, Guildford Dudley, were tainted by association. Though they had in no way been involved in the rebellion, the Duke's own role as a conspirator sealed their fates. Reluctantly, Mary signed their death warrants, and on the morning of 12 February both were executed.[100] Jane met her end with a courage and bravery that impressed those who witnessed it, and on 23 February her father too was beheaded.

Jane was perhaps three years younger than Elizabeth, but her youth and her royal blood had not been enough to save her. Mary had done her utmost to avoid sending her cousin to the block, but the treachery of others had alerted her to the fact that while Jane lived, her royal blood made the Queen a vulnerable target for dissenters. Jane's death, however, removed only one figurehead and Mary was all too aware of the rumours connecting Elizabeth to the conspiracy. She had long been under pressure to move against her sister, and the Wyatt Rebellion provided Elizabeth's enemies with the perfect justification they needed to push Mary into action. Even so, the Queen gave no indication as to how she would deal with her sister, and lying sick at Ashridge, Elizabeth was unaware of Mary's thoughts and feelings. Her cousin Jane Grey had been innocent of any complicity, yet had still paid a heavy price for her identity, her death serving as a warning of the most chilling kind – one that had a lasting impact on Elizabeth. With evidence linking her to Wyatt's conspirators, she had good reason to fear that the consequences for her would be equally brutal. Indeed, she may have perceived that the fight for her life had only just begun.

Part Three

1554–8

'After so long restrainment, so great dangers escaped, such blusterous storms overblown, so many injuries digested, and wrongs sustained, by the mighty protection of our merciful God, to our no small comfort and commodity, hath been exalted and erected out of thrall to liberty, out of danger to peace and quietness, from dread to dignity, from misery to majesty, from mourning to ruling.'

JOHN FOXE, *ACTS AND MONUMENTS*

CHAPTER 14

'False Traitor'

'Being a true woman in thought, word, and deed, towards her
majesty, might not be committed to so notorious and doleful
a place.'

ELIZABETH TO THE COUNCIL IN FOXE'S *MIRACULOUS*
PRESERVATION, 16 MARCH 1554

T
HE RAIN POURED ceaselessly on Palm Sunday, 18 March. The
importance of the religious celebration commemorating Christ's triumphant entry into Jerusalem, coupled with the downpour, ensured
that in London citizens remained sheltered indoors, having been ordered to
go to church and carry their palms. Nobody in their right mind would
choose to be out in such a tireless rainstorm. But not everybody had a choice.

This day of remembrance for all good Christians was also a day of
unspeakable fear for one in the realm. Beneath the lashing rain, Elizabeth
was led out from the Palace of Whitehall to a waiting barge on the Thames.
As she approached the vessel she looked up at the palace windows in
desperation, hoping to catch a glimpse of the Queen, on whose orders
she was now leaving. But though her eyes searched hopefully, nobody
was there. Resignation was her only choice. As she boarded the barge and
it pushed away from the palace wharf, Elizabeth began the most fateful
journey of her life. Her destination was the palatial prison that had, in
recent years, acquired a chilling reputation: the Tower.

Never in her worst nightmares could Elizabeth ever have imagined
that events would transpire in this way, with her being taken to a place
that had a reputation for doom and fear. Her incarceration was necessary,

according to the Queen, in order that Elizabeth might be questioned over her complicity in the disastrous Wyatt Rebellion – the rebellion that had, in an ironic twist, originally been planned for that very day. As she was rowed through the angry waves of the Thames in the pouring rain, her mind was in turmoil at what awaited her. The journey must have held a particularly bitter poignancy for her, given that her mother had lost her life within the Tower's walls less than two decades earlier. Perhaps she now feared that history was about to repeat itself with the next generation.

Elizabeth had every reason to be afraid, for the recent death of her cousin Lady Jane Grey in the same prison for which she was now bound confirmed that nobody was safe from the executioner's axe. Moreover, Elizabeth was all too aware that the rebels had acted not in Jane's name, but in hers. She also knew that prisoners who entered the walls of the ancient fortress rarely emerged alive.

After Wyatt's treason had been suppressed, it was not long before Mary's agents came knocking at Elizabeth's door, as she had known they would. On 11 February, her uncle Lord William Howard, Sir Edward Hastings and Sir Thomas Cornwallis arrived at Ashridge.[1] It was gone ten o'clock at night when the men unceremoniously made their way up to her bedchamber, an intrusion to which Elizabeth did not take kindly. She did not mince her words as she told them tartly that she was 'not glad to see you here, at this time of the night'.[2] Yet she was still weak from illness and had no choice but to listen as they informed her that the Queen had given orders she must accompany them to London, 'either quick or dead'.[3] Just a couple of weeks earlier, Elizabeth had resisted Mary's attempt to cage her when invited to court, declaring that she was too ill to travel the twenty miles to the capital. But now the danger posed by Wyatt and his rebels had passed, and Elizabeth had to be brought to heel.

Once more, Elizabeth, determined to put up a fight, had no intention of submitting gracefully to the Queen's commands. She again pleaded ill health, announcing to Mary's officers that she could not undertake the journey 'without peril of life'. She often fell ill when suffering from stress, her symptoms exacerbated by the situation in which she found herself. But it was a performance Mary had swallowed once too often, and though the trio of men were convinced that her malady was genuine, on this occasion her feeble pleas were ignored. Elizabeth had pressed Mary to send the royal physicians, and two of these accompanied Howard, Hastings and Cornwallis to Ashridge. Dr Owen and Dr Wendy had both served Elizabeth's father and brother and had been sent to examine Elizabeth 'to find out whether she is still unwell or only pretending'.[4] They declared that, though undoubtedly sick, Elizabeth could make the journey 'without danger of life'.[5] She had no choice but to obey the summons. Even this, though, did not prevent her from employing stalling tactics, Elizabeth begging to recoup and regain her strength before travelling. Her plea was denied. Howard, Hastings and Cornwallis advised her that she must be ready to depart Ashridge at nine o'clock the following morning to begin the journey to London. As a courtesy, however, at her own request they did at least send word to court seeking a lodging for her away from the water, and thus the damp that came with it.[6]

Elizabeth realized she could play for time no longer. On 12 February, the same day the axe severed Lady Jane Grey's head in a single stroke, she left Ashridge with a sense of foreboding over what she might face. The main source for this period of Elizabeth's life and the details that follow is John Foxe, whose *Miraculous Preservation of the Lady Elizabeth* painted Elizabeth as a victim who was cruelly handled by her sister. Some of what Foxe wrote is likely to have been exaggerated or embellished to reinforce that Elizabeth was callously treated by Mary, but parts of the story are corroborated by other sources, including Renard's reports. Foxe writes that as Elizabeth approached the litter on that winter morning at Ashridge, she was 'very faint and feeble', still so unwell that 'she was ready to swoon three or four times'.[7]

Elizabeth's state of mind can be determined from what came next, for her illness ensured that the journey to London was a long and arduous one. The ever-hostile Renard reported that Elizabeth 'is so unwell that she only travels two or three leagues a day', and 'has such a stricken conscience that she cannot stand on her feet and refuses meat or drink'.[8] Her malady forced the party to make several stops, including at both St Albans and Highgate, yet her symptoms did not abate and she remained severely unwell. Her weakened state necessitated the use of a litter, in which she was carried for the entirety of the journey. To add insult to injury, in a sting that would have caused Elizabeth great distress, Renard reported a rumour that 'it is taken for certain that she is with child'.[9] It was not the first time Elizabeth had been confronted with such talk, and if gossip was indeed in circulation, it may have been spread in an attempt to slur her reputation. This was reinforced a few days later when, in his correspondence with Prince Philip, Renard apprised him that Elizabeth had 'lived loosely like her mother'.[10] Anne Boleyn's character was once again being used to tarnish her daughter.

Between four and five o'clock on the afternoon of 23 February, Elizabeth's litter reached the capital. In a show of adoration that would have dismayed Mary, citizens flocked to see her. Elizabeth seized on this opportunity, and having ensured that she had a captive audience, she had the curtains of her litter drawn back so the people could see her pitiful state. Crucially, this also provided her with a means of showing that despite the vicious rumours, she was not pregnant. Dressed in white and already paler than usual as a result of her illness, Elizabeth made a startling impression against the backdrop of her guards, whose livery was blood-red. Renard could not resist noting that, when confronted with the people, she 'kept a proud, haughty expression in order to mask her vexation'.[11] It was a clever ploy on Elizabeth's part, designed to move the people to sympathy on her behalf. It worked. And it was precisely the type of display Mary had hoped to avoid. Elizabeth was duly conducted through the city to the Palace of Whitehall.

Once the palace gates had closed and Elizabeth was no longer in view of the people, the Queen's disfavour became apparent. Elizabeth was conveyed to lodgings in a remote part of the Palace, 'out of which neither she nor any of her suite can pass without crossing the guard'.[12] Her retinue was reduced to two gentlemen, six ladies and four other servants, while the rest of her household was lodged in the city.

For two weeks, Elizabeth was 'kept as close prisoner', her only visitors being the Lord Chamberlain, Sir John Gage, and the Vice-Chamberlain, Sir Henry Jerningham – neither of whom were friends.[13] The wait for news must have been hard to bear, heightened by the fact that Margaret Douglas, Countess of Lennox, whose apartment lay directly above Elizabeth's, had resolved to make life even worse for her cousin. The Countess gave orders for some of her rooms to be turned into a kitchen, so Elizabeth was constantly troubled by the smells and noises such a setting entailed.[14] Moreover, if Elizabeth had been hoping that she could soothe her sister with her words or play on her sympathies in her time of sickness, she was to be sorely disappointed. Mary utterly refused to see her, leaving Elizabeth in a state of anxiety as she waited to hear her fate.

Though Mary would not meet with her sister, Elizabeth was still very much in her thoughts. The day after Elizabeth's arrival in London, Renard, who had long been wholeheartedly advocating her removal to the Tower, notified the Emperor that the Queen's advisors had been urging her to do the same. There was good cause for doing so, he believed, for by now Elizabeth had been 'accused by Wyatt, mentioned by name in the French ambassador's letters, suspected by her own counsellors, and it is certain that the enterprise was undertaken for her sake'.[15] Renard was misinformed on the first point; though Wyatt had admitted to sending Elizabeth a message, he had said nothing more. Likewise, there was no real, direct evidence of her complicity in the rebellion, though Renard was certainly hopeful that more would be forthcoming. For Elizabeth's enemies, her plight was the perfect opportunity through which the Queen could rid herself of her popular sister: if she did not take it, Renard – the scheming diplomat who wielded such influence over Mary – warned that 'the Queen will never be secure'.[16]

Mary was determined not to let Elizabeth slip through the net. Convinced of her sister's guilt, the Queen scathingly told Renard that 'Elizabeth's character was just what she had always believed it to be'.[17] It is difficult to establish precisely what Mary meant by this comment, for prior to her accession and aside from Elizabeth's decision to remain with Katherine Parr rather than join Mary, there is no real indication of any early tension between the siblings. It seems plausible that her attitude was influenced not only by an acute sense of betrayal, but also by the painful memories of her childhood and the role Elizabeth's mother, Anne

Boleyn, had played in them. As Linda Porter has pointed out, as a result of the destruction of her family life and the subsequent cruelty inflicted on her, nobody had a more lasting impact on Mary than Anne Boleyn.[18] Her bitterness towards the stepmother she hated had never dissipated, but Elizabeth's blood ties with Anne could not be removed. The characteristics of Anne that manifested themselves in Elizabeth – the dark eyes, the proud demeanour and bearing – all of which had become more apparent as she grew, had perhaps begun to grate on Mary. Such traits, coupled with the Queen's suspicions of Elizabeth's treachery, continued to fuel Mary's hostility.

After Elizabeth had spent almost a month in limbo at Whitehall, by 13 March Renard believed that Mary had the upper hand as evidence against the conspirators continued to stack up. He felt sure that both Courtenay and Elizabeth would be put on trial, but the very next day he acknowledged that there seemed to be some doubt over this.[19] There remained no direct proof of Elizabeth's guilt. To Mary, however, this mattered not. All too aware of Elizabeth's grim associations with the Tower and eager to force her sister to crack, the Queen hoped that a spell in the capital's fortress would break Elizabeth's resolve of innocence. Several members of her Council were hesitant, feeling that 'there was not sufficient evidence against her, that her rank must be considered and that she might perfectly well be confined elsewhere than in the Tower'.[20] As an alternative, the possibility of placing Elizabeth under the custodianship of one of the Queen's Council was discussed, but it was a responsibility nobody was prepared to take. The Tower appeared to be the only viable option.

On 16 March, Lord Chancellor Gardiner and nineteen other Council members visited Elizabeth to question her about the rebellion. She 'utterly denied' any involvement, 'affirming that she was altogether guiltless'.[21] They did not believe her. They proceeded to inform her that it was the Queen's will that she be taken to the Tower. Elizabeth was 'aghast' and once more protested her innocence, begging the lords to speak to the Queen on her behalf, she being 'a true woman in thought, word, and deed'.[22] But the lords answered only that 'there was no remedy, for that the Queen's majesty was fully determined that she should go unto the Tower'.[23]

Left to compose her thoughts, Elizabeth was barely afforded an opportunity to digest this fearful news when Gardiner returned. This time, he was accompanied by the Marquess of Winchester, the Lord Steward, and the Earl of Sussex, who brought with them an armed guard. This was frightening enough, but much to Elizabeth's distress she was then separated from most of her servants. Kate Astley was among them, and it is in fact possible that she had already been placed in the custodianship of Sir Roger Cholmeley, the former Lord Chief Justice, from whom she would not be released until the following spring.[24] The remainder of Elizabeth's servants were forbidden access to her, and Elizabeth was left with just one gentleman-usher, three of her women and two grooms. They were joined by three of the Queen's men and three of her ladies. Elizabeth was distraught.

The following day, William Paulet, Marquess of Winchester, and Henry Radcliffe, Earl of Sussex, returned to escort Elizabeth to her prison. In their manner and deportment the two men could not have been more different: in his late sixties but looking older with his grizzled grey beard and moustache, Winchester had been well favoured by Elizabeth's father and even attended the trial of Anne Boleyn's alleged lovers. Even so, he was well liked by Elizabeth.[25] Sussex, on the other hand, was in his mid-forties. A seasoned courtier, he was also great-uncle to Elizabeth.[26] These familiar faces may have provided Elizabeth with some comfort, but the task they were to perform did not. It was time to leave, the pair now told her, for a barge was being prepared and 'the tide now ready, which tarrieth for nobody'.[27] In that moment, as it suddenly dawned on Elizabeth that Mary truly did intend for her to go to the Tower, she panicked. She asked if they might wait for the next tide but was told that 'neither time nor tide was to be delayed'.[28]

Renard later heard that 'when the tide was rising Elizabeth prayed to be allowed to speak to the Queen, saying the order could not have been given with her knowledge, but merely proceeded from the Chancellor's hatred of her' – she clearly knew who her enemies were.[29] But the Queen still utterly refused to see her. Elizabeth begged to be allowed to write to Mary, but Winchester dared not permit it.[30] However, according to Foxe, 'the other lord, more courteous and favourable (who was the Earl of Sussex), kneeling down, told her Grace that she should have liberty to write, and, as he was a true man, he would deliver it to the Queen's Highness, and bring an answer of the same, whatsoever came thereof'.[31]

Seeing that Elizabeth's turmoil was so great, Sussex could not help but relent. Elizabeth seized her opportunity. Though terrified, she took up her quill and composed her thoughts. As she put pen to paper, she knew the stakes could not have been higher: she was writing for her life.

If any ever did try this old saying, 'that a King's word was more than another man's oath', I most humbly beseech your majesty to verify it to me, and to remember your last promise and my last demand, that I be not condemned without answer and due proof, which it seems that I now am; for without cause proved, I am by your council from you commanded to go to the Tower, a place more wanted for a false traitor than a true subject, which though I know I desire it not, yet in the face of all this realm it appears proved.

This was how Elizabeth began her letter, begging Mary to remember that she had assured her she would not be condemned unheard. She continued to protest her innocence steadfastly and desperately:

I pray to God I may die the shamefullest death that any ever died, if I may mean any such thing; and to this present hour I protest before God (who shall judge my truth, whatsoever malice shall devise), that I never practiced, counselled, nor consented to anything that might be prejudicial to your person any way, or dangerous to the state by any means. And therefore I humbly beseech your majesty to let me answer afore yourself, and not suffer me to trust to your councillors, yea, and that afore I go to the Tower, if it be possible; if not, before I be further condemned. Howbeit, I trust assuredly your highness will give me leave to do it afore I go, that thus shamefully I may not be cried out on, as I now shall be; yea, and that without cause.

Elizabeth longed to lay her case before Mary personally, feeling sure that if only she could speak to the Queen she would be able to convince her that she had committed no crime. She was in great fear of entering the Tower and did not need to be reminded of the fate of many of those who had done so before her. She was also painfully aware that she had enemies among the Queen's Council, chiefly Lord Chancellor Gardiner, and was anxious to absolve herself in person.

Let conscience move your highness to pardon this my boldness, which innocency procures me to do, together with hope of your natural kindness, which I trust will not see me cast away without desert, which what it is I would desire no more of God but that you truly knew. Which thing I think and believe you shall never by report know, unless by yourself you hear. I have heard in my time of many cast away for want of coming to the presence of their prince; and in late days I heard my Lord of Somerset say that if his brother had been suffered to speak with him he had never suffered; but persuasions were made to him so great that he was brought in belief that he could not live safely if the Admiral lived, and that made him give consent to his death. Though these persons are not to be compared to your majesty, yet I pray God the like evil persuasions persuade not one sister against the other, and all for that they have heard false report, and the truth not known.

Her pleas to be admitted to the Queen's presence became increasingly urgent, and it is extraordinary that at this moment she remembered and referenced the fate of Thomas Seymour, using his own ties of kinship with his brother and Somerset's subsequent regret to reinforce her point. Similarly, that she was able to draw comparisons between the Admiral's fall and her own circumstances is reflective of the deep impression Thomas's end had made on her. Reminding Mary of their own blood relationship, she implored the Queen not to listen to the evil words of her councillors, or probably more specifically Gardiner, and allow Elizabeth to share a similar fate. But Elizabeth had not finished yet and proceeded to beg for an audience:

*Therefore, once again, kneeling with humbleness of heart, because
I am not suffered to blow the knees of my body, I humbly crave to
speak with your highness, which I would not be so bold as to desire if
I knew not myself most clear, as I know myself most true. And as for
the traitor Wyatt, he might peradventure write me a letter, but on my
faith I never received any from him.*

Having maintained her innocence, implored and pleaded, Elizabeth
had done all she could. When she finished, though, she had only filled a
quarter of her second page. Even in this moment of extreme stress, when
she could have been forgiven for lacking clarity of thought, she realized
that the remaining space left her vulnerable and provided an opportunity
for someone to add forged words. Showing great presence of mind, she
scored lines through the rest of the page, at the bottom making one final
attempt to soften Mary: 'I humbly crave but one word of answer from
yourself.' She signed herself as 'Your highness's most faithful subject, that
hath been from the beginning, and will be to my end'.[32]

The 'Tide Letter', as it has become known, is one of, if not the most
famous of Elizabeth's letters and is a poignant and tangible reminder of an
occasion when she was in genuine fear for her life. It is thus called because
when she had finished putting pen to paper, part of her desired outcome
had been achieved: 'While she was writing the tide rose so high that it was
no longer possible to pass under London Bridge, and they had to wait til
the morrow.'[33] She had played for time and managed to delay her fateful
journey for a day. Though she remained at Whitehall that night, sleep
almost certainly evaded her as thoughts of the Tower must have loomed
large. Doubtless, she hoped and prayed that her letter would receive a
favourable response and that Mary would think again about sending her
to the fortress. But, once more, she was soon to be disappointed.

When the Queen learned that her orders had been disobeyed and
Elizabeth remained at Whitehall, she was furious. Renard claimed that
she was 'very angry with the Council for this'.[34] She fiercely berated them,
declaring that they would 'never have dared to do such a thing in her
father's lifetime, and she only wished he might come to life again for a

month'.[35] She was unmoved by Elizabeth's final attempt to plead her innocence and reprimanded the Earl of Sussex for allowing her to write. Ignoring the letter, Mary was adamant that there would be no more delays: Elizabeth would go to the Tower.

At nine o'clock the following morning, Palm Sunday, Sussex and Winchester once more appeared before a restless Elizabeth. The significance of the day would not have been lost on her, for Palm Sunday marked the day when Jesus made his triumphal entry into Jerusalem shortly before his death. It is feasible that Elizabeth's thoughts may not have been far from death, for on hearing that there was no response from the Queen, her final hope drained away. 'If there be no remedy then I must be contented,' she told the lords, resignedly.[36] She had no choice but to comply, and, accompanied by the small group of servants she had been allowed to retain, she followed the men into the palace gardens and the heavy rain to the waiting barge. The choice to transport Elizabeth by water rather than by road was deliberate. Though the people had been ordered to 'keep the church, and carry their palms', there were fears that if the citizens caught sight of the well-loved youth on her way to the country's most notorious jail, it would lead to uproar in the city.[37] As Elizabeth was rowed away from Whitehall, her heart filled with dread. Even the company of her servants did not serve to comfort her, and the situation intensified when the short journey proved to be more perilous than expected. As the barge passed under London Bridge, 'the stern of the boat struck upon the ground, the fall was so big, and the water was so shallow, that the boat being under the bridge, there staid again awhile'.[38] For Elizabeth, any time spent away from the Tower was a blessing, but it was to be of short duration as the boatmen managed to steer the barge clear and the gloomy Tower came into sight.

Minutes later the barge landed at Tower Wharf, and there, once again, Elizabeth employed delaying tactics. She 'denied to land at those stairs where all traitors and offenders customably used to land', meaning Traitors' Gate. Here, Foxe recounts that Elizabeth remained steadfastly seated in the barge in the pouring rain while Winchester and Sussex alighted. After some coaxing, she finally removed herself and chose this moment to make another defiant stand of her innocence: 'Here landeth as true a subject, being prisoner, as ever landed at these stairs; and before thee, O God! I speak it, having no other friends but thee alone.'[39] It is a moving speech and story, but it is unlikely to be true; we know that Elizabeth entered her prison via the Byward Tower, in the same manner as her mother had done.[40] Regardless of the truth of the tale, the outcome was the same.

The rain had continued to pour, and Elizabeth's fine clothes were drenched. But this did not move her to proceed further, for the rain seemed more favourable than what lay beyond. Observing Sir John Brydges, the Lieutenant of the Tower, and the large gathering of servants and warders who had gathered for her arrival, all shivering in their soaking garments, she enquired, 'What needed all this?' The reply came that it was standard practice 'when any prisoner comes thither'. Not satisfied, 'I beseech you that they may be dismissed,' she demanded. This won her the admiration of the grateful guards, who 'kneeled down, and with one voice desired God to preserve her Grace'.[41] She was determined not to make her captivity easy for those intent on imprisoning her.

As Elizabeth finally began to pass into the Tower precincts by the Byward Tower, the route lined with guards and echoing with the distant roar of lions from the menagerie, despite the abysmal weather she decided that she could go no further and sat down upon a stone to rest. Realizing that this was without doubt another stalling tactic, Sir John Brydges entreated her: 'Madam, you were best to come out of the rain; for you sit unwholesomely.' Once again, Elizabeth was steadfast and defiantly replied, 'It is better sitting here, than in a worse place; for God knoweth, I know not whither you will bring me.'[42] Her remarks have a ring of those made by her mother when Anne was brought to the Tower, but though clearly fearful of her surroundings, Elizabeth was probably aware that her status meant it was unlikely she would be led to one of the dungeons, where the screams of the tortured vibrated through the Tower walls. It was nevertheless a scene that bore a striking similarity to her mother's final journey, a fact of which Elizabeth may have been all too conscious. Foxe related that, upon hearing her words, her gentleman-usher began to weep. Elizabeth did not take kindly to this, however, asking him what he meant by such an outburst, 'seeing she took him to be her comforter, and not to dismay her; especially for that she knew her truth to be such, that no man should have cause to weep for her'.[43] Finally, realizing that she could delay matters no longer, she roused herself to face her woeful prison.

The sources are silent on the location of Elizabeth's lodgings within the Tower, but though Foxe tells us that 'the doors were locked and bolted upon her, which did not a little discomfort and dismay her Grace', she was not taken to a dungeon.[44] Like her mother before her, Elizabeth was probably escorted to the royal apartments, which lay next to the White Tower. As she approached, she may just have caught a glimpse of Lady Jane Grey's scaffold, upon which the teenager had met her end mere days ago and that stood close to where Elizabeth was now lodged. The scaffold was placed on the same spot at which Anne Boleyn had died.

The reminder of her mother would perhaps have been all the more poignant if Elizabeth were indeed housed, by chance or design, in the rooms Anne had occupied in her final days. Tracy Borman has suggested that these may have been chosen to exacerbate Elizabeth's terror, and though the rooms were by no means as dire as those endured by other Tower prisoners, there is still little doubt that they were not allocated for her comfort.[45] Twenty years earlier, the royal apartments had been lavishly refurbished for Anne Boleyn's coronation and were the most magnificent in the Tower complex. Hung with costly tapestries laced with gold thread and ornate furnishings of the finest quality, they provided the very best in luxury and splendour. By the time of Elizabeth's arrival, the rooms that had once dazzled her mother had fallen into disrepair; the gold had begun to fade and the tapestries to unravel. As the doors were locked behind her, there was no mistaking the fact that Elizabeth was now, officially, a Tower prisoner.

With Winchester and Sussex departed and Elizabeth's liberty removed, the enormity of her situation hit her. Not for the first time, she became greatly distressed, and though she still had a handful of servants for company, for Elizabeth it was not enough. She turned to the only other comfort she had. Ordering one of her ladies to bring her book – presumably a Bible – in a reference to Scripture she desired God 'not to suffer her to build her foundation upon the sands, but upon the rock, whereby all blasts of blustering weather should have no power against her'.[46] Elizabeth was, in other words, grounding her faith in Christ to guide her to the most wise course lest the storms of life should blow her away. Plagued with uncertainty as to what would happen next, her trust was now in God. Elizabeth prayed that he would give her the courage she needed to survive her ordeal.

CHAPTER 15

'What Shall Be Done With Her?'

'You shall not do more to me than God hath appointed; and so God forgive you all.'

ELIZABETH TO THE COUNCIL IN FOXE'S *MIRACULOUS*
PRESERVATION, GOOD FRIDAY 1554

FOUR YEARS LATER, when Elizabeth was on the brink of queenship, she told Count de Feria defiantly that she felt 'it was not dishonourable to admit that she had been a prisoner; on the contrary, it was those who had put her there who were dishonoured, because she had never been guilty of having acted or said anything against the Queen, nor would she ever confess otherwise'.[1] She resented her imprisonment, yet in the spring of 1554, as she languished in the Tower, Elizabeth had no idea of what her fate might be – or if she would survive.

As she agonized, Elizabeth had only her gentlewomen beside her to offer what little comfort they could. Intriguingly, one of these appears to have been Etheldreda Harington (née Malte), who may have been an illegitimate daughter of Henry VIII.[2] Etheldreda's husband, John, was a former servant of Thomas Seymour and had himself been imprisoned in the Tower following the Wyatt Rebellion, for carrying a letter to Elizabeth from the Duke of Suffolk.[3] John Harington remarked on the fact that 'my wife is her servant, and doth but rejoice in this our misery', noting that Elizabeth 'doth honour us in tender sort, and scorneth not to shed her tears with ours'.[4] We do not know how or when Etheldreda came to be among Elizabeth's household – certainly it was after 1547, but further details of her presence are a mystery.[5]

Another of Elizabeth's ladies was Elizabeth Sandes, one of her most devoted servants whom she in turn adored. Sandes was soon to create problems, though, for within two days of Elizabeth's arrival at the Tower an order was received that she was to attend mass. Like Elizabeth, Sandes was a Protestant, but one who had no intention of conforming to such a demand. When she refused to attend, she was dismissed from Elizabeth's service and replaced by a Mrs Coldburn, who joined one Mrs Marborow – probably Isabella Markham, who had entered Elizabeth's household by 1549 and was the daughter of the former Lieutenant of the Tower, Sir John Markham.[6] The removal of her attendant only made an already unbearable situation worse for Elizabeth, but there was more to come.

Before leaving the Tower, the Earl of Sussex had expressed to his colleagues his view that they should exercise caution in their handling of Elizabeth. 'My Lords,' he implored them, 'let us take heed, and do no more than our commission will bear us out in.' They should also, he said, 'consider that she was the King our master's daughter', thereby reminding them that Elizabeth's status demanded a certain level of respect.[7] Sussex was right, for whether Mary liked it or not, Elizabeth was still the heir to the throne, as the Council knew all too well. Even so, Mary, once again encouraged by Renard, was convinced of Elizabeth's complicity in the treason against her and was determined to wring a confession from her.

On 15 March, shortly before Elizabeth's arrival at the Tower, Thomas Wyatt stood trial at Westminster Hall. The Queen's attorney rebuked him with the words: 'You attempted the second person of this realm, who should have been all our comforts, whereby her honour is brought into question.'[8] Wyatt admitted that he had received an oral message from Elizabeth by her servant William St Loe, but the content provided nothing incriminating. According to the chronicler Wingfield, Wyatt was 'overwhelmed by the enormity of his crime and immediately confessed his treason' without awaiting the verdict.[9] Significantly for Elizabeth, this included nothing concerning her. He was nevertheless remorseful and hoped the Queen would show mercy. There was to be none forthcoming, however, and the trial was little more than a formality. Wyatt was found guilty and sentenced to die, having provided Mary with nothing she could use against her sister. The search for evidence continued.

AFTER SEVERAL RESTLESS days and nights in the Tower, on Good Friday, Elizabeth came face to face with the Council. That she had been conveyed to the fortress and was now to be questioned during one of the most significant periods in the Christian calendar conveys the severity of her circumstances, and Mary's determination to deal with her. The men were headed by her enemy, Lord Chancellor Gardiner, the 'ruler of the roost'.[10] Sensing what would follow, Elizabeth was confronted with a gruelling interrogation. She was asked about Sir James Croft's visit to Ashridge and her supposed intended move to Donnington Castle. What did she mean by such a thing? the Council demanded of her. Elizabeth was solely reliant on her wits and her own counsel, but despite her surroundings and the anxiety she must have felt, she was too astute to give anything away. She did not recall owning such a place, she answered, but her memory soon caught up with her: 'I do now remember that I have such a place, but I never lay in it in all my life. And as for any that hath moved me thereunto, I do not remember,' she told them.[11]

According to Foxe's account, to force a confession from her the Council then had Croft brought before her. 'What had she said to him?' Gardiner demanded of her. She had little to say to him, Elizabeth replied, or indeed to any of the rebels who were imprisoned in the Tower. She intended to reinforce her innocence, accusing the Council of wrongdoing, because 'you do examine every mean prisoner of me, wherein, methinks, you do me great injury. If they have done evil, and offended the Queen's Majesty, let them answer to it accordingly. I beseech you, my Lords, join not me, in this sort, with any of these offenders.' She admitted that Croft had spoken to her of the move to Donnington, but 'what is that to the purpose, my Lords, but that I may go to mine own houses at all times?'[12] Her outward composure and refusal to admit to any wrongdoing frustrated Gardiner, but Foxe claimed that it left others troubled. At Elizabeth's declaration the Earl of Arundel, Mary's Lord Steward, knelt before her. Evidently embarrassed at the line of questioning, he professed his apologies: 'Your Grace saith true, and certainly we are very sorry that we have so troubled you about so vain matters.' Elizabeth responded graciously, but though her first interrogation was over, her troubles were not at an end.

In the coming days, Elizabeth's servants were allowed to leave the Tower to buy food for her – costs that she was forced to cover – although much of it was commandeered by the 'common rascal soldiers' at the Tower gates.[13] When the servants complained to the Lord Chamberlain, Sir John Gage, they found him unsympathetic, and the matter was only resolved when it was agreed that he too might have his food prepared by Elizabeth's own cook.[14] Meanwhile, the Queen and Council were busy pondering her fate. Renard did his best to try to influence Mary, attempting to convince her that it was necessary to order 'the trials and executions of criminals, especially Courtenay and the Lady Elizabeth, [be] concluded before his Highness arrives'.[15] Now that the Queen and Philip were betrothed, Renard had the perfect opportunity to push Mary into dealing with Elizabeth once and for all.[16]

Jane Dormer recalled that most of the Council wanted to proceed against Elizabeth, but the Queen's 'goodness' deferred it.[17] This is most likely an exaggeration, as aside from Gardiner the Council members were largely divided as to how she ought to be dealt with and all were fully aware that Elizabeth stood as heir to the throne. The reality of the situation was that, because of Elizabeth's popularity, Mary recognized that without compelling evidence, to put her on trial would be extremely risky.

With Wyatt failing to implicate Elizabeth, by 3 April even Renard was forced to admit that there was little to prove her complicity. Deep down Mary knew this too but, convinced of her sister's treachery, she claimed that 'fresh proof is coming up against her every day, and there were several witnesses to assert that she had gathered together stores and weapons in order to rise with the rest and fortify a house in the country whither she had been sending her provisions' – this being Donnington.[18] There were already those among the Queen's Council who thought differently, including William Paget.

Paget had always been against the idea of sending Elizabeth to the Tower and his thoughts had not changed. Now, however, he 'had talked at great length with Elizabeth' and told Renard that 'if sufficient evidence to put her to death were not discovered he saw no better means of keeping her quiet than to marry her to a foreigner'. Already he was acknowledging what would become glaringly clear in the coming days: there would be no further proof against Elizabeth. Paget had once been of the opinion that a marriage between Elizabeth and Courtenay might be wise, but although that was now out of the question, he did believe that matrimony was the best way to solve the problem. It was his view that Elizabeth should marry a foreign prince, and what was more, he already had a candidate in mind. If, for example, 'a match with the Prince of Piedmont [Duke of Savoy] could be arranged, Parliament and the Council would readily consent that the succession should go to them in case the Queen had no children'.[19] Savoy was not the only candidate, though, and Renard acknowledged that Don Luis of Portugal had also been suggested.[20]

On 11 April, meanwhile, Wyatt left the Tower for the last time. Perhaps Elizabeth heard or saw the guards pass as they escorted the convicted traitor to nearby Tower Hill, where he was to meet his end. He appears to have hoped for a reprieve until the very last minute – a carrot that the Council had probably dangled in the hope he would yet incriminate Elizabeth. He did no such thing and, his guards having pushed him through the crowds to the scaffold, in his final speech he cleared both Elizabeth and Courtenay of any wrongdoing. A severed head was only the first part of Wyatt's sentence, for once this had been done 'his bowels and members [were] burnt beside the scaffold'.[21] His lifeless and bloodied remains were then quartered, with the four parts 'hanged on gibbets in chains' at four places outside London to serve as a grisly warning. His head was 'set on the gallows at the park pale beyond St James's'.[22] Within days it would be stolen.

The following day, Elizabeth was questioned once again, with members of the Council using every persuasion they could think of to convince her to make some admission of guilt. Their efforts were in vain. With each passing day it was becoming clearer that there was no reason for her to do so, and with Wyatt dead and the remainder of the plotters having fled or refused to implicate her, the chances of a conviction seemed slimmer than ever. By 17 April, much to his disappointment, Renard knew for sure that there was not 'sufficient evidence to condemn Elizabeth'.[23] Her fate appeared to rest on a decision not of life or death but of imprisonment or freedom.

Mary was likewise aware that she had no grounds to take further action against her sister, and Renard conceded that the resolution 'leaves the Queen in perplexity whether to leave her in the Tower, for it would not be wise to set her at liberty so soon, and it would be neither honourable, safe nor reasonable to let her follow the Court'. The Council, similarly, could not agree on the best way forward, as while 'some think it would be well to send her to a castle in the north, where the people are good Christians and lovers of peace', others opposed this and, like Paget, felt that 'the best thing would be to marry her to a foreigner'. A consensus could not be reached, and thus, 'the question of the day is: what shall be done with her?'[24] Whatever the answer, the danger of Elizabeth losing her life appeared to have passed. By now Elizabeth herself must have realized that the Council had no proof against her, and thus that the threat of execution was diminishing. But nevertheless, she remained in the Tower suffering an agony of emotional torment as she waited for Mary to make her next move.

A decision on Elizabeth's fate was now even more imperative because on 12 April an Act of Parliament had confirmed the marriage treaty between Mary and Philip, and plans for the wedding were gathering pace. Elizabeth was probably made aware of this, but her thoughts were elsewhere. Her living conditions were comfortable enough, but, still held in the Tower, reminders of her mother's demise within these walls surrounded her. Moreover, as so often happened during times of strain, she fell ill, asking for a physician to attend her.[25] After a month in the Tower she was understandably 'very evil at ease therewithal', and she sent for Sir John Gage and Sir John Brydges, Lieutenant of the Tower, who had been created Baron

Chandos just days earlier on 8 April.[26] When the men arrived before her, Elizabeth 'requested them that she might have liberty to walk in some place, for that she felt herself not well'. They were sorry, came the response, but 'they had commandment to the contrary, which they durst not in any wise break'. If that were so, then might she at least walk into the Queen's lodging? she asked. This too was denied her. 'Well,' she replied. 'My Lords, if the matter be so hard, that they must be sued unto for so small a thing, and that friendship be so strict, God comfort me.'[27]

The newly ennobled Lord Chandos, a kindly man, felt troubled at having to deny Elizabeth's supplication. So much so that he approached the Council to seek permission 'for further liberty' for her. Even on this small point the men were divided, however, 'for that there were so many prisoners in the Tower'. After some debate they agreed that Elizabeth might walk in the Queen's apartments on condition that she was accompanied by Lord Chandos, the Lord Chamberlain and three of the Queen's gentlewomen. In a further ridiculous twist that reflected their concerns about the esteem in which Elizabeth was held and possible reactions should she be seen by the populace, the Council ruled that, while doing so, the windows must be shut and Elizabeth 'not suffered to look out at any of them'.[28] Lord Chandos was able to deliver this slightly heartening news to her the following day, 'wherewith she contented herself, and gave him thanks for his good will in that behalf'.[29] Before long this privilege was extended, and she was allowed to walk in the Privy Garden of the Tower, 'the doors and gates being shut up'.[30] As one who had always been fond of fresh air and exercise, Elizabeth was grateful for this small concession.

According to some reports, Elizabeth was also comforted at this time by the small offerings of a little boy who regularly brought her gifts of flowers.[31] This tale has often been supposed apocryphal, but Renard refers to it too in his reports. Foxe claimed that this young child soon drew the suspicions of the Lord Chamberlain, who told the 'crafty boy' that 'thou shalt be whipped, if thou come any more to the Lady Elizabeth, or the Lord Courtenay'. Rather than being afraid, however, the boy defiantly answered, 'I will bring my Lady my mistress more flowers,' causing the Chamberlain to order the boy's father to keep him away. The following day, Elizabeth was walking in the garden when the boy, 'peeping in at a hole in the door, cried unto her, saying, "Mistress, I can bring you no more flowers."' Elizabeth smiled but said nothing, understanding full well the reasoning.[32] Clearly, there was a fear that the child was being used as a means of communication between Courtenay and Elizabeth, for on 1 May Renard suggested that the former was using the boy, 'a child of five, the son of one of the soldiers in the Tower, to present his commendations to Elizabeth'.[33] Writing in the seventeenth century, clergyman John Strype noted that this boy was the child of one Martin, keeper of the wardrobe, and also claimed that Elizabeth was visited by a little girl named Susanna, who was 'not above three or four years old'. Susanna 'once innocently brought her some little keys she had got, and telling her, she had brought her keys now, that she might go abroad'.[34]

Aside from Renard's suspicions, there is no evidence that Elizabeth was communicating with Courtenay during her time in the Tower, and frankly she was too preoccupied with her own circumstances to have any wish to be. Neither is there anything to suggest she was in contact with another Tower prisoner with whom she was familiar: her friend and, later, suitor, Robert Dudley. Robert had been imprisoned in the Tower since the previous summer, along with his brothers John, Ambrose and Henry (Guildford had been executed alongside Lady Jane Grey), for the roles they had played in challenging Mary's claim to the throne, and though Robert had been condemned in January, no further action had been taken against him.[35] It is possible that he and Elizabeth may have caught the occasional glimpse of one another during their time as prisoners, but given the restrictions on Elizabeth's liberty it seems improbable that there was anything further.

Elizabeth was, in fact, intent on doing her utmost to be seen to conform as far as possible. She would later tell Sir Henry Bedingfield a tale whereby her attendant, Lady Anne Grey (although this may, perhaps, have been Honora Grey, rather than Anne), produced an English prayer book a few days after Elizabeth's arrival at the Tower.[36] Knowing this to be a flagrant sign of Protestantism, Elizabeth had told Lady Grey that unless the Lord Chamberlain permitted her to use it, she would refrain from doing so. Permission was duly granted, and it was only then that Elizabeth proceeded to make use of the book.[37] Displaying the caution that she had been forced to put into practice over the course of both her brother Edward's reign and Mary's, she was determined not to antagonize the Queen or give her cause to move against her while she remained in the Tower.

An incomplete pocket-sized copy of Coverdale's 1538 translation of the New Testament, now in the British Library, contains a short poem written by Elizabeth, possibly around this time and addressed to Anne Poyntz.[38] How Elizabeth came to own the book is unknown, but it is tantalizing to consider the possibility that she may have composed the poem if not while in the Tower, then some time shortly after. It is certainly likely that it was written either in the 1540s or the early 1550s, as her signature does not contain the customary 'R' (Regina) that she habitually used when signing her name following her accession. The book could have been given to her by Katherine Parr, or perhaps Coverdale himself. Either way, Elizabeth was just halfway through the third word of the poem when she seems to have felt unhappy or that she had made some error, prompting her to abandon the page altogether and begin afresh on the next.[39] In her neat hand, she wrote:

> *Among good things*
> *I prove and find, the quiet*
> *life doth much abound,*
> *and sure to the contented*
> *mind, there is no riches*
> *may be found.*
>
> *Your loving mistress [the word 'friend', which was originally*
> *chosen, has been deleted]*
> *Elizabeth*[40]

The content of the poem, referencing as it does a 'quiet life', suggests it was written at a time when Elizabeth was living away from court, perhaps during or in the aftermath of her spell of imprisonment on the orders of her sister when she yearned for freedom. The poem that Anne wrote on the opposite page in response – at the end of which she signed herself 'your friend Anne Poyntz' – somewhat corroborates this. In a nod to the fleetingness of youth, she observed that 'our young days fly away then age calls for his right', before ending with the poignant lines: 'so life by death and death by life shall bring us all to well or woe'.[41] Could this have been a reference to the uncertain future Elizabeth faced? Although there is no reference to Anne Poyntz joining Elizabeth in the Tower or during her subsequent imprisonment, she was a member of her household, corroborated by Elizabeth referring to herself as her friend's 'mistress'.[42] We cannot know for certain if Elizabeth and Anne wrote their poems in this dangerous period of Elizabeth's life, but the book survives as a tangible reminder of an intriguing possibility.

ON 22 APRIL Renard reaffirmed what everybody already knew: 'The lawyers find no sufficient evidence to condemn her.'[43] Moreover, 'even if there were evidence, they would not dare to proceed against her because her relative, the Admiral, has espoused her cause, and controls all the forces of England. If she is released, the heretics will probably proclaim her Queen.'[44] The Admiral of whom he spoke was Lord William Howard, the same maternal relative who had escorted Elizabeth from Ashridge to London earlier that year.[45] Howard had only recently received the position of Lord Admiral and had also been created Baron Howard of Effingham, but there is no other evidence of him speaking up on Elizabeth's behalf. Indeed, several years later Count de Feria believed that she 'does not hold him in high esteem'.[46] Howard was not alone in his support for Elizabeth, for most Council members recognized that she could not be lawfully condemned. Yet still the debate concerning her future dragged on, and by 1 May Renard noted, 'As for her, no decision has yet been arrived at.'[47]

Elizabeth's fears were heightened, though, when on 5 May Sir Henry Bedingfield replaced Lord Chandos as the Lieutenant of the Tower. Bedingfield was unfamiliar to Elizabeth, and she was seriously alarmed when he arrived at the Tower with one hundred soldiers. As she saw them marching into the complex wearing their blue coats, she panicked that their coming indicated her own imminent removal. Terrified, she asked her servants 'whether the Lady Jane's scaffold were taken away or no'. Her cousin's fate, and likely also her mother's, were evidently haunting her, and she was relieved when she was told that the scaffold had been taken down. This calmed her, though she was still sufficiently anxious to wonder why Bedingfield had been sent. Could it be that 'her murdering were secretly committed to his charge'?[48] She would soon discover that Bedingfield was not cut from that cloth.

While Elizabeth remained locked away, many of the arrested rebels were gradually freed. There were rumours that Courtenay would be set at liberty, though he would in fact be removed from the Tower on 25 May, to be sent to the old Yorkist stronghold of Fotheringhay under the custodianship of Sir Thomas Tresham.[49] Sir James Croft was also later pardoned, as were Elisabeth Brooke's brothers. These men would all, in time, serve Elizabeth.[50]

As for Elizabeth herself, she would not have to endure the excruciating wait for much longer. It was becoming ever more difficult to find grounds to keep her in the Tower, and Mary was forced to grudgingly acknowledge that an alternative would have to be found. Yet she was by no means content to release Elizabeth entirely, and thus it was finally decided to send her to the old royal palace of Woodstock, where she would remain under house arrest. Unlike her mother, then, Elizabeth survived the Tower.

ELIZABETH'S IMPRISONMENT IN the Tower came to an end when, at around three o'clock in the afternoon of 19 May 1554, she was taken from its walls. In what was probably a deliberate irony, it was the eighteenth anniversary of Anne Boleyn's execution. Elizabeth's incarceration in the ancient fortress had lasted for nine weeks, but she had survived the ordeal and emerged from the Tower physically unscathed, though not emotionally. Her time there had a profound and lasting impact, instilling in her an intense hatred for the Tower, and she would never forget her experience. As Elizabeth 'went through London Bridge in her barge', though she understood that she was still a prisoner, she was relieved to leave the Tower behind her.[51] She must also have been heartened at the sight of the Londoners; the disgusted Imperial ambassadors noted that 'the people rejoiced at her departure, thinking she had been set at liberty'.[52] Several citizens, sensing that this was the case, fired cannons in celebration, much to the displeasure of the Queen and the Council when they heard of it. According to the seventeenth-century clergyman John Strype, a number of people took to boats on the Thames in order to catch a glimpse of her, and though they were happy to see her they were 'heavy for her trouble'.[53] For Elizabeth's trials were not at an end: as she arrived at Richmond Palace, her ordeal of house imprisonment had only just begun.

CHAPTER 16

'Worse Case than the Worst Prisoner in Newgate'

'We have appointed our sister the Lady Elizabeth, for divers good considerations, to be removed from our Tower of London unto our manor of Woodstock, there to remain until we shall otherwise determine.'

MARY I TO SIR HENRY BEDINGFIELD, 21 MAY 1554

LIZABETH MAY HAVE been relieved to reach the familiar surroundings of Richmond Palace, but her stay was to be of short duration. It was probably while she was there that a story was reported whereby a guard, known as Allen, 'brought her a dish of apples, and thought also to have delivered her book, supposing that she had been delivered, and no prisoner'. The unfortunate guard was supposedly committed to prison himself for his mistake, on the orders of the man who had now been charged with overseeing Elizabeth's continued imprisonment: Sir Henry Bedingfield.[1] Elizabeth was panicked when she found that Bedingfield's soldiers guarded her room, and once again wondered if she was to be secretly assassinated. 'Calling her gentleman-usher to her, she desired that he might pray for her, for this night, "I think to die."' Horrified, he cried, 'God forbid that any such wickedness should be pretended against your grace.'[2] Bedingfield was no assassin, but to Elizabeth's great frustration he would follow his instructions regarding her custodianship to the letter.

Mindful of both the cost and the responsibility that such a post entailed, none among Mary's Council had volunteered for the role of Elizabeth's jailer, forcing the Queen to make a choice. Sir Henry Bedingfield was a man of unswerving loyalty who had wholeheartedly supported Mary during the coup of 1553. At nearly fifty years old and sporting a grey beard and moustache, he hailed from a Catholic family of Norfolk origin, and Henry VIII had appointed his father, Edmund, to oversee the household of Katherine of Aragon at Kimbolton Castle after he had separated from her.[3] It was therefore either a strange coincidence or a deliberate peculiarity that Mary now opted to appoint the son of the man who had watched over her mother to guard her sister.[4] Sir Henry was obviously considered a safe pair of hands when it came to guarding royal persons. He was well rewarded for his loyalty to Mary, for he had already been appointed to the Privy Council prior to obtaining the post of Lieutenant of the Tower, in addition to an annual pension of £100 (£20,000). His role as Elizabeth's jailer, however, was one that would cause him an extraordinary level of stress and anxiety.

AFTER A STAY of just one night, Elizabeth left Richmond on the first stage of her journey to Woodstock, there to remain at the Queen's pleasure. On what would be a four-day journey, she was escorted by Sir Henry Bedingfield, his brother Edmund and Henry VIII's former Master of the Jewels, Sir John Williams.[5] Thanks to Bedingfield's letters, which survive among his carefully preserved papers and in which he detailed every particular, we know that what was intended to be the transportation of a prisoner transpired to be a kind of progress that showcased Elizabeth's popularity with her sister's subjects to the extreme. It was a progress with one crucial difference, though: Elizabeth was not Queen.

Elizabeth was joined by the few ladies and members of her household who had been allowed to accompany her, including Lady Grey (whether Anne or Honora) and possibly Etheldreda Malte and Isabella Markham too – according to Isabella's son, at some time following her liberation from the Tower in 1554 Elizabeth gave Isabella a rare copper engraving of herself 'as a token of her affection'.[6] Thus it is possible that, as she journeyed, Elizabeth was at least with some of those of whom she was fond. The party's first stop was Windsor, where Elizabeth was lodged in the Dean's House, 'a place more meet indeed for a priest than a princess'.[7] From there, she was taken in a litter on the next stage of her journey, accompanied not only by Bedingfield but also by Sir John Norris, brother of the executed Sir Henry Norris. People gathered in Windsor to watch as Elizabeth left, escorted by Norris's servants in their tawny coats. She passed by Eton College, where the scholars came out to greet her, and in every village people lined the streets to cheer her. Women tossed homemade cakes and wafers into the passing litter, a kind gesture for which Elizabeth was grateful.[8] However, the gifts eventually became so numerous that she was obliged to ask the people to stop. It was little wonder she was exhausted by the time she reached West Wycombe, where she was to lodge in the house of Sir William Dormer. Greeted by Sir William half a mile from his home, as Elizabeth arrived at the house she was welcomed by Lady Dormer and Sir William's daughter Jane – the same Jane who served the Queen and is one of the sources for Elizabeth's life.[9] It is perhaps unsurprising, then, given Jane's loyalties, that Elizabeth chose to retire straight to her chamber for the evening, although Bedingfield noted that her host was very hospitable towards her.[10]

After a night spent in the Dormer household, Elizabeth climbed into her litter once more. Yet again people had gathered to see her, but there was no opportunity for her to engage with them. As she left West Wycombe, the litter made its way across fifteen miles of bumpy country roads to the Buckinghamshire village of Aston Clinton, where four men were so eager to welcome their guest that they rushed to the ancient church of St Michael and All Angels to ring the bells; an unimpressed Bedingfield had the men punished.[11] Elizabeth rested that evening at Thame, in the home of Sir John Williams, who treated her with great kindness. Lady Williams was waiting to greet her, and she and other gentlewomen 'did entertain her grace' before Elizabeth retired to her rooms, where she took supper with Lady Williams.[12]

According to Foxe, Bedingfield was most displeased with the level of ceremony employed at Thame, and reminded Sir John that Elizabeth was 'the Queen's Majesty's prisoner'. He was aware of that, came Williams' response, but 'her grace might and should in his house be merry'.[13] Despite the circumstances, Elizabeth seems to have liked Sir John's home and relished the chance to stroll in his garden the following morning. Such pleasures had been few and far between in recent months. She was given a brief opportunity to inspect Sir John's 'great gallery', but it was not long before she was once more stepping into her litter as she bade Lady Williams farewell.[14]

In each town and village she passed through, people thronged to see her, crying out their well wishes and craning their necks for a glimpse of her. The party journeyed through Wheatley, Stanton St John, Islip – where a minstrel began to strum a tune for her – and Gosworth.[15] After Gosworth the litter finally approached its destination: Woodstock. By now, Elizabeth had become used to the townsfolk and villagers gathering to see her, and upon her arrival at Woodstock on 23 May her reception was no different. Her litter made its way through the gates of the old royal palace and people cried out their welcome, but Elizabeth, utterly exhausted after four days of uncomfortable roads and continued unease concerning her circumstances, immediately retired to her lodgings. She was painfully aware that she had reached her next prison, with no idea of when – or if – she would leave.

The royal palace that would now be Elizabeth's prison had a long history. Initially a hunting lodge that had been transformed into a palace by Henry II, Woodstock had enjoyed both prestige and popularity with its royal owners.[16] In 1330, Edward III and Philippa of Hainault's eldest son, the Black Prince, was born at Woodstock, and one of his daughters was married there in 1361.[17] Elizabeth's grandfather, Henry VII, also favoured the palace, on which he spent a vast sum and chose to celebrate Prince Arthur's betrothal to Katherine of Aragon there in 1497. Woodstock had then been a luxurious residence that boasted two great halls, a jewel house and a gatehouse, all of which contained equally lavish interiors. The Venetian ambassador, Andrea Trevisano, who visited the King there in 1497, had been awestruck not only by the monarch but also by Woodstock's furnishings. In 1554, however, there was little of this splendour to be seen, for the Palace had become neglected and fallen into a state of disrepair.[18] It was now damp and cold and difficult for Bedingfield to secure, given that only three of the doors in the entire Palace could be bolted and barred.[19] The lack of security proved to be a cause of constant worry to him, 'to the great disquiet and trouble of mind', heightened by the fact that he was not only unfamiliar with the area but also responsible for such an important charge.[20] Although Woodstock's dilapidation rendered it highly unsuitable for someone of Elizabeth's status, it was to become her 'home' for almost a year.

Elizabeth was disappointed when Sir John Williams, who had accompanied her the whole way from Richmond, took his leave the day after their arrival. She was fond of him but knew Mary had given orders that none save the Queen's own servants and a handful of Elizabeth's were to be allowed access to her.[21] She had probably also learned from the paranoid Bedingfield that the Queen had issued him with a set of written orders that detailed the way in which Elizabeth was to be treated. These made it clear that, though her sister had not yet been fully absolved of that which she stood accused, it was Mary's wish that Elizabeth should be treated 'in such good and honourable sort as may be agreeable to our honour and her estate and degree'.[22] Judging by the instructions from both the Queen and Council, coupled with her clashes with Bedingfield in the coming months, Elizabeth would have refuted that she ever received such treatment.

Elizabeth was lodged in four rooms in the gatehouse of her grandfather's creation, which were decorated with a mixture of Mary's belongings and her own. For Elizabeth, who had long since grown used to presiding over her own household, with whole estates to command, such confinement came as a huge blow. Given her love of the outdoors, the saving grace was that Mary had given permission for her to walk in the palace gardens. Less agreeable to her was that when doing so she had always to be accompanied by Bedingfield, who took care to ensure that 'the doors were fast locked up' between her lodgings and the gardens.[23] This caused Elizabeth so much irritation that on one occasion she called him her jailer. Mortified, Bedingfield knelt before her and begged her not to call him so, for he had merely been appointed to be one of her officers. 'From such officers,' she retorted, 'good Lord deliver me!'[24]

Bedingfield's presence was not the only trial Elizabeth was forced to endure. Her laundry was to be collected and delivered by the Queen's women, and anything brought to Woodstock for her was first to be searched by Bedingfield or one of his brothers, who had joined him at the dilapidated Palace.[25] Bedingfield was to monitor any conversation she might have, and Elizabeth was forbidden from sending or receiving messages or tokens. Sir Henry was so concerned about incurring the Queen's wrath that he questioned the Council over every minute detail. For example, did the conversations with 'suspected persons' that Elizabeth had been banned from having relate solely to strangers, or did it also apply to members of her household?[26] Bedingfield also forbade Elizabeth's gentleman-usher, Francis Cornwallis, from hanging up her cloth of estate, a tangible sign of her status, until he received the Council's orders. The list of his concerns went on and on, and as it did so, Elizabeth's patience became ever more frayed.[27]

To begin with, Bedingfield reported that his charge was 'in reasonable health and quietness', but it is hardly surprising that before long Elizabeth had grown bored and frustrated by her captivity.[28] She resented having her wings clipped, and Bedingfield's stringency only made an already difficult situation infinitely worse. During the course of her time at Woodstock, she is supposed to have used a diamond to make an engraving on a windowpane: 'Much suspected by me, Nothing proved can be, Quoth Elizabeth prisoner'.[29] It was an accurate summary of her situation.

Much of Elizabeth's only solace came from the handful of servants who had been allowed to accompany her. In addition to her two grooms and single yeoman, she relied on her three ladies to help her while away the tedious and long hours of captivity. Elizabeth Sandes, the servant who had been removed from Elizabeth in the Tower for her refusal to attend mass, had been allowed to re-join her mistress – but this was to be of short duration as her Protestant views once again created trouble, causing such offence that Bedingfield received orders to remove her. The

Queen referred to Sandes distastefully as 'a person of an evil opinion, and not fit to remain about our said sister's person'.[30] Realizing she could do nothing to prevent the dismissal of her lady, Elizabeth tried desperately to have Sandes replaced with either Dorothy Bradbelt or Elizabeth Norwich, the latter of whom had certainly been a part of her household and of whom she was evidently fond – both women would serve her when she became Queen.[31] Her request was denied. Instead, Elizabeth Marbery, whose husband also served Elizabeth, was brought in.[32] When Bedingfield arrived in Elizabeth's rooms to implement the removal of Sandes at two o'clock in the afternoon on 5 June, both women were greatly distressed. Sir Henry was unmoved by their tears, however, and Sandes was escorted home to her family.[33]

Elizabeth could, at least, still rely on the services of her cofferer Thomas Parry, who took up residence in a nearby inn, The Bull, in Woodstock.[34] From there he continued to oversee Elizabeth's affairs, including the management of her estates, but a suspicious Bedingfield thought that so many people visited the cofferer – forty a day, including both Elizabeth's servants and Parry's own – that plots were bound to be afoot. Parry also tried to send his mistress books, but Bedingfield, always a stickler for the rules, refused to allow this until the Council gave their permission.[35]

By 9 June, a little over two weeks after her arrival at Woodstock, Elizabeth began to feel unwell with 'swelling in the visage at certain times'.[36] Probably exacerbated – once again – by stress, as the month progressed her symptoms grew worse. Soon the swelling had spread to other parts of her body, causing her great discomfort. Unwell and miserable, Elizabeth became progressively more snappy with her jailer, an attitude Bedingfield suspected was also on account of the removal of Elizabeth Sandes.[37] Turning to her faith and abandoning the compliance she had earlier shown, she demanded an English Bible and was unhappy when told that she could only have a Latin version. Within half an hour, Bedingfield reported that 'in the most unpleasant sort that ever I saw her since her coming from the Tower', she had accused him of neglecting to pass on her numerous requests to the Council. Bedingfield denied this, insisting that the Council had important business that prevented it responding to her pleas immediately. She then pressed him to seek permission for her to write directly to the Queen, to which Bedingfield promised he would. She would, though, he told her, have to wait patiently for an answer. She must have been heartened a little, then, when she was told that the Council had granted her request for an English Bible – and that she was allowed to write to Mary.[38]

Elizabeth's letter has not survived, but we can get some sense of its contents from the replies, which came via Bedingfield from the Council and from Mary herself. In her illness, Elizabeth had asked for Dr Robert Huicke, her usual physician, to attend her. Huicke was sick, however, and as none of the usual royal physicians were available, the Council suggested alternatives local to Oxford.[39] Dr Owen even wrote to Bedingfield offering advice.[40] Elizabeth was unimpressed with these answers, refusing to see a physician she was not familiar with. By the time, though, that the Queen and Council sent their responses, they had more pressing affairs to deal with than Mary's complaining sister: they had left London bound for Winchester – and a royal wedding.

Mary was now preoccupied with plans for her impending marriage to Philip. It had been agreed that the fast-approaching wedding would take place in the ancient city of Winchester, which, given the recent troubles in London and the anti-Spanish mood there, seemed a safer alternative. In June, Mary and her court set out from Richmond on the first stage of their journey, but try as she might the Queen could not shake away all thoughts of Elizabeth. Her sister's letter, which had not been written in the most deferential of terms, had, apparently, once again reiterated Elizabeth's innocence, but the Queen remained sceptical. Mary felt that she had 'used more clemency and favour toward her then in the like matters hath been accustomed', and thus Elizabeth had been fortunate.[41] Showing one of Elizabeth's letters to Renard, he remarked that it was 'as bold as anything I have ever seen, never addressing the Queen except as "you", without qualifying her by the title of Highness or Majesty'.[42] But Mary was adamant that Elizabeth would not spoil her moment.

On 13 July, after much delay Philip finally set sail for England, leaving the port of La Coruña – and Spain – behind. The crossing was terrible,

Philip's friend and confidant Ruy Gómez later recollecting that 'since the world began there never was such a voyage as ours across the sea'.[43] Philip was among those who suffered from awful seasickness thanks to the rough waves of the Bay of Biscay. Eventually, he landed at Portsmouth and, on 23 July, he arrived in Winchester 'accompanied with noblemen as well of England as of his own country, with trumpets blowing and bells ringing'.[44] Two days later, on the feast day of St James, Philip and Mary's marriage was celebrated by Bishop Gardiner with 'the greatest solemnity' within Winchester Cathedral.[45] Mary was determined to make a magnificent impression, and having always adored finery she wore 'a rich dress and adorned with jewels'.[46] Philip's equally lavish costume had been designed to match.[47] The Queen's wedding ring, a band of plain gold, served as a contrast to the rest of the opulence. Following the hour-long ceremony, the newlyweds proceeded to Wolvesey Castle, the Winchester residence of Bishop Gardiner and a stone's throw from the Cathedral, where a sumptuous celebratory feast had been prepared for their enjoyment.[48] The day 'was spent in pleasure, and part of the night'.[49] Mary, and England, now had a Spanish, Catholic consort.

Elizabeth, and any thought of her, had no place in this most joyous of moments in Mary's life, and instead all of her energies were focused firmly in Philip's direction. She felt 'a violent love for him', and the day after the wedding she wrote to the Emperor, expressing her joy and gratitude for his role in allying her with 'a Prince so full of virtues'.[50] For the twenty-seven-year-old Philip, however, the marriage was merely a matter of policy, and shortly after the wedding his friend Gómez articulated a view that probably echoed Philip's own. Though he conceded that Mary 'is a very good creature', she was 'rather older than we had been told'.[51] Three years later, the Venetian ambassador Giovanni Michiel observed disparagingly that Mary had some wrinkles, 'caused more by anxieties than by age, which make her appear some years older'. By the same token, 'her voice is rough and loud, almost like a man's, so that when she speaks she is always heard a long way off'.[52] Despite Mary's age – by the time of her wedding she was thirty-eight – the loyal Gómez said, 'His Highness is so tactful and attentive to her that I am sure they will be very happy.'[53] Philip would do as he had been bid, but there was little in the way of romantic sentiment on his part for the woman a decade his senior.

Once the wedding celebrations had concluded, Mary and Philip made their way steadily back towards the capital, stopping at both Basing House and Windsor, before arriving at Richmond on 11 August. They then proceeded to Suffolk Place, from where they made their ceremonial entry into London amid the many pageants that had been especially devised for the occasion. The pageantry, nonetheless, did not reflect the mood of the people, who still loathed the idea of a Spanish consort. They particularly hated Philip's Spanish entourage, and Renard reported a story whereby a servant of the Lord Privy Seal 'tried to beat two Spaniards in the street at three o'clock in the afternoon, but seeing that he was not getting the best of it he pulled out a pistol from under his cloak, aimed it at one of them and then, when he was seven or eight houses off, fired it into the air to show what a brave man he was'.[54] This was just one example of anti-Spanish feeling, and in the years that followed, Mary's subjects would have further reason to resent Philip and mourn the day he ever set foot in England.

BACK AT WOODSTOCK, by the beginning of July Elizabeth had recovered from her malady sufficiently to walk in the gardens again, but her temper was still easily flared. The tension between her and Bedingfield had continued to grow, and by now he had refused to write to the Council on her behalf. As she savoured the fresh air one day, Elizabeth took the opportunity to upbraid him. Bedingfield listened as Elizabeth beseeched him that if he continued in his refusal to write, 'I shall be in worse case than the worst prisoner in Newgate.'[55] She believed that with no friend to speak for her, her cause was lost.

Elizabeth was becoming desperate in her craving for freedom. She must have been dispirited to learn, then, that she was no longer permitted to write directly to Mary, no doubt because of what was perceived to be a lack of respect in her letters. On 30 July, she again begged Bedingfield to write to the Council for her, 'considering her long imprisonment and restraint of liberty, either to charge her with special matter to be answered unto and tried, or to grant her liberty to come unto her Highness's presence'. She would not have asked to do so, 'were it not she knoweth herself to be clear even before God'.[56] She was utterly depressed, feeling as though she had been forgotten and left in limbo, neither free nor condemned.

Elizabeth waited impatiently for some word from the Queen, but Mary, besotted with her husband, was in no hurry to provide one. By late August, Elizabeth had resorted to other tactics, and going against her principles in a bid to gain Mary's attention, she took the Catholic Holy Sacrament. Just before doing so, she summoned Bedingfield and one of the Queen's women and before them protested that she 'in all her life, had done nothing, nor intended to do, that was perilous to the person of the Queen's highness'.[57] Such shows achieved nothing, however, and she remained incarcerated. As autumn approached, relations between Elizabeth and Bedingfield continued to be fraught, and this was exacerbated in October when Elizabeth once again became ill. She sent a further plea for the royal physicians, Doctors Wendy, Owen and Huicke to attend her, and for a surgeon to let her blood. Mary conceded to her request, and Wendy and Owen duly arrived at Woodstock to tend to her. At court it was said that they had 'bled her in order to stop a running cold in the head from which she was suffering'.[58] Elizabeth was bled first from the arm and then from the foot, after which a relieved Bedingfield reported that she appeared to be a little better.[59]

Having regained her strength, in November Elizabeth petitioned Bedingfield to ask if it might be possible to move closer to London, perhaps even to one of her own houses, there to remain at the Queen's pleasure.[60] Her request was denied. What was more, though she had now recognized that her life was no longer in danger, she had greater reason than ever to feel insecure about her position: the Queen was believed to be pregnant.

On 18 September, Renard informed the Emperor that he had been told by the Queen's physician that 'she is very probably with child; and if it is true everything will calm down and go smoothly here'.[61] Indeed, he caused a rumour to be started to that effect. Although she was distant from London, it seems likely that Elizabeth would have come to hear the reports by means of one of her servants, and they must have left her uneasy. It was true that Mary was experiencing many of the symptoms of pregnancy, including sickness and swollen breasts, and by early November Renard was in no doubt that the physician had been right, for her 'stomach clearly shows it and her dresses no longer fit her'.[62] On 27 November, the news was confirmed when Mary believed she felt the baby stir within her; it was publicly proclaimed throughout London: the royal baby was expected in May. On both a personal and a political level, the Queen was over-joyed, believing she would soon succeed in doing her duty to provide her husband and her country with a Catholic heir. How and when Elizabeth officially heard the tidings of her sister's pregnancy is unknown, but she must have started to wonder what her own future held. If Mary did indeed succeed in bearing a child, where would Elizabeth fit in?

The fact that Elizabeth remained a prisoner, albeit in far less fearful surroundings than she had experienced in the Tower, was not popular among the English people. In January 1555, Renard believed that the brother of the French ambassador Noailles was plotting both on her behalf and with her, with a view to marrying her to Courtenay and enticing the people to revolt. He revealed, 'Several persons have been arrested, who had been holding nightly meetings and heretic rites, praying for the said Elizabeth's freedom and prosperity. Writings have been found in several public places praying God to deliver Elizabeth soon from her captivity.'[63] By March, Renard had heard that Elizabeth had turned to religion in her desperation to win her freedom, and was doing all she could to be seen as a good Catholic:

> According to the reports of the person who is in charge with Elizabeth, she has obtained the indulgencies that have been published in this kingdom, attends mass every day and does her utmost to give the impression that she has changed her religion. Nevertheless, he sees that she is plotting, because she withdraws two or three hours every day under colour of wishing to pray, and has a treasurer and purveyor who often speak to her apart, pretexting special business. However, she is too clever to get herself caught.[64]

Elizabeth's apparent willingness to conform to Catholicism in her times of trouble or moments of vulnerability gives us an insight into her tumultuous state of mind, but it was already obvious – and would later become clearer still – that she had been disingenuous in this regard. We do not know whether there was any truth to the rumours that she was plotting – given her yearning for liberty it is conceivable that she did share dangerous conversations, but it is also feasible that she employed other tactics in her attempts to gain it. After all, she was intuitive enough to recognize that she was being closely watched, and attending Catholic devotions provided a tangible means of appearing to counteract the risk she posed to Mary. She would have been aware that she had plenty of supporters, and Renard was convinced that 'this kingdom will never be at peace until the Elizabeth and Courtenay matter is settled'.[65]

With talk of Elizabeth widespread, it was unsurprising that her future had again become a topic of conversation at court. Renard's reports show that there was still division and confusion, for while both Mary and the Council recognized that Elizabeth could not remain under house imprisonment indefinitely, there seemed to be no viable alternative. While she was held captive she would always be a figure of dissent to those who opposed Mary and the idea of Spanish rule, but the same would be true if she were free. In either scenario, on a political level Elizabeth posed a threat, thus underscoring the difficulty of any decision over her future. Talk of marrying her off to neutralize her was once again rife. Not for the first time, Paget told Renard that this, in his view, was the best way of dealing with her, perhaps with a German prince.[66] He even thought that Courtenay would be a good possibility, but it is probable that this was a suggestion made with one eye on his own future should Mary not produce an heir. The Emperor was very much of the opinion that Elizabeth ought to be removed in some way, but nobody quite knew how. Perhaps she could be sent abroad, it was proposed.[67] Gardiner was a strong advocate of having Elizabeth declared formally illegitimate, a move that was opposed by Philip, who now also became a part of the conversations on her fate. His reasoning was his desire to keep England under Spanish control if Mary either failed to provide an heir or died, for he had no desire to give the French any opportunity to push for the candidacy of Mary, Queen of Scots, who was living at the French court and betrothed to the Dauphin, which they were likely to do if Elizabeth was declared illegitimate. He instead made it clear that his preferred method of dealing with Elizabeth was to see her married in order to control her position and nullify the potential threat she posed, and he already had a contender in mind.

Emmanuel Philibert, Prince of Piedmont and titular Duke of Savoy, was Philip's cousin, an ally of Spain and, crucially, a Catholic. He was also, according to the Venetian ambassador Giovanni Michiel, a man of 'pleasing presence, and was educated in conformity with Italian manners and customs'.[68] From Philip's perspective he was the ideal candidate, for if Mary should die childless, then with Elizabeth married to one of his allies his interests in England would still be protected. For the time being, however, marriage with Savoy remained nothing more than an option.

AT THE END of March 1555, Renard, who had formerly been so confident of Mary's pregnancy, expressed doubt that she was with child at all. It was this uncertainty that led him to confide his fears for the future of the realm to Philip:

> The kingdom is in uncertainty as to the succession to the Crown. Supposing the Queen is not with child and dies without issue there will certainly be strife, and the heretics will espouse the cause of the Lady Elizabeth. If she is set aside, the next heir would be the Queen of Scotland. But if Elizabeth does succeed, the kingdom will certainly return to heresy and to alliance with the French unless adequate measures are taken to prevent it. If Elizabeth is married to an Englishman, she will prevail upon her husband to adopt the new religion, even if he is a Catholic. If a foreign husband is found for her, it will be necessary to make sure that he is constant and faithful to your Majesty, for it is essential to keep England on good terms with your states and to prevent the enemy from getting a foothold here.[69]

Renard was not telling Philip anything he did not already know, and Mary's husband had already resolved that it would be wise to court the friendship of the next in line to the throne. This became even more pertinent when Courtenay was freed from Fotheringhay in April, making a decision on Elizabeth's future more pressing than ever. Seizing an opportune moment, Lord Admiral Howard, Elizabeth's uncle, proposed to the Council that 'it would also be fit to release the other less guilty prisoners, meaning by that the Lady Elizabeth, for otherwise it would be unjust'. The Council agreed, and much to Renard's disappointment, 'it was then decided to bring Elizabeth here to court in a few days, before the Queen's confinement takes place. Thus both she and Courtenay are going to be reinstated or forgiven, and the Queen will remain in the same uncertainty and fear.'[70] In Elizabeth's case, however, reinstatement and forgiveness were far from Mary's mind.

At the beginning of April, Mary and Philip withdrew to Hampton Court, where the Queen took to her chamber to await the birth of her child. While Courtenay had been sent abroad following his liberation, Mary, encouraged by Philip, decided that the best course of action was to keep Elizabeth close at hand. The Queen was believed to be 'in better humour', and it seems she may also have wanted Elizabeth nearby when she bore the child that was to displace her sister from the succession, for with her pregnancy Mary felt that both Elizabeth and Courtenay posed less of a threat.[71] Thus, there was no longer any need to keep them so closely guarded. There was probably another reason too, at least from Philip's perspective, for if Mary did not survive the ordeal of childbirth, Elizabeth would be nearby and thus easier for him to control. Yet this did not mean Elizabeth would be welcomed back with open arms.

On 17 April, Elizabeth was summoned to join the Queen and attend her lying in: her spell of imprisonment at Woodstock was finally at an end. She wasted no time in making her preparations as per Mary's orders – though she was not yet rid of Bedingfield, who was to escort her to Hampton Court. Once there, Elizabeth would continue to be a thorn in Mary's side, but temporarily at least the spotlight was no longer on the Queen's sister. All eyes now turned to the Queen: it was down to Mary to bear an heir.

CHAPTER 17

Think Me To Be Your True Subject'

'Her Majesty willeth me to tell you, that you must tell another tale ere that you be set at liberty.'

BISHOP GARDINER TO ELIZABETH IN FOXE'S *MIRACULOUS PRESERVATION*, MAY 1555

FTER ALMOST A year spent within the confines of the damp and dilapidated Woodstock, the red-brick magnificence of Hampton Court was a welcome sight indeed. It was also bittersweet, for despite the change of scene Elizabeth was still escorted by Bedingfield and had yet to be granted her full liberty. As her litter drew into the courtyard of the Palace some time towards the end of April, she must have wondered what lay in store for her as she prepared to witness this moment of Mary's hoped-for triumph: would she be welcomed in a spirit of reconciliation, or would she be forced to endure humiliation as the fruits of Mary's belly – and her own demotion in status – were paraded in front of her?

The circumstances of Elizabeth's arrival at the Palace that her father had spent such great sums on extending and beautifying were a far cry from the joyous reception she had received when joining Katherine Parr there during the summer of her regency, just over a decade earlier. Now, only three or four ladies and several gentlemen accompanied her as she arrived quietly, there to be housed, according to Foxe, in the apartment Elizabeth's brother had once occupied during childhood.[1] She must have

THINK ME TO BE YOUR TRUE SUBJECT'

known that Mary's retreat into confinement as she awaited the birth of her child made it improbable she would be granted an audience immediately, and she was right. A fortnight passed with Elizabeth living quietly at the Palace, and most of Mary's courtiers, aware that she was still in disgrace, avoided her rooms. Soldiers guarded her door – but one day they allowed a visitor to pass. The face of her uncle, Lord Admiral Howard, who had petitioned for her release from the Tower, perhaps came as a relief to Elizabeth, despite the fact she was later believed to have no fondness for him. At this moment, however, Howard 'marvellous honourably used her grace', and she entreated him to beg an audience with the Council for her.[2] Sure enough, before long Lord Chancellor Gardiner, the Earl of Arundel, the Earl of Shrewsbury and Lord Petre visited and 'with great humility, humbled themselves to her Grace'. She finally had the opportunity she had long been craving to speak to those closest to Mary: 'My Lords, I am glad to see you: for methinks I have been kept a great while from you desolately, alone. Wherefore I would desire you to be a means to the King and Queen's Majesties, that I may be delivered from prison, wherein I have been kept a long space, as to you, my Lords, it is not unknown.'[3]

Listening intently, though Gardiner disliked Elizabeth he now kneeled before her and urged her to submit herself to Mary's grace, for 'in so doing he had no doubt but that her Majesty would be good to her'. He was advising her to confess that she had plotted against the Queen, but Elizabeth was not going to admit to any wrongdoing now. She resolutely told Gardiner that 'she would [rather] lie in prison all the days of her life'.[4] She did not seek mercy, for she had done no wrong. Renard heard that the councillors, recognizing that imprisonment had not weakened Elizabeth's resolve, took the opportunity to 'induce her to go to Flanders' in the hope of removing her from the realm, thereby solving the problem of her future. From Mary's perspective, they felt this was the safest course of action, as 'if Elizabeth stays in this kingdom, the country and the Queen will always have trouble'. Renard acknowledged and agreed with Philip's viewpoint, though, for Mary's husband 'considers that it would be better to keep her here until after the Queen's confinement; and there may be something in this, as the confinement is so near'.[5]

The day after Elizabeth's meeting with Mary's councillors, Gardiner paid her another visit. He had consulted with Mary and knelt once more as he informed her that the Queen marvelled at her refusal to confess to any wrongdoing, 'so that it should seem that the Queen's Majesty had wrongfully imprisoned her Grace'. Sensing danger, Elizabeth was cautious. 'Nay,' she replied. 'It may please her to punish me as she thinketh good.' This was not good enough for Gardiner, and in an attempt to force her to admit to plotting against Mary, he told Elizabeth that the Queen would not release her unless she confessed. Elizabeth refused to be drawn into the trap: she would not admit to something she had not done, she told him, but would rather 'be in prison with honesty and truth, as to be abroad, suspected of her majesty'.[6] A stalemate was reached: Gardiner left without the confession he had been hoping for, while Elizabeth remained under guard.

Another week passed before, at ten o'clock one evening, Elizabeth received a summons. She was so 'amazed' at having been sent for so suddenly that, thinking the worst, she 'desired her gentlemen and gentle-women to pray for her'. Escorted by Bedingfield and Mary's most trusted servant, Susan Clarencius, Elizabeth was led through the darkness across the garden to the foot of a staircase that led to Mary's lodgings. Her gentle-man-usher and grooms lit the stairway with their torches as Elizabeth ascended, followed by her ladies. All save Clarencius were commanded to remain outside, though, as Elizabeth was taken to the Queen's bedcham-ber. According to Foxe, Mary's husband, Philip, stood behind a cloth in the room to witness the first meeting that took place between the two sisters in over a year – his first glimpse of his sister-in-law. We can only imagine what Elizabeth and Mary felt as they observed one another for the first time since one sister had been accused of plotting against the other, but at this moment Elizabeth did not hesitate and immediately knelt before her sister. Mary's eyes were 'so piercing that they inspire, not only respect, but fear, in those on whom she fixes them', and at this moment they rested firmly on Elizabeth.[7]

After desiring 'God to preserve her Majesty', Elizabeth wasted no time in declaring to Mary that which she had longed to for more than a year:

her innocence. She insisted that Mary 'should not find her to the contrary, whatsoever report otherwise had gone of her'. But the Queen's response was cool, with not even a hint of familial warmth: 'You will not confess your offence, but stand stoutly to your truth: I pray God it may so fall out.' 'If it doth not,' Elizabeth replied, 'I request neither favour nor pardon at your Majesty's hands.' Mary was not impressed: 'You stiffly still persevere in your truth. Belike you will not confess but that you have been wrongfully punished.' Aware that Mary was scrutinizing her every word, Elizabeth demurely answered, 'I must not say so if it please your Majesty, to you.' But, her senses heightened, Mary immediately shot back: 'Belike you will to others.' Elizabeth denied this: 'I have borne the burden, and must bear it. I humbly beseech your Majesty to have a good opinion of me, and to think me to be your true subject, not only from the beginning hitherto, but for ever, as long as life lasteth.' Elizabeth, though admitting no wrongdoing, was begging for the Queen's forgiveness, but Mary remained unmoved. She would not be swayed by words, and with that their meeting came to an end. As a crestfallen Elizabeth departed for her lodgings, she realized that the rift between herself and Mary was far from healed. Indeed, it appeared worse than ever.

Though the Queen remained hostile she felt less threatened by her sister, and Foxe noted that a week after the meeting with Mary, Bedingfield and his soldiers were discharged from watching over the young woman that he had guarded so carefully, although unsurprisingly, Renard in particular remained mistrustful of Elizabeth.[8] Everything now depended on Mary's safe delivery, for if she were to produce an heir, Elizabeth's own position in the line of succession would be significantly undermined and the future security of the Catholic faith and Spain's own grip on English affairs would be secured. Back on 1 April, the Venetian ambassador Giovanni Michiel had reported that to encourage the Queen in the days approaching her own delivery, 'three most beautiful infants were brought last week for her Majesty to see, they having been born a few days previously at one birth, of a woman of low stature and great age like the Queen'. The woman had survived the birth, and the sight of her and her children 'greatly rejoiced her Majesty'.[9] Her subjects were also jubilant when at the end of the month it was falsely reported in London that the Queen had been delivered of a son, 'with little pain and no danger'.[10] Hearty celebrations erupted on the capital's streets, with roaring bonfires and the ringing of church bells. But the news was erroneous.

As May began, the Queen's delivery was expected daily, yet Mary showed no signs of labour. Initially, the delay was blamed on a miscalculation, but the days soon turned into weeks. As the end of June drew near, Renard declared that the royal baby was expected within the next eight to ten days.[11] By this time it was noticed that although Elizabeth had not been seen outside of her apartments, her attendants were allowed to come and go as they pleased. Doubtless they passed on word of the gossip surrounding the Queen's pregnancy, for though the wait continued, no baby appeared. It was now becoming glaringly obvious to all save Mary that she was not pregnant at all. By July, Mary's continued hope of producing a child was becoming an embarrassment. There was no longer any doubt among those around her that there was no child, and she herself was soon forced to face that humiliating reality. Over the past months, the Queen's women had continually assured her that she was undoubtedly pregnant, save one, Frideswide Strelley, much to Mary's displeasure.[12] But now, in her sorrow she sent for Frideswide. 'Ah, Strelley, Strelley, I see they be all but flatterers and none true to me but thou,' she lamented sadly.[13]

Several theories have been offered for Mary's condition in late 1554 and 1555, but it seems probable that she was experiencing a phantom pregnancy, during which she had many of the symptoms of the real thing.[14] It is impossible not to feel sympathy for Mary's plight, as on both a personal and a political level her longing for a child was genuine. It is rather sad that, while Mary was going through one of the most traumatic experiences of her life, Elizabeth, though still at court, remained a distant figure unable to offer comfort or support. Whatever had passed between them, it is difficult to imagine that Elizabeth did not feel some compassion for her sister and the humiliation Mary endured. Mary was mocked and became a subject of ridicule, and for Philip the situation was also a great embarrassment. It seriously undermined his position in his wife's country, for as father to the heir to the throne his importance would have been cemented. Without a child, he continued to see the advantages of keeping Elizabeth both alive and on-side. This worked in her favour too, and Venetian ambassador Giovanni Michiel later observed that the Queen's sister 'contrived so to ingratiate herself with all the Spaniards, and especially with the King, that ever since no one has favoured her more than he does'.[15] For her part, Elizabeth would later admit to Philip's envoy Count de Feria that she was grateful to the King, as he had 'shown her favour and helped to obtain her release'. Similarly, Jane Dormer recalled that it was Philip who 'dealt with the Queen to be merciful to [Elizabeth], and so delivered her not only from extreme punishment but procured her liberty to return to the Court'.[16] Disfavoured by Mary Elizabeth may have been, but there really was no further justification for leaving her under such close observation. What was more, Elizabeth recognized that her position was now stronger than ever before: while Mary remained child-less, she still stood as next in line to the throne.

LATER IN JULY, her hopes crushed, Mary was seen walking in the gardens at Hampton Court and she also began attending once more to matters of state. No official announcement about her condition was made, and the whole affair was put quietly to bed. In a sign that a line had been firmly drawn under the situation, on 4 August Mary and Philip left Hampton Court for the nearby Oatlands. Soon afterwards, Elizabeth was also given permission to leave Hampton Court, to allow the Palace to be thoroughly cleansed, and was told to 'withdraw with all her attendants to a house distant three miles from her Majesty's'. Ambassador Giovanni Michiel thought that Mary and Philip would soon return to Hampton Court, but Elizabeth would not. Instead, she would perhaps travel to one of her homes, 'as she is completely free'.[17]

Elizabeth may now have been at liberty, but Mary was still wary of her and never again would the two sisters be close. Rather than returning to one of her estates, Elizabeth remained near the royal couple throughout the summer of 1555, perhaps not completely of her own choice. Mary and Philip made a brief return to Hampton Court, but later in August Elizabeth joined them when they travelled to Greenwich.

Given that his wife had been unsuccessful in her hopes of providing him with a child, Philip saw no reason to remain in England, especially as his father the Emperor urgently needed his assistance in the Habsburg wars against France, wars that he himself was now too careworn to oversee. Much to Mary's sorrow, on 29 August Philip left Greenwich on the first stage of his journey to Spain. Though 'evidently deeply grieved internally', Mary conducted herself with the utmost dignity as she bade her beloved husband farewell. When she returned to her apartments, 'placing herself at a window which looks on the river, not supposing herself any longer seen or observed by any one, it was perceived that she gave free vent to her grief by a flood of tears, nor did she once quit the window until she had not only seen the King embark and depart, but remained looking after him as long as he was in sight'.[18] On 4 September, Philip set sail from Dover. Though he had assured his wife that his absence would be of short duration, Philip knew this to be a lie. It would be eighteen months before he set foot on English soil once more.

With Philip gone, Mary was desolate. She had been prone to bouts of anxiety and depression since the tumultuous days of her youth, but with no husband or child by her side she now sank into a deep state of melan-choly.[19] Unable to face putting the past to bed, she found no comfort in Elizabeth, with whom her relationship remained strained. In fact, Mary persisted in her resolve to remove Elizabeth from the line of succession. The lack of an heir of her body made this altogether trickier, but the idea of replacing Elizabeth with Mary's cousin, Lady Margaret Douglas, Countess of Lennox, reared its head once more. It was quickly abandoned when the Queen again recognized that excluding Elizabeth would mean attempting to overturn their father's will, and as the events of Mary's own accession had shown, this would be disastrously unpopular; the people, let alone the Council, would never accept it.

Instead, for reasons of his own, Philip advised his wife to treat Elizabeth courteously and wrote her regular letters in which he advocated such a course. To please her husband Mary tried, and even the French ambassador Noailles admitted that Elizabeth was 'more in favour than she used to be'.[20] It was later said that Mary 'dissembles her hatred and anger as much as she can, and endeavours when they are together in public to receive her with every sort of graciousness and honour, nor does she ever converse with her about any but agreeable subjects'.[21] But it was all an act; Mary took her role as Philip's wife seriously and his advice to heart. Though she attempted to be civil, it was nothing more than a placatory gesture employed with her husband's advice in mind.

Elizabeth probably recognized that Mary's courtesy was insincere, but must have been thrilled to be reunited with her former tutor, Roger Ascham, who had taken on the role of Mary's secretary. Ascham was delighted that at court, 'Lady Elizabeth and I read together in Greek the orations of Aeschines and Demosthenes on the Crown. She reads it first to me, and at first sight understands everything, not only the peculiarity of the language and the meaning of the orator.'[22] For Elizabeth and Ascham at least, it was like old times. However, in all other respects, Elizabeth's life had altered immeasurably, and in one respect in particular: religion. On 4 September, Elizabeth joined Mary for her religious observances, for on that day the whole court fasted and was pardoned for its sins.[23] It was a day full of the symbolism and ritual of Catholicism, but Elizabeth's heart was not in it and Mary knew it. The deterioration of her once sisterly relationship with Mary was heightened by the religious persecution that was by now taking hold in the realm. Throughout this, Elizabeth's popularity became glaringly apparent, while Mary's, once riding high, was rapidly dwindling.

LESS THAN A year after Mary's accession, in January 1554 the first English Protestants started to flee. By 12 November that year, Parliament had repealed an attainder against Mary's cousin Cardinal Reginald Pole, which had been implemented by Henry VIII because of Pole's extremely vocal opposition to his separation from Katherine of Aragon, which took the form of a defamatory treatise – so incensed had the King been that he took a terrible revenge against Pole's family.[24] Mary was eager for Pole's assistance in returning England to the folds of the Catholic Church in Rome, and upon the lifting of the attainder he travelled to England immediately, arriving just days later. Working as papal legate, Pole set to work straight away, intent on establishing a counter-reformation that would firmly bring England back under the wing of Rome.[25] The situation was quickly becoming worse for English Protestants, as Parliament had by now reintroduced all the former heresy laws, allowing Protestants to be tried and executed if they were found guilty of having beliefs at odds with those of the Catholic Church.

On 4 February 1555, the first Protestant burning of Mary's reign took place. At Smithfield, John Rogers, who had been condemned by Bishop Gardiner, was burned. Some wept as they watched the poor man's flesh become engulfed by the flames, others prayed for him, and many felt a great hatred for Mary's Catholic bishops who had been given the authority to root out and investigate those suspected of heresy.[26] Even Renard felt that the bishops had proceeded too hastily, and shared his view with Philip that the burnings should be prevented 'unless the reasons are overwhelmingly strong and the offenses committed have been so scandalous as to render this course justifiable in the eyes of the people'.[27] Five days later, Bishop John Hooper suffered at Gloucester and another clergyman, Rowland Taylor, was burned in Hadleigh.[28] These men were just the first of those who would face burning for their religious beliefs during Mary's reign, and among those who were also sentenced to face the flames was Elizabeth's godfather, Thomas Cranmer, the former Archbishop of Canterbury. Cranmer had already been condemned for treason, but would later be tried for heresy.[29] Having been 'disgraded of all his orders and dignities', despite his having recanted, he was burned at Oxford on 21 March 1556, retracting his recantations before he died.[30]

Death at the stake was truly terrible, and many of those who died in the flames were deemed martyrs to the Protestant faith. Mary has received an extremely bad press on account of the burnings that were staged throughout her reign, which have earned her the nickname of 'Bloody Mary'. This was largely thanks to the work of John Foxe, whose *Acts and*

Monuments – better known as the *Book of Martyrs* – first published in 1563 during Elizabeth's reign, formed the basis for Mary's reputation and charted the course of the burnings. Recent scholarship has done much to rehabilitate her image and highlight her successes as a Queen regnant and the challenges she faced as England's first crowned female monarch, and this reassessment is in many respects both welcome and justified.[31] When considering the burnings it is important to place Mary within the context of her European contemporaries in order to gain an accurate sense of perspective. It then becomes clear that her actions mirrored both those of the Habsburgs in the Netherlands and central Europe, and of François I in France, all of whom were, like Mary, intent on rooting out heresy, which these rulers considered to be their duty.[32] Yet it is she, rather than her male contemporaries, who has been censured for her stringency in doing so. This does not detract, though, from the fact that it was Mary alone who had the power to authorize the English burnings, in doing so ignoring both her husband and Gardiner who advised her to be cautious.[33] Neither can one escape from the reality that the numbers of those persecuted during her reign were unprecedented in England, a fact for which Mary must bear much culpability.[34] It is nevertheless clear that even in her own time not everyone believed her to be fully responsible. William Camden, Elizabeth's first biographer, acknowledged that Mary's 'days have been ill spoken of' but said that this was 'by reason of the barbarous cruelty of the Bishops, who with a most sad spectacle, in all places polluted England by burning Protestants alive'.[35] He, in other words, placed the blame on Mary's advisors. Bishop Gardiner had in fact quickly become shocked by the burnings, and he died at the end of 1555, leaving Mary's government without a strong figurehead.[36] There were others, however, notably Pole and Edmund Bonner, Bishop of London, nicknamed 'Bloody Bonner', who must bear partial responsibility for the burnings, which continued long after Gardiner's death. It was clear that nobody was safe, and between 4 February 1555 and 10 November 1558, a total of 283 Protestants – 227 men and 56 women – were burned.[37]

Elizabeth continued outwardly to conform to Mary's religious policies; her proximity to the Queen made it expedient for her to do so.

Others among her friends and family, however, were not prepared to be so compliant, and it therefore came as no surprise when some made the decision to flee. Several European cities were far more accommodating to Protestants than London, including Geneva, Frankfurt, Basel and Strasbourg, and it was in these that many of those leaving England sought refuge. Among them were Elizabeth's one-time servant Elizabeth Sandes, and John Cheke, Edward VI's former tutor, who had left following the Wyatt Rebellion.[38] Most painful for Elizabeth, though, was the departure of her cousin Katherine Carey, Lady Knollys. Elizabeth had evidently spent enough time with Katherine during her youth for the two to become close, and may have been the godmother of Katherine's daughter, Elizabeth, born in 1549. It is also possible, although by no means certain, that Katherine entrusted one of her daughters, Lettice, to Elizabeth's care as she prepared to leave England with four of her eleven children, to join her husband and son who had gone on ahead.[39] As Katherine prepared to depart, Elizabeth wrote her a touching letter in which she reassured her kinswoman: 'Relieve your sorrow for your far journey with joy of your short return, and think this pilgrimage rather a proof of your friends, than a leaving of your country. The length of time, and distance of place, separates not the love of friends, nor deprives not the show of goodwill.' She signed the letter 'Cor Rotto [broken heart]'.[40] The next time Elizabeth saw Katherine, the circumstances would be remarkably different.

By the latter part of 1555, the atmosphere in the capital was uneasy and the citizens were sickened by the burnings. Ambassador Giovanni Michiel had been right in his observation that 'such sudden severity is odious to many people', and anger against Mary was growing.[41] Yet there was more to it than the religious persecution. There were also economic problems, for September had witnessed a torrent of rain and floods across the country to the extent that in 'divers places both men and cattle drowned'.[42] To top it all off, anti-Spanish feeling remained widespread, and on the morning of 18 October, a pair of gallows were set up in Fleet Street, where two men were hanged for robbing a Spaniard, and there they remained for the whole day in the pouring rain.[43] It was a depressing scene. Little wonder, then, that Elizabeth now sought permission to leave court. Having been fully under

Mary's control for more than eighteen months, she was greatly relieved when this was granted. On the same morning as the thieves were punished in Fleet Street, Elizabeth left London for Hatfield to re-establish her household. Despite the sombre mood in the capital, as she passed through the streets she was cheered in the same manner as the people had once applauded Mary. Her popularity had remained unchanged, and the populace was glad to see that she was finally, of a sort, free. Unsurprisingly, however, and indicating just how paranoid she was by this point in her reign, Mary, still distrustful of Elizabeth's motives, had set spies to watch over her.

With Elizabeth having been absent for more than two years, her return to the familiar surroundings of Hatfield came as a relief. The beginnings of Mary's reign had pushed her to her limits and she had faced the greatest dangers of her life, yet she had survived. Thomas Parry fully resumed his role as her cofferer, now able to communicate with his mistress freely without the interference of Sir Henry Bedingfield. The greatest source of joy, however, came in November, when Elizabeth's beloved Kate Astley, having been freed from the detention of Sir Roger Cholmeley as one 'who hath of long time remained in his custody', also returned.[44] Isabella Markham was there too, as was Elizabeth Norwich and several other ladies, including Mary St Loe, daughter of Elizabeth's former servant Sir William.[45] It was a great comfort to Elizabeth to once again be surrounded by the familiar faces of those whose loyalty and devotion to her was unswerving. Just as life seemed as though it might finally settle down for her, however, danger attached itself to her name once more.

Barely had Elizabeth returned to Hatfield when, by November, the seeds of a further plot were being sown. The following month they were beginning to take root, and as with the Wyatt Rebellion, this too had Mary's replacement by Elizabeth at its core. On this occasion, however, Mary was to be sent abroad to join her husband.[46] Once again, the scheme was driven by hatred of the Spanish, who remained fiercely unpopular in England, as well as by the fear of Philip's rumoured coronation, which it was thought would lead to Elizabeth's removal from the kingdom.[47] As with the Wyatt Rebellion, the plotters once again hoped to marry Elizabeth to Courtenay.

It became known as the Dudley Conspiracy, though the man who gave his name to the plot – Henry Dudley – was just one of several architects. Dudley was a second cousin of the executed Duke of Northumberland, who had once done his utmost to ingratiate himself with Elizabeth before supporting her disinheritance.[48] Dudley had been thrown into the Tower following the coup to place Jane Grey on the throne, but unlike Northumberland he had been released in October 1553. His fortunes were nevertheless ruined, and he failed to gain any kind of position under Mary. Dudley's father-in-law, Christopher Ashton, was another key conspirator, and he adored Elizabeth. Ashton hailed from Berkshire and, significantly, had been married – before she died in 1537 – to none other than Lady Katherine Gordon, a distant cousin of James IV of Scotland and widowed wife of another former executed traitor, Perkin Warbeck.[49] Lord Bray, the grandson of Sir Reginald Bray who had once served Henry VII and Margaret Beaufort so faithfully, was also involved and had declared that 'if my neighbour of Hatfield might once reign (meaning the Lady Elizabeth), he should have his lands and debts given him again, which he both wished for and trusted once to see'.[50] John Throckmorton, a distant relative of Katherine Parr, was another key plotter. Ultimately for the conspirators, 'the day they longed for was that of the accession of Elizabeth'.[51] And they were confident of success.

To fund their enterprise Dudley planned to steal money from the Exchequer, in which lay £50,000 (£13,735,000) in Spanish silver bars.[52] In order to gain access to the money, the conspirators bribed the keeper, William Rossey, a friend of Dudley's.[53] Their plans progressed, but the plot was discovered in early March 1556 when one of the conspirators, Thomas White, 'either from hope of reward, or to exculpate himself', informed Cardinal Pole.[54] Both Dudley and Ashton were in France, where they were attempting to gain support for their plans, but the Council was in no rush arrest the plotters. Instead, as related by David Loades, they 'waited for the fruit to ripen a little, and then plucked it'.[55] On 18 March, 'divers gentlemen' were rounded up and taken to the Tower for questioning, and on 4 April a proclamation was read in London that declared 'certain gentlemen' who had fled overseas to be traitors.[56] These included both Dudley and Ashton, who were still safely in France.

None would admit that Elizabeth herself was involved in the conspiracy, but there was no doubt that many of those close to her were. It came as no surprise when it was discovered that the French ambassador Noailles had played a part, and in May he swiftly left the country before action could be taken against him. The plotters had hoped that the French King would fund part of the rebellion, but this had been thwarted when, in February 1556, Henri II signed the truce of Vaucelles with Philip, suspending French and Spanish hostilities for five years.[57] Of those conspirators who were hauled off to the Tower, many were kept in miserable conditions while they faced questioning. One Daniel, for example, was imprisoned in 'a filthy and unwholesome dungeon'.[58] In light of such treatment, unsurprisingly all save one, Throckmorton, showed themselves eager to confess.

Closer to home, when the conspiracy was discovered, Elizabeth's London residence, Somerset House, was searched. A chest full of Protestant books was uncovered, but there was far worse.[59] A cabinet, believed to belong to Elizabeth's beloved Kate Astley, was also found and discovered to contain incriminating evidence against the Queen, including 'those writings and scandalous books against the religion and against the King and Queen which were scattered about some months ago, and published all over the kingdom'.[60] Thus it was no surprise when, in May, Kate was once more arrested and taken to the Tower. Neither was she alone, for Giovanni Battista Castiglione, Elizabeth's Italian tutor, was seized at the same time, along with another gentleman named Francis Verney. Verney's brother, Edmund, and his brother-in-law, Henry Peckham, seem also to have been involved.[61] Not for the first time, the removal of members of Elizabeth's household from Hatfield caused 'great general vexation'.[62]

Under questioning, Castiglione denied any involvement in the plot, insisting that he had only visited London once that year, and that was solely for the purpose of purchasing lute strings for Elizabeth. Kate too denied any knowledge of the conspiracy, but by 2 June Ambassador Giovanni Michiel reported, 'I am told that they have all already confessed to having known about the conspiracy; so not having revealed it, were there nothing else against them, they may probably not quit the Tower alive, this alone subjecting them to capital punishment.'[63] The fact that they had admitted to an awareness of the plot without reporting it was almost as bad as having personally participated, for they were thereby guilty of concealing treason. Thus the punishment was expected to be heavy, and the complicity of those closest to Elizabeth would once again inflame Mary's antipathy towards and suspicion of her.

Despite the situation in which she found herself, Elizabeth remained composed while those in her household were arrested, and she was allowed to remain at Hatfield. Mary, who interpreted Elizabeth's poise as confirmation of her misgivings, was desperate to act against her but first sought her husband's advice. She sent a courier, Francesco Piamontese, 'in haste to Brussels', for 'nothing is done, nor does anything take place, without having the King's opinion about it, and hearing his will'.[64] Elizabeth's destiny now seemingly lay in Philip's hands.

CHAPTER 18

'Of a Prisoner Made a Princess'

'So great is the effect produced by recollection, not only of past
offences but also of present ones, for it unfortunately appears
that never is a conspiracy discovered in which either justly or
unjustly she or some of her servants are not mentioned.'

GIOVANNI MICHIEL, VENETIAN AMBASSADOR TO THE
VENETIAN SENATE, 13 MAY 1557

A S THE FRESHNESS of spring turned to the soft warmth of summer, in early June 1556 two visitors arrived at Hatfield. Sir Edward Hastings was the Queen's Master of Horse and Sir Francis Englefield one of her councillors, and it was on Mary's orders that they came. Elizabeth is likely to have been wary, given that Hastings had escorted her on that unpleasant journey from Ashridge to Whitehall in March 1554, but he and his colleague carried no warrants of arrest. They came instead in the spirit of friendship. As Elizabeth received the two men, who were both highly thought of by the Queen, they explained to her that they had been sent 'to console and comfort her on behalf of her Majesty', knowing that the arrest of her servants would have left her 'distressed and dejected'.[1] Moreover, as 'a token of loving salutation' and a gesture of the Queen's goodwill, they presented her with a ring.[2] Hastings and Englefield proceeded to detail the arrests of those closest to Elizabeth, while 'assuring her of the Queen's good will and disposition, provided she continue to live becomingly, to her Majesty's liking'.[3] Elizabeth must have been struck by the change in Mary's attitude towards her, for the councillors now assured her that 'she is neither neglected nor hated, but loved and esteemed by her Majesty'.[4] They also invited her to court on the Queen's behalf – an invitation that she declined. The reality was that these honeyed words delivered at Mary's behest could not have been further from the truth.

The reasons behind Mary's clemency were threefold: her lack of an heir, Elizabeth's ever-growing popularity, and Philip's attitude towards her troublesome sister. To suit his own agenda, Philip had always advised caution where Elizabeth was concerned, and the aftermath of the Dudley Conspiracy proved no different. According to Jane Dormer, the Council would have 'examined and chastised' Elizabeth for her knowledge and involvement, but 'the King again protected her from this danger'.[5] Not only did Philip recognize the esteem Elizabeth was held in, but he was also fully aware that Mary's lack of an heir had strengthened Elizabeth's position immeasurably. Driven by 'fear of a popular insurrection' should Elizabeth be punished, his inclination towards clemency was reinforced.[6] Although it was Mary who gave the orders, she was eager to obey her husband, and so it was Philip who had decided how Elizabeth should be dealt with. As a result of the leniency with which she had been treated, however, Elizabeth now 'sensed the strength of her position'.[7] Her confidence would grow considerably in the coming months and years.

It was not only Elizabeth who evaded punishment but most of the conspirators too. Though a handful were executed over the summer, most remained in prison, and 'thus terminated this miserable and foolish plot'.[8] With Philip's distant hand to steady her, Mary dared not act against her sister, but she did at least see the Dudley Conspiracy as an opportunity to reform Elizabeth's household 'with a different sort of persons to those now in her service'. The likes of the disruptive Kate Astley would now be replaced with 'such as are entirely dependent on her Majesty', and Mary already had a candidate in mind.[9]

Having delivered Mary's message, Hastings and Englefield prepared to journey back to London. Before they left, however, they informed Elizabeth that her household was to be overseen by Sir Thomas Pope, 'a rich and grave gentleman, of good name, both for conduct and religion'.[10]

Giovanni Michiel had heard that Pope had been reluctant to take on such an assignment, but Elizabeth 'accepted him willingly'. He was, though, to be assisted by one to whom Elizabeth did not feel so warmly: Robert Gage, son of the Lord Chamberlain Sir John Gage, who had been unsympathetic to her plight while imprisoned in the Tower, and had died in April.[11] Additionally, a 'widow gentlewoman' was appointed to join the household, but the identity of this lady is unknown.[12]

Though now surrounded by those who were loyal to Mary, Elizabeth quickly discovered that, unlike Sir Henry Bedingfield, Sir Thomas Pope – a member of Mary's Privy Council – 'behaved with the utmost tenderness'.[13] Rather than sticking rigorously to the rules, he treated Elizabeth 'rather as an indulgent and affectionate guardian, than as an officious or rigorous governor'.[14] Jane Dormer held a different view, asserting that Elizabeth, with 'her courteous behaviour and cunning, and by her public profession of Catholic religion with show of zeal, did deceive these gentlemen'.[15] At roughly fifty years old, Pope was of Oxfordshire origin and, like Elizabeth, was highly educated.[16] He had been fortunate enough to enjoy the patronage of Henry VIII's former Lord Chancellor, Lord Audley, and though not a particularly prominent member of court, Pope had been knighted in 1537 and was well favoured by Mary because of his Catholic faith. Agnes Strickland described Pope as someone of 'honourable and friendly conditions', and there is no doubt that he and Elizabeth got along very well.[17] Scholarship was a common interest, and Elizabeth would assuredly have been impressed by the fact that Pope had just founded Trinity College, Oxford. When he died in 1559, his widow would erect a monument to his memory and his remains would be moved there.[18]

At the end of July, Pope had only been at Hatfield a matter of weeks when he apprised Elizabeth of the fact that there had been another failed plot against the Queen. This time, one Cleobury, who had been impersonating Courtenay (who was still abroad), had proclaimed Elizabeth and Courtenay King and Queen in Suffolk.[19] The rebellion came to nothing, however, and Cleobury was swiftly executed. On this occasion nobody even took the trouble to question Elizabeth, and she remained unmolested at Hatfield. It was now almost expected that, given her position and proximity to the throne, her name would always be connected with plots against the Queen. Elizabeth nevertheless judged it expedient to write to Mary on 2 August, expressing her disgust with the rebels: 'When I revolve in mind (most noble Queen) the old love of paynims [pagans] to their prince and the reverent fear of Romans to their Senate, I can but muse for my part and blush for theirs, to see the rebellious hearts and devilish intents of Christians in names, but Jews in deed, toward their anointed King.'[20] She took care to stress to her sister that, 'like as I have been your faithful subject from the beginning of your reign, so shall no wicked persons cause me to change to the end of my life'.[21] It was a not-so-subtle reassertion by Elizabeth that she was a loyal subject who had never plotted against Mary.

The small wave caused by Cleobury was to be the last occasion on which Elizabeth's name was linked with that of Courtenay, for in September the latter died in Padua amid rumours of poison.[22] His death must have been a cause of some relief to both Elizabeth and Mary, for with Courtenay gone one small cause of strain on their relationship had been removed, and thus 'the Queen grew less jealous' of Elizabeth.[23] It was likely as a result of this that life took a further turn in Elizabeth's favour, for on 19 October Sir Thomas Pope was released from his role as her custodian. His removal signified Elizabeth's true freedom; she was now finally at full liberty with nobody to watch over her or guard her movements. She was also relieved to learn that same month that Kate Astley was freed from the Fleet Prison, though she was 'deprived not only of her office as governess, but forbidden ever again to go to her ladyship'.[24] For Elizabeth this was a high price to pay.

Although suspicion lingered, there were signs that relations between the two sisters were thawing, and in late November Elizabeth arrived in London, where she was due to spend Christmas at court. This time she travelled without any sense of trepidation; instead it is a sign of her growing confidence in her position that she came with 'a handsome retinue, having with her, including lords and gentlemen, upwards of 200 horsemen clad in her own livery, and dismounted at her own house [Somerset House], where she has remained ever since, to the infinite pleasure of this entire population, though she was not met by any of the lords or gentlemen of the court, but many visited her subsequently'.[25]

It was Elizabeth's first visit to the capital in just over a year, and three days after her arrival she came to see the Queen. She was apparently received 'very graciously and familiarly' by her sister and took the opportunity to call on Cardinal Pole, who had never shown her any warmth.[26] This meeting took place in his chamber, 'he never having seen her until then, although last year they both resided at the court for a whole month with their apartments very near each other'.[27] Though on opposite sides of the religious spectrum, Pole, recognizing her growing standing, was now the epitome of kindness towards her.

Though Giovanni Michiel believed Elizabeth had 'with great earnestness solicited to come' to court, this was not the case.[28] It later came to light that Mary had sent for Elizabeth, with a view to informing her of Philip's desire that she should be wed to his cousin Emmanuel Philibert. Conscious that his wife had thus far had no child and that her health was not robust, Philip was by now determined to safeguard his interests in England by marrying Elizabeth to one whose loyalty to Habsburg interests was assured. She would later admit that Philip had 'tried very hard' to persuade Mary to this course of action, but, despite the leniency with which he had treated her and the support he'd given, Elizabeth would not be swayed.[29] Her reaction bordered on hysterical, for in an answer that confirms her attitude to marriage by this point, she told the Queen that 'the afflictions suffered by her were such that they had not only ridded her of any wish for a husband, but that they had induced her to desire nothing but death, and then by a flood of tears she brought them also to the eyes of the Queen'.[30]

Mary could see that no good would come of attempting to force Elizabeth, and she felt no more enthusiasm for the marriage herself. After all, why should the progeny of Anne Boleyn be married to a European Catholic prince? It was more than she deserved. But she would not permit Elizabeth's disobedience either. She declared her intention to summon Parliament with a view to, once again, preventing her sister from succeeding. If Elizabeth would not marry a Catholic, then Mary would certainly not willingly leave her the throne. Here, the Queen found herself in opposition to most of her Council, as many continued to oppose Elizabeth's exclusion. This did not prevent Mary from 'obstinately maintaining that she was neither her sister nor the daughter of the Queen's father, King Henry, nor would she hear of favouring her, as she was born of an infamous woman, who had so greatly outraged the Queen her mother, and herself'.[31] It was an outburst that underscored Mary's recognition of her own insecurity, for she was painfully conscious that, to her sorrow, her lack of a child cleared the way for Elizabeth to succeed her. Lashing out, as she had done before, she threw her strongest weapon at her sister, aimed squarely at Elizabeth's Achilles' heel: her illegitimacy.

With the Queen's temper flaring, Elizabeth's visit was destined to be brief; Mary sent her from court before they could spend Christmas together. Leaving suddenly and under a cloud, on 3 December 'came riding from her place my Lady Elizabeth's grace, from Somerset Place down Fleet Street, and through Old Bailey, and through Smithfield, with a great company; and her servants all in red guarded with velvet; and so her grace took her way toward Bishop's Hatfield'.[32]

Hatfield was destined to remain Elizabeth's base for the next two years, but though gone from London she was anything but removed from Mary's mind – or Philip's. Less than two weeks after her visit, new supporters were beginning to flock to Elizabeth, including some of those on the Queen's Council.[33] Mary ignored this, despite the claim of Giovanni Michiel the following year that 'what disquiets her most of all is to see the eyes and hearts of the nation already fixed on this lady as successor to the Crown'.[34] Instead, she attempted to gloss over the bad feeling between them by sending her sister the traditional gifts that were exchanged at New Year. As 1557 dawned, Elizabeth received three gilt bowls, two cups and a jug.[35] Although these items were slightly more generous than those Mary gave to Cardinal Pole and Anne of Cleves, there was nothing to indicate any kind of sisterly warmth, for they were very much in keeping with the gifts the Queen gave to her courtiers.[36] Elizabeth put more thought into what she sent in return, gifting Mary items of clothing that had been richly embroidered, but these were a far cry from the personalized offerings she had once made to her father and brother.[37] Perhaps, with her own position growing stronger by the day, Elizabeth sensed she no longer needed to curry her sister's favour as she once had. The exchange of gifts was almost certainly little more than a formality, and the tension between the sisters remained.

This strained relationship was becoming ever more apparent to those around them, for later in 1557, Michiel claimed that Mary bore her sister an 'evil disposition', which, 'although dissembled, it cannot be denied that she displays in many ways the scorn and ill will she bears her'.[38] This was no exaggeration. Mary would remain distrustful of her sister, and, despite having no grounds for doing so, she nonetheless continued to send 'many spies and guards in the neighbourhood who keep strict watch on all persons passing to and fro'.[39] This ensured that Elizabeth, though growing in confidence, was nevertheless 'obliged to act very cautiously'.[40]

MUCH TO MARY'S disappointment, her husband showed himself to be in no hurry to return to England. His father, after all, had abdicated in January 1556, making Philip King of Spain and other Habsburg territories in his own right. England, by comparison, was of little interest to him. In an indication of Mary's frustration, Gilles de Noailles, brother of the former French ambassador, who served as agent for the French King in England for several months in 1556, was told by some of those close to the Queen that she had been seen 'scratching the portraits of her husband the King of Spain which she keeps in her room', so vexed was she by Philip's absence.[41] There were two matters, however, in which Philip needed Mary's assistance, so in the spring of 1557, he landed in England once more. On 20 March, after an absence of eighteen months and much to Mary's elation, he arrived at Greenwich. Despite Philip's outward shows of courtesy, though, her feelings were not reciprocated and unbeknown to Mary he had only come in the hope of concluding issues of business. The first was to convince his wife to back his war against France, which had been reignited when the truce of Vaucelles was broken. But he was also determined to conclude the Emmanuel Philibert, Duke of Savoy, match for Elizabeth. Regarding the second point, at least, he would have a fight on his hands.

Elizabeth sensed that Philip intended to pressurize her into agreeing to the Savoy match, but she was not prepared to dance to the Habsburg tune. She was aware of Philip's continuing unpopularity within the realm, as well as Mary's, observed by the recently arrived Venetian ambassador Michiel Surian, who noted that 'the Spaniards are so greatly hated, that neither his Majesty nor the Queen are well looked on by the multitude'.[42] Perhaps suspecting that Elizabeth would be difficult to bring to heel, Philip had brought his sister, the Duchess of Parma, and his cousin, the Duchess of Lorraine – whom Elizabeth's father had once hoped to marry – with him to England.[43] It was hoped that they would 'bring back with them Madama Elizabeth to this side of the sea', but Elizabeth knew that nobody could force her.[44]

Elizabeth had every reason to stand her ground, evidenced when Ambassador Giovanni Michiel had described her:

She is a young woman, whose mind is considered no less excellent than her person, although her face is comely rather than handsome, but she is tall and well formed, with a good skin, although swarthy; she has fine eyes and above all a beautiful hand of which she makes a display; and her intellect and understanding are wonderful, as she showed very plainly by her conduct when in danger and under suspicion. As a linguist she excels the Queen, for besides Latin she has no slight knowledge of Greek, and speaks Italian more than the Queen does, taking so much pleasure in it that from vanity she will never speak any other language with Italians. She is proud and haughty, as although she knows that she was born of such a mother, she nevertheless does not consider herself of inferior degree to the Queen, whom she equals in self-esteem.[45]

The French King, Henri II, was just as eager as Elizabeth to prevent this match, for the last thing he wanted was for the Habsburgs to have a further foothold in England. The French ambassador François – another of the de Noailles brothers – was so alarmed when he heard of Philip's plan that he sent Elizabeth's friend, Elisabeth Brooke, Marchioness of Northampton, with a warning that there was a plan to kidnap her and thereby force her to marry Savoy.[46] Thanking him for alerting her, Elizabeth assured him that she would rather die than allow either of these things to pass. She would not yield; she refused to meet with Philip's relatives.[47] Much to Elizabeth's relief, Philip's attentions were soon distracted elsewhere, leaving him unable to push her further.

Philip finally succeeded in persuading Mary to declare war on France in June. This was prompted by Thomas Stafford – embarrassingly, Cardinal Pole's nephew – who, backed by French support, successfully seized Scarborough Castle at the end of April.[48] Jane Dormer suspected that Elizabeth had been in communication with Stafford and was in on his plans, 'they supposing themselves strong enough against Queen Mary'.[49] She also claimed that, upon taking Scarborough, Stafford hoped that Elizabeth 'would send her forces to fetch him, or with them to come to him herself'.[50] Elizabeth certainly had links with Stafford, for he was the brother of her friend Dorothy Stafford, later one of her closest ladies.[51] Yet having avoided directly implicating herself in previous plots, it seems unlikely that she did so now. Moreover, the threat was immediately quelled due to lack of support, and Stafford and his followers were captured by the Earl of Westmorland.[52] Stafford was executed, and, as Jane Dormer recounted, Elizabeth once again – whether she was involved or not – thanks to Philip's 'singular favour [...] again escaped this plunge'.[53] The French, however, did not.

Having been pressured by Philip, Mary capitulated to her husband's wishes and her kingdom now became embroiled in conflict.[54] In early July, Philip left England – and Mary – behind to partake in the war. Mary would never see her husband again. The war began well for England, but was extremely unpopular in the realm, even after a victory at St Quentin in August, led by Elizabeth's would-be suitor Emmanuel Philibert, Duke of Savoy. Three of the sons of the executed Northumberland also joined the campaign, including Robert Dudley, who witnessed the tragic death of his younger brother Henry, hit by a cannonball. Crucially, there were no spare funds to allow the victory at St Quentin to be consolidated further.

Involving her country in Philip's wars was about to cost Mary dearly. In the aftermath of St Quentin, it was clear that the French would fight back, and when they did the results were disastrous. On New Year's Day 1558, an attack was launched on Calais by the French army, headed by the Duke of Guise. It had always been Henri II's 'most cherished dream' to recover this important town from the English, and his wish was about to be granted.[55] Before long, the town – the last of England's possessions in France, which had been acquired in 1347 during the Hundred Years' War – fell to the French. The news came as a devastating blow to the English people, and they would never forgive either Philip or Mary for the defeat. The love that her subjects had harboured for Mary upon her accession four and a half years previously, and the popularity she had then enjoyed, had long since vanished, and the Queen now found herself completely isolated.

The loss of Calais and Philip's departure left Mary spiralling into depression. Yet she believed there was one reason to be hopeful: in January – six months after he left – she sent word to her husband, via Cardinal Pole, that she was pregnant. Though he responded in positive terms, assuring Pole that the news has 'given me greater joy than I can express to you, as it is the one thing in the world I have most desired', it was obvious Philip was unconvinced.[56] He was not alone, for nobody truly believed the Queen to be with child, and it is telling that on this occasion no preparations were made for the birth. The former Venetian ambassador Giacomo Soranzo surmised that 'no one believes in the possibility of her having progeny, so that day by day she sees her authority and the respect induced by it diminish'.[57] Nevertheless, it was perhaps to confirm this in her own mind that Elizabeth visited Mary. On 25 February, 'came riding to London my Lady Elizabeth the Queen's sister, with a great company of lords and noblemen and noblewomen, to her place called Somerset Place'.[58] Presumably having satisfied herself that there would be no child, after a week spent at Somerset House, on the morning of 4 March, Elizabeth left the capital with 'many lords, knights, and ladies, and gentlewomen, with a goodly company of horse', and returned to Hatfield.[59] She and Mary would never see one another again.

In March, Count de Feria, one of Philip's most trusted councillors, wrote his master a frank letter. His views on the Queen's pregnancy were plain, for 'it seems to me she is making herself believe that she is with child, although she does not own up to it'.[60] Feria had accompanied Philip to England in 1554, and having witnessed the outcome of the Queen's first pregnancy he did not hesitate to share his scepticism on this occasion. He was right to be doubtful, and by this point even Simon Renard had grudgingly conceded that as far as Mary's subjects were concerned, Elizabeth 'is now honoured and recognized (as heiress to the crown)'. Renard had left England in the autumn of 1555, but still took an avid interest in the country's affairs. He thought it inevitable now that Elizabeth would succeed, but, recognizing that the issue of the succession was of great concern to Spain, he took the opportunity to express his concerns to Philip. His dislike of Elizabeth had not dissipated, and he assured his master that she

> hates the Queen and has many supporters who are suspect from the point-of-view of religion. If she succeeds, and marries an Englishman, religion will be undermined, everything sacred profaned, Catholics ill-treated, churchmen driven out, those monasteries which have been restored will again suffer, churches will be destroyed, affairs which had taken a favourable turn will once more be compromised. The heretics have no other intentions. Moreover, the ancient amity, good neighbourliness and understanding that have so far been maintained, albeit with difficulty, between England and your Majesty's realms, will not only be impaired but disappear altogether.[61]

Renard knew that when Elizabeth succeeded, there would be no place for Catholicism in the realm. It was with this and safeguarding Spanish interests in mind that he once again urged Philip to push for Elizabeth's marriage to Emmanuel Philibert.

Mary, though, was convinced enough of her pregnancy to be more determined than ever to make one last-ditch attempt to cut Elizabeth out, drawing up her will on 30 March. Believing – or hoping – herself to be with child, she gave orders in the document that the crown was to be inherited by any progeny she produced, with Philip acting as the infant's guardian.[62] But as before, Mary's hopes were dashed for there was to be no child. By April, Mary was forced to come to terms with the fact that she was not pregnant and would never have a child of her own. The reality of her failure to produce a Catholic heir left her heartbroken, as once again the whole matter was very quietly dropped.

As Mary's position weakened, Elizabeth's grew stronger by the day. Throughout the course of Mary's reign her younger sister had been faced with uncertainty and danger that placed her very life in jeopardy. Yet she had survived. And her confidence was now mounting, for the events of the past two years had shown that Mary dared not move against her, by reason of both her popularity – particularly among the common people – and her proximity to the throne.

Elizabeth made no secret of the fact that support for her cause was growing, for she knew that the Council would not countenance her removal from the succession. Even Renard was aware that 'frequent communications reach and leave her, secretly, in regard to the succession'.[63] She must inwardly have rejoiced, for despite Mary's treatment of her there was nothing the Queen could do now to threaten Elizabeth's future: everyone knew that it was only a matter of time before she received that which had once seemed so remote, and they looked towards her with hope for the future. The crown was no longer a possibility for Elizabeth but a certainty: all she need do was wait for her moment.

Yet while Elizabeth remained at Hatfield, from where she gathered supporters, she knew that it would be unwise to antagonize Mary further, so she moved carefully to avoid any 'increase of the Queen's hatred and anger'.[64] This became apparent in the spring when an envoy from the King of Sweden, Gustav I, arrived at Hatfield with a proposal of marriage on behalf of his son. The envoy had completely ignored the expected etiquette by failing to obtain Mary's prior consent or approval, instead offering the proposal directly to Elizabeth. Mary was furious, and more so because she was worried Philip would think she had encouraged Gustav's suit in a way she had failed to do for Emmanuel Philibert's. Sir Thomas Pope was dispatched to Hatfield to see what Elizabeth had to say on the matter, and it was through him that, at the end of April, she gave the Queen her response. Elizabeth's views on marriage were genuine, as she reiterated what she had once told her brother: that, despite having been offered prospective husbands in Edward's reign, she preferred 'to remain in that estate I was, which of all other best liked, and pleased me'. In fact, even now, 'I so well like this estate, as I persuade unto myself, there is not any kind of life comparable unto it', even were she offered 'the greatest prince of all Europe'.[65] Pope returned to London, where, having delivered to his mistress the news that 'the Lady Elizabeth has answered that she does not wish to marry', he was able to report that 'the Queen has calmed down; but she takes a most passionate interest in the affair'.[66] As she long had been on the question of marriage, Elizabeth was sincere: she had no desire for wedlock.

Mary was by now seriously unwell, suffering with a number of ailments that included headaches and fever.[67] On 1 May Count de Feria informed Philip that 'she sleeps badly, is weak and suffers from melancholy'.[68] Later in the month she moved to St James's Palace and she would spend the summer at Hampton Court, but the decline in her health even prevented her from writing her usual letters to her husband. Used to hearing from his wife on a regular basis, in June Philip was concerned enough to confide to Feria that 'she has not written to me for some days past, and I cannot help being anxious'.[69] There was an influenza epidemic in England that year, which killed many of Mary's subjects and which, in August, the Queen herself seems to have been unfortunate enough to contract. Though she appeared to recover from this, she remained weak, and it was clear that preparations for the future had already begun.

Philip recognized that Mary's health was deteriorating and, thinking ahead lest her life should soon draw to a close, he turned his attentions to Elizabeth in an attempt to retain as much control over England and English affairs as he could. He had been unsuccessful in his hopes of wedding her to Emmanuel Philibert, but was now also considering the possibility of marrying her himself. Though Philip did not share this latter thought with his messenger, in June, he instructed Count de Feria to visit Elizabeth at Hatfield. She welcomed Philip's envoy and he, in turn, felt gratified by their conversation. He recalled that she was 'very much pleased; and I was also, for reasons I will tell your Majesty when I arrive over there'.[70] Feria soon returned to his master, but before long it would become clear that his hopes of Elizabeth's compliance with Spain's wishes were misplaced.

By the autumn Mary's health had worsened, and as it did so, Elizabeth's plans to assume power over her sister's realm began to take further shape. She was busy consolidating her supporters, with Parry sending letters on her behalf to Sir John Thynne, the Comptroller of her household, among others.[71] She even secured the assistance of captains on garrison duty at Berwick, to march to her aid if needs be.[72] Such preparations would prove unnecessary.

In late October, Philip received word from St James's Palace that his wife was 'grievously ill, and her life in danger', and it was this that prompted him to dispatch Count de Feria to England again without delay.[73] On 9 November, Feria arrived, and five days later he delivered Philip the news that there was 'no hope of her life, but on the contrary, each hour I think that they will come to inform me of her death, so rapidly does her condition deteriorate from one day to the next'.[74] Even a physician Philip had sent with Feria could do nothing for Mary.[75] She cut a lonely figure, abandoned by her husband and, assuming the news reached her, saddened following the death of her cousin and lifelong supporter, Philip's father the Emperor Charles V, on 21 September.[76] Still, Mary could barely stand any mention of Elizabeth and until the end she 'would never call her sister, nor be persuaded that she was her father's daughter'.[77]

The Queen found it painfully difficult to accept that all eyes were now firmly turned in Elizabeth's direction, but finally she had no choice but to accept reality. In October, she had added a codicil in her will, but at that time she had refrained from mentioning who her successor would be. To her sorrow, motherhood had evaded her, and so it was with great reluctance that on 6 November she eventually acknowledged Elizabeth as her heir. The following day the Comptroller, Sir Thomas Cornwallis, and the Master of the Rolls, John Boxall, were sent to deliver the news to Mary's sister, informing Elizabeth that 'the Queen is willing that she succeed in the event of her own death, but that she asks two things of her: one, that she will maintain the old religion as the Queen has restored it;

and the other that she will pay the Queen's debts'.[78] Elizabeth's moment was swiftly approaching.

ON 10 NOVEMBER, Count de Feria arrived at Brocket Hall, about four miles from Hatfield. Elizabeth had been to Brocket Hall on a couple of occasions as the guest of John Brocket (or Brockett), who had recently come into his inheritance, and she had known the family for many years.[79] She seems to have been there readying her supporters, and it probably provided a better base than Hatfield, as it was more easily defendable and offered better communications via river.[80] Upon Feria's arrival, Elizabeth received him graciously enough, though he was dismayed that she did so 'not as joyfully as she did the last time'.[81] Knowing that Feria had been sent to obtain from her what he could on Spain's behalf, she invited him to dine with her.

Feria remembered that 'During the meal we laughed and enjoyed ourselves a great deal', but Elizabeth knew he was there on business.[82] Accordingly, once the meal had come to an end she invited him to speak with her if he so wished, for she would order everyone from the room apart from two or three of her women who spoke only English. Feria, though, declared, 'I would prefer the whole kingdom to hear what I wished to say to her' before professing the goodwill and 'brotherly love' that Philip had for her. Elizabeth acknowledged her gratitude for this, and although she was very open with him, Feria could not help but express his opinion that she was 'a very vain and clever woman. She must have been thoroughly schooled in the manner in which her father conducted his affairs.' He knew that she would be no friend to Catholicism, 'for I see her inclined to govern through men who are believed to be heretics and I am told that all the women around her definitely are'.[83] Elizabeth assured him, however, of her desire to remain on good terms with Spain, although she was at pains to stress that her situation was in no way thanks to Philip or his assistance. She would not be indebted to anyone and was insistent that 'it was the people who put her in her present position'.[84] She felt confident of their love and support, a fact that Feria could not deny.

He perceived that 'Madam Elizabeth already sees herself as the next Queen' and considered it obvious who she would favour.[85] Among them were William Cecil, 'an able and virtuous man', and Robert Dudley, to whom she would later become famously close.[86] Very little is known of her relationship with the latter at this time, but Elizabeth would later say of Robert that 'when she was deserted by everybody in the reign of her sister not only did he never lessen in any degree his kindness and humble attention to her, but he even sold his possessions that he might assist her with money'.[87] Evidently, therefore, the foundations of their friendship were already solidly established: it would not be long before they began to blossom. Elizabeth had also become close to Sir John Mason, the stepfather of her friend Mary Cheke.

Upon Feria's return to London, the ambassador met with the Council, making a point of emphasizing that Philip had long ago wanted Elizabeth to be named as Mary's successor. Sir John Mason was present, and Feria knew that 'he is greatly favoured by Madam Elizabeth and would report to her all that had passed between us'.[88] Mason was not alone in ingratiating himself with Elizabeth, for by now, as the Venetian ambassador Michiel Surian noted, 'many persons of the kingdom flocked to the house of my lady Elizabeth, the crowd constantly increasing with great frequency'.[89] It was as though Elizabeth were already Queen.

The behaviour of those around her as they hurried to cultivate the favour of the twenty-five-year-old woman who would soon rule over them was not lost on Elizabeth, who was deeply affected by the manner in which they abandoned a dying monarch in order to find glory with a new one. She knew that Mary had only the company of the most loyal of her ladies left to comfort her, and it was to one of these that the Queen now entrusted a message to her sister: 'This good Queen had commended in private divers things to Jane Dormer to give to the Lady Elizabeth her sister, and to tell her who was to succeed her in the kingdom; which she performed with dutiful fidelity, giving her the rich and precious jewels, that were in her custody.'[90] It was Jane Dormer, one of those who had witnessed the friction between the two sisters first-hand, that Mary tasked with apprising Elizabeth of her final wishes. But Mary was no longer in any condition to leave Elizabeth beholden to her.

In her bedchamber at St James's, as her end approached, Mary attempted to comfort her grieving ladies with thoughts of 'what good dreams she had, seeing many little children like Angels play before her'.[91] On the morning of 17 November, she heard mass as she did each day and 'although sick to death', heard it with 'good attention, zeal, and devotion'.[92] Soon afterwards, Mary slipped peacefully into death, and in so doing brought her five-year reign to an end. In a strange quirk of fate, within a few hours Cardinal Pole, who had also lain sick, died too. With them both died Mary's hopes of restoring her land to the Catholic faith to which she had been committed all her life. Aside from her most devoted servants, there were few who mourned Mary's passing, for many were eagerly anticipating the reign of her successor.

It has been said that the news of Mary's death was delivered to Elizabeth while she sat under an oak tree in the park at Hatfield, but this tale has no basis in truth. She had, by this time, returned to her childhood home, and when she was told of the death of her sister, her outward reaction, at least, was one of grief. 'My Lords,' she declared to those around her, 'the law of nature moveth me to sorrow for my sister: The burden that is fallen upon me maketh me amazed.'[93] Though she claimed to have shed tears for Mary's passing, there were none who witnessed them. Instead, Elizabeth appears to have been relieved at her sister's passing, for with Mary died the bitterness – it is fair to say on both sides – that had come to dominate the last few years of their relationship. In the latter part of Mary's reign Elizabeth had written to the Marquess of Winchester, criticizing her sister for 'none of my state hath been and yet is, more misused with them of mine own family than myself' – evidence of the resentment she felt at the treatment she had received at Mary's hand.[94] One of the pageants staged for Elizabeth's entertainment the day before her coronation featured an old man who represented 'Time' accompanied by his daughter 'Truth' – a play on Mary's motto 'Truth is the Daughter of Time'. When these figures spoke, they inferred that the old man was 'the past state', and his daughter 'the present' – Truth had triumphed over Time in a way that Elizabeth considered herself to have triumphed over Mary. Mary was the past, whereas Elizabeth very much considered herself to be the future.[95]

Everything about Elizabeth's life thus far had been unconventional, and her path to the throne was no different. For most of her years, wearing the crown had seemed unlikely. The fates of Elizabeth and Mary were intertwined from the beginning, and the tragedy that had engulfed Mary had given Elizabeth the opportunity to prepare for this moment. Mary's death marked the beginning of a brand-new era, and its significance was not lost on Elizabeth. For the first time in her life, she, and she alone, would choose the path of her own future and that of the realm – her realm. 'She is determined to be governed by no one,' Count de Feria observed.[96] She was twenty-five years old, and she was Queen of England. From this moment, she would begin crafting her name and her identity on the pages of history. In so doing, she created a legacy that has echoed down through the passage of time and continues to spark debate – one of a Queen who defied convention by choosing not to marry, who would persecute Catholics in a similar manner to her sister's persecution of Protestants, who executed a fellow anointed Queen, whose forces defeated a mighty Spanish Armada, and who lived through and patronized an age of exploration. Yet her legacy was one that began from the moment of her birth. Her early experiences shaped not only the young woman she was, but the Queen she would become.

Elizabeth had been born her father's heir, yet before her third birthday and as a result of her mother's fall, this position had been taken from her. She had nevertheless spent the remainder of Henry's life trying to please him and ingratiate herself, and was forced to continue this under her brother Edward when her place in the world was more uncertain. She had done so successfully, and, despite the trouble in which she found herself following Edward's death, she managed to navigate the dangerous waters of her sister's reign. In so doing she achieved a queenship she had never presumed to expect. Nothing about her life had been easy. She had trodden paths few before her could possibly have tackled and that could have resulted in her demise. She had never really been destined for the throne, yet here she was: her father's only surviving and acknowledged direct heir – the female heir he had never anticipated or hoped for. The responsibility of ruling England now lay squarely on Elizabeth's shoulders. In the moment of her anointing on that chilly day, 15 January 1559, the future – her future – was hers to command: hers, and hers alone.

'She being the true posterity of the families of the White and Red Roses.'

'I STOOD IN DANGER of my life,' Elizabeth once told her Parliament, 'my sister was so incensed against me.'[1] Yet on the day of Elizabeth's accession, all fear had vanished. On this day, 'the bells in all the churches in London rung in token of joy; and at night bonfires were made, and tables set out in the streets, where was plentiful eating and drinking, and making merry'.[2] The joy expressed by her subjects was genuine and heartfelt, and her admirer William Camden expressed his belief that she was 'of beauty very fair and worthy of a Crown'.[3] By reason of 'experience and adversity', Elizabeth had 'gathered wisdom above her age', which was just as well because the business of ruling her kingdom began immediately.[4] It was a task she approached with the utmost seriousness, and before she had even left Hatfield Elizabeth began appointing those whose role it would be to advise her: her Privy Council.

It came as no surprise that Elizabeth chose William Cecil to be her Principal Secretary – a role he was awarded on the very same day as Elizabeth's accession. Though Cecil's advice was not always welcome, she trusted him implicitly and he did not disappoint. A man of great intelligence, he was an integral part of Elizabeth's government for many years. He would remain loyal to Elizabeth for the rest of his life, and on a personal level she was fond of him, giving him the affectionate nickname of her 'Spirit'. Ten of Mary's former councillors were retained, including the Marquess of Winchester and the Earls of Shrewsbury, Pembroke, Arundel and Derby. Robert Dudley was given the position of Master of Horse, and his relationship with Elizabeth would soon set tongues wagging.

On 23 November, joined by her thousand-strong entourage, Queen Elizabeth left her childhood home of Hatfield behind as she began her journey to the capital: the setting for the next chapter of her life. To her delight, as she travelled her new subjects flocked to see her. They greeted her 'with so lively representations of love, joy and hope, that it far exceeded her expectation'.[5] Elizabeth had always been popular with the English people, but the beginning of her rule signified the start of a truly special relationship with her subjects.

When Elizabeth entered her capital, the Palace of Whitehall, which would become her primary seat, was not yet ready to receive her. Instead, her first five days in London were spent as the guest of Lord North at the Charterhouse in Smithfield, where 'the whole of London turned out and received her with great acclamations'.[6] At the time of Elizabeth's accession, London was one of the largest cities in Europe, with a population totalling around two hundred thousand. Although just the previous year Ambassador Giovanni Michiel had described the city as 'the metropolis of the kingdom, and truly royal, being with reason regarded as one of the principal cities of Europe', it was noisy and overcrowded.[7] It had 'handsome streets and buildings', including the cathedral of Old St Paul's and the royal palaces, but it was also poor, with poverty and vagrancy rife, having been financially crippled by the foreign wars of Elizabeth's brother-in-law Philip, which it had been forced to fund.[8] The country was weak and vulnerable, and people looked towards their new Queen to change this. Though hopes for Elizabeth were high, given the problems with which the country was riddled, including a crippled economy laden with debts, religious divides, and generally low standards of living, genuine expectations were few.[9] But Elizabeth was determined to bring about change, and what was more, she was prepared to work for it.

On 14 December, Queen Mary's body was taken by chariot from St James's for burial in Westminster Abbey. Though in her will she had declared her wish for her mother to be buried with her, Katherine of Aragon remained in Peterborough and Mary was laid to rest in Henry

VII's Lady Chapel, her grandfather's creation. The scars that Elizabeth bore from her sister's reign were still visible, and Count de Feria was not alone in his view that 'it is evident that she is highly indignant about what has been done to her during the Queen's lifetime'.[10] No monument was ever erected to Mary's memory – though in an ironic twist she and Elizabeth now share the same vault. Elizabeth's monument bears the inscription:

Partners both in throne and grave, here rest we two sisters,
Elizabeth and Mary, in the hope of the Resurrection.

Preparations for the first Christmas of Elizabeth's reign and her coronation were now underway, and though she had made a brief visit to the Tower, on 23 December Elizabeth settled at Whitehall, where her court quickly began to fill with those who sought her favour. Places in her household were more highly sought after than ever, but there were some whose special relationship with the new Queen guaranteed them a place. The choicest position went to Kate Astley, who was appointed Chief Gentlewoman of the Privy Chamber, while her husband, soon to return from his foreign exile, was made Master of the Jewel House. Thomas Parry was given a knighthood and made Comptroller of the Household, while his stepson, John Fortescue, became Master of the Wardrobe. The devoted Blanche Parry was made a Gentlewoman of Elizabeth's Privy Chamber and Keeper of the Queen's Books. With the appointment of the Queen's ladies there came too a shift in the balance of power at court: women became intercessors on account of their proximity to Elizabeth, notwithstanding the fact that, as Count de Feria recounted, 'a few days after the Queen's accession she made a speech to the women who were in her service commanding them never to speak to her on business affairs'.[11]

The Christmas festivities were lavish indeed, and the new Venetian ambassador Il Schifanoya remarked that 'they are intent on amusing themselves and on dancing till after midnight'.[12] No expense was spared, the entertainments all organized by Robert Dudley, who was already in high favour. On New Year's Day, Elizabeth received her first gifts as sovereign and among them were a 'fair cushion all over richly embroidered and set with pearl' from her cousin Frances, Duchess of Suffolk; 'a fair chain set with pearl' from Robert Dudley; and 'the Queen's picture finely painted upon a card' by the miniaturist Levina Teerlinc.[13]

Once the New Year's celebrations were concluded, all attention turned to Elizabeth's coronation. The preparations took many craftsmen several weeks, and platforms were erected close to Westminster Abbey in the week of Christmas, in readiness for the pageants that had been planned to mark the occasion. When choosing a date for her coronation, Elizabeth had consulted the renowned astrologer, mathematician and alchemist Dr John Dee, who may have been recommended to her by Robert Dudley.[14] On consulting his astrological charts, he suggested that 15 January would be a most propitious date for a glorious reign and, trusting his word, Elizabeth agreed.[15] On 12 January, Elizabeth left Whitehall by barge to take up residence at the Tower, in keeping with tradition. Given her previous experience there, it was perhaps a tradition she could have done without; despite her dramatic change in circumstance she still viewed the Tower with revulsion. However, Elizabeth would, at least, visit her former prison in fine style. The spectacle of the Queen's arrival was splendid, with 'ships, galleys, brigantines', all of which had been 'prepared as sumptuously as possible to accompany her Majesty and her Court thither by the Thames'. So magnificent was it that it reminded Il Schifanoya of Ascension Day in Venice, 'when the Signory go to espouse the sea'.[16] The magnificent festivities were all as the Queen had hoped and planned, and there was more to come.

On the morning of 14 January, Elizabeth prepared to make her state entry into her capital city. It was a bitterly cold day, with even a light sprinkling of snow, but this did not detract from the majesty of the occasion. An impressed Il Schifanoya wrote that 'the whole Court so sparkled with jewels and gold collars that they cleared the air'.[17] Houses throughout the city were decorated and people placed sand and gravel in front of their homes to make the mud caused by the bad weather more easily passable. As the cavalcade accompanying the Queen passed through the city, *last of all came her Majesty in an open litter, trimmed down to the ground with gold brocade, with a raised pile, and carried by two very handsome mules covered with the same material, and surrounded by a multitude of footmen in crimson velvet jerkins, all studded with massive gilt silver, with the arms of a white and red rose on their breasts and backs, and laterally the letters E. R. for Elizabeth Regina wrought in relief, the usual livery of this Crown, which makes a superb show.*[18]

Elizabeth was sumptuously attired in 'a royal robe of very rich cloth of gold', while on her head, over a coif of cloth of gold, had been placed 'a plain gold crown without lace, as a princess, but covered with jewels, and nothing in her hands but gloves'.[19] Behind the Queen's litter came Robert Dudley, her Master of Horse, who was 'mounted on a very fine charger'. Then came 'the Lord Chamberlain and other Lords of her Majesty's Privy Chamber, who were followed by nine pages dressed in crimson satin on very handsome chargers richly caparisoned, with their Governor and Lieutenant'.[20] With the Queen's trumpeters blowing and her cavalcade awash with colour, it was a dazzling scene.

The desire to mark the onset of this new and eagerly anticipated reign ensured that the citizens spared no expense in preparing a spectacular assortment of displays for the Queen's enjoyment, all in an attempt to 'express their love and joy' for her.[21] Elizabeth's relationship with her people would always be completely unique, and on this day in particular she took the time to acknowledge their efforts. She listened to each speech and each entertainment carefully, thanking those who were respon- sible, and thus many of her citizens were left that day with a personal impression and memory of their Queen. Each of these displays had been carefully chosen with a mind to extolling Elizabeth's virtues and lineage – some reflected her experiences and the adversity she had faced. When she reached Gracechurch Street, the first of a series of triumphal arches had been prepared, divided into three floors. Intended to highlight her royal lineage, on the first of these floors were her grandparents, the founders of her dynasty, 'King Henry the Seventh, of the House of Lancaster, with a large white rose in front of him, and his wife, the Queen Elizabeth, of the House of York, with another large red rose in front of her, both in royal robes'. More poignant for Elizabeth were the figures on the second floor, which showed 'King Henry VIII with a white and red rose in front of him, with the pomegranate between them, and Queen Anne Boleyn, mother of the present one, with a white eagle and a gold crown on its head and a gilt sceptre in its right talon (*nella destra griffa*), the other resting on a hillock; and surrounded in front of her by small branches of little roses, the coat of arms and device (*arma et impresa*) of the said Queen'.[22] For Elizabeth this must have been a significant moment, for not since her own time as Queen had Anne Boleyn been depicted alongside Elizabeth's father in such a majestic and favourable guise.[23] It was symbolic of Elizabeth's pride in her roots and this was reinforced by the scene on the third floor of the arch, in which 'a Queen was seen in majesty, to represent the present one, who is descended from the aforesaid'.[24] As Elizabeth approached, a little boy 'briefly interpreted the whole subject, and her Majesty listened to him most attentively, evincing much satisfaction'.[25]

Elizabeth's magnificent procession continued to Cornhill, where a further display had been staged. This one had evidently been prepared with a view to criticizing Mary, for it contained an inscription 'purporting that hitherto religion had been misunderstood and misdirected, and that now it will proceed on a better footing, which was exemplified by a queen seated aloft on her throne'. On one side of the Queen were people dressed with labels inscribed in Latin: '*Religio pura*; *Justicia gubernandi*; *Intelligentia*; *Sapientia*; *Prudentia*; *Timor Dei*'. To the other side, however, in an even clearer dig at the late Queen, were those wearing costumes inscribed with '*Ignorance, Superstition, Hypocrisy, Vain Glory, Simulation, Rebellion,* and *Idolatry*'.[26] Another contemporary source relates that a further pageant on the day featured both Henry VIII and Edward VI; it was clear which of Elizabeth's relatives were to be revered, and who was to be reviled.[27]

After Cornhill, the royal procession reached Cheapside, where there were more entertainments, and it was here that Elizabeth was presented with a copy of the New Testament in English. Finally free to express her faith openly, she took the book, 'which the Queen clasped in her arms and embraced passionately, returning thanks'.[28] From there the party travelled to Fleet Street, the entertainments concluding with an oration from the scholars of the City of London School. After what had been a truly splendid day of celebrations, Elizabeth retired for the evening to prepare for her big moment.

The following morning, the Queen emerged from Westminster Hall magnificently arrayed in her coronation robes and began the short walk to the Abbey. The Duchess of Norfolk was given the honour of carrying the Queen's train as she walked on the costly purple carpet that adorned her path. No sooner had Elizabeth stepped on a piece than the souvenir hunters were out in full force, for 'the cloth was cut away by those who could get it'.[29] Once inside, the peers of the realm watched in awe as Elizabeth was anointed Queen of England. Her reign had well and truly begun.

Edward VI was just nine years old when he became King in 1547. Elizabeth
prided herself in being 'the right excellent Princess the Lady Elizabeth her grace,
the King's Majesty's most honourable sister'.

ABOVE: Katherine Parr, the stepmother Elizabeth adored. The relationship between the pair was one of the most important of Elizabeth's life but ended on a sad note.

ABOVE: Thomas Seymour, the man who put Elizabeth's reputation at risk and abused her vulnerability.

BELOW: Chelsea Manor, the home that Elizabeth shared with Katherine Parr. It was at Chelsea that many of the dangerous scenes involving Thomas Seymour played out.

LEFT: A copy of a copper engraving of Elizabeth, which she reputedly gave to one of her ladies, Isabella Markham.

BELOW: The letter that Elizabeth wrote to Katherine Parr soon after leaving her household. Elizabeth regretted the pain that had been caused to the woman who had cared so deeply for her.

Although I coulde not be plentiful in giuinge thankes for the manifolde kimdems receyue
at your hithnis hande at my departure, yet I am some thinge to be borne with al, for
truly g was replete with sorowe to departe frome your highnis, especially leuinge you
vndoubful of helthe, and albeit I answered litel I wayed it more dipper whan you
sayd you wolde warne me of al euelles that you shulde hire of me, for if your grace
had not a good opinion of me you wolde not haue offered frindeship to me that
way, that al men iuge the contrarye, but what may I more say, thanke God for pro-
uidinge suche frendes to me, desiringe God to enriche me with ther longe life, and
me grace to be in hart no les thankeful to receyue it, than I nowe am glad in wri-
tinge to shewe it. and althougth I haue plentye of matter, hire I wil staye, for I
knowe you ar not quiet to rede . Frome Cheston this present saterday .

LEFT: Edward Courtenay, first Earl of Devon. During the reign of Mary I, Elizabeth's name was often linked with Courtenay's, and there were several plots involving the couple's marriage.

BELOW LEFT: Stephen Gardiner, Bishop of Winchester. An enemy to Elizabeth, Gardiner believed that she was plotting against her sister Mary and was deeply mistrustful of her.

BELOW: Thomas Parry, Elizabeth's cofferer. He became fully embroiled in the scandal surrounding Elizabeth and Thomas Seymour and was one of the few who knew the details of what transpired. He served Elizabeth loyally, even when she was under house imprisonment at Woodstock.

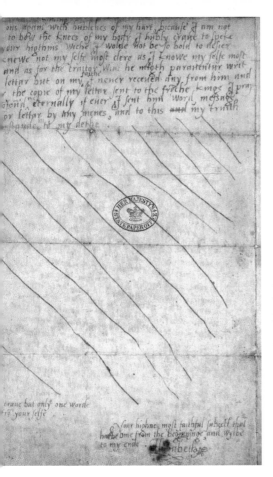

LEFT: Written at the most terrifying moment of her life, the 'Tide Letter' was Elizabeth's attempt to plead with her sister. The lines she scored to prevent forged words being added are a tangible reminder of her fear.

BELOW: The site of the former royal apartments at the Tower of London. Elizabeth was likely held here during her captivity in 1554.

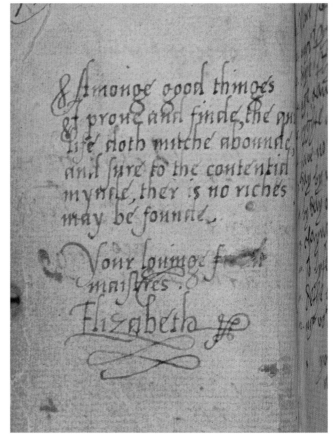

ABOVE: Woodstock Palace, where Elizabeth spent almost a year in house imprisonment under the custodianship of Sir Henry Bedingfield.

RIGHT: A poem composed by Elizabeth, written in an incomplete copy of the New Testament. It is possible that Elizabeth wrote this while in the Tower or when under house imprisonment.

LEFT: Philip and Mary, Elizabeth's brother-in-law and sister. Philip encouraged his wife to deal leniently with Elizabeth but had his own agenda for keeping her on side.

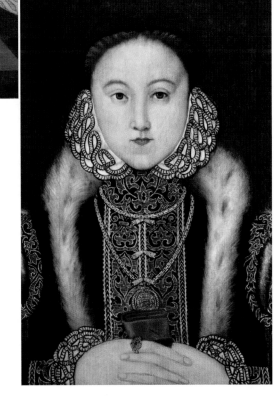

RIGHT: Young Elizabeth, probably painted shortly after her accession when demand for her likeness was high. This painting now hangs at Hever Castle, the childhood home of Elizabeth's mother.

Wearing full regalia, this image of Elizabeth reflects her appearance at her coronation, which was the ultimate moment of triumph after an uncertain youth.

APPENDIX 1

Elizabeth's Health

THROUGHOUT THE COURSE of researching *Young Elizabeth*, I was struck by the frequency with which Elizabeth suffered illness, notably during periods of stress or pressure. I am always wary of attempting to offer medical theories or explanations in relation to historical figures, but I was intrigued enough to want to at least explore some of the possibilities. At my husband's suggestion, I spoke with my brother-in-law Stephen Peters, and his business partner, Seb Kane, who has been studying neuroscience for more than twenty years. I outlined the details of Elizabeth's early life and the symptoms from which she suffered, interested to see what their take might be. The outcome of our conversations was astonishing and left me with a completely different perspective.

Using an approach that centred on his research into the brain and how it functions, Seb explained that some of the scenarios with which Elizabeth was faced during her earliest days could and would have led to certain physical symptoms she experienced. Before she was even born, Seb believed that the stress endured by her mother Anne Boleyn as a result of the pressure on her to produce a boy would have been transmitted to Elizabeth, manifesting itself physically throughout her life. Likewise, the trauma and grief she experienced at various points – caused by the deaths of her parents and stepmothers, and by increasing stress as her relationship with her sister Mary deteriorated – would not only have led to anxiety and depression, but also made her prone to digestive issues. Seb explained that Elizabeth would also probably have been a shallow breather; a phenomenon closely linked with the body's 'fight or flight' response when it finds itself in moments of stress. This is given further traction by the claim of Sir

Robert Tyrwhit in February 1549 that Elizabeth was 'much abashed, and half breathless', when told of Kate Astley's confession.[1]

Elizabeth almost certainly suffered from migraines, and on one occasion she apologized to her brother for a delay in writing that was caused by 'an affliction of my head and eyes' – not the only time she would be troubled by such complaints.[2] Similarly, the swelling of her body that she experienced, most notably in early 1554 at Ashridge and later at Woodstock, may, as hinted at earlier, potentially be accounted for by nephritis. Nephritis, inflammation of the kidneys, is often caused by autoimmune disease, which in itself can be triggered by stress. Or it can come about as the result of something as simple as a sore throat. In either scenario, it can lead to swelling of the body, as well as possible headaches, stomach pains, and a general feeling of being unwell. It is possible that this too may have been exacerbated by childhood trauma.

We cannot pinpoint the precise causes or diagnose all of Elizabeth's illnesses with certainty, but what we can surely say is that the unresolved issues of trauma, grief, as well as neglect from a father who was primarily occupied with ruling his kingdom, which Elizabeth was forced to contend with, had a profound and instrumental effect on her physical health and wellbeing. She would be forced to suffer these for the rest of her life.

APPENDIX 2

❦

Following in Elizabeth's Footsteps – Places to Visit

MANY OF THE places in which Elizabeth spent her youth have now vanished completely or survive only as the product of a later century. These include Greenwich, the place of her birth; Chelsea, where much of the scandal involving Thomas Seymour was staged; and Woodstock, where Elizabeth endured imprisonment. There are enough surviving fragments, though, to paint a picture of some of the surroundings in which Elizabeth grew up.

Eltham Palace, London

Much of Eltham Palace is now the product of the 1930s, when it was redesigned by the millionaires Stephen and Virginia Courtauld. Fortunately, Edward IV's magnificent Great Hall survives as the centrepiece, a statement room with which Elizabeth would have been familiar. There are also fragments of other parts of the Palace that Elizabeth would have known, including a fifteenth-century bridge that crosses the moat.

Hampton Court Palace, Surrey

Elizabeth came to know her father's Palace well, although it did not always harbour happy memories. Not only had she awaited the outcome of Mary's confinement at Hampton Court in 1555, but in 1562 she nearly died at the Palace when she caught smallpox. Hampton Court underwent great changes in the seventeenth century during the reign of William and

Mary, but much of the Palace Elizabeth was familiar with remains. The spectacular Great Hall, which features her mother's carved initials, and the Chapel Royal, where Elizabeth attended the christening of her brother Edward VI in 1537, are notable examples.

Hatfield House, Hertfordshire

One wing known as the Old Palace is all that survives of the Hatfield in which Elizabeth passed much of her youth, and this contains the Banqueting Hall complete with original roof timbers. Hatfield House itself was built in 1611 by Robert Cecil, first Earl of Salisbury, the son of Elizabeth's chief advisor. The House nevertheless contains some magnificent reminders of Elizabeth, including the splendid Rainbow Portrait and the Ermine Portrait. Likewise, some of Elizabeth's letters, written as the Seymour scandal unfolded, survive among the Cecil Papers in the archives – tangible reminders of a dangerous point in her youth.

Tower of London

Elizabeth's associations with the mighty fortress were not happy, yet they are impossible to overlook. The royal apartments in which she is likely to have been lodged during her imprisonment in 1554 have long since vanished, but traces of the ordeals of those close to her remain. Her mother, Thomas Seymour, the Duke of Northumberland, and Lady Jane Grey are all buried in the Chapel of St Peter ad Vincula within the Tower precincts, somewhere that Elizabeth would have become familiar with from the outside if not from within. Likewise, inscriptions reflecting the imprisonment of the Dudleys can be seen in the Beauchamp Tower, and those made by Elizabeth's Italian tutor, Giovanni Battista Castiglione, can be seen elsewhere in the Tower.

ABBREVIATIONS

The following abbreviations are used in the Notes and References

BL   British Library

CPR   *Calendar of Patent Rolls*

CSPD   *Calendar of State Papers, Domestic: Edward VI, Mary and Elizabeth*, R. Lemon (ed.) (London, 1856)

CSPF   *Calendar of State Papers, Foreign*, J. Stevenson *et al.* (eds), 23 vols (London, 1863–1969)

CSPS   *Calendar of State Papers, Spain*, G.A. Bergenroth *et al.* (eds), 13 vols (London, 1862–1954)

CSPV   *Calendar of State Papers, Venice*, R. Brown *et al.* (eds), 38 vols (London, 1864–1947)

L & P   *Letters and Papers, Foreign and Domestic, of the Reign of Henry VIII, 1509–1547*, J. Brewer *et al.* (eds), 21 vols (London, 1862–1932)

NPG   National Portrait Gallery

SoA   Society of Antiquaries

SP   State Papers

TNA   The National Archives

NOTES AND REFERENCES

Notes on Sources

1. D. Starkey, *Elizabeth: Apprenticeship* (London, 2001), pp. 155-6.
2. Viscount Strangford (ed.), *Household Expenses of the Princess Elizabeth During Her Residence at Hatfield, October 1, 1551, to September 30, 1552* (London, 1853), p. 40.
3. There are several similar versions of this portrait.

Prologue

1. Otherwise known as the Coronation Chair, the Chair was made on the orders of Edward I. It has been used at the coronation of every English monarch since 1308 and remains in Westminster Abbey to this day.
2. See https://www.westminster-abbey.org/about-the-abbey/history/cosmati-pavement.
3. CSPV, vii (10).
4. Ibid.
5. Sadly, the Crown Jewels used by Elizabeth were broken up and melted down during the Interregnum. The only piece she would have been familiar with is the Spoon, first used at the coronation of King John in 1199. There is, though, evidence that part of St Edward's Crown, made for the coronation of Charles II in 1660, pre-dates his reign and may have been part of the original medieval crown that was used for Elizabeth's coronation.
6. Unknown English artist, *Queen Elizabeth I*, c. 1600, The National Portrait Gallery, NPG 5175. For further details of this portrait see J. Arnold, 'The "Coronation" Portrait of Queen Elizabeth I', *Burlington Magazine*, 120:908 (1978), pp. 726–39, 741.

Introduction

1. W. Camden, *The Historie of the Most Renowned and Victorious Princesse Elizabeth, Late Queene of England*, 3rd edition (London, 1675), pp. 6–7.
2. Bryson and Evans say twenty-three letters, written in a variety of languages. See A. Bryson and M. Evans, 'Seven Rediscovered Letters of Princess Elizabeth Tudor', *Notes and Documents*, Institute of Historical Research, 90 (2017), p. 829.
3. H. Clifford, *The Life of Jane Dormer, Duchess of Feria*, ed. J. Stevenson (London, 1887), p. 22.
4. Starkey, *Elizabeth: Apprenticeship*.

Chapter 1

1. Humphrey, Duke of Gloucester, was arrested on charges of treason on 20 February 1447. Three days later he died, possibly as the result of a stroke.
2. J.O. Halliwell (ed.), *Letters of the Kings of England*, i (London, 1848), p. 305.
3. CSPV, ii (1287).

4. The Tudor dynasty had been established in 1485 when Henry Tudor had defeated (and killed) Richard III at the Battle of Bosworth on 22 August. Henry VII had subsequently married Elizabeth of York, the eldest daughter of Edward IV by Elizabeth Wydeville.

5. Arthur had been born in Winchester in September 1486 and was named after the legendary king of the same name. For more on Arthur see S. Cunningham, *Prince Arthur: The Tudor King Who Never Was* (Stroud, 2017).

6. Edmund had been born on 21 February 1499 and was styled Duke of Somerset. He was buried in Westminster Abbey, where his sister Elizabeth had also been laid to rest.

7. It has been noted that Henry's handwriting and that of his sister Mary bears a marked resemblance to that of Elizabeth of York. This seems to indicate that she had some hand in teaching the children their letters. D. Starkey, *Henry: Virtuous Prince* (London, 2008), pp. 118–20.

8. CSPV, ii (1287).

9. Katherine had been born on 16 December 1485 near Madrid. She was the youngest daughter of Ferdinand of Aragon and Isabella of Castile. Arthur died on 2 April 1502 at Ludlow Castle. He was buried in Worcester Cathedral, where the tomb and chantry erected to his memory can still be seen. For Arthur's final illness see A. Weir, *Elizabeth of York: The First Tudor Queen* (London, 2013), pp. 371–4. See also J. Guy, *The Children of Henry VIII* (London, 2013), pp. 2–4.

10. Elizabeth of York was buried in Westminster Abbey, where the splendid double tomb she shares with her husband survives. Her daughter Katherine was also buried there.

11. Margaret's wedding took place at Holyrood Abbey on 8 August 1503. She and James would have six children together before James was slain at the Battle of Flodden in 1513. Only one of these, the future James V, survived infancy.

12. CSPS, i (398).

13. Starkey, *Virtuous Prince*, pp. 239–40.

14. CSPS, i (552).

15. CSPV, i (942).

16. See D. Starkey (ed.), *The Inventory of King Henry VIII*, trans. P. Ward (London, 1998), which reveals the level of material wealth that surrounded Henry by the time of his death in 1547.

17. Katherine of Aragon had endured much hardship in the aftermath of Arthur's death. Though she had been betrothed to Prince Henry, her mother's death in 1504 greatly diminished her value in the marriage market. Several years of tussles over her dowry ensued, while Katherine herself lived in penury, largely at Durham House on London's Strand. See T. Earenfight, *Catherine of Aragon: Infanta of Spain, Queen of England* (Pennsylvania, 2021), pp. 81–5.

18. Shortly after their wedding both Henry and Katherine wrote to her father assuring him of their happiness within the marriage. For Henry's letter see Starkey, *Virtuous Prince*, p. 327–8.

19. Katherine's first pregnancy had resulted in the birth of a stillborn girl on 31 January 1510. The following year, on 1 January, a son, Henry, Duke of Cornwall, was born. He died on 22 February. In 1513 and 1514 she gave birth to two short-lived boys, before Mary's birth in 1516. Katherine's final child, a girl, was born on 10 November 1518. She died a few hours later. For more on Katherine's pregnancies see Earenfight, *Catherine of Aragon*, pp. 104–18.

20. CSPV, ii (1287).

21. CSPV, ii (1230).

22. Taken from John Skelton's *Speculum principis*, which was presented to Henry by Skelton at Eltham in 1501. Cited in Starkey, *Virtuous Prince*, p. 326.

23. Fitzroy was born in 1519 and was created Duke of Richmond in June 1525. See Guy, *Children of Henry VIII*, pp. 20–2.

24. Mary Boleyn had two children, Katherine and Henry. For evidence that Katherine may have been the King's daughter see A. Weir, *Mary Boleyn: 'The Great and Infamous Whore'* (London, 2011), pp.148–51. There may also have been another daughter, Etheldreda, who is referred to in Chapter Fifteen.

25. Anne Boleyn's date of birth has been the subject of much debate, and various dates have been suggested. It is now generally accepted that she was born around 1500–01, although some historians still contest this. Eric Ives was of the opinion that *c.* 1501 was correct. See E. Ives, *The Life and Death of Anne Boleyn* (Oxford, 2004), p. 15. For an alternative viewpoint see R.M. Warnicke, *The Rise and Fall of Anne Boleyn* (Cambridge, 1989), p. 9. Equally, Jane Dormer stated that at the time of her death in 1536 Anne 'was not twenty-nine years of age'. Clifford, *Life of Jane Dormer*, p. 18. She was probably born at Blickling in Norfolk.

26. Camden, *Historie*, p. 1. The Boleyns came from Salle in Norfolk. Henry VI knighted Geoffrey Boleyn, and his term as mayor dated from 1457–8. He died in 1463 and was buried in London. For more on Geoffrey and the family see O. Emmerson and C. Ridgway, *The Boleyns of Hever Castle* (Lucar, 2021).

27. Two further sons, Thomas and Henry, died, Thomas in 1520 when he was in his twenties. He was buried in the church at Penshurst in Kent where his tomb brass survives. See Weir, *Mary Boleyn*, p. 105. Henry's brass survives in St Peter's Church, Hever.

28. Emmerson and Ridgway, *Boleyns of Hever Castle*, p. 36.

29. Margaret was the daughter of the Holy Roman Emperor, Maximilian, and Mary of Burgundy. When she was seventeen she married Katherine of Aragon's brother, Prince Juan. However, Juan died after just six months of marriage. In 1501 she married Philibert II, Duke of Savoy, but he died in 1504. Three years later Margaret was named governor of the Low Countries and guardian of her nephew, Charles. For more on Margaret's life and experiences see S. Gristwood, *Game of Queens: The Women Who Made Sixteenth-Century Europe* (London, 2016).

30. As highly debated as Anne's date of birth is the order in which she and her siblings were born. There have been suggestions that Anne was older than her sister Mary, but it is more likely that she was the younger of the two. For differing viewpoints see R.M. Warnicke,' Anne Boleyn's Childhood and Adolescence', *Historical Journal*, 28:4 (1985), pp. 942–3; Ives, *Life and Death*, pp. 15–17; Weir, *Mary Boleyn*, pp. 12–15.

31. Eleanor would become both Queen of Portugal and Queen of France, while Isabella was Queen of Denmark, Norway and Sweden. Mary was Queen of Hungary and Bohemia and would later become Governor of the Netherlands.

32. Cited in Ives, *Life and Death*, p. 19.

33. Ibid.

34. Ibid. The letter later came into the possession of Anne's chaplain, Matthew Parker. It was Parker who bequeathed it to Corpus Christi College, Cambridge, in whose possession it is today.

35. Ives, *Life and Death*, p. 27.

36. Weir, *Mary Boleyn*, p. 54.

37. Although the name of Anne's sister, Mary, appears on a list of companions who accompanied Mary Tudor to France from England, Anne's name is not listed. This

suggests that she travelled directly from Margaret's court. Ives, *Life and Death*, pp. 27–8; Weir, *Mary Boleyn*, p. 55.

38. The couple had been married on 9 October at Abbeville, and Mary was crowned on 5 November.
39. The date of the wedding is uncertain, but it may have taken place as early as February 1515. B.J. Harris, 'Power, Profit, and Passion: Mary Tudor, Charles Brandon, and the Arranged Marriage in Early Tudor England', *Feminist Studies*, 15:1 (1989), p. 77.
40. It was agreed that the newlyweds would pay Henry £1,000 (£484,000) a year until the sum of £24,000 (£7,200,000) by way of compensation had been settled. Mary was also forced to hand over her jewels. However, the settlement was not heavily enforced. L & P, ii (436).
41. Claude was the daughter of Louis XII by his second wife, Anne of Brittany. She was born on 13 October 1499.
42. Both Blois and Amboise are still extant, and it remains possible to imagine what they would have been like during Claude's residency.
43. Claude had seven children in eight years. Of these, one later succeeded his father as Henri II, and two other sons died unmarried and childless. Two daughters died young, and Madeleine died aged sixteen shortly after her marriage to James V of Scotland. Margaret went on to marry the Duke of Savoy.
44. CSPV, ii (1287).
45. Cited in Ives, *Life and Death*, p. 45.
46. Cardinal Wolsey would recount that 'he himself was responsible for her [Anne's] recall, because he intended, by her marriage, to pacify certain quarrels and litigation between Boleyn and other English nobles'. CSPS, Further Supplement to Volumes 1 and 2, p. 30.
47. N. Sander, *Rise and Growth of the Anglican Schism*, ed. D. Lewis (London, 1877), p. 25.
48. Mary was married to William Carey on 4 February 1520 at Greenwich Palace. The King was among the wedding guests. Weir, *Mary Boleyn*, p. 92.
49. G. Cavendish, *The Life and Death of Cardinal Wolsey*, ed. R.S. Sylvester (London and New York, 1959), p. 59.
50. E. Hall, *The Union of the Two Noble and Illustre Famelies of York and Lancaster*, ed. H. Ellis (London, 1809), p. 631.
51. Henry Percy was the eldest son of the fifth Earl of Northumberland by Catherine Spencer. He was probably about a year younger than Anne.
52. Cavendish, *Life and Death*, p. 59.
53. Ibid.
54. See Ives, *Life and Death*, p. 65.
55. The date of Percy's marriage to Mary Talbot is unknown, but it was an extremely unhappy match. In 1532 Mary unsuccessfully attempted to have the marriage annulled. The couple had no children, and Percy died in 1537. Mary never remarried, and died in 1572.
56. Cavendish, *Life and Death*, p. 64. Wolsey ended his career in disgrace due to his failure to obtain an annulment from the Pope for Henry's marriage to Katherine of Aragon. Accused of treason in 1530, he set out for London from Yorkshire, but died in Leicester on 29 November.
57. Cavendish, *Life and Death*, p. 64.
58. Wyatt's wife was Elizabeth Brooke, a sister of Lord Cobham. Following Wyatt's death she remarried, taking Sir Edward Warner as her second husband; Ives, *Life and Death*, pp. 67–8, 73–8; G.W. Bernard, *Anne Boleyn: Fatal Attractions* (New Haven and

London, 2010), pp. 15–18; N. Shulman, *Graven with Diamonds: The Many Lives of Thomas Wyatt* (London, 2011), pp. 89–110.

59. Cited in Shulman, *Graven with Diamonds*, p. 107.
60. CSPV, iv (824).
61. Halliwell (ed.), *Letters*, i, pp. 305, 306.
62. See Ives, *Life and Death*, p. 83; Warnicke, *Rise and Fall*, pp. 53–4.
63. D. Starkey, *Six Wives: The Queens of Henry VIII* (London, 2003), pp. 203–4.
64. For more details see Starkey, *Six Wives*, pp. 285–433; A. Weir, *The Six Wives of Henry VIII* (London, 1991), pp. 171–244.
65. It was reported that Mary had used 'opprobrious language' against Anne. CSPV, iv (761).
66. Tracy Borman has noted that the letters patent issued to Anne in early 1533 include the first known use of the falcon as her official badge. See *Anne Boleyn and Elizabeth I: The Mother and Daughter Who Changed History* (London, 2023), p. 25; CSPS, iv (995).
67. Starkey, *Six Wives*, p. 461.
68. According to Chapuys, who reported the information to Charles V in May, the marriage was celebrated on the day of the Conversion of St Paul, 25 January. See L & P, vi (465). Archbishop Cranmer, who confirmed that, contrary to contemporary rumours, he had not performed the couple's marriage ceremony, supported this view. See H. Ellis, *Original Letters*, iii (London, 1825–46), pp. 34–9. Instead, the ceremony is likely to have been performed by Bishop Rowland Lee, an associate of Thomas Cromwell who would later be appointed Bishop of Coventry and Lichfield. See J. Denny, *Anne Boleyn* (London, 2004), p. 186.
69. L & P, vi (351).
70. Clifford, *Life of Jane Dormer*, p. 18.
71. BL, Egerton MS 985, f. 55v.
72. Ives, *Life and Death*, p. 179.
73. L & P, vi (584).
74. L & P, vi (142). See also L & P, vi (585).
75. L & P, vi (918).
76. L & P, vi (1069).
77. L & P, vi (1004).
78. L & P, vi (1069).
79. L & P, vi (1111).
80. L & P, vi (1112).
81. L & P, vi (1089); BL, Harley MS 283, f. 75r.
82. Ives, *Life and Death*, p. 186.
83. BL, Harley MS 283, f. 75r.
84. L & P, vi (1112).
85. L & P, vi (1125).

Chapter 2

1. Agnes Tilney was the second wife of Thomas Howard, Earl of Surrey and then second Duke of Norfolk. Howard's first wife died on 4 April 1497, and he married Agnes just months later. The couple had seven children, several of whom attended Elizabeth's christening. Agnes was the stepmother of Anne Boleyn's mother, and therefore step-grandmother to Anne herself. After her husband's death in 1524 Agnes never remarried.

2. Henry's younger brother Edmund had also been christened here in 1499, as had his daughter Mary in 1516.
3. J.W. Kirby, 'Building Works at Placentia 1532–1533', *Transactions of the Greenwich and Lewisham Antiquarian Society*, 5:1 (1957), p. 50.
4. L & P, vi (1111).
5. Ibid.
6. Margaret Wootton was the paternal grandmother of Lady Jane Grey and her sisters. The court artist Hans Holbein drew a sketch of her, which survives in the Royal Collection.
7. L & P, vi (1112).
8. John Stokesley had supported Henry VIII's separation from Katherine of Aragon, but later fell out of favour with his royal master; L & P, vi (1125).
9. L & P, vi (1125).
10. In July 1534 two friars who had attended Elizabeth's christening were arrested for saying that she had been christened in hot water, but 'it was not hot enough'. L & P, vii (939); C. Wriothesley, *A Chronicle of England during the Reigns of the Tudors, from AD 1485 to 1559*, ed. W.D. Hamilton, Camden Society (London, 1875, 1877), i, p. 23.
11. Initially it was agreed that Hertford Castle should be Elizabeth's base, but this was struck out and replaced with Hatfield.
12. As mentioned in Chapter One, Henry VIII's nursery and that of most of his siblings was established at Eltham Palace.
13. This tale is recounted by David Starkey, who notes that there is no contemporary evidence to support this. See Starkey, *Six Wives*, p. 511.
14. In August 1582 Blanche Parry sought Lord Burghley's intercession on behalf of 'Mr Pendryth, whose wife nursed the Queen'. HMS Salisbury, ii (1198); HMC Salisbury, i, pp. 133–4 lists an intriguing document that had been forwarded by an anonymous author to John Garnons in 1601, who duly sent it to Sir Robert Cecil. In the letter the anonymous writer claims that 'My mother was chosen and brought to the Court by my Lady Herbert, of Troy, to have been her Majesty's nurse, and had been chosen before all other had her gracious mother had her own will therein.' The identity of the lady in question is a mystery. Ruth Richardson also references this document in *Mistress Blanche: Queen Elizabeth I's Confidante* (Eardisley, 2018), p. 37.
15. M.A.S. Hume (trans.), *Chronicle of King Henry VIII of England: Being a Contemporary Record of Some of the Principal Events of the Reigns of Henry VIII and Edward VI* (London, 1889), p. 42.
16. L & P, vi (1510).
17. L & P, vi (1528).
18. It was not until 1538 that Hatfield would officially become Crown property. See H.M. Colvin, D.R. Ransome and J. Summerson (eds), *The History of the King's Works*, iv (London, 1982), p. 149. Morton was one of Henry VII's ministers. Only one part of the original Palace survives, known today as the Old Palace. This contains the Banqueting Hall, which is frequently used for events.
19. The church was named after the patron saint of the bishops of Ely, and parts date from the thirteenth century. On 16 July 1517 Elizabeth's cousin, Lady Frances Brandon, had also been born at Hatfield and christened in the church of St Etheldreda. Frances was the daughter of Mary Tudor, Henry VIII's younger sister, and her husband Charles Brandon, Duke of Suffolk. She was later the mother of Lady Jane Grey and her two sisters. Today, the church contains the tomb of Robert Cecil, first Earl of Salisbury. Two prime ministers, Lord Melbourne and Lord Salisbury, are also buried in St Etheldreda's.

20. Anne Shelton was Thomas Boleyn's sister, as was Alice Clere. Alice was her parents third daughter, and the second wife of Sir Robert Clere. She died in 1538. In her will, she left 'a pair of beads of gold which Queen Anne gave me with divers precious stones' to her son, Thomas. TNA, PROB 10/7459/5.

21. Lady Bryan married three times: her first husband was Sir John Sandys, a match that had been arranged during Margaret's childhood. She then married Sir Thomas Bryan, who had been a knight of the body to both Henry VII and Henry VIII, as well as Vice-Chamberlain of Katherine of Aragon's household. Following his death in 1517 she took as her third husband David Souche. See B.J. Harris, 'The View from My Lady's Chamber: New Perspectives on the Early Tudor Monarchy', Huntingdon Library Quarterly, 60:3 (1997), p. 239.

22. Lady Bryan had assumed this role for Mary by 1518, and had been replaced by Margaret Pole, Countess of Salisbury, by the spring of 1520. See L. Porter, Mary Tudor: The First Queen (London, 2007), pp. 14, 16.

23. Margaret was the daughter of Sir Humphrey Bourchier and Elizabeth Tilney. Sir Humphrey was killed at the Battle of Barnet in 1471, and his widow remarried Thomas Howard, second Duke of Norfolk. Among their many children was Anne Boleyn's mother, born Elizabeth Howard.

24. Clifford, Life of Jane Dormer, p. 11. Sir Francis Bryan was greatly favoured by Henry VIII, and much of his life was spent at court. He lost an eye during a jousting tournament at Greenwich, and was forced to wear an eye patch as a result. He later became known as 'The Vicar of Hell'.

25. T. Borman, Elizabeth's Women: The Hidden Story of the Virgin Queen (London, 2009), p. 24; L & P, xi (203).

26. Mary's laundress was Avice Wood, Alice Baker was her gentlewoman, and Sir Henry Rowte was her chaplain. L & P, ii, The King's Book of Payments; L & P, x (1187).

27. Richardson, Mistress Blanche, p. 37.

28. Mary's rockers were Margery Parker, Anne Bright, Ellen Hutton and Margery Cousin, all of whom were paid sixty shillings in October 1516 for three-quarters of a year's wages. L & P, ii, The King's Book of Payments.

29. The reference to rocking Elizabeth's cradle comes from the epitaph adorning the empty tomb that Blanche commissioned for herself in St Faith's Church, Bacton. Blanche was born between March 1507 and March 1508, the daughter of Henry Myles and Alice Milborne. Richardson, Mistress Blanche, pp. 7, 20.

30. By the time of Henry VIII's death in 1547, Lady Troy had almost certainly been responsible for the appointment of at least one other relative, for a Mistress Whitney was listed among Elizabeth's ladies as being one of those who received material for mourning clothes for the late King. Nothing else is known of her, but Lady Troy's first husband had been James Whitney. It is therefore plausible that Mistress Whitney may have been a granddaughter, or perhaps a niece. TNA, LC 2/2, f. 48v.

31. L.S. Marcus, J. Mueller and M.B. Rose (eds), Elizabeth I: Collected Works (Chicago, 2000), p. 34.

32. L & P, viii (440); TNA, E 101/421/12.

33. Kirby, 'Building Works', p. 50; J.B. Heath, 'An Account of Materials Furnished for the Use of Queen Anne Boleyn, and the Princess Elizabeth, by William Loke, The King's Mercer, between the 20th January 1535 and the 27th April, 1536', Miscellanies of the Philobiblon Society, Vol. VII (London, 1862–3), p. 12.

34. CSPV, vi (884).

35. Ibid.
36. L & P, vi (1125).
37. L & P, vi (1392).
38. L & P, vi (1558).
39. L & P, vii (14).
40. L & P, vii (83).
41. Thomas Cromwell was the son of a Putney blacksmith, Walter, but travelled abroad during his youth. When he returned he eventually joined Wolsey's household, where before long he had risen to become one of the Cardinal's most trusted advisors. Following Wolsey's fall, Cromwell managed to retain the King's favour and steadily rose in prominence.
42. L & P, vii (83).
43. L & P, vii (171).
44. L & P, vii (214).
45. L & P, vii (296).
46. L & P, vii (373); L & P, vii (337). This incident occurred on 16 March, Chapuys reported it to the Emperor the following day.
47. A. Somerset, *Elizabeth I* (London, 1991), p. 6.
48. L & P, vii (393).
49. Thomas More was the son of a lawyer, Sir John More, and grew in influence with Henry during the early years of his reign. He was appointed Lord Chancellor in 1529. John Fisher was the confessor and close friend of Henry's grandmother, Margaret Beaufort. He was made Bishop of Rochester in 1504 during the reign of Henry VII.
50. John Fisher was executed on 22 June 1535, while Sir Thomas More was executed the following month on 6 July. Pope Pius XI canonized both men on 19 May 1935.
51. S. Lawson (ed.), *Eltham Palace* (London, 2011), p. 29.
52. Ibid., pp. 3, 14.
53. Ibid., pp. 27, 40.
54. S. Thurley, *The Royal Palaces of Tudor England: Architecture and Court Life 1460–1547* (New Haven and London, 1993), p. 79. Accounts note the repairing of the glass in this gallery in 1535, and in the same year Queen Anne's badge was set in the glazing of the gallery. See Colvin, Ransome and Summerson (eds), *History of the King's Works*, iv, p. 82.
55. Ibid.
56. L & P, vii (393).
57. L & P, vii (509).
58. L & P, vii (556).
59. Weir, *Mary Boleyn*, p. 195.
60. L & P, vii (1193).
61. L & P, vii (1095).
62. Ibid.
63. L & P, vii (530).
64. L & P, vii (1129). William Butts was educated at Cambridge and became a member of the College of Physicians in 1529. He had three sons, who married three sisters, Joan, Bridget and Anne Bures.
65. L & P, vii (1297).
66. Ibid.
67. Ibid.
68. L & P, vii (1437).
69. Formerly the royal palace of Sheen, Henry had it rebuilt following a catastrophic fire

there in 1497. He named it Richmond in honour of his previous earldom, and it became a masterpiece of Renaissance architecture.

70. L & P, vii (1297).
71. Ibid.
72. L & P, vii (469).
73. It seems probable that at least one ambassador saw Elizabeth again later in 1534, for on 29 September Sir Anthony Browne wrote to Cromwell noting that he had received a letter requesting that he accompany the ambassador on his visit to the Princess. L & P, vii (1198).
74. Charles had been born on 22 January 1522, and following his brother's death would become Duke of Orléans. A popular and lively young man, Charles died at the age of twenty-three, probably of the plague.
75. L & P, viii (174).
76. The Treaty of the More had been signed at The More on 30 August 1525, having been negotiated by Cardinal Wolsey and Louise of Savoy, working on behalf of her son François I, who was then the captive of the Emperor Charles V.
77. CSPS, v, part 1 (213).
78. N. Orme, *Tudor Children* (New Haven and London, 2023), p. 69.
79. E. Norton, *The Lives of Tudor Women* (London, 2016), p. 35.
80. L & P, viii (440).
81. Thurley, *Royal Palaces*, p. 237.
82. Hunsdon had apparently been begun by Sir William Oldhall, chamberlain to Richard, Duke of York. Colvin, Ransome and Summerson (eds), *King's Works*, iv, pp. 154–5.
83. Heath, 'An Account of Materials'.
84. Ibid., p. 10.
85. Ibid., pp. 10, 13.
86. Hans Holbein, 'Drawing', 1532–43, The British Museum, SL,5308.77; Hans Holbein, 'Drawing', 1532–43, SL,5308.84.
87. D. Scarisbrick, *Tudor and Jacobean Jewellery* (London, 1995), p. 14.
88. This fountain was given to Henry at New Year 1534, and was described as 'A goodly gilt bason, having a rail or board of gold in the midst of the brim, garnished with rubies and pearls, wherein standeth a fountain, also having a rail of gold about it garnished with diamonds; out thereof issueth water, at the teats of three naked women standing at the foot of the same fountain.' L & P, vii (9). For more on Holbein and Anne see F. Moyle, *The King's Painter: The Life and Times of Hans Holbein* (London, 2021), pp. 289–90.
89. Anne's 'B' necklace appears in the following portrait: *Anne Boleyn*, unknown English artist, late sixteenth century, based on a work of *c*. 1533–6, The National Portrait Gallery, NPG 668. See also one of Holbein's designs of a jewel combining the initials HA: Hans Holbein, 'Drawing', 1532–43, The British Museum, SL,5308.115.
90. Lucas Horenbout, *Queen Mary I*, *c*. 1525, The National Portrait Gallery, NPG 6453.
91. Norton, *Lives of Tudor Women*, p. 35.
92. L & P, ix (568).
93. Weir, *Six Wives*, p. 277.
94. CSPV, v (54).

Chapter 3

1. L & P, x (141). Kimbolton Castle is now a school.
2. A. Weir, *The Lady in the Tower: The Fall of Anne Boleyn* (London, 2009), p. 19.

3. L & P, viii (59).
4. L & P, x (141).
5. Ibid.
6. CSPS, v, part 2 (9).
7. Ibid.
8. L & P, x (141).
9. L & P, x (200).
10. This is now Peterborough Cathedral, where the site of Katherine's burial can still be seen. Her tomb was vandalized by Oliver Cromwell's troops in 1643, and her present memorial dates from 1895; L & P, x (284).
11. L & P, x (282).
12. Wriothesley, *Chronicle*, i, p. 33. Chapuys reported that Norfolk had informed Anne of her husband's accident 'in a way that she should not be alarmed or attach much importance to it'. L & P, x (282).
13. L & P, x (351).
14. L & P, x (282).
15. L & P, x (351).
16. L & P, x (352).
17. L & P, x (351).
18. L & P, x (901).
19. L & P, x (282).
20. L & P, x (601).
21. Ibid.
22. Ibid.
23. L & P, x (901).
24. L & P, x (913).
25. Weir, *Lady in the Tower*, p. 17.
26. Borman, *Anne Boleyn and Elizabeth I*, pp. 69–70.
27. L & P, viii (601).
28. L & P, x (615).
29. Weir, *Lady in the Tower*, p. 59.
30. L & P, x (752).
31. Ives, *Life and Death*, p. 306.
32. Ibid., p. 307.
33. Carew had been born in around 1496 and was highly favoured by the King. He and Elizabeth Bryan would have five children together, one of whom was the mother-in-law of Sir Walter Raleigh. Carew was later executed on 3 March 1539, having become entangled in the Exeter Conspiracy; Weir, *Lady in the Tower*, p. 33.
34. L & P, x (752).
35. See Weir, *Lady in the Tower* p. 84; L & P, x (873).
36. L & P, x (873).
37. Alison Weir's *Lady in the Tower* analyses this evidence and thereby provides a convincing argument that this was indeed the case. See p. 68.
38. CSPS, v, part 2 (61).
39. HMC Rutland, i, p. 107.
40. In 1572 Parker would refer to himself as being Anne's 'poor countryman'. See J. Bruce (ed.), *Correspondence of Matthew Parker, Archbishop of Canterbury* (Cambridge, 1853), p. 400.
41. Ibid.

42. Ibid., p. 59.
43. Ibid., p. 391.
44. L & P, x (953). The Countess of Worcester was the second wife of Henry Somerset, second Earl of Worcester. Together the couple would have at least eight living children. Following her death in 1565 the Countess was buried in the Priory Church of St Mary, Chepstow, where the tomb effigy in memory of her and her husband can still be seen.
45. CSP Foreign, Elizabeth I, i (1303).
46. L & P, x (782).
47. CSP Foreign, Elizabeth I, i (1303).
48. Ibid.
49. Weir, *Lady in the Tower*, p. 122.
50. Ibid., p. 125.
51. See Ives, *Life and Death*, pp. 326–7.
52. See Weir, *Lady in the Tower*, p. 129. Norris was a widower with three children. He had been in the King's service since he was a youth, and Henry trusted him implicitly. This is evident from both his position at the time of his fall, and the numerous posts and grants that he had received throughout the course of the King's reign.
53. L & P, x (782).
54. L & P, x (797).
55. L & P, x (782).
56. This detail comes from Ales, who personally heard the cannon. CSP Foreign, Elizabeth I, i (1303).
57. L & P, x (793).
58. Ibid.
59. L & P, x (797).
60. See Weir, *Lady in the Tower*, pp. 138–9 for possible reasons for Lady Shelton's grievance with Anne.
61. Mary Kingston had been born Mary Scrope, and had first married Edward Jerningham, by whom she had five children. Following the death of her husband in 1515, she remarried William Kingston. The date of their wedding is unknown, but it had taken place by 1532.
62. L & P, x (793).
63. Cited in Weir, *Lady in the Tower*, p. 213.
64. L & P, x (793); Weir, *Lady in the Tower*, p. 120.
65. L & P, x (793).
66. Sir Richard Page began his career in the household of Cardinal Wolsey, and later became a gentleman of Henry VIII's Privy Chamber. He had also been Vice-Chamberlain in the household of Henry's illegitimate son, Henry Fitzroy. Page not only survived the events of May 1536 but was also restored to the King's favour once more. He died in 1548.
67. L & P, x (797).
68. L & P, x (908).
69. See Bernard, *Fatal Attractions*.
70. See Weir, *Lady in the Tower*, p. 184.
71. L & P, xxi, part 2 (554).
72. L & P, x (908).
73. L & P, x (848).
74. L & P, x (908).
75. L & P, x (873).

76. Weir, *Lady in the Tower*, p. 205.
77. Henry Percy had succeeded his father as the sixth Earl of Northumberland in 1527. He died in 1537.
78. L & P, x (908).
79. Weir, *Lady in the Tower*, p. 212.
80. L & P, x (908).
81. Camden, *Historie*, p. 4.
82. Cited in Weir, *Lady in the Tower*, p. 218.
83. L & P, x (908).
84. Ibid.
85. Ibid.
86. L & P, x (792).
87. L & P, x (890).
88. L & P, x (909).
89. Ibid.
90. CSP Foreign, Elizabeth I, i (1303).
91. Clifford, *Life of Jane Dormer*, p. 18.
92. L & P, x (908).
93. L & P, x (1036).
94. Weir, *Lady in the Tower*, p. 238.
95. L & P, x (910).
96. L & P, x (1036).
97. L & P, x (908); L & P, x (918).
98. L & P, x (911).
99. Cited in Ives, *Life and Death*, pp. 357–8.
100. L & P, x (911).
101. CSP Foreign, Elizabeth I, i (1303).
102. In 1876 during restoration of the Chapel, bones believed to be Anne's were found. However, Weir convincingly argues that the bones believed to be Anne's probably belonged to someone else. See *Lady in the Tower*, pp. 324–5.
103. L & P, x (968).
104. It seems likely that, at the latest, Elizabeth had at least some knowledge of what had happened to her mother by 1545 when she was eleven/twelve, for that same year she was painted wearing her mother's necklace.
105. CSP Foreign, Elizabeth I, i (1303).
106. Borman, *Anne Boleyn and Elizabeth I*, pp. 149–50.
107. Borman, *Anne Boleyn and Elizabeth I*.
108. Weir, *Lady in the Tower*, p. 307.
109. Ibid.; V & A 19-1887.
110. See Weir, *Mary Boleyn*, pp. 148–51.
111. Ibid., p. 214.
112. Henry had become Anne Boleyn's ward following the death of his father, William Carey. He was later sent to Syon Abbey where in 1535 the vicar of Isleworth, John Hale, scathingly referred to him as being the King's bastard. According to Hale, he had been introduced to 'young Master Carey', whom he had been told 'was our sovereign lord the King's son by our sovereign lady the Queen's sister, whom the Queen's grace might not suffer to be in the court', L & P, viii (609). No other contemporary source refers to Henry as being the King's son, and the claim was almost certainly incorrect.

113. The book is now on display at Anne's childhood home, Hever Castle. I am greatly indebted to Kate McCaffrey for allowing me to see some of the extensive research she conducted for her MA on this topic. Kate's research has made an invaluable contribution to our knowledge and understanding of the book, and will be published in the future.

114. For more on the ring see S. Doran (ed.), *Elizabeth and Mary: Royal Cousins, Rival Queens* (London, 2021), pp. 44–5.

115. Unknown artist, *The Family of Henry VIII, c.* 1545, Royal Collection Trust, RCIN 405796.

116. Some were overlooked, however, and remain in place today at St James's Palace, Hampton Court, and King's College Chapel, Cambridge.

117. Starkey (ed.), *Inventory*, pp. 12–13, 34–5 for several examples, including a pair of pots that contained 'Queen Anne's cipher upon the lids', p. 35.

Chapter 4

1. L & P, x (1047). Arthur Plantagenet, Lord Lisle, was the illegitimate son of Edward IV by an unconfirmed lady.
2. L & P, x (1022).
3. L & P, x (968).
4. Ibid.
5. L & P, x (991).
6. L & P, x (1022).
7. L & P, x (1110).
8. L & P, xi (7).
9. L & P, x (1129).
10. L & P, x (1137).
11. Thomas Wriothesley was born in 1505, the son of York Herald, William Wriothesley. Through the influence of Stephen Gardiner, Wriothesley attracted the notice of Thomas Cromwell, whose service he entered in 1524. Wriothesley served Henry VIII faithfully for the remainder of the King's reign, and on Henry's wishes was ennobled as Earl of Southampton on 16 February 1547.
12. L & P, x (1186).
13. BL, Cotton MS Vespasian C XIV, f. 246v.
14. L & P, xi (639).
15. Blanche was the daughter of Simon Milborne and Jane Baskerville and had been married twice. First, to James Whitney, by whom she had four children. After his death in 1500, between then and 1502 she married Sir William Herbert of Troy as his second wife. He was an illegitimate son of Sir William Herbert, first Earl of Pembroke.
16. Cited in Richardson, *Mistress Blanche*, p. 40.
17. Ibid., p. 41.
18. Ibid.
19. Ibid., p. 42.
20. Ibid., p. 40.
21. Ibid., p. 44.
22. An Elizabeth Cavendish appears as a recipient of those who received jewels after Jane Seymour's death, so it is possible that she transferred to Jane's service. L & P, xii, part 2 (973). However, if she did so she may have re-joined Elizabeth's household after Jane's

death, as the Lady Mary's expenses show a payment in January 1540 to Elizabeth's lady, Mistress Cavendish. F. Madden (ed.), *The Privy Purse Expenses of Princess Mary* (London, 1831), p. 84.

23. The Countess of Kildare was the daughter of Thomas Grey, first Marquess of Dorset (and son of Elizabeth Wydeville by her first marriage), and Cecily Bonville. She had served in the household of Mary Tudor in France and had afterwards remained in the household of Queen Claude with Anne Boleyn. Like Anne, she later served Katherine of Aragon. Given her links with Anne, it is possible that the Countess was personally chosen by Anne to attend on her daughter. In around 1522 the Countess married Gerald FitzGerald, a widower, with whom she had many children.

24. Sir John Norris was favoured by Henry VIII, to whom he had been Usher of the Outer Chamber – he would later fulfil the same post for Edward VI. He married Elizabeth Braye, but the couple had no children. Thus, when he died in 1564, all his estates were settled on his nephew.

25. L & P, xii, part 2 (1060); L & P, xii, part 2 (973). After a short marriage to the captain of the *Mary Rose*, Sir George Carew, who drowned in the ship's sinking in 1545, Mary went on to marry Sir Arthur Champernowne, nephew of Katherine.

26. BL, Cotton MS Vespasian C XIV. Interestingly, Dorothy Bradbelt would become one of Elizabeth's ladies, and her name appears among several lists of those who gave Elizabeth New Year's gifts when she became queen. There was almost certainly a familial relationship and continuity with Jane Bradbelt. See J.A. Lawson (ed.), *The Elizabethan New Year's Gift Exchanges 1559–1603* (Oxford, 2013), p. 80, for example.

27. Elizabeth's two grooms of the chamber, Richard Foster and William Russell, were rewarded by the Lady Mary in October 1538, and in Russell's case he was still serving Elizabeth in 1552. Madden (ed.), *Privy Purse Expenses*, p. 80.

28. L & P, x (1187). Many of these names also appear on the list of Elizabeth's household who were to receive materials for mourning clothes following Henry VIII's death. TNA, LC 2/2, f. 48v–r.

29. BL, Cotton MS Vespasian C XIV, f. 75v.

30. L & P, xi (40).

31. L & P, x (1204); L & P, xi (40).

32. L & P, xi (29).

33. L & P, xi (41).

34. HMC Rutland, i, p. 310.

35. Henry Fitzroy died at St James's Palace at the age of seventeen. There has been speculation as to the cause of his death. He was buried in St Michael's Church, Framlingham, where his beautiful tomb can still be seen.

36. L & P, xi (132).

37. Madden (ed.), *Privy Purse Expenses*, pp. 50, 88.

38. On 3 August Chapuys observed that Mary was not without company, 'even the followers of the little Bastard'. L & P, xi (219).

39. Madden (ed.), *Privy Purse Expenses*, p. 4.

40. L & P, xi (148).

41. Ibid.

42. Ibid.

43. BL, Cotton MS Otho C X, f. 234r. The husband to whom she referred was David Souche, Lady Bryan's third husband.

44. L & P, xi (203).

45. Tracy Borman offers an alternative explanation: that Lady Bryan was perhaps being disingenuous in an attempt to ensure that Elizabeth was not forgotten by her father. She rightly points out that Anne Boleyn was ordering clothes for her daughter until shortly before her death. See *Anne Boleyn and Elizabeth I*, pp. 99–100.
46. L & P, xi (203).
47. Ibid.
48. Ibid.
49. For Shelton's letter to Cromwell see L & P, xi (312).
50. Mary wrote to Cromwell from Hertford on 2 October; however, Elizabeth's gentle-woman Katherine Champernowne wrote from Hunsdon on 10 October. This suggests either that Elizabeth did not travel to Hertford with Mary, or that the trip to Hertford was only short.
51. TNA, LC 5/31, p. 8; M. Hayward, *Dress at the Court of King Henry VIII* (Leeds, 2007), p. 209.
52. Aske hailed from an old Yorkshire family, and had prominent family connections. For more on this see G. Moorhouse, *The Pilgrimage of Grace: The Rebellion that Shook Henry VIII's Throne* (London, 2002), pp. 72, 74.
53. Lady Eleanor Clifford was the youngest daughter of Henry's sister, Mary, and her second husband Charles Brandon. She married Henry Clifford, heir of the first Earl of Cumberland, and became Countess of Cumberland when her father-in-law died in 1542. Little is known of Eleanor, and just one of her letters survives. Written to her husband, she complained of ill health, and she died on 27 September 1547. She is buried in Skipton, Yorkshire.
54. L & P, xi (860).
55. Ibid.
56. See L & P, xi (8) and L & P, xi (285), for example.
57. Colvin, Ransome and Summerson (eds), *History of the King's Works*, iv, p. 103.
58. Thurley, *Royal Palaces*, p. 81.
59. L & P, xii, part 1 (815).
60. Ibid.
61. L & P, xiii, part 2 (14).
62. Madden (ed.), *Privy Purse Expenses*, p. 42.
63. L & P, xii, part 2 (889).
64. Ibid.
65. L & P, xii, part 2 (911).
66. L & P, xii, part 2 (905).
67. L & P, xii, part 2 (894).
68. L & P, xii, part 2 (911).
69. Ibid. This definition of a chrisom is taken from C. Hibbert, *Elizabeth I: A Personal History of the Virgin Queen* (London, 1992), p. 21.
70. Madden (ed.), *Privy Purse Expenses*, p. 42.
71. L & P, xii, part 2 (911).
72. Ibid.
73. A. Weir, *Jane Seymour: The Haunted Queen* (London, 2018), pp. 511–13.
74. L & P, xii, part 2 (971).
75. L & P, xii, part 2 (972).
76. BL, Royal MS 7 C XVI, f. 21v.
77. Ibid.

78. Following Henry VIII's death he too was interred at Windsor. A marble slab in the Chapel, installed in 1837 on the orders of William IV, marks their resting place.

Chapter 5

1. Cited in C. Skidmore, *Edward VI: The Lost King of England* (London, 2007), p. 22.
2. L & P, xiv, part 1 (655). Sir Edward Baynton also had some hand in questioning the men accused of adultery with Anne Boleyn. His second wife, who joined him in supervising Elizabeth and Mary's household, was Isabel Leigh, a sister of Katherine Howard.
3. Part of an elegy composed for Lady Troy by Lewys Morgannwg, a bard from Glamorgan. Cited in Richardson, *Mistress Blanche*, p. 40.
4. Lady Troy's name does not appear on the second list of Elizabeth's household staff, which is likely to date from 1546. L & P, x (1187). However, there is evidence that she did not leave until 1547.
5. Madden (ed.), *Privy Purse Expenses*, p. 51.
6. Ibid., p. 52.
7. Ibid., pp. 54, 58. On the first of these occasions, a bonnet was also given to the Prince's nurse. These are likely to have been New Year's gifts.
8. Ibid., p. 72.
9. L & P, xiii, part 1 (1290).
10. L & P, xiv, part 1 (5).
11. See V. Schutte, *Princesses Mary and Elizabeth Tudor and the Gift Book Exchange* (Leeds, 2021), p. 61.
12. Madden (ed.), *Privy Purse Expenses*, p. 48; T. Borman, *The Private Lives of the Tudors: Uncovering the Secrets of Britain's Greatest Dynasty* (London, 2016), p. 249.
13. Ibid., pp. 3, 62, 107. Both Anne of Cleves and Katherine Parr also had parrots. S. James, *Catherine Parr: Henry VIII's Last Love* (Stroud, 2008), p. 106.
14. Starkey (ed.), *Inventory*, p. 252.
15. See J. Childs, *Henry VIII's Last Victim* (London, 2006), pp. 130–3.
16. CSPS, xiii, p. 387.
17. L & P, xiv, part 1 (1145).
18. L & P, xiii, part 1 (402).
19. L & P, xiii, part 2 (898).
20. Hayward, *Dress*, p. 209; L & P, xiv, part 2 (238).
21. Richardson, *Mistress Blanche*, p. 42; Orme, *Tudor Children*, p. 126.
22. Katherine's family originated in Devon. She is often referred to as Kat, but Elizabeth Norton convincingly argues that Elizabeth would have called her Kate, hence the reason that this name has been adopted throughout the book. See E. Norton, *The Temptation of Elizabeth Tudor* (London, 2015), p. 70.
23. Marcus, Mueller and Rose (eds), *Collected Works*, p. 34.
24. There is no evidence that Mary was assigned a tutor until 1525 when she was nine years old. See also A. Whitelock, *Mary Tudor: England's First Queen* (London, 2009), pp. 25–6; A. Pollnitz, 'Christian Women or Sovereign Queens? The Schooling of Mary and Elizabeth', in A. Hunt and A. Whitelock (eds), *Tudor Queenship: The Reigns of Mary and Elizabeth* (Basingstoke, 2010), p. 129.
25. R. Ascham, *The Whole Works of Roger Ascham*, ed. J.A. Giles, i (London, 1864–5), p. 86.
26. Cited in A.F. Pollard, *Tudor Tracts 1532–1588* (New York, 1964), p. 334.
27. Marcus, Mueller and Rose (eds), *Collected Works*, p. 96.

28. Madden (ed.), *Privy Purse Expenses*, p. 10.
29. Bruce (ed.), *Correspondence of Matthew Parker*, p. ix.
30. Marcus, Mueller and Rose (eds), *Collected Works*, pp. 135–51, 175, for example.
31. A. Weir, *Henry VIII: King and Court* (London, 2001), p. 418.
32. M. Dowling, *Humanism in the Age of Henry VIII* (Beckenham, 1986), p. 90.
33. See J.P. Carley, *The Books of King Henry VIII and His Wives* (London, 2004), p. 26.
34. Lawson (ed.), *Gift Exchanges*, p. 78.
35. Madden (ed.), *Privy Purse Expenses*, p. 24; L & P, xiv, part 2 (781).
36. Camden, *Historie*, p. 6.
37. For more on Elizabeth's interest in music see K. Butler, "'By Instruments her Powers Appear": Music and Authority in the Reign of Queen Elizabeth I', *Renaissance Quarterly*, 65:2 (2012), pp. 353–84.
38. Originally a Norman castle, by the mid-sixteenth century Hertford Castle was a comfortable residence dating largely from the fifteenth century. Hertford had been in royal hands for centuries, with the coat of arms of Elizabeth's paternal great-grandfather Edward IV adorning the porch of the gatehouse. Little of the original structure survives, and Hertford Castle is now used to host private events.
39. L & P, xiv, part 2 (697).
40. L & P, xii, part 2 (1004).
41. L & P, xii, part 2 (1172).
42. In January 1566 the Earl of Sussex would tell the Spanish ambassador that Elizabeth 'had always declared she would never marry a man she had not seen first'. CSP Simancas, i (335).
43. Jane's portrait, one of Holbein's most spectacular masterpieces, is now in the Kunsthistoriches Museum, Vienna, Inv. No. 881.
44. Anne's likeness is part of the collection at the Louvre, Paris, INV 1348; MR 756.
45. Mary Tudor, the King's sister, had died on 25 June 1533, several months before Elizabeth's birth. On the day of Elizabeth's birth, however, Charles Brandon, Duke of Suffolk, had remarried. His bride was Katherine Willoughby, and it was she who joined her husband to welcome Anne of Cleves to England.
46. L & P, xiv, part 2 (572).
47. L & P, xv (22).
48. L & P, xv (6).
49. Ibid.
50. L & P, xv (822).
51. L & P, xv (334).
52. A. Strickland, *The Life of Queen Elizabeth* (London, 1906), p. 9.
53. Madden (ed.), *Privy Purse Expenses*, p. 88.
54. L & P, xv (872).
55. Although Thomas Boleyn attended the christening of Prince Edward and visited court, he appears to have led a largely quiet life after the executions of his children. He died at Hever Castle on 12 March 1539 and was buried in the nearby church where his magnificent tomb brass can be seen. Elizabeth, Thomas's wife, predeceased him, having died on 3 April 1538. She was buried in the Howard family vault of St Mary's Church, Lambeth. It is unknown how much contact Elizabeth had with her maternal grandparents following her mother's execution but given that Thomas Boleyn had attended Prince Edward's christening it is likely that Elizabeth at least knew who he was. In October 1538 he had been described as 'of small power, wise,

and little experience'. L & P, xiii, part 2 (732). His surviving daughter, Mary, had been banished from court in 1534 following her marriage to William Stafford, a man beneath her in social status. Evidence for the remainder of Mary's life is patchy, but she died on 19 July 1543.

56. Henry VIII had acquired Oatlands in 1538 and rebuilt it, transforming it into a palace. Subsequent Tudor and Stuart monarchs used Oatlands, but it was demolished soon after the execution of Charles I.

57. Katherine Howard was the daughter of Edmund Howard (brother of Anne Boleyn's mother) and Joyce Culpeper. Her date of birth is unknown and has been much debated. Katherine's biographer, Gareth Russell, suggests that 1522 or 1523 are the most likely years of her birth. See *Young and Damned and Fair: The Life and Tragedy of Catherine Howard at the Court of Henry VIII* (London, 2017), pp. 16–19.

58. L & P, xvi (12).

59. A portrait miniature now in the Royal Collection shows a woman thought to be Katherine Howard (RCIN 422293). If the sitter is indeed Katherine, then her jewels match with some of those that can be seen in Hans Holbein's portrait of Jane Seymour.

60. In December 1540 Chapuys reported that the Queen was offended with Mary 'because the Princess did not treat her with the same respect as her two predecessors', attempting to dismiss two of her ladies by means of punishment. See L & P, xvi (314). By New Year 1541, however, although Mary had reportedly not yet visited the Queen, relations had apparently thawed after Mary sent the Queen a gift, receiving two from the King and Queen in response. See L & P, xvi (436).

61. BL, Stowe MS 559, f. 57v.

62. Ibid.

63. Suffolk Place was once located on Borough High Street in Southwark, and was the former property of Charles Brandon, Duke of Suffolk. It was exchanged with the Crown in 1536, and in 1545 a Royal Mint was established there. Suffolk Place remained in royal hands until it was demolished in 1557. A modern office block stands on the site it once occupied.

64. Katherine came from Baynard's Castle, which once stood in the City of London. It was used as a base by the House of York during the Wars of the Roses, and it was from Baynard's that Edward IV was declared king. It remained in royal ownership until Edward VI granted it to the Earl of Pembroke. Sadly, Baynard's Castle was destroyed during the Great Fire of London.

65. Russell, *Young and Damned*, p. 380.

66. Katherine's biographer Josephine Wilkinson believes that Katherine was the victim of abuse. See J. Wilkinson, *Katherine Howard: The Tragic Story of Henry VIII's Fifth Queen* (London, 2016), pp. 20–4, for example. Gareth Russell is of the opinion that though the relationships were inappropriate, they did not amount to abuse. See *Young and Damned*, pp. 62–3.

67. L & P, xvii (100).

68. Ibid.

69. Marcus, Mueller and Rose (eds), *Collected Works*, p. 59.

70. CSPV, vi (884).

71. Ibid.

72. Ibid.

73. HMC Rutland, i, p. 30.

74. Madden (ed.), *Privy Purse Expenses*, p. 96; Strickland, *Life of Queen Elizabeth*, p. 9.

Chapter 6

1. Margaret Douglas was the daughter of Henry VIII's elder sister, Margaret, Queen of Scots, by her second husband Archibald Douglas. She had been born on 8 October 1515 at Harbottle Castle and was largely raised at the English court. She had previously served in the household of Elizabeth's mother.
2. Thomas Cranmer had granted the marriage licence just two days earlier at Lambeth. L & P, xviii, part 1 (854). Katherine's sister Anne had married William Herbert, who became first Earl of Pembroke, in 1538. Their descendants still hold the title of earls of Pembroke and live in Wilton House, the land of which was first acquired by William Herbert.
3. L & P, xviii, part 1 (873).
4. Sir Thomas was the son of Sir William Parr and Elizabeth FitzHugh. Through his mother Sir Thomas could claim descent from Edward III. His wife, Maud Green, was the daughter of Sir Thomas Green by Jane Fogge. She hailed from Northamptonshire and was a highly educated woman.
5. Sir Thomas was buried in St Anne's Church, Blackfriars, where Maud Green would later join him, following her death in 1531. A splendid tomb was erected, but sadly the church was destroyed in the Great Fire of London.
6. Katherine's first husband had been Edward Burgh, who she had married in 1529. He died in 1533, and the following year Katherine married Lord Latimer. Following his death, Latimer was buried in Old St Paul's Cathedral.
7. See L. Porter, *Katherine the Queen: The Remarkable Life of Katherine Parr* (London, 2010), p. 153.
8. Dent-Brocklehurst MS, Sudeley Castle; J. Mueller (ed.), *Katherine Parr: Complete Works and Correspondence* (Chicago, 2011), p. 131.
9. L & P, xvii (100).
10. L & P, xviii, part 1 (44).
11. L & P, xviii, part 1 (740).
12. John Neville was born in 1520, and Margaret Neville was born in 1525. Their mother, Dorothy de Vere, had been Lord Latimer's first wife, but had died in 1527. In 1545 John Neville would marry Lucy Somerset, the daughter of the Earl and Countess of Worcester – the same Countess who had testified against Anne Boleyn and in whose household Lady Troy had once been a member. Together they would have four daughters. Sadly, Margaret Neville died in 1546 before she could be married.
13. J.J. Scarisbrick, *Henry VIII* (London, 1968), pp. 625–6.
14. James, *Catherine Parr*, pp. 99, 105; Porter, *Katherine the Queen*, p. 150.
15. The cloth of silver was a New Year's gift, intended to be made into kirtles. Anne of Cleves received the same. TNA, E 315/161, f. 210r.
16. L & P, xviii, part 1 (894).
17. In August Chapuys remarked that while Mary was with the Queen, Elizabeth and Edward were together. L & P, xviii, part 2 (39).
18. TNA, E 315/161, f. 112; James, *Catherine Parr*, p. 142.
19. James, *Catherine Parr*, p. 115.
20. St John's had been founded in 1511, two years after Lady Margaret's death. She had also been responsible for endowing Christ's College, Cambridge, in 1505.
21. Ascham, *Whole Works*, i, p. lv.
22. Little is known of Grindal's life, but many of his contemporaries believed him to be an

excellent scholar. It was Roger Ascham who claimed that Grindal's Greek was second to none. See Ascham, *Whole Works*, i, p. xliii.

23. Somerset, *Elizabeth I*, p. 14.

24. In his letter to Kate in 1545, Roger Ascham mentioned the favour she had shown to Grindal. See Ascham, *Whole Works*, i, p. 86. Astley was also referred to as Ashley. John Astley's mother was Anne Wood, whose sister, Elizabeth, married Sir James Boleyn. This made James and Elizabeth the aunt and uncle of Anne Boleyn.

25. In 1483 Margaret is known to have purchased a copy of *Blanchardyn and Eglantine*, a French romance. She liked it so much that she also ordered an English translation. M.K. Jones and M.G. Underwood, *The King's Mother: Lady Margaret Beaufort, Countess of Richmond and Derby* (Cambridge, 1992), p. 182.

26. Camden, *Historie*, Introduction.

27. CSPV, ix (1169).

28. Jane earned the admiration of many of her male contemporaries, including Roger Ascham and the Swiss Scholar, John of Ulm, who wrote of her: 'For my own part I do not think there ever lived anyone more deserving of respect than this young lady.' Ellis, *Original Letters*, p. 430.

29. Castiglione was born in Piedmont and had once served in the army of Charles V. He seems to have begun teaching Elizabeth later in 1544, but the date is uncertain. He probably fought with Henry's troops earlier that year, and returned to England with them in the autumn. See Guy, *Children of Henry VIII*, p. 113.

30. Doran (ed.), *Elizabeth and Mary*, p. 29; R.C. Manning (ed.), 'State Papers relating to the Custody of the Princess Elizabeth at Woodstock in 1554', *Norfolk Archaeology*, 4 (1855), p. 161.

31. Marcus, Mueller and Rose (eds), *Collected Works*, p. 5.

32. Margaret was married to Matthew Lennox, and the two became parents to Lord Henry Darnley, consort of Mary, Queen of Scots.

33. Marcus, Mueller and Rose (eds), *Collected Works*, p. 5.

34. Ibid., pp. 5–6.

35. Starkey, *Elizabeth*, p. 36.

36. Marcus, Mueller and Rose (eds), *Collected Works*, p. 6.

37. L & P, xix, part 1 (780).

38. During Katherine of Aragon's regency, the English army had victoriously defeated the Scots at the Battle of Flodden on 9 September. James IV, Henry's brother-in-law, was killed in the battle.

39. L & P, xix, part 1 (864).

40. Sir William Sidney was well favoured by Henry VIII and had attended the Field of the Cloth of Gold. He had married Anne Pakenham, by whom he had four daughters. In 1552 Edward VI would grant Penshurst Place to Sidney, who died there two years later and is buried in the church; for Sidney's initial appointment to Edward's household see L & P, xiii, part 1 (579); L & P, xix, part 1 (864).

41. *Psalms or Prayers* was published in late April by the King's own printer, Thomas Berthelet. See James, *Catherine Parr*, p. 170.

42. Ibid., p. 152.

43. SP 1/190, f. 155r. Cited in Mueller (ed.), *Katherine Parr*, p. 59. This letter was written on 25 July, and others expressing similar sentiments were written on 31 July, 9 and 25 August.

44. Ellis, *Original Letters*, ii, p. 130.

45. James, *Catherine Parr*, p. 154; Porter, *Katherine the Queen*, p. 348; Starkey, *Elizabeth*, pp. 40–41.

46. See BL, Harley MS 442, f. 164r, for example.

47. The work of Cassie Auble has shown how, during her reign, Elizabeth was able to use her jewels to create an image of sovereign power. This is an area in which Katherine is likely to have been highly influential. See C. Auble, 'Bejeweled Majesty: Queen Elizabeth I, Precious Stones, and Statecraft', in D. Barrett-Graves (ed.), *The Emblematic Queen: Extra-Literary Representations of Early Modern Queenship* (Basingstoke, 2013), p. 37.

48. See Master John, 'Katherine Parr', *c.* 1545, National Portrait Gallery, NPG 4451.

49. See James, *Catherine Parr*, pp. 104–5, and N. Tallis, *All the Queen's Jewels 1445–1548: Power, Majesty and Display* (Abingdon, 2023), pp. 179–81.

50. S.E. James, 'Lady Jane Grey or Queen Kateryn Parr?' *Burlington Magazine*, 138 (1996), pp. 20–24. The portrait of Katherine Parr was auctioned at Sotheby's in July 2023: further details in Chapter Seven; BL, Royal MS Appendix 68, f. 26r. Anne of Denmark later owned the crown ouche but ordered it to be broken down.

51. There has been a building on the site of Woking Palace since 1272, and it was acquired by Margaret Beaufort in 1466. She adored Woking and spent much of her time there. Henry VII and Henry VIII both owned the Palace, and Elizabeth herself would later pay for works to be carried out there. Sadly, Woking Palace is now a ruin, but excavations have revealed much about the footprint of the building and life there.

52. L & P, xix, part 2 (246); BL, Harley MS 442, f. 164r.

53. L & P, xix, part 2 (688).

54. Ibid. Nothing remains of Mortlake, which remained royal property until Elizabeth granted it to Sir Thomas Cecil. The manor at Byfleet had been inherited by Henry VIII, but the house was largely rebuilt in the seventeenth century, and it is this that survives today. Guildford Castle was built at around the time of the Norman Conquest and was a royal property. It is now a museum. The manor at Chobham was acquired by Henry VIII, and later sold by Mary I.

55. L & P, xix, part 2 (688).

56. L & P, xix, part 2 (251).

57. Henry VIII acquired Otford Palace from Thomas Cranmer in 1543. It had until then been an archbishop's palace. It is now a ruin.

58. James, *Catherine Parr*, p. 153; TNA, E 315/161, f. 129.

59. L & P, vi (692); L & P, ix (378).

60. Starkey, *Elizabeth*, pp. 48–9; see also Schutte, *Gift Book Exchange*, p. 36.

61. Cited in Marcus, Mueller and Rose (eds), *Collected Works*, p. 6.

62. Ibid., p. 7.

63. Ibid., p. 7.

64. Ibid.

65. Ibid.

66. Jones and Underwood, *The King's Mother*, p. 184.

67. The gift is now in the collection of the National Record Office of Scotland, reference number RH13/78.

68. See Hosington, B.M., '"How we ovght to knowe God": Princess Elizabeth's Presentation of her Calvin Translation to Katherine Parr', Université de Montréal/University of Warwick (2018), p. 1.

69. Marcus, Mueller and Rose (eds), *Collected Works*, p. 10.

70. Ibid., p. 12.
71. Ibid.
72. BL, Royal MS 7 D X.
73. S. Watkins, *In Public and in Private: Elizabeth I and Her World* (London, 1998), p. 19.
74. Ibid.
75. In Elizabeth's reign, Paul Hentzner, who was a German visitor, noted that during a visit to the Palace of Whitehall he saw a book written in French in the royal library. Inside, it was inscribed in the hand of the young Elizabeth and addressed to her father. See H. Walpole (trans.), *Paul Hentzner's Travels in England During the Reign of Queen Elizabeth* (London, 1797), p. 21.
76. Marcus, Mueller and Rose (eds), *Collected Works*, p. 9.
77. Ibid.
78. Ibid., p. 10.
79. Ibid.; see also Schutte, *Gift Book Exchange*, p. 43.
80. Schutte explains that there were once at least two other dedications that Elizabeth made to her father, which no longer survive. *Gift Book Exchange*, p. 50.
81. BL, Kings MS 395, ff. 33v–34r. The images of Henry VIII, Katherine of Aragon and Mary I were completed by one artistic hand, while those of Elizabeth, her brother and Henry's subsequent wives were added later; Boughton House also owns a seventeenth-century copy of a lost original portrait that shows young Elizabeth with her father, half-siblings, and Will Somers.
82. Unknown Artist, *The Family of Henry VIII, c.* 1545, Royal Collection Trust, RCIN 405796.
83. Starkey, *Elizabeth*, p. 31; Guy, *Children of Henry VIII*, p. 106.
84. Mary's jewel inventory records several pieces that were given to Elizabeth, but there are no items that match with the initial pendant. See Madden (ed.), *Privy Purse Expenses*, p. 175–201. It is interesting to note, though, that Mary did own initial jewels, including a jewelled 'M'. Madden (ed.), *Privy Purse Expenses*, p. 176.
85. There are items in Mary's jewel inventory which almost certainly came from her mother or had been made with her mother in mind, whether directly or after Katherine's death. For example, a 'book of gold with the King's face and her grace's mother's'. Madden (ed.), *Privy Purse Expenses*, p. 178.
86. BL, Cotton MS Otho C X, f. 216r.
87. Little is known of Scrots, but he worked as court painter to Mary of Hungary before travelling to England, where he seems to have begun working in 1545.
88. Starkey (ed.), *Inventory*, p. 240.
89. Attributed to William Scrots, *Edward VI*, 1546, Royal Collection Trust, RCIN 404441. Hunsdon can be seen in the background.
90. S. Clarke and L. Collins, *Gloriana: Elizabeth I and the Art of Queenship* (Cheltenham, 2022), p. 36.
91. A. Reynolds, *In Fine Style: The Art of Tudor and Stuart Fashion* (London, 2013), p. 19.
92. The portrait was auctioned at Sotheby's in July 2023; further details in Chapter Seven.
93. See SOA, MS, ff. 178r, 179v for two possible examples.
94. R. Strong, *Portraits of Queen Elizabeth* (Oxford, 1963), p. 53.
95. J. Scott, *The Royal Portrait: Image and Impact* (London, 2010), p. 59.
96. Clarke and Collins, *Gloriana*, p. 38.
97. L & P, xxi, part 1 (969).
98. L & P, xxi, part 1 (1464).

99. L & P, xxi, part 2 (14).
100. L & P, xxi, part 1 (1383:96); Porter, *Katherine the Queen*, p. 269.
101. Jane Dudley was one of the few who attended Henry VIII and Katherine Parr's wedding. L & P, xviii, part 1 (873).
102. C.I. Merton, 'The Women Who Served Queen Mary and Queen Elizabeth: Ladies, Gentlewomen and Maids of the Privy Chamber, 1553–1603', unpublished PhD thesis (University of Cambridge, 1992), p. 32.
103. Ibid. Skipwith is referenced in a poem by John Harington as one of six ladies who were in Elizabeth's service while she was living at Hatfield in the 1550s. See R. Hughey, *John Harington of Stepney: Tudor Gentleman* (Ohio, 1971), p. 104.
104. Elisabeth's parents were George Brooke, ninth Baron Cobham, and his wife Anne. The family hailed from Kent.
105. H.J. Graham-Matheson, 'All wemen in thar degree shuld to thar men subiectit be': The Controversial Court Career of Elisabeth Parr, Marchioness of Northampton, *c.* 1547–1565', unpublished PhD thesis (University College London, 2015), pp. 9, 14. See also TNA, E 179/69/41, f. 1.
106. Graham-Matheson, 'All wemen', p. 84.
107. BL, Cotton MS Vespasian C XIV, f. 75v; TNA, LC 2/2, f. 48v–r.
108. Cited in Richardson, *Mistress Blanche*, p. 44. Interestingly, in the list Kate's name still appears as Champernowne rather than Astley, suggesting that she may have been appointed prior to her marriage. There is no further evidence to pinpoint when her role in Elizabeth's household changed. L & P, x (1187).
109. L & P, xiv, part 1 (1145).
110. The chamberers and two of the gentlemen remained the same, as did the chaplain and laundress. There were now two different grooms, one of whom, William Man, was described as 'the eldest groom' in a document dating from 1546 in which he was granted pay of 4d a day. L & P, xxi, part 2 (199).
111. BL, Cotton MS Vespasian C XIV, f. 75v.
112. L & P, xxi, part 2 (605).
113. Ibid.
114. Cited in J. Nichols, *The Progresses and Public Processions of Queen Elizabeth*, i (London, 1823), p. 43.
115. Ibid.

Chapter 7

1. CSPS, ix, p. 6.
2. S. Lipscomb, *The King is Dead: The Last Will and Testament of Henry VIII* (London, 2015), p. 133.
3. See Weir, *Henry VIII*, pp. 504–5.
4. Skidmore, *Edward VI*, p. 49.
5. Sir J. Hayward, *The Life and Raigne of King Edward the Sixth* (London, 1630), p. 4.
6. L & P, xx, part 2 (890); L & P, xx, part 2 (904).
7. TNA, E 23/4/1. The will remains controversial and was probably signed with a dry stamp (although this is not entirely certain).
8. This portrait was formerly in the collection of the Earl of Jersey, but was auctioned by Sotheby's in July 2023 – it is now in a private collection. Dendrochronological analysis has revealed that the three boards on which the portrait is painted derived

from trees felled from *circa* 1546 to before *circa* 1576. If this was the case, then the portrait could potentially have been painted in the last year of Henry VIII's life.

9. Linda Porter points out that Katherine sought advice on the matter, citing a note from Roger Cholmeley, a lawyer, in which he referred to Katherine's affairs. See *Katherine the Queen*, p. 283.

10. Lipscomb, *The King is Dead*, p. 139.

11. L & P, xxi, part 2 (686).

12. Halliwell (ed.), *Letters*, ii, p. 25.

13. TNA, E 23/4/1, f. 24. See also Lipscomb, *The King is Dead*, p. 139.

14. Lipscomb, *The King is Dead*, p. 139.

15. J. Strype, *Annals of the Reformation, Ecclesiastical Memorials*, ii (Oxford, 1820–40), p. 17.

16. Will Somers, as noted previously, also appears in *The Family of Henry VIII*. Very little is known of his life, but he first appears in the royal accounts in 1535. He served Henry VIII for the rest of the King's life, and continued to serve under Mary and, briefly, Elizabeth. He was listed under those who received clothes for Elizabeth's coronation. He probably died in 1560. TNA, E 101/429/3, f. 21r.

17. TNA, LC 2/2, ff. 5r, 48v–r; Elizabeth had referenced this pain in her letter to Edward VI on 14 February. See Marcus, Mueller and Rose (eds), *Collected Works*, p. 13.

18. The closet still survives, decorated with Katherine of Aragon's pomegranate badge.

19. Henry VIII and Jane Seymour also share their vault with Charles I and an infant of Queen Anne's. For more details on Henry's resting place see https://www.stgeorges-windsor.org/wp-content/uploads/2017/08/HenryVIIIRestingPlace.pdf.

20. CSPS, ix, p. 19.

21. See Skidmore, *Edward VI*, p. 62.

22. Marcus, Mueller and Rose (eds), *Collected Works*, p. 14; BL, Harley MS 6986, ff. 19r–20v.

23. The decision had been made by 7 March, as the Imperial ambassador referred to the two living together in his despatch of that date. See CSPS, ix, pp. 48–9.

24. Somerset, *Elizabeth I*, p. 28. It is unclear precisely when Parry entered Elizabeth's service, but it must have been in the aftermath of Henry VIII's death as his name does not appear on any of her earlier household lists.

25. Cited in Richardson, *Mistress Blanche*, p. 44.

26. Victoria County History, *A History of the County of Middlesex*, xii (London, 2004), pp. 108–15. Available at British History Online, https://www.britishhistory.ac.uk/vch/middx/vol12/xii.

27. S. Haynes, *Collection of State Papers Relating to Affairs in the Reigns of King Henry VIII, King Edward VI, Queen Mary and Queen Elizabeth, From the Year 1542 to 1570 … Left by William Cecil, Lord Burghley … at Hatfield House* (London, 1740), p. 96.

28. Graham-Matheson, 'All wemen', pp. 43, 45; CSPS, ix, pp. 253–4. It was by no means a smooth match, for within days of the wedding William Parr was ordered 'to put her away and never speak to her again on pain of death', by reason that his first wife was still living.

29. Cited in Porter, *Katherine the Queen*, p. 307.

30. For more on this see Mueller (ed.), *Katherine Parr*, 425–8.

31. Ascham, *Whole Works*, i, p. lxiii.

32. Miles Coverdale studied in Cambridge, but he fled abroad at the end of 1528 for fear of persecution for his religious views. He spent many years in Europe, and dedicated his translation of the Bible to Henry VIII.

33. Hayward, *Edward the Sixth*, p. 81; James, *Catherine Parr*, p. 261.

34. CSPS, ix, p. 20.

35. Van der Delft claimed that this was what·John Dudley had told Thomas Seymour. CSPS, ix, p. 341.
36. Cited in Mueller (ed.), *Katherine Parr*, p. 135.
37. Thomas referenced this in a letter to Katherine, in which he told her that Anne 'waded further with me touching my being with your highness at Chelsea'. Cited in Mueller (ed.), *Katherine Parr*, p. 137.
38. CSPS, ix, p. 104.
39. Haynes, *State Papers*, p. 102. In the seventeenth century the Italian Gregorio Leti claimed that Elizabeth wrote a letter responding to Thomas's proposal of marriage, in which she claimed that she would need a two-year mourning period for her father before considering it. Leti is, however, a dubious source and there is no other evidence corroborating this. The letter is cited in M.A. Everett Wood (ed.), *Letters of Royal and Illustrious Ladies of Great Britain*, iii (London, 1846), pp. 191–2.
40. Haynes, *State Papers*, p. 102.
41. CSPS, ix, p. 340.
42. Marcus, Mueller and Rose (eds), *Collected Works*, p. 29.
43. James, *Catherine Parr*, p. 269. Linda Porter places the wedding probably in the last two weeks of May, or else earlier in the month. See *Katherine the Queen*, p. 290. Starkey places the wedding in mid-April. See *Elizabeth*, p. 67.
44. Ellis, *Original Letters*, ii, p. 131; Mueller (ed.), *Katherine Parr*, p. 147.
45. Mueller (ed.), *Katherine Parr*, p. 147.
46. Ibid., p. 131. For Katherine's dislike of the Duchess see Porter, *Katherine the Queen*, pp. 297–9.
47. BL, Lansdowne MS, 1236, f. 26.
48. Leti cites a letter that Elizabeth supposedly wrote to Mary; however, its tone is not in keeping with any of her other known letters. It is cited in Wood (ed.), *Letters of Royal and Illustrious Ladies*, iii, pp. 193–4.
49. Haynes, *State Papers*, p. 99.
50. Ibid.
51. Ibid.
52. Marcus, Mueller and Rose (eds), *Collected Works*, pp. 25–6.
53. Haynes, *State Papers*, p. 99.
54. Ibid. According to her testimony, Kate could not recall whether this incident took place at Chelsea or Hanworth.
55. Ibid.
56. Ibid.
57. Ibid.
58. Ibid.
59. Norton, *Temptation*, p. 90.
60. Marcus, Mueller and Rose (eds), *Collected Works*, p. 30.
61. Norton, *Temptation*, pp. 85–6.
62. Haynes, *State Papers*, p. 96.
63. Ibid., p. 99.
64. Ibid., p. 93.
65. Ives, *Life and Death*, p. 156; Colvin, Ransome and Summerson (eds), *King's Works*, iv, p. 148.
66. Haynes, *State Papers*, p. 99.
67. Marcus, Mueller and Rose (eds), *Collected Works*, p. 28.

68. Haynes, *State Papers*, p. 96.
69. Ibid., pp. 100, 99.
70. Ibid., p. 100.

Chapter 8

1. Ascham, *Whole Works*, i, p. lv.
2. Ibid.
3. Ibid.
4. Ibid., p. lvi.
5. James, *Catherine Parr*, p. 162.
6. Ascham, *Whole Works*, i, p. lvi.
7. Ibid.
8. Ibid.
9. Ibid.
10. Ibid.
11. James, *Catherine Parr*, p. 290.
12. Haynes, *State Papers*, p. 62.
13. On occasion, Katherine sent Cheke gifts of game. James, *Catherine Parr*, p. 116.
14. Ascham, *Whole Works*, i, p. lvii.
15. Camden, *Historie*, p. 6.
16. Ascham, *Whole Works*, i, p. lvii.
17. Ibid., p. lxiv.
18. Ibid., p. lxiii.
19. Ibid., p. lxiv.
20. R. Ascham, *The Schoolmaster*, ed. L.V. Ryan (New York, 1967), p. 96.
21. Ascham, *Whole Works*, i, p. lxiii.
22. Haynes, *State Papers*, p. 99.
23. Ibid., p. 62; Norton, *Temptation*, p. 125.
24. Haynes, *State Papers*, p. 96.
25. Ibid.
26. Ibid., p. 62.
27. Ibid., p. 96.
28. Norton, *Temptation*, pp. 133–4.
29. Haynes, *State Papers*, p. 96.
30. Ibid.
31. It was Kate Astley who later recalled that Elizabeth left Katherine at this time. See Haynes, *State Papers*, p. 101; SP 10/2, f. 84c. Cited in Mueller (ed.), *Katherine Parr*, pp. 171–2.
32. SP 10/2, f. 84c. Cited in Mueller (ed.), *Katherine Parr*, pp. 171–2.
33. Haynes, *State Papers*, p. 101. Kate would later claim that 'what communication she doth not remember'.
34. Cheshunt had been built around a courtyard and boasted a forty-foot-long hall. See A. Weir, *Children of England: The Heirs of King Henry VIII* (London, 1996), p. 54; CSPS, ix, p. 21.
35. One of these, Sir Edward Denny (born in 1547), became a privateer during Elizabeth's reign. He married Margaret Edgcumbe, by whom he had ten children. Edward's tomb monument can still be seen in Waltham Abbey, Essex. Joan Denny was believed to have had some influence with Henry VIII, for in 1539 Lady Lisle approached her

about a matter regarding Elizabeth's household. It probably concerned her hope for the placement of one of her daughters, but Lady Lisle's agent informed her that, though Joan Denny had offered to ask her husband to speak to the King on her behalf, 'the King answered that she should no more'. L & P, xiv, part 1 (1145).

36. BL, Cotton MS Otho C X, f. 236v. Also cited in Marcus, Mueller and Rose (eds), *Collected Works*, p. 20.
37. Marcus, Mueller and Rose (eds), *Collected Works*, pp. 18–19.
38. SP 10/2, f. 84c. Cited in Mueller (ed.), *Katherine Parr*, pp. 171–2.
39. CSPS, ix, p. 278.
40. James, *Catherine Parr*, p. 289.
41. Sir Robert Tyrwhit referred to a walk he shared with Katherine in the park at Sudeley on one occasion that summer. See Haynes, *State Papers*, p. 104.
42. Strype, *Ecclesiastical Memorials*, ii, p. 61.
43. BL, Cotton MS Otho C X, f. 236v. The letter has been damaged by fire, but it appears to have potentially been written from Windsor. It is possible that Elizabeth was visiting the King, although he spent most of the summer at Hampton Court. Perhaps he paid a shorter visit to Windsor, making the time to see his sister while he was there.
44. Ibid.
45. Ibid.
46. Ibid.
47. Mueller (ed.), *Katherine Parr*, p. 175.
48. Haynes, *State Papers*, p. 103.
49. Ibid.
50. Ibid.
51. Ibid.
52. Ibid.
53. Mueller (ed.), *Katherine Parr*, pp. 180–2.
54. Katherine's original tomb was destroyed, and the monument that marks her resting place today was created in the nineteenth century by Sir George Gilbert Scott.
55. Cited in Mueller (ed.), *Katherine Parr*, p. 183.
56. Marcus, Mueller and Rose (eds), *Collected Works*, p. 25.
57. Clifford, *Life of Jane Dormer*, p. 20.
58. Ibid.
59. Ibid.
60. Marcus, Mueller and Rose (eds), *Collected Works*, p. 22.
61. Cited in D. Loades, *Elizabeth I: The Golden Reign of Gloriana* (London, 2003), p. 16.
62. Haynes, *State Papers*, p. 77.
63. Bradgate Park, though now a magnificent ruin, can still be visited. It lies within the park that would have been largely familiar to the Grey family.
64. Haynes, *State Papers*, p. 76.
65. Ibid., p. 101.

Chapter 9

1. Haynes, *State Papers*, p. 102.
2. Ibid.
3. Ibid.
4. Ibid.

5. Ibid., p. 100.
6. Ibid., p. 73.
7. This is apparent from Wightman's confession, in which he says that Thomas asked Mary what she thought of his conduct towards Elizabeth when they were in the same household. See Haynes, *State Papers*, p. 73.
8. Ibid., pp. 73, 100.
9. Lady Browne's husband, Sir Anthony, died on 6 May 1548. She would not remarry until 1552.
10. Thomas asked William Wightman to inform Lady Browne that, had he died any time since making his will prior to his departure for Boulogne with Henry VIII in 1544, then 'she should have been no loser by him'. See Haynes, *State Papers*, p. 72.
11. Haynes, *State Papers*, p. 72.
12. Ibid.
13. Ibid.
14. In a display of Elizabeth's generosity, she would later give money to Lady Denny, the woman she had known since girlhood. Strangford (ed.), *Household Expenses*, p. 37.
15. Elizabeth Norton believes that the John Seymour in question was in fact the eldest son of the Lord Protector, who had been disinherited because of the infidelity of his mother, Katherine Fillol (the Protector's first wife). See *Temptation*, p. 201.
16. Haynes, *State Papers*, p. 100.
17. Ibid.
18. Ibid., p. 97.
19. Ibid., pp. 96, 101.
20. Marcus, Mueller and Rose (eds), *Collected Works*, p. 26.
21. Ibid., pp. 26–7.
22. Haynes, *State Papers*, p. 70. Edmund Allen had links with Katherine Parr, and thus it is likely that this is how he came to know Elizabeth. He was a fellow of Corpus Christi College, Cambridge, and during the reign of Mary I would flee abroad into exile. See C. Garrett, *The Marian Exiles* (Cambridge, 1938), p. 70.
23. Haynes, *State Papers*, p. 97.
24. Ibid., p. 95.
25. Ibid., p. 98.
26. Ibid., p. 102.
27. Ibid., p. 97.
28. Ibid.
29. Ibid., p. 95.
30. Ibid.
31. Ibid., p. 103.
32. Ibid., p. 98.
33. Ibid.
34. Ibid., p. 75.
35. CSPS, ix, p. 341.
36. See Norton, *Temptation*, pp. 202–3, 226–9.
37. Weir, *Children of England*, pp. 58–9.
38. CSPS, ix, p. 332.
39. Ibid.
40. Ibid.
41. Ibid.

42. The Fleet Prison was originally built at the end of the twelfth century and would gain fame as a debtor's prison. It was closed in the nineteenth century and demolished in 1846.
43. Haynes, *State Papers*, p. 70.
44. Ibid.
45. Ibid.
46. Ibid.
47. Ibid.
48. Ibid., p. 71.
49. Ibid., p. 88.
50. Ibid., p. 89.
51. Ibid.
52. Ibid.
53. Ibid.
54. Ibid.
55. Ibid., p. 90.
56. Ibid.
57. Marcus, Mueller and Rose (eds), *Collected Works*, p. 30.
58. Haynes, *State Papers*, pp. 95–7.
59. Ibid., p. 95.
60. Smith hailed from Essex and was an educated man, attending Queen's College, Cambridge. He was knighted in 1548, and although he later lost favour with Mary I, upon Elizabeth's accession he was restored to prestige and the Queen trusted him. He died in 1577.
61. Haynes, *State Papers*, p. 101.
62. Ibid., p. 94.
63. Ibid.
64. Ibid.
65. Ibid., p. 103.
66. Ibid., p. 102.
67. Ibid., p. 107.
68. Ibid., p. 108.
69. Ibid., p. 104.
70. Ibid., p. 108.
71. Ibid., p. 76.
72. Ibid., p. 74.
73. Ibid.
74. Ibid., p. 108; CSPS, ix, p. 350.
75. Haynes, *State Papers*, p. 88.
76. CSPS, ix, p. 349.
77. Porter, *Katherine the Queen*, p. 336. Elizabeth Norton pointed out that Katherine Howard was condemned in the same manner. See Norton, *Temptation*, p. 270.
78. CSPS, ix, p. 349.
79. Ibid.
80. J.R. Dasent *et al.* (eds), *Acts of the Privy Council*, ii (London, 1890–1907), p. 261. This took place at the Palace of Whitehall on 10 March.
81. Ibid., p. 262.
82. It is probable that Mary Seymour died at the age of two while in the Duchess's care. No further records confirm her existence after this time, and thus she has been lost to

history. Susan James suggested that she probably died at Grimsthorpe Castle and is buried in the church at Edenham. *Catherine Parr*, p. 300.
83. H. Latimer, *Sermons by Hugh Latimer*, ed. G.E. Corrie, i (Cambridge, 1844), p. 161.
84. Ibid., p. 162.
85. CSPS, ix, p. 349.
86. Latimer, *Sermons*, p. 161.
87. Ibid.
88. G. Leti, *Historia overo vita de Elisabetta, Regina d'Inghilterra* (Amsterdam, 1693), cited in Norton, *Temptation*, p. 279.
89. SP 11/4/2, f. 3r–v.
90. Latimer, *Sermons*, p. 162.
91. Norton notes that in 1567 John Harington presented her with a portrait of Thomas, which she had hung at Somerset House. See *Temptation*, p. 291.

Chapter 10

1. H. Robinson (ed.), *Original Letters Relative to the English Reformation*, i (Cambridge, 1846–7), p. 278.
2. Ascham, *Whole Works*, i, p. lxiii.
3. Schutte, *Gift Book Exchange*, p. 14. See p. 15 for more on the dedication of Belmain in 1550, in which he recommended single life.
4. MS. Bodl. 6; Starkey, *Elizabeth*, p. 88. It is uncertain in which year this was given, but 1548 is a possibility.
5. Cited in M. Perry, *The Word of a Prince: A Life of Elizabeth I* (Woodbridge, 1990), p. 49.
6. Ibid.
7. Ibid., pp. 49–50.
8. Ibid., p. 50.
9. CSPS, ix, p. 489.
10. Ibid.
11. CSPS, ix, p. 361.
12. See D. Loades, *Mary Tudor* (Stroud, 2012), pp. 110–15.
13. CSPV, v (934).
14. Marcus, Mueller and Rose (eds), *Collected Works*, pp. 37–8
15. Ibid., pp. 33–4.
16. BL, Lansdowne MS 1238, f. 30r–v. This letter is undated, but the subject matter makes it clear that it was composed at around this time.
17. Born in 1520, Cecil was the son of Sir Richard Cecil and his wife Jane Heckington; the other secretary of state was Sir William Petre, who had served Henry VIII and would also serve Mary I in the same role. For further reading on Cecil see S. Alford, *Burghley: William Cecil at the Court of Elizabeth I* (London, 2011).
18. Somerset, *Elizabeth I*, p. 36.
19. Cecil had a son by Mary Cheke, Thomas, born in 1542. He was later created Earl of Exeter, and his descendants are the Marquesses of Exeter. Mary died in childbirth in 1544, and Cecil took as his second wife Mildred Cooke, by whom he had several children who survived to adulthood.
20. Bryson and Evans, 'Seven Rediscovered Letters', p. 831; BL, Add MS 70518, ff. 11–12v. This letter has been said to date from 1547 and was written from Enfield. However, the year cannot be correct as Elizabeth was not at Enfield at this time. I have tentatively

placed it the previous year in 1546, when we know that Elizabeth was indeed at Enfield.
21. BL, Add MS 70518, ff. 11–12v. See also Bryson and Evans, 'Seven Rediscovered Letters', p. 848.
22. BL, Lansdowne MS 1238, f. 30r–v.
23. They must have been reinstated before September, for that month Parry was writing to the Lord Protector. See also A.J. Collins (ed.), *Jewels and Plate of Queen Elizabeth I: The Inventory of 1574* (London, 1955), p. 202.
24. CSPD Edward VI, viii (64).
25. Ascham, *Whole Works*, i, p. lxiii.
26. Dasent *et al.* (eds), *Acts of the Privy Council*, iii, p. 52; CPR Edward VI, iii, 71, 364–5, 415. She legally obtained Hatfield in September 1550. Somerset, *Elizabeth I*, p. 36.
27. Durham Place got its name from Richard le Poor, Bishop of Durham, who probably built it in the thirteenth century. See G.H. Gater and E.P. Wheeler (eds), 'Durham Place', in *Survey of London: Volume 18, St Martin-in-The-Fields II: the Strand* (London, 1937), pp. 84–98. *British History Online*, http://www.british-history.ac.uk/survey-london/vol18/pt2/pp84-98 [accessed 1 August 2022].
28. CSPS, x, p. 214.
29. Cited in F. von Raumer, *The Political History of England, During the 16th, 17th and 18th Centuries*, i (London, 1837), p. 141.
30. Ascham, *Whole Works*, i, p. lxxii.
31. Ibid.
32. Somerset, *Elizabeth I*, p. 26. When Elizabeth became Queen, she made him her Latin secretary with a pension of £20 a year. He died in 1568.
33. BL, Lansdowne MS 1238, f. 30r–v.
34. Starkey (ed.), *Inventory*, p. 381.
35. Ibid.
36. Charles VI and Isabeau of Bavaria were related to Elizabeth, for their daughter, Katherine of Valois, was the wife of Henry V. Following Henry's death, she had a relationship – and possible marriage – with Owen Tudor, by whom she had several children. Katherine and Owen's great-grandson was Henry VIII.
37. Starkey (ed.), *Inventory*, pp. 381–2.
38. Ibid., p. 382.
39. Ibid., pp. 376–80.
40. Walter Buckler was an educated man who had also served Henry VIII in a diplomatic capacity. He was knighted soon after the coronation of Edward VI and seems to have joined Elizabeth's household in 1550. He left in 1553 on the orders of the Council. Strangford (ed.), *Household Expenses*.
41. Ibid., pp. 43–4.
42. Ibid., pp. 5, 7, 10, 18, 19.
43. Ibid., pp. 7–11.
44. Ibid., pp. 27–8.
45. Ibid., p. 11.
46. Ibid., p. 33.
47. Ibid., p. 31.
48. Ibid., p. 32.
49. Cited in Wood, *Letters of Royal and Illustrious Ladies*, iii, p. 234.
50. Strangford (ed.), *Household Expenses*, p. 34. Huicke appears in many of the gift rolls from Elizabeth's reign, and was one of those who regularly gave her a gift at New

Year. In 1565 for example, he gave her a pot of green ginger and another of 'flowers of oranges'. See Lawson (ed.), *Gift Exchanges*, p. 109.

51. Strangford (ed.), *Household Expenses*, pp. 30, 33.
52. Ibid., pp. 33, 38.
53. Ibid., p. 34.
54. Ibid., p. 33.
55. Ibid., p. 34.
56. Ibid., p. 37.
57. Ibid., p. 40; L & P, xiv, part 2 (554).
58. Strangford (ed.), *Household Expenses*, p. 42.
59. Ibid., p. 40.
60. Ibid., p. 34.
61. Ibid., pp. 41, 38, 39. Henry Carey was well rewarded by Elizabeth when she became Queen, and was created Baron Hunsdon two days before her coronation. He died in 1596 and is buried in Westminster Abbey. His wife, Anne Morgan, served in Elizabeth's Privy Chamber, and was also awarded the post of Keeper of Somerset House in 1595. She outlived both her husband and Elizabeth, dying in 1607. She shares her husband's tomb and monument in Westminster Abbey.
62. Ibid., p. 35.
63. Continuing relationships between royal children and their wet nurses were very common. Henry VIII, for example, made his wet nurse, Anne Oxenbridge, several gifts throughout his reign. See L & P, i (82), L & P, i (132), L & P, ii (658), L & P, ii (659). I am very grateful to Elizabeth Norton for sharing these references with me.
64. Strangford (ed.), *Household Expenses*, p. 42.
65. M.S. Lovell, *Bess of Hardwick: First Lady of Chatsworth* (London, 2005), p. 70; Strangford (ed.), *Household Expenses*, p. 41 also shows money paid to a 'Mr Cavendish', who was probably Sir William.
66. Strangford (ed.), *Household Expenses*, p. 34.
67. Ibid., p. 41.
68. Bryson and Evans, 'Seven Rediscovered Letters', pp. 838, 850.
69. Ibid., pp. 838–9, 851. This letter was written from Hatfield on 20 May 1552 – interestingly, Elizabeth's expenses note that the previous day she gave Wingfield money. Perhaps he had petitioned her, and she promised to write the letter immediately.
70. Ibid., p. 852.
71. Ibid.
72. Cawarden had served Henry VIII as Master of Revels and Tents in Boulogne in 1544 and was knighted there by the King. He was also Keeper of Nonsuch Palace from 1543 until 1556. He fulfilled various other commissions, and died in 1559.
73. Guy, *Children of Henry VIII*, p. 136.
74. Cited in Wood, *Letters of Royal and Illustrious Ladies*, iii, p. 228.
75. P.F. Tytler, *England under the Reigns of Edward VI and Mary, Illustrated in a Series of Original Letters*, i (London, 1839), p. 251.
76. CSPD Edward VI, viii (33); Tytler, *Reigns of Edward VI and Mary*, i, p. 248.
77. Edward VI's journal noted the event in an emotionless tone: 'The Duke of Somerset had his head cut off upon Tower Hill between eight and nine o'clock in the morning.' J. North (ed.), *England's Boy King: The Diary of Edward VI 1547-1553* (Welwyn Garden City, 2005), p.132. In the next century, following the abolition of the monarchy, Oliver Cromwell would be Lord Protector of England between 1653 and 1658.

78. Edmund Dudley had served as a financial agent to Henry VII, but had been extremely unpopular. He was executed on a treason charge in August 1510. For more on this see J. Paul, *The House of Dudley: A New History of Tudor England* (London, 2022), pp. 44–60.
79. CSPS, x, p. 43.
80. CSPS, x, p. 216.
81. Guy, *Children of Henry VIII*, p. 134.
82. For more information on the family see Paul, *House of Dudley*. For Northumberland's children and their birth dates see pp. 461–3.
83. North (ed.), *England's Boy King*, p. 98.
84. In his journal the young King noted that the wedding celebrations had been followed by a gruesome entertainment, when 'certain gentlemen tried to see who could be the first to take away a goose's head which was hanged alive on two crossed posts'. North (ed.), *England's Boy King*, p. 56.
85. CSPS, x, p. 215.
86. CSPS, x, p. 206.
87. CSPS, x, p. 203.
88. Camden, *Historie*, Intro.
89. CSPS, x, p. 216.
90. CSPS, x, p. 209.
91. CSPS, x, p. 213.
92. CSPS, x, p. 258.
93. North (ed.), *England's Boy King*, p. 76.
94. Ibid., pp. 76–7.
95. CSPS, ix, p. 278.
96. CSPS, x, p. 286. Mallet had once served Katherine Parr and had joined Mary's household in 1544. When Mary became Queen, Mallet was made Dean of Lincoln. He died in 1570.
97. Strangford (ed.), *Household Accounts*, p. 1; Bryson and Evans, 'Seven Rediscovered Letters', pp. 844–5.
98. Marcus, Mueller and Rose (eds), *Collected Works*, p. 35.
99. Dasent *et al.* (eds), *Acts of the Privy Council*, iii, p. 376.
100. Levina Teerlinc, *Katherine Parr, c.* 1544–5, Sudeley Castle. Katherine's sister, Anne, also served as Levina's patron. James, *Catherine Parr*, p. 133.
101. Nichols, *Progresses and Public Processions*, i, p. 117.
102. CSPS, x, p. 299.
103. CSPS, x, p. 394; North (ed.), *England's Boy King*, p. 70.
104. CSPF, Edward VI (633).
105. Strangford (ed.), *Household Expenses*, p. 36.
106. Ibid.
107. J.G. Nichols (ed.), *The Diary of Henry Machyn: Citizen and Merchant-Taylor of London, from AD 1550 to AD 1563* (London, 1848), p. 16.
108. Ibid.
109. Starkey, *Elizabeth*, p. 106.
110. Strangford (ed.), *Household Expenses*, p. 38.
111. Ibid.
112. Nichols (ed.), *Diary of Henry Machyn*, p. 16.
113. CSPS, x, p. 493.

114. At the end of Mary I's reign, Elizabeth told Sir Thomas Pope that she had 'made my humble suit' to Edward that with his blessing, she would like to remain unmarried. She made no mention of Edward's response. BL, Add MS 48062, ff. 297–8b.
115. Strangford (ed.), *Household Expenses*, p. 38.
116. Ibid., pp. 41–2.

Chapter 11

1. BL, Harley MS 6986, f. 23r; Marcus, Mueller and Rose (eds), *Collected Works*, p. 38.
2. Ibid.
3. Ibid. The date of this letter is uncertain, but it seems plausible that it was written in around February 1553. See Starkey, *Elizabeth*, p. 108.
4. CSPS, xi, p. 9.
5. CSPS, xi, p. 16.
6. Marcus, Mueller and Rose (eds), *Collected Works*, p. 36.
7. CSPS, xi, p. 35.
8. Ibid.
9. Ibid.
10. Cited in Wood, *Letters of Royal and Illustrious Ladies*, iii, p. 229.
11. CSPS, xi, p. 40. In his biography, Chris Skidmore states his belief that Edward suffered from tuberculosis. See *Edward VI*, p. 260.
12. CSPS, xi, p. 40.
13. Guildford was of a similar age to Jane, and was named after his maternal grandfather, Sir Edward Guildford.
14. Strype, *Ecclesiastical Memorials*, iv, p. 485; CSPS, xi, p. 36. A royal warrant containing clothes that were to be provided for Elisabeth Brooke for the wedding suggests that she had indeed had some hand in bringing the marriage to pass. However, Helen Graham-Matheson has suggested that Elisabeth may not necessarily have supported the plan to overlook Elizabeth in the succession in Jane's favour, and may instead have been reacting to events. See 'All wemen', p. 132.
15. R. Wingfield, 'Vitae Mariae Reginae', trans. D. MacCulloch, Camden Miscellany XXVIII, 4th series, XXIX (London, 1984), p. 245.
16. John had married Anne Seymour, eldest daughter of the Lord Protector, on 3 June 1550. She would later be declared a lunatic and died in 1588. She is buried in All Saints Church, Faringdon, with her second husband, Sir Edward Unton.
17. CSPS, xi, p. 38.
18. The other couples were Jane's sister, Katherine Grey, who was married to Henry Herbert, heir of the Earl of Pembroke, and Henry Hastings, heir of the Earl of Huntingdon, who was married to Northumberland's daughter Katherine.
19. New College Library, Oxford, MS 328, f. 29; CSPS, xi, p. 40.
20. Wingfield, 'Vitae Mariae', p. 245.
21. CSPS, xi, p. 45.
22. Ibid. The daughter was Margaret of Valois, later the consort of Henri IV of France.
23. Marcus, Mueller and Rose (eds), *Collected Works*, p. 40.
24. Elisabeth Brooke was frequently at court during the reign of Edward VI, and seems to have been well liked and favoured there. See Graham-Matheson, 'All wemen', p. 48.
25. CSPS, xi, p. 107.
26. Wingfield, 'Vitae Mariae', p. 247.

27. Ibid.
28. Inner Temple Library, Petyt MS 538.47.
29. The terms of this will were probably based on an earlier one that has not survived, but that probably coincided with the Act of Succession in 1544.
30. See N. Tallis, *Crown of Blood: The Deadly Inheritance of Lady Jane Grey* (London, 2016), pp. 54–5 for more on the possible reasons for Frances's exclusion.
31. Inner Temple Library, Petyt MS 538.47.
32. Ibid.
33. CSPS, xi, p. 55.
34. Wingfield, 'Vitae Mariae', p. 248.
35. CSPS, xi, p. 46.
36. Ibid.
37. CSPS, xi, p. 71.
38. For more on this see Skidmore, *Edward VI*, pp. 258–60. On 4 July Scheyfve had also reported that 'It seems there is at present about the King a certain woman who professes to understand medicine, and is administering certain restoratives, though not independently of the physicians.' This may have bolstered the rumours of poison. CSPS, xi, p. 70.
39. CSPS, xi, p. 66.
40. CSPS, xi, p. 69.
41. Cited in Skidmore, *Edward VI*, p. 258.
42. Camden, *Historie*, Introduction.
43. Wingfield, 'Vitae Mariae', p. 251; CSPS, xi, p. 73.
44. CSPS, xi, p. 73.
45. CSPS, xi, p. 72.
46. CSPS, xi, p. 80.
47. Kenninghall had formerly been the property of the Duke of Norfolk, but was later seized by Henry VIII, who gave it to Mary. Little survives of the house.
48. CSPS, xi, p. 82.
49. Wingfield, 'Vitae Mariae', p. 255. For details of Mary's movements at this time see A. Whitelock and D. MacCulloch, 'Princess Mary's Household and the Succession Crisis, July 1553', *Historical Journal*, 50:2 (2007), p. 266.
50. Weir, *Children of England*, p. 172.
51. CSPS, xi, p. 88.
52. J.G. Nichols (ed.), *The Chronicle of Queen Jane and of Two Years of Queen Mary*, Camden Society, 48 (London, 1850), p. 7.
53. CSPS, xi, p. 88.
54. Wingfield, 'Vitae Mariae', p. 255.
55. CSPS, xi, pp. 91–2.
56. CSPS, xi, p. 94.
57. George Talbot, sixth Earl of Shrewsbury, is better known as the fourth husband of Bess of Hardwick and jailer of Mary, Queen of Scots. Sir John Mason hailed from Berkshire, but attended Oxford. He served the Tudor monarchs as a diplomat, and died in 1566.
58. CSPS, xi, pp. 95–6.
59. CSPS, xi, p. 96.
60. Ibid.
61. Clifford, *Life of Jane Dormer*, p. 12.
62. CSPS, xi, p. 109; CSPS, xi, p. 113.

63. CSPS, xi, p. 115.
64. Ibid.
65. CSPS, xi, p. 116.
66. Ibid.
67. CSPS, xi, p. 125.
68. Nichols (ed.), *Chronicle of Queen Jane*, p. 12.
69. Wriothesley, *Chronicle*, ii, p. 92.
70. Wingfield, 'Vitae Mariae', p. 271.
71. CSPS, xi, p. 151.
72. Ibid.
73. Nichols (ed.), *Diary of Henry Machyn*, p. 38.
74. CSPS, xi, p. 150.
75. Wingfield, 'Vitae Mariae', p. 271.
76. CSPS, xi, p. 150.
77. A. de Guaras, *The Accession of Queen Mary*, ed. and trans. R. Garnett (London, 1892), p. 100.
78. Wingfield, 'Vitae Mariae', p. 272; CSPS, xi, p. 152.
79. CSPS, xi, p. 152.
80. J. Foxe, *The Acts and Monuments of John Foxe*, ed. S.R. Cattley, viii (London, 1839), p. 606.
81. CSPS, xi, p. 169.
82. Nichols (ed.), *Chronicle of Queen Jane*, p. 19.
83. Northumberland's associates Sir John Gates and Sir Thomas Palmer were also executed on the same day; CSPS, xi, p. 210; Paul, *House of Dudley*, pp. 224–6.
84. CSPS, xi, p. 169.
85. Camden, *Historie*, no page number.
86. In 1495 Katherine was married to William Courtenay, first Earl of Devon. William was later arrested, however, for conspiring with Edmund de la Pole against Henry VII. He was pardoned by Henry VIII but died in 1511. The couple's son, Henry, was Edward Courtenay's father.
87. CSPS, xi, p. 196.

Chapter 12

1. Elizabeth's friend Elisabeth Brooke, Marchioness of Northampton, had been told to remove herself from Winchester Palace in Southwark, which was then taken over by Gardiner.
2. CSPS, xi, p. 217.
3. Julius III was Pope from 1550 until his death in 1555. His term in office, however, was marked by several scandals.
4. Edward was buried beneath the original altar of Henry VII's Lady Chapel, close to the tomb of his grandparents, Henry VII and Elizabeth of York.
5. CSPS, xi, p. 157.
6. Ibid.
7. CSPS, xi, pp. 173–4.
8. CSPS, xi, p. 220.
9. Ibid.
10. Ibid.
11. Clifford, *Life of Jane Dormer*, p. 17.

12. CSPS, xi, p. 221.
13. CSPS, xi, p. 240.
14. CSPS, xi, p. 228.
15. There was little evidence against the Marquess, but he had engaged in a correspondence with Cardinal Pole, who had spoken out about the King's separation from the Church of Rome. He was executed on 9 December 1538.
16. The Marchioness was released from the Tower in 1540.
17. CSPS, xi, p. 114.
18. CSPS, xi, p. 213.
19. CSPS, xi, p. 114.
20. CSPS, xi, p. 242.
21. CSPS, xi, p. 240.
22. BL, Harley MS 7376, ff. 3r, 4v, 6r.
23. Madden (ed.), *Privy Purse Expenses*, pp. 194, 188.
24. Ibid., p. 197.
25. Her jewel inventory shows that on another occasion Mary had given Elizabeth 'a green tablet garnished with gold having the picture of the Trinity in it', and 'a pomander of gold with a dial in it'. Madden (ed.), *Privy Purse Expenses*, p. 178.
26. CSPS, xi, pp. 252–3.
27. CSPS, xi, p. 253.
28. Nichols (ed.), *Chronicle of Queen Jane*, p. 22.
29. Ibid.
30. Ibid.
31. CSPS, xi, p. 259.
32. Wingfield, 'Vitae Mariae', p. 275.
33. CSPS, xi, p. 262.
34. For a contemporary account of Mary's coronation, see Nichols (ed.), *Chronicle of Queen Jane*, pp. 22–4.
35. CSPV, vi (884).
36. CSPV, v (934).
37. CSPS, xi, p. 281.
38. CSPS, xi, p. 292.
39. CSPS, xi, p. 307. On 19 October Renard reported that 'Courtenay is in disgrace with the Lady Elizabeth for having spoken otherwise than she had looked for about *amourettes* said to have existed between them.'
40. On 4 November Renard remarked that Elizabeth 'has not gone into the country as I had been told'. CSPS, xi, p. 334.
41. CSPS, xi, p. 241.
42. CSPS, xi, p. 359.
43. CSPV, v (934).
44. Nichols (ed.), *Chronicle of Queen Jane*, p. 25.
45. CSPS, xi, p. 393.
46. CSPS, xi, pp. 393–4.
47. CSPS, xi, pp. 393–4, 395.
48. CSPS, xi, p. 454.
49. CSPS, xi, p. 400.
50. CSPS, xi, p. 418.
51. Ibid.

52. Ibid.
53. Ibid.
54. CSPS, xi, p. 440.

Chapter 13

1. CSPV, v (934).
2. Ibid.
3. Following Stephen's death though, Matilda's son succeeded to the throne as Henry II. He would rule for thirty-five years.
4. CSPS, xi, p. 213.
5. CSPS, xi, p. 441.
6. CSPS, xi, p. 300.
7. CSPS, xi, p. 289.
8. Charles's wife, Isabella of Portugal, had died in 1539. Charles was devastated and continued to mourn Isabella for the rest of his life, never remarrying. His terrible gout severely restricted his mobility as he grew older.
9. CSPS, xi, p. 289.
10. Philip had been married to Maria Manuela of Portugal in 1543, but she had died two years later just days after giving birth to the couple's only child, a son. The young Don Carlos was mentally unstable and suffered from numerous health problems. He died in 1568 at the age of just twenty-three.
11. CSPS, xi, p. 367. Mary of Hungary also instructed Renard to tell Mary that the portrait 'will serve to tell her what he is like, if she will put it in a proper light and look at it from a distance, as all Titian's paintings have to be looked at. She will of course know that the likeness is no longer exact, as it was painted so long ago, and she will be able to imagine, from what he was then, the progress he will have made in the last three years. So you will present the portrait to her under one condition: that I am to have it again, as it is only a dead thing, when she has the living model in her presence.'
12. CSPV, vii (274).
13. CSPS, xi, p. 328.
14. E.H. Harbison, *Rival Ambassadors at the Court of Queen Mary* (London, 1940), p. 69.
15. Susan Clarencius had been a member of Mary's household since Mary was a child. She and Mary were extremely close, and Susan was well rewarded for her loyalty and devotion. She had a brief marriage, but her husband died less than two years later and Susan never remarried. She outlived Mary, dying in around 1564.
16. CSPS, xi, p. 328.
17. Wingfield, 'Vitae Mariae', p. 279.
18. CSPS, xi, p. 343.
19. CSPS, xi, p. 443.
20. CSPS, xi, p. 363.
21. CSPS, xi, pp. 363–4.
22. CSPS, xi, p. 364.
23. M.J. Rodriguez-Salgado and S. Adams, 'The Count of Feria's Dispatch to Philip II of 14 November 1558', *Camden Miscellany,* Camden Fourth Series, 29 (1984), p. 334.
24. Wingfield, 'Vitae Mariae', p. 279.
25. D. Loades, *Two Tudor Conspiracies* (Cambridge, 1965), p. 52.
26. Carew had previously declared his support for Mary in the summer of 1553, but the

Spanish marriage was more than he could stomach; Rodriguez-Salgado and Adams, 'Count of Feria's Dispatch', p. 332; Loades, *Two Tudor Conspiracies*, p. 16.

27. As early as 17 December Renard had heard that Thomas and John Grey were among those 'conspiring to prevent his Highness from landing'. CSPS, xi, p. 441.
28. CSPS, xi, p. 87.
29. Wingfield, 'Vitae Mariae', p. 279.
30. In 1557 the Venetian ambassador Giovanni Michiel reported that 'the Queen's hatred is increased by knowing her [Elizabeth] to be averse to the present religion, she having not only been born in the other, but being versed and educated in it; for although externally she showed, and by living catholically shows, that she has recanted, she is nevertheless supposed to dissemble, and to hold to it more than ever internally'. CSPV, vi (884).
31. CSPS, xi, p. 314.
32. Somerset, *Elizabeth I*, p. 47.
33. Guy, *Children of Henry VIII*, p. 155. Astley would not return until Elizabeth's accession, when she created him Master of the Jewel House. Cheke, meanwhile, was kidnapped in 1556 on Philip's orders and returned to England and the Tower. He was eventually released, but died in 1557.
34. CSPS, xi, p. 439.
35. Elizabeth herself acknowledged this in her letter to Mary on 26 January 1554. See CSPS, xii, p. 50.
36. Sir Anthony Browne was the stepson of Elizabeth's friend, Elizabeth FitzGerald. He was nevertheless wholly loyal to Mary, and would become Philip's Master of Horse after their marriage.
37. Nichols (ed.), *Diary of Henry Machyn*, p. 50; Nichols (ed.), *Chronicle of Queen Jane*, p. 25.
38. Nichols (ed.), *Chronicle of Queen Jane*, p. 26.
39. CSPS, xii, p. 2.
40. Ibid.
41. CSPS, xii, p. 22.
42. CSPS, xii, p. 50.
43. CSPS, xii, p. 16.
44. Ibid.
45. Carew was arrested in Flanders in May 1556 alongside Sir John Cheke and returned to England. He was incarcerated in the Tower until October, when he was released after the payment of a debt to the Crown. He died in 1580 having taken part in the English campaign to conquer Ireland and is buried in Waterford Cathedral. A monument to his memory was also erected in Exeter Cathedral.
46. Loades, *Two Tudor Conspiracies*, p. 23.
47. Harbison, *Rival Ambassadors*, p. 126; CSPS, xii, p. 41.
48. CSPS, xi, p. 472.
49. CSPS, xii, p. 33.
50. CSPS, xii, p. 42.
51. Donnington Castle was built in the fourteenth century by Sir Richard Abberbury, an associate of the Black Prince. It was later held by Thomas Chaucer, son of the poet Geoffrey. Donnington is now in ruins, having been largely demolished during the English Civil War. It is administered today by English Heritage.
52. Strype, *Ecclesiastical Memorials*, iii, p. 150.
53. Nichols (ed.), *Chronicle of Queen Jane*, p. 46. St Loe survived the Tower, and upon her

accession Elizabeth appointed him her Captain of the Guard. He was also the third husband of Bess of Hardwick, whom he married in 1559.

54. Guy, *Children of Henry VIII*, p. 159.
55. Strype, *Ecclesiastical Memorials*, iii, p. 126.
56. Ibid.
57. Nichols (ed.), *Chronicle of Queen Jane*, p. 37.
58. Jane's younger sisters were Katherine and Mary. During Elizabeth's reign, both sisters would end their lives in tragic circumstances.
59. Wingfield, 'Vitae Mariae', p. 280.
60. Loades, *Two Tudor Conspiracies*, p. 62. Allington Castle was originally built in the twelfth century, and had become the home of the Wyatt family by the end of the fifteenth.
61. Wingfield, 'Vitae Mariae', p. 279.
62. Loades, *Two Tudor Conspiracies*, p. 63.
63. Astley Castle was named after the family who built it, but by the early fifteenth century it had been inherited by the Greys. Astley served as a base for the Parliamentarians during the Civil War, but by the late twentieth century it was largely ruinous. It has since been restored and turned into a holiday let.
64. CSPS, xii, p. 85.
65. CSPS, xii, pp. 51–2; Nichols (ed.), *Chronicle of Queen Jane*, p. 25.
66. Loades, *Two Tudor Conspiracies*, p. 64.
67. Wingfield, 'Vitae Mariae', p. 280.
68. Henry Jerningham was born in around 1509/10, the son of Edward Jerningham and Mary Scrope. Henry's father died in 1515, and his stepfather was Sir William Kingston. In 1536 Henry married Frances Baynham, by whom he had five children.
69. CSPS, xii, p. 63.
70. Ibid.
71. Starkey, *Elizabeth*, p. 132.
72. CSPS, xii, p. 55.
73. CSPS, xii, p. 56.
74. Ibid.
75. Manning (ed.), 'State Papers', p. 182.
76. CSPS, xii, p. 56.
77. J.G. Nichols (ed.), *Chronicle of the Grey Friars of London*, Camden Society (London, 1851), p. 86.
78. CSPS, xii, p. 79.
79. Ibid.
80. Ibid.
81. Loades, *Two Tudor Conspiracies*, p. 67.
82. CSPS, xii, p. 86.
83. Nichols (ed.), *Diary of Henry Machyn*, p. 54.
84. Ibid.
85. Wingfield, 'Vitae Mariae', p. 281.
86. Nichols (ed.), *Chronicle of Queen Jane*, p. 36.
87. Ibid.
88. Ibid.
89. Wingfield, 'Vitae Mariae', p. 284.
90. Nichols (ed.), *Chronicle of Queen Jane*, p. 37.

91. CSPS, xii, p. 86.
92. CSPS, xii, p. 94.
93. CSPS, xii, p. 89; see H.R. Darsie, *Anna, Duchess of Cleves: The King's 'Beloved Sister'* (Stroud, 2020), pp. 260–2.
94. In August 1554 Anne wrote to Mary from Hever thanking her for the favour that had been shown to her. She expressed her desire to pay court to Mary and Philip, but it seems that she never had an opportunity to do so. CSPD Mary, iv (18). When Anne made her will, she left her best jewel to Mary, and her second-best jewel to Elizabeth. TNA, PROB 11/39/368, f. 262v.
95. CSPS, xii, p. 94.
96. CSPS, xii. 87.
97. Harbison, *Rival Ambassadors*, p. 158.
98. CSPS, xii, p. 106.
99. CSPS, xii, p. 87.
100. The remains of both Jane and Guildford were interred in the Chapel of St Peter ad Vincula within the Tower of London. A memorial plaque commemorates their final resting place.

Chapter 14

1. Sir Edward Hastings was a Privy Councillor and Mary's Master of Horse. He played no role in the affairs of the realm after Mary's death and died in 1572. Sir Thomas Cornwallis was also a Privy Councillor and likewise largely retired from public life during Elizabeth's reign. He died in 1604.
2. Foxe, *Acts and Monuments*, viii, p. 606.
3. Ibid.
4. Dr George Owen was a fellow of Merton College, Oxford, while Dr Thomas Wendy had attended Cambridge. Wendy had also served Katherine Parr; CSPS, xii, p. 94.
5. Foxe, *Acts and Monuments*, viii, p. 606.
6. CSPD Mary, iii (21).
7. Foxe, *Acts and Monuments*, viii, p. 607.
8. CSPS, xii, p. 106.
9. Ibid.
10. CSPS, xii, p. 120.
11. CSPS, xii, p. 125.
12. Ibid.
13. Foxe, *Acts and Monuments*, viii, p. 607.
14. Borman, *Elizabeth's Women*, p. 148.
15. CSPS, xii, p. 125.
16. Ibid.
17. CSPS, xii, p. 140.
18. Porter, *Mary Tudor*, p. 51.
19. CSPS, xii, p. 151.
20. CSPS, xii, p. 167.
21. Foxe, *Acts and Monuments*, viii, p. 607.
22. Ibid., pp. 607–8.
23. Ibid., p. 608.
24. Dasent *et al.* (eds), *Acts of the Privy Council*, v, p. 129.

25. In later years, Elizabeth is reported to have said of Winchester, 'for, by my troth, if my lord treasurer were but a young man, I could find it in my heart to have him for a husband before any man in England'.

26. Sussex's first wife, Elizabeth Howard, was sister to Elizabeth's maternal grandmother of the same name. Elizabeth Howard had died when Elizabeth was very young, and Sussex took as his second wife Anne Calthorpe. Anne had served Katherine Parr, but in September 1552 she was sent to the Tower accused of sorcery. Though she was released after a few months, she fled abroad during Mary's reign to avoid persecution for her Protestant beliefs. Her marriage to Sussex was unsuccessful and they finally divorced in 1555.

27. Foxe, *Acts and Monuments*, viii, p. 608.

28. Ibid.

29. CSPS, xii, p. 167.

30. Foxe does not specifically name Winchester, but he does seem to be the most probable candidate.

31. Foxe, *Acts and Monuments*, viii, p. 608.

32. SP 11/4.

33. CSPS, xii, p. 167.

34. Ibid.

35. Ibid.

36. Foxe, *Acts and Monuments*, viii, p. 608.

37. Ibid., p. 609.

38. Ibid.

39. Ibid.

40. The Byward Tower was built by Henry III in the thirteenth century and contains beautiful medieval wall paintings.

41. Foxe, *Acts and Monuments*, viii, p. 609.

42. Ibid.

43. Ibid.

44. Ibid.

45. Borman, *Anne Boleyn and Elizabeth I*, p. 133.

46. Foxe, *Acts and Monuments*, viii, p. 609.

Chapter 15

1. Rodriguez-Salgado and Adams, 'Count of Feria's Dispatch', p. 330.

2. Weir, *Mary Boleyn*, pp. 156–8.

3. Nichols (ed.), *Chronicle of Queen Jane*, p. 38.

4. Cited in Hughey, *John Harington*, p. 45.

5. For further details of Etheldreda's life see Weir, *Mary Boleyn*, pp. 156–8.

6. Strype, *Ecclesiastical Memorials*, iii, p. 129.

7. Foxe, *Acts and Monuments*, viii, pp. 609–10.

8. W. Cobbett, *State Trials and Proceedings for High Treason and Other Misdemeanours*, i (London, 1820), p. 863.

9. Wingfield, 'Vitae Mariae', p. 289.

10. Foxe, *Acts and Monuments*, viii, p. 610.

11. Ibid.

12. Ibid.

13. Ibid., p. 611.
14. Sir John Gage had served Henry VII, Henry VIII and Edward VI, and had been made a Knight of the Garter in 1541. His main seat was Firle Place in Sussex.
15. CSPS, xii, p. 196.
16. This is particularly interesting given that, as Dr Joanne Paul highlighted to me, Mary's maternal grandfather, Ferdinand of Aragon, had pushed Henry VII to order the execution of Edward, Earl of Warwick, before allowing Katherine of Aragon to come to England and marry Prince Arthur. Warwick was executed in 1499, an occurrence over which Katherine seems to have felt much guilt.
17. Clifford, *Life of Jane Dormer*, p. 20.
18. CSPS, xii, p. 201.
19. Ibid.
20. CSPS, xii, p. 218.
21. Strype, *Ecclesiastical Memorials*, iii, p. 187.
22. Wriothesley, *Chronicle*, ii, p. 115.
23. CSPS, xii, p. 218.
24. Ibid.
25. Manning (ed.), 'State Papers', p. 191.
26. Foxe, *Acts and Monuments*, viii, p. 612. Brydges was also granted Sudeley Castle, where Katherine Parr had died in 1548. His successors would later entertain Elizabeth at Sudeley. He had attended Lady Jane Grey on the scaffold, and she had inscribed her prayer book for him with a message of farewell.
27. Foxe, *Acts and Monuments*, viii, p. 612.
28. Ibid.
29. Ibid.
30. Ibid.
31. There is also a tale that at this time Lady Tyrwhit made Elizabeth a gift of a girdle prayer book, which now survives in the British Museum. Although the girdle undoubtedly belonged to Lady Tyrwhit, there is no substantive evidence that she ever gave it to Elizabeth. It is nevertheless an interesting story. See H. Tait, 'The "tablet" and the girdle-prayerbook at the Renaissance court of Henry VIII', *Jewellery Studies*, 2 (1985), pp. 29–58.
32. Foxe, *Acts and Monuments*, viii, pp. 612–13.
33. CSPS, xii, p. 230.
34. Strype, *Ecclesiastical Memorials*, iii, p. 129.
35. The Dudley brothers were released from the Tower in the autumn, but sadly John died immediately afterwards. Henry was killed at the Battle of St Quentin in 1557, and only Robert and Ambrose lived to see Elizabeth reign.
36. Working out Lady Grey's identity has been somewhat of a puzzle, and I am indebted to Melita Thomas for her assistance in helping me with this. John Harington later wrote of a Grey attendant on Elizabeth, and Hughey suggests that this was Honora, daughter of Sir William Grey, thirteenth Baron Grey of Wilton. See *John Harington*, p. 270. Whatever her identity, she is not to be confused with the branch of the Grey family from which Lady Jane Grey stemmed.
37. Manning (ed.), 'State Papers', p. 219.
38. BL, C.45.a.13. See https://www.bl.uk/collection-items/coverdale-new-testament-with-manuscript-dedication-by-elizabeth-tudor. Little is known of Anne aside from that she was the daughter of Sir Nicholas Poyntz and his wife Joan Berkeley, who had welcomed

Elizabeth's parents to their home at Acton Court, Gloucestershire, during their 1535 progress. The sumptuous lodgings Poyntz had built for the visit still survive at Acton Court. Scholar Helen Graham-Matheson suggested that Anne may have been a distant relative of Elisabeth Brooke, for her name also appears in the Book of Hours at Hever. If this was indeed the case, then it may have been Elisabeth who introduced Anne to Elizabeth. Graham-Matheson, 'All wemen', p. 174.

39. BL, C.45.a.13., f. 3r.
40. Ibid., f. 4v.
41. Ibid., f. 5r. Though not conclusive, the fact that Anne signed herself by her maiden name suggests that the inscription may date from prior to her marriage to Sir Thomas Heneage, which took place at some time in 1554 – perhaps Elizabeth later gave the book to Anne to mark that occasion.
42. Though there is no mention of Anne in any of Elizabeth's household lists, in February 1554 the Imperial ambassador Simon Renard referred to 'a certain gentleman named Poyntz', who 'has a son and a daughter living with her [Elizabeth]'. It is likely that this was Anne, who would also serve Elizabeth when she became Queen. CSPS, xii, p. 82.
43. CSPS, xii, p. 221.
44. Ibid.
45. Lord William Howard was the son of Thomas Howard, second Duke of Norfolk by Agnes Tilney. He had enjoyed a military career and was a member of Mary's Privy Council. He would later serve Elizabeth, and died in 1573.
46. Rodriguez-Salgado and Adams, 'Count of Feria's Dispatch', p. 331.
47. CSPS, xii, p. 230.
48. Foxe, *Acts and Monuments*, viii, p. 613.
49. Fotheringhay Castle later gained notoriety as the final prison – and site of execution – of Mary, Queen of Scots, in 1587. Only a fragment of the castle now remains, but the nearby church contains many reminders of its medieval past. Sir Thomas Tresham was a prominent Catholic gentleman hailing from Northamptonshire. He was responsible for building both the extraordinary Rushton Triangular Lodge and the unfinished Lyveden New Bield nearby. He was also the father of one of the gunpowder plotters, Francis Tresham.
50. Sir James Croft survived to serve Elizabeth, and was eventually invited to join the Privy Council and become Comptroller of the Queen's Household. He died in 1590 and is buried in Westminster Abbey.
51. Wriothesley, *Chronicle*, ii, p. 116.
52. CSPS, xii, p. 261.
53. Strype, *Ecclesiastical Memorials*, iii, p. 199.

Chapter 16

1. Strype, *Ecclesiastical Memorials*, iii, p. 129.
2. Foxe, *Acts and Monuments*, viii, p. 614.
3. Oxburgh Hall had been built by Sir Henry's grandfather, Edmund, in 1482. Though he had once been loyal to Richard III, following his death Edmund later transferred his allegiance to Henry VII. He hosted the King and his wife, Elizabeth of York – Elizabeth's grandparents – as well as Lady Margaret Beaufort, at his new home. Although it is now owned and administered by the National Trust, Sir Henry's descendants still live at Oxburgh Hall today.

4. Edmund Bedingfield was married to Grace Marney, the daughter of Henry Marney of Layer Marney in Essex. Henry Marney had been one of Henry VIII's great favourites.

5. Sir John Williams shared his role of Master of the Jewels with Thomas Cromwell and had enjoyed Henry VIII's favour. He had been imprisoned by Edward VI but was favoured by Mary. He married twice, and the tomb he shares with one of his wives is in St Mary's Church, Thame.

6. It is uncertain if Isabella Markham did accompany Elizabeth to Woodstock, but she was certainly back at Hatfield with Elizabeth by the end of 1555. If Elizabeth did indeed gift her the copper portrait in 1554, however, then she must have been at Woodstock at some point. See Hughey, *John Harington*, p. 239. The sitter in the image does not, though, bear any resemblance to Elizabeth, so it is possible that it represents someone else.

7. Foxe, *Acts and Monuments*, viii, p. 615.

8. Manning (ed.), 'State Papers', p. 149. The original papers are in the British Library, BL, Add MS 34563, ff. 1v–66v.

9. Jane was the product of Sir William Dormer's first marriage to Mary Sidney. Following Mary's death, however, by 1550 Sir William had married Dorothy Catesby and it was she who welcomed Elizabeth to West Wycombe.

10. Manning (ed.), 'State Papers', p. 150.

11. Ibid., p. 151.

12. Ibid.

13. Foxe, *Acts and Monuments*, viii, p. 615.

14. Manning (ed.), 'State Papers', p. 152.

15. Ibid., p. 153.

16. Woodstock became famed as a trysting location for Henry II and his mistress, Rosamund Clifford.

17. This was Mary, who married John, Duke of Brittany, at the Palace in the summer of 1361. Tragically though, Mary died within a few months of her marriage. She was sixteen years old.

18. Nothing survives of Woodstock Palace, which now stands in the grounds of Blenheim Palace. A single stone marks the site it once occupied.

19. Manning (ed.), 'State Papers', p. 154.

20. Ibid.

21. Ibid., p. 141.

22. Ibid., p. 158.

23. Ibid.; Foxe, *Acts and Monuments*, viii, p. 616.

24. Ibid.

25. Manning (ed.), 'State Papers', p. 158.

26. Ibid., p. 159.

27. Ibid., p. 163.

28. Ibid., pp. 160–1.

29. Cited in Marcus, Mueller and Rose (eds), *Collected Works*, p. 46.

30. Manning (ed.), 'State Papers', p. 166.

31. Ibid., p. 169. Elizabeth Norwich had served Elizabeth since at least the beginning of 1547 – probably earlier – for her name appears in the list of members of Elizabeth's household who received material for mourning garments following Henry VIII's death. She would marry Sir Gawain Carew. TNA, LC 2/2, f. 48v.

32. Elizabeth Marbery became one of Elizabeth's chamberers upon her accession. TNA, E 101/429/3, f. 53v.
33. Ibid., p. 170.
34. The Bull Inn is now No. 16 Market Place, and the location of NatWest Bank.
35. Manning (ed.), 'State Papers', p. 161.
36. Ibid., p. 174.
37. Ibid., p. 176.
38. Ibid., pp. 178–9.
39. Ibid., pp. 180–1.
40. Ibid., pp. 186–7.
41. Ibid., p. 182.
42. CSPS, xii, p. 286.
43. CSPS, xii, p. 316.
44. Wriothesley, *Chronicle*, ii, p. 119.
45. CSPS, xiii, p. 1.
46. G.F. Commendone, *The Accession, Coronation and Marriage of Mary Tudor*, ed. C.V. Malfatti (Barcelona, 1956), p. 51.
47. Porter, *Mary Tudor*, p. 322.
48. Wolvesey Castle is now a ruin, having been abandoned in the 1680s. It is administered by English Heritage and is open to visitors.
49. CSPS, xii, p. 322.
50. CSPV, vi (884); CSPS, xii, p. 318.
51. CSPS, xiii, p. 2.
52. CSPV, vi (884).
53. CSPS, xiii, pp. 2–3.
54. CSPS, xiii, pp. 49–50.
55. Manning (ed.), 'State Papers', p. 193.
56. Ibid., p. 203.
57. Ibid., p. 208.
58. CSPS, xiii, p. 84.
59. Manning (ed.), 'State Papers', p. 223.
60. Ibid., pp. 224–5.
61. CSPS, xiii, p. 51.
62. CSPS, xiii, p. 78.
63. CSPS, xiii, p. 135.
64. CSPS, xiii, p. 145.
65. Ibid.
66. Ibid.
67. CSPS, xiii, p. 148. In his report Renard observed: 'Still other persons think that four Privy Councillors had better be sent to her to tell her plainly of the plots that are being woven, and to inform her that the Queen thinks she had better go to Flanders for some time, making a show of authority if she demurs, and have her taken away by force.'
68. CSPV, vi (884).
69. CSPS, xiii, p. 151.
70. CSPS, xiii, p. 166.
71. Strype, *Ecclesiastical Memorials*, iii, p. 336.

Chapter 17

1. Foxe, *Acts and Monuments*, viii, p. 620.
2. Ibid.
3. Ibid.
4. Ibid.
5. CSPS, xiii, p. 169.
6. Foxe, *Acts and Monuments*, viii, p. 621.
7. CSPV, vi (884).
8. Foxe, *Acts and Monuments*, viii, p. 621.
9. CSPV, vi (42).
10. CSPV, vi (72).
11. CSPS, xiii, p. 224.
12. Frideswide was the daughter of John Knight and had formerly served Katherine of Aragon. She married Robert Strelley, a gentleman of Mary's household, and became a gentlewoman of Mary's Privy Chamber.
13. HMC Rutland, i, p. 311.
14. See Porter, *Mary Tudor*, pp. 337–8; Weir, *Children of England*, pp. 314–15.
15. CSPV, vi (884); Rodriguez-Salgado and Adams, 'Count of Feria's Dispatch', p. 330.
16. Clifford, *Life of Jane Dormer*, p. 20.
17. CSPV, vi (174).
18. CSPV, vi (204).
19. In the summer of 1554, the Venetian ambassador Giacomo Soranzo would refer to Mary's anxiety, and it is clear that she had been suffering from such symptoms at various points throughout her life. CSPV, v (934).
20. Cited in Porter, *Mary Tudor*, p. 349.
21. CSPV, vi (884).
22. Ascham, *Whole Works*, p. lxxxvi.
23. Nichols (ed.), *Diary of Henry Machyn*, p. 94.
24. Pole's family were punished by Henry VIII for their apparent involvement in the Exeter Conspiracy of 1538. His brother, Sir Geoffrey Pole, was arrested but pardoned. Pole's other brother, Henry Pole, Baron Montagu, was executed, as was his mother, Margaret Pole, Countess of Salisbury. The death of the Countess, Mary's former governess, which took place in 1541, caused shockwaves given that she was in her sixties and met her end in a particularly brutal manner.
25. For more on this in Mary's reign see D. MacCulloch, *Reformation: Europe's House Divided 1490–1700* (London, 2003), pp. 280–6; Weir, *Children of England*, pp. 289–94.
26. CSPS, xiii, p. 138.
27. Ibid.
28. Loades, *Mary Tudor*, p. 177.
29. Following Cranmer's condemnation for treason in 1553, he had remained imprisoned and was moved to Oxford in 1554. His heresy trial did not take place until 12 September 1555.
30. Wriothesley, *Chronicle*, ii, p. 133; Nichols (ed.), *Chronicle of the Grey Friars*, p. 97.
31. See Porter, *Mary Tudor*; S. Duncan and V. Schutte (eds), *The Birth of a Queen: Essays on the Quincentenary of Mary I* (Basingstoke, 2016); V. Schutte and J.S. Hower (eds), *Writing Mary I: History, Historiography, and Fiction* (Basingstoke, 2022).

32. MacCulloch, *Reformation*, p. 285.
33. Weir, *Children of England*, p. 293.
34. Ibid.; E. Duffy, *Fires of Faith: Catholic England Under Mary Tudor* (New Haven and London, 2009), p. 7.
35. Camden, *Historie*, p. 20.
36. Weir, *Children of England*, p. 293. Gardiner died on 12 November. He is buried in Winchester Cathedral, where his chantry tomb can be seen.
37. J. Ridley, *Bloody Mary's Martyrs: The Story of England's Terror* (London, 2001), p. 1.
38. Garrett, *Marian Exiles*, p. 73.
39. See N. Tallis, *Elizabeth's Rival: The Tumultuous Tale of Lettice Knollys, Countess of Leicester* (London, 2017), pp. 29–30.
40. Cited in Wood, *Letters of Royal and Illustrious Ladies*, iii, p. 280. Wood incorrectly dates this letter to 1553. Given that Katherine probably did not leave England until early in 1557, this cannot have been the case.
41. CSPV, vi (116); Weir, *Children of England*, p. 296.
42. Nichols (ed.), *Diary of Henry Machyn*, pp. 94–5.
43. CSPV, vi (884); Nichols (ed.), *Diary of Henry Machyn*, p. 96.
44. Dasent *et al.* (eds), *Acts of the Privy Council*, v, p. 129.
45. See Hughey, *John Harington*, pp. 103–5, 270–1.
46. J. Bruce (ed.), *Letters and Papers of the Verney Family* (London, 1853), p. 63.
47. Loades, *Two Tudor Conspiracies*, p. 190; Harbison, *Rival Ambassadors*, p. 290.
48. Dudley's mother was Cecily, a daughter of Thomas Grey, first Marquess of Dorset. He had at one time served Thomas Cromwell.
49. Lady Katherine Gordon was the daughter of the second Earl of Huntly, George Gordon. She had been married to Warbeck at the instigation of James IV of Scotland, and joined the household of Elizabeth of York when Warbeck was captured in 1497. Henry VII treated her kindly, and after Warbeck's execution in 1499 Katherine married three more times. Her second husband was James Strangeways, and in 1517 she married her third husband Matthew Craddock. Finally, she married Christopher Ashton.
50. Bruce (ed.), *Verney Papers*, p. 75.
51. Ibid., p. 57.
52. Ibid., p. 64.
53. Ibid., p. 65.
54. CSPV, vi (434).
55. Loades, *Two Tudor Conspiracies*, p. 211.
56. Nichols (ed.), *Diary of Henry Machyn*, p. 103.
57. Starkey, *Elizabeth*, p. 196.
58. Bruce (ed.), *Verney Papers*, p. 67.
59. Guy, *Children of Henry VIII*, p. 169.
60. CSPV, vi (505).
61. Peckham's father would later be an executor to the will of Anne of Cleves. Bruce (ed.), *Verney Papers*, p. 57.
62. CSPV, vi (505).
63. Ibid.
64. Ibid.

Chapter 18

1. CSPV, vi (510).
2. Ibid.
3. Ibid.
4. Ibid.
5. Clifford, *Life of Jane Dormer*, p. 20.
6. Harbison, *Rival Ambassadors*, p. 290.
7. Ibid., p. 291.
8. Lord Bray was pardoned and released in the spring of 1557. Following his release he travelled to Europe and fought alongside Philip's forces at the Battle of St Quentin in August. Here he was injured, and having returned to England he died on 19 November; Bruce (ed.), *Verney Papers*, p. 75.
9. CSPV, vi (510).
10. CSPV, vi (514).
11. The double tomb that Sir John Gage shares with his wife, Philippa, can be seen in St Peter's Church at West Firle, Sussex.
12. CSPV, vi (514).
13. T. Warton, *The Life of Sir Thomas Pope* (London, 1772), p. 81.
14. Ibid.
15. Clifford, *Life of Jane Dormer*, p. 20.
16. Pope's father was a farmer, and Pope himself had been fortunate enough to attend Eton College.
17. Strickland, *Life of Queen Elizabeth*, p. 58. Pope may already have been familiar to Elizabeth in some capacity, for her 1551/52 payments record a reward given to Lady Pope's servant. Pope was married three times. Strangford (ed.), *Household Expenses*, p. 38.
18. James P. Carley has noted that many of the books formerly in Henry VIII's library at Greenwich, now at Trinity College, were acquired for the college by Pope. *Books of King Henry VIII and His Wives*, p. 28. Trinity is the only college in either Oxford or Cambridge that contains the tomb of its founder.
19. Somerset, *Elizabeth I*, pp. 65–6; Warton, *Life of Sir Thomas Pope*, pp. 90–1.
20. Marcus, Mueller and Rose (eds), *Collected Works*, p. 43.
21. Ibid., p. 44.
22. Weir, *Children of England*, p. 335.
23. Wharton, *Life of Sir Thomas Pope*, p. 100.
24. Cited in Collins (ed.), *Jewels and Plate*, p. 207.
25. CSPV, vi (743).
26. Ibid.
27. Ibid.
28. Ibid.
29. Rodriguez-Salgado and Adams, 'Count of Feria's Dispatch', p. 334.
30. CSPV, vi (775).
31. CSPV, vi (1274).
32. Nichols (ed.), *Diary of Henry Machyn*, p. 120.
33. Somerset, *Elizabeth I*, p. 67.
34. CSPV, vi (884).
35. BL, Add MS 62525, f. 1r.
36. Ibid., ff. 1r–5v.

37. Ibid., f. 6v.
38. CSPV, vi (884).
39. Ibid.
40. Ibid.
41. Cited in Harbinger, *Rival Ambassadors*, p. 301.
42. CSPV, vi (852).
43. Margaret, Duchess of Parma, was an illegitimate daughter of Charles V, and would serve as Governor of the Netherlands from 1559 to 1567. She died in 1586. The Duchess of Lorraine is better known to history as Christina of Denmark, who famously quipped that she would be happy to marry Henry VIII if she had two heads. Christina was born in 1521 and had two marriages. First, to Francis, Duke of Milan, and then to Francis, Duke of Lorraine. She died in 1590.
44. CSPV, vi (866).
45. CSPV, vi (884).
46. L. Wiesener, *La Jeunesse d'Élisabeth d'Angleterre, 1533–1558* (Paris, 1878), p. 358.
47. Ibid.
48. CSPS, xiii, pp. 293–4.
49. Clifford, *Life of Jane Dormer*, p. 20.
50. Ibid.
51. Through their mother Thomas and Dorothy Stafford were the grandchildren of Margaret Pole, Countess of Salisbury. Dorothy married William Stafford, the widower of Elizabeth's aunt, Mary Boleyn, by whom she had six children. The Staffords spent much of Mary's reign living abroad in exile, but Dorothy returned home upon Elizabeth's accession – her husband had died in 1556. She remained close to Elizabeth for the rest of her life, and outlived her by a year. She died in 1604 and was buried in St Margaret's Church, Westminster.
52. CSPV, vi (870).
53. Clifford, *Life of Jane Dormer*, p. 20.
54. Harbinger, *Rival Ambassadors*, p. 297.
55. Ibid., p. 309.
56. CSPS, xiii, pp. 340–1.
57. CSPV, vi (884).
58. Nichols (ed.), *Diary of Henry Machyn*, pp. 166–7.
59. Ibid., p. 167.
60. CSPS, xiii, p. 367.
61. CSPS, xiii, p. 372.
62. See A. Whitelock, *Mary Tudor: England's First Queen* (London, 2009), pp. 299–300.
63. CSPS, xiii, p. 362.
64. CSPV, vi (884).
65. BL, Add MS 48062, ff. 297–8b.
66. CSPS, xiii, p. 380.
67. Whitelock, *Mary Tudor*, p. 300.
68. CSPS, xiii, p. 378.
69. CSPS, xiii, p. 398.
70. CSPS, xiii, p. 400.
71. Starkey, *Elizabeth*, p. 225; Bryson and Evans, 'Seven Rediscovered Letters', p. 843.
72. Somerset, *Elizabeth I*, p. 71.
73. CSPV, vi (1274).

74. Rodriguez-Salgado and Adams, 'Count of Feria's Dispatch', p. 328.
75. Philip referred to this physician in a letter written to his sister, Joanna, in which he informed her of Mary's ill health. CSPS, xiii, p. 440.
76. Charles V died at the Monastery of Yuste, and is buried in El Escorial.
77. Clifford, *Life of Jane Dormer*, p. 18.
78. CSPS, xiii, p. 438.
79. The will of Brocket's father had only been proved in May. Brocket himself was a few years younger than Elizabeth, having been born in around 1540. Elizabeth had also been at Brocket Hall on 28 October. Her earlier accounts show a payment made as well to a servant of 'Mr Brocket', so she had evidently been communicating with her Hertfordshire neighbours for many years. Strangford (ed.), *Household Expenses*, p. 39. Brocket Hall later became better known as the home of Lord Melbourne, Queen Victoria's Prime Minister. It has greatly altered since Elizabeth's day and is now a wedding venue and home to a fine golf course.
80. Starkey, *Elizabeth*, p. 225.
81. Rodriguez-Salgado and Adams, 'Count of Feria's Dispatch', p. 329.
82. Ibid., p. 330. Elizabeth was also joined by her childhood friend Elizabeth FitzGerald, now Lady Clinton as a result of her marriage to Edward Clinton, which had taken place in 1552.
83. Ibid., p. 331.
84. Ibid.
85. Ibid., p. 335.
86. Ibid., p. 332.
87. Cited in D. Wilson, *Sweet Robin: Robert Dudley, Earl of Leicester 1533–1588* (London, 1981), p. 76.
88. Rodriguez-Salgado and Adams, 'Count of Feria's Dispatch', p. 332.
89. CSPV, vi (1549).
90. Clifford, *Life of Jane Dormer*, p. 17.
91. Ibid.
92. Ibid.
93. J. Harington, *Nugae Antiquae: Being a Miscellaneous Collection of Original Papers in Prose and Verse: Written in the Reigns of Henry VIII, Queen Mary, Elizabeth, King James, etc*, II (London, 1779), p. 312; Thurley, *Royal Palaces*, p. 209.
94. Cited in Perry, *Word of a Prince*, pp. 76–7.
95. CSPV, vii (10).
96. Rodriguez-Salgado and Adams, 'Count of Feria's Dispatch', p. 331.

Epilogue

1. Cited in Perry, *Word of a Prince*, p. 2.
2. Nichols, *Progresses and Public Processions*, i, p. 36.
3. Camden, *Historie*, p. 6.
4. Ibid., p. 12.
5. Sir J. Hayward, *Annals of the First Four Years of the Reign of Queen Elizabeth*, ed. J. Bruce, Camden Society, vii (London, 1840), p. 6.
6. The Charterhouse was a former Carthusian monastery that had been purchased by Lord North in 1545. It was he who transformed the property into a luxurious residence; CSP Simancas, i, p. 5.

7. CSPV, vi (884).
8. Ibid.
9. A. Weir, *Elizabeth the Queen* (London, 1998), pp. 3–4.
10. Rodriguez-Salgado and Adams, 'Count of Feria's Dispatch', p. 331.
11. CSP Simancas, i, p. 21.
12. CSPV, vii (2).
13. Lawson (ed.), *Gift Exchange*, pp. 35, 38, 41.
14. There is no real previous indication that Elizabeth had been interested in alchemy, and when and where she first met Dee is unknown.
15. Weir, *Elizabeth the Queen*, p. 33.
16. CSPV, vii (10).
17. Ibid.
18. Ibid.
19. Ibid.
20. Ibid.
21. Nichols, *Progresses and Public Processions*, i, p. 43.
22. CSPV, vii (10).
23. Tracy Borman has also made this point. See *Anne Boleyn and Elizabeth I*, p. 153.
24. CSPV, vii (10).
25. Ibid.
26. Ibid.
27. Nichols (ed.), *Diary of Henry Machyn*, p. 186.
28. CSPV, vii (10).
29. Ibid.

Appendix 1

1. Haynes, *State Papers*, p. 94.
2. Marcus, Mueller and Rose (eds), *Collected Works*, p. 21.

Manuscript Sources

British Library, London

Additional	4149, 33271, 34563, 48062, 62525, 70518, 74745
	C.45.a.13.
Cotton	Otho C X, Vespasian C XIV, Vespasian F III, Vitellius C XVI
Egerton	985
Harley	283, 442, 6986, 7376
Kings	395
Lansdowne	1236, 1238
Royal	Appendix 68, 7 C XVI, 7 D X
Sloane	1786
Stowe	554, 559

National Archives, Kew

Exchequer

E 23	Treasury of Receipt, Royal Wills
E 101	King's Remembrancer, Various Accounts
E 179	King's Remembrancer, particulars of account and other records relating to lay and clerical taxation
E 315	Court of Augmentations and Predecessors, Miscellaneous Books

Lord Chamberlain's Department

LC 2	Records of Special Events
LC 5	Miscellaneous Records
LC 9	Accounts and Miscellanea

Prerogative Court of Canterbury

PROB 11	Registered Copy Wills
T 38/500	

Society of Antiquaries, London

MS 129	Inventory of King Henry VIII

Inner Temple Library, London

Petyt MS 538.47

Sudeley Castle, Gloucestershire
Dent-Brocklehurst MS

New College Library, Oxford
MS 328

Bodleian Library, Oxford
MS. Bodl. 6

National Library of Scotland, Edinburgh
RH13/78

Printed Primary Sources

Ascham, R., *English Works*, ed. Wright, W.A. (Cambridge, 1904).
Ascham, R., *The Schoolmaster*, ed. Ryan, L.V. (New York, 1967).
Ascham, R., *The Whole Works of Roger Ascham*, ed. Giles, J.A., 3 vols (London, 1864–5).
Bell, D.C., *Notices of the Historic Persons Buried in the Chapel of St Peter ad Vincula* (London, 1877).
Boyle, J. (ed.), *Memoirs of the Life of Robert Carey ... Written by Himself* (London, 1759).
Bruce, J. (ed.), *Correspondence of Matthew Parker, Archbishop of Canterbury* (Cambridge, 1853).
Bruce, J. (ed.), *Letters and Papers of the Verney Family* (London, 1853).
Byrne, M. St C. (ed.), *The Lisle Letters* (Chicago, 1980).
Camden, W., *The Historie of the Most Renowned and Victorious Princesse Elizabeth, Late Queene of England*, 3rd edition (London, 1675).
Cavendish, G., *The Life and Death of Cardinal Wolsey*, ed. Sylvester, R.S. (London and New York, 1959).
Clifford, H., *The Life of Jane Dormer, Duchess of Feria*, ed. Stevenson, J. (London, 1887).
Cobbett, W., *State Trials and Proceedings for High Treason and Other Misdemeanours*, i (London, 1820).
Collins, A.J. (ed.), *Jewels and Plate of Queen Elizabeth I: The Inventory of 1574* (London, 1955).
Colvin, H.M., Ransome, D.R. and Summerson, J. (eds), *The History of the King's Works*, iv (London, 1982).
Commendone, G.F., *The Accession, Coronation and Marriage of Mary Tudor*, ed. Malfatti, C.V. (Barcelona, 1956).
Crawford, A. (ed.), *Letters of the Queens of England* (Stroud, 2002).
Dasent, J.R., et al. (eds), *Acts of the Privy Council*, XXXVI vols (London, 1890–1907).
Ellis, H., *Original Letters*, 3 series, 10 vols (London, 1825–46).
Feuillerat, A. (ed.), *Documents relating to the Revels at Court in the time of King Edward VI and Queen Mary* (Louvain, 1914).
Foxe, J., *The Acts and Monuments of John Foxe*, ed. Cattley, S.R., viii (London, 1839).

Grafton, R., *An Abridgement of the Chronicles of England* (London, 1564).

Guaras, A. de, *The Accession of Queen Mary*, ed. and trans. Garnett, R. (London, 1892).

Hall, E., *The Union of the Two Noble and Illustre Famelies of York and Lancaster*, ed. Ellis, H. (London, 1809).

Halliwell, J.O. (ed.), *Letters of the Kings of England*, 2 vols (London, 1848).

Harington, J., *Nuguae Antiquae: Being a Miscellaneous Collection of Original Papers in Prose and Verse: Written in the Reigns of Henry VIII, Queen Mary, Elizabeth, King James, etc* (London, 1779).

Harrison, G.B. (ed.), *The Letters of Queen Elizabeth I* (London, 1968).

Haynes, S., *Collection of State Papers Relating to Affairs in the Reigns of King Henry VIII, King Edward VI, Queen Mary and Queen Elizabeth, From the Year 1542 to 1570 ... Left by William Cecil, Lord Burghley ... at Hatfield House* (London, 1740).

Hayward, M. (ed.), *The 1542 Inventory of Whitehall* (London, 2004).

Hayward, Sir J., *The Life and Raigne of King Edward the Sixth* (London, 1630).

Hayward, Sir J., *Annals of the First Four Years of the Reign of Queen Elizabeth*, ed. Bruce, J., Camden Society, VII (London, 1840).

Heath, J.B., 'An Account of Materials Furnished for the Use of Queen Anne Boleyn, and the Princess Elizabeth, by William Loke, The King's Mercer, between the 20th January 1535 and the 27th April, 1536', *Miscellanies of the Philobiblon Society*, Vol. VII (London, 1862–3).

Historical Manuscripts Commission, *Calendar of the Manuscripts of the Marquis of Salisbury, Preserved at Hatfield House, Herts*, i–xiv (London, 1883–1930).

Historical Manuscripts Commission, *The Manuscripts of His Grace the Duke of Rutland, Preserved at Belvoir Castle*, i (London, 1888).

Hoby, T., *The Book of the Courtier* (London, 1900).

Hughey, R. (ed.), *The Arundel Harington Manuscript of Tudor Poetry*, i (Ohio, 1960).

Hume, M.A.S. (ed.), *Calendar of Letters and State Papers relating to English Affairs, preserved principally in the Archives of Simancas, Elizabeth I*, 4 vols (London, 1892–9).

Hume, M.A.S. (trans.), *Chronicle of King Henry VIII of England: Being a Contemporary Record of Some of the Principal Events of the Reigns of Henry VIII and Edward VI* (London, 1889).

Hume, M.A.S., Tyller, R., *et al.* (eds), *Calendar of Letters, Despatches, and State Papers, relating to the Negotiations between England and Spain, preserved in the Archives at Simancas and Elsewhere, 1547–1558* (London, 1912–54).

Jordan, W.K. (ed.), *The Chronicle and Political Papers of King Edward VI* (London, 1966).

Latimer, H., *Sermons by Hugh Latimer*, ed. Corrie, G.E., i (Cambridge, 1844).

Lawson, J.A. (ed.), *The Elizabethan New Year's Gift Exchanges 1559–1603* (Oxford, 2013).

Leti, G., *Historia overo vita de Elisabetta, Regina d'Inghilterra* (Amsterdam, 1693).

Madden, F. (ed.), *The Privy Purse Expenses of Princess Mary* (London, 1831).

Manning, R.C. (ed.), 'State Papers relating to the Custody of the Princess Elizabeth at Woodstock in 1554', *Norfolk Archaeology*, 4 (1855).

Marcus, L.S., Mueller, J. and Rose, M.B. (eds), *Elizabeth I: Collected Works* (Chicago, 2000).

Mueller, J. (ed.), *Katherine Parr: Complete Works and Correspondence* (Chicago, 2011).

Mueller, J. and Scodel, J. (eds), *Elizabeth I: Translations 1544–1589* (Chicago, 2009).

Mumby, F.A., *The Girlhood of Queen Elizabeth* (Boston, 1909).

Newton, T., 'An epitaph upon the worthy and honourable lady, the Lady Knowles' (1569).

Nichols, J., *The Progresses and Public Processions of Queen Elizabeth*, i (London, 1823).

Nichols, J.G. (ed.), *The Diary of Henry Machyn: Citizen and Merchant-Taylor of London, from AD 1550 to AD 1563* (London, 1848).

Nichols, J.G. (ed.), *The Chronicle of Queen Jane and of Two Years of Queen Mary*, Camden Society, 48 (London, 1850).

Nichols, J.G. (ed.), *Chronicle of the Grey Friars of London*, Camden Society (London, 1851).

Nichols, J.G. (ed.), *The Literary Remains of King Edward VI*, 2 vols (London, 1851).

North, J. (ed.), *England's Boy King: The Diary of Edward VI 1547–1553* (Welwyn Garden City, 2005).

Orchard Halliwell, J. (ed.), *The Private Diary of John Dee*, Camden Society, XIX (London, 1842).

Orchard Halliwell, J. (ed.), *Letters of the Kings of England*, 2 vols (London, 1846).

Payne Collier, J., *The Egerton Papers: A Collection of Public and Private Documents, Chiefly Illustrative of the Times of Elizabeth and James I*, Camden Society (London, 1840).

Pollard, A.F., *Tudor Tracts 1532–1588* (New York, 1964).

Robinson, H. (ed.), *Original Letters Relative to the English Reformation*, i (Cambridge, 1846–7).

Rodriguez-Salgado, M.J. and Adams, S., 'The Count of Feria's Dispatch to Philip II of 14 November 1558', *Camden Miscellany, Camden Fourth Series*, 29 (1984).

Sander, N., *Rise and Growth of the Anglican Schism*, ed. Lewis, D. (London, 1877).

Starkey, D. (ed.), *The Inventory of King Henry VIII*, trans. Ward, P. (London, 1998).

Steuart, A.F. (ed.), *Memoirs of Sir James Melville* (London, 1929).

Stevenson, J. *et al.* (eds), *Calendar of State Papers, Foreign Series, of the Reign of Elizabeth I, 1558–1591* (London, 1863–1969).

Stow, J., *A Survey of London*, ed. Kingsford, C.L., 2 vols (Oxford, 1908).

Stow, J., *Two London Chronicles*, ed. Kingsford, C.L., Camden Miscellany (London, 1910).

Strangford, Viscount (ed.), *Household Expenses of the Princess Elizabeth During Her Residence at Hatfield, October 1, 1551 to September 30, 1552* (London, 1853).

Strype, J., *Annals of the Reformation, Ecclesiastical Memorials*, 6 vols (Oxford, 1820–40).

Turnbull, W.B., Stevenson, J., Crosby, A.J., Butler, A.J., Lomas, S.C., Hinds, A.B. and Wernham, R.B. (eds), *Calendar of State Papers, Foreign*, 23 vols (London, 1861–1950).

Tytler, P.F., *England under the Reigns of Edward VI and Mary, Illustrated in a Series of Original Letters*, 2 vols (London, 1839).

Vertot, R.A. de and Villaret, C. (eds), *Ambassades de Meisseurs de Noailles en Angleterre*, II (Paris, 1763).

Wingfield, R., 'Vitae Mariae Reginae', trans. MacCulloch, D., Camden Miscellany, XXVIII, 4th series, XXIX (London, 1984).

Wood, M.A.E., *Letters of Royal and Illustrious Ladies of Great Britain*, 3 vols (London, 1846).

Wriothesley, C., *A Chronicle of England during the Reigns of the Tudors, from AD 1485 to 1559*, ed. Hamilton, W.D., Camden Society (London, 1875, 1877).

Secondary Sources

Adamson, J. (ed.), *The Princely Courts of Europe 1500–1750* (London, 1999).

Alford, S., *Burghley: William Cecil at the Court of Elizabeth I* (London, 2011).

Archer, J.E., Goldring, E. and Knight, S. (eds), *The Progresses, Pageants, and Entertainments of Queen Elizabeth I* (Oxford, 2007).

Arnold, J., 'The "Coronation" Portrait of Queen Elizabeth I', *Burlington Magazine*, 120:908 (1978), pp. 726–39, 741.

Arnold, J., 'The "Pictur" of Elizabeth I When Princess', *Burlington Magazine*, 123:938 (1981), pp. 302–4.

Ashdown, D.M., *Tudor Cousins: Rivals for the Throne* (Stroud, 2000).

Attreed, L. and Winkler, A., 'Faith and Forgiveness: Lessons in Statecraft for Queen Mary Tudor', *Sixteenth Century Journal*, 36:4 (2005), pp. 971–89.

Auble, C., 'Bejeweled Majesty: Queen Elizabeth I, Precious Stones, and Statecraft', in Barrett-Graves, D. (ed.), *The Emblematic Queen: Extra-Literary Representations of Early Modern Queenship* (Basingstoke, 2013).

Auerbach, E., 'Portraits of Elizabeth I', *Burlington Magazine*, 95 (1953), pp. 196–205.

Baldwin Smith, L., *A Tudor Tragedy: The Life and Times of Catherine Howard* (London, 1961).

Baldwin Smith, L., 'The Last Will and Testament of Henry VIII: A Question of Perspective', *Journal of British Studies*, 2:1 (1962), pp. 14–27.

Beer, B.L., 'John Stow and Tudor Rebellions, 1549–1569', *Journal of British Studies*, 27:4 (1988), pp. 352–74.

Bernard, G.W., 'The Fall of Anne Boleyn', *English Historical Review*, 106:420 (1991), pp. 584–610.

Bernard, G.W., 'The Fall of Anne Boleyn: A Rejoinder', *English Historical Review*, 107:424 (1992), pp. 665–74.

Bernard, G.W. (ed.), *The Tudor Nobility* (Manchester, 1992).

Bernard, G.W., *Anne Boleyn: Fatal Attractions* (London, 2010).

Betteridge, T. and Lipscomb, S. (eds), *Henry VIII and the Court: Art, Politics and Performance* (Farnham, 2013).

Bolland, C. and Cooper, T., *The Real Tudors: Kings and Queens Rediscovered* (London, 2014).

Borman, T., *Elizabeth's Women: The Hidden Story of the Virgin Queen* (London, 2009).

Borman, T., *The Private Lives of the Tudors* (London, 2016).

Borman, T., *Anne Boleyn and Elizabeth I: The Mother and Daughter Who Changed History* (London, 2023).

Bradford, G., *Elizabethan Women* (New York, 1969).

Bryson, A. and Evans, M., 'Seven Rediscovered Letters of Princess Elizabeth Tudor', *Notes and Documents, Institute of Historical Research*, 90 (2017), pp. 829–58.

Bundesen, K., '"No Other Faction But My Own": Dynastic Politics and Elizabeth I's Carey Cousins', unpublished PhD thesis (University of Nottingham, 2009).

Burton, E., *The Elizabethans at Home* (London, 1958).

Butler, K., '"By Instruments her Powers Appeare": Music and Authority in the Reign of Queen Elizabeth I, *Renaissance Quarterly*, 65:2 (2012), pp. 353–84.

Carley, J.P., *The Books of King Henry VIII and His Wives* (London, 2004).

Castor, H., *Elizabeth I* (London, 2018).

Childs, J., *Henry VIII's Last Victim* (London, 2006).

Clarke, S. and Collins, L., *Gloriana: Elizabeth I and the Art of Queenship* (Cheltenham, 2022).

Colvin, H., 'Edward VI at Hunsdon House', *Burlington Magazine*, 113:817 (1971), pp. 210–11.

Cooper, T., *A Guide to Tudor and Jacobean Portraits* (London, 2008).

Cunningham, S., *Prince Arthur: The Tudor King Who Never Was* (Stroud, 2017).

Darsie, H.R., *Anna, Duchess of Cleves: The King's 'Beloved Sister'* (Stroud, 2020).

De Lisle, L., *Tudor: The Family Story* (London, 2013).

Denny, J., *Anne Boleyn* (London, 2004).

Dickens, A.G. (ed.), *The Courts of Europe: Politics, Patronage and Royalty 1400–1800* (London, 1977).

Dmitrieva, O. and Murdoch, T. (eds), *Treasures of the Royal Courts: Tudors, Stuarts and the Russian Tsars* (London, 2013).

Dodson, A., *The Royal Tombs of Great Britain: An Illustrated History* (London, 2004).

Doran, S. (ed.), *Henry VIII: Man and Monarch* (London, 2009).

Doran, S. (ed.), *Elizabeth and Mary: Royal Cousins, Rival Queens* (London, 2021).

Dowling, M., *Humanism in the Age of Henry VIII* (Beckenham, 1986).

Dowling, M. (ed.), 'William Latymer's Cronickille of Anne Bulleyne', *Camden Fourth Series*, 39 (London, 1990).

Duffy, E., *Fires of Faith: Catholic England under Mary Tudor* (New Haven and London, 2009).

Duncan, S. and Schutte, V. (eds), *The Birth of a Queen: Essays on the Quincentenary of Mary I* (Basingstoke, 2016).

Dunlop, I., *Palaces and Progresses of Elizabeth I* (London, 1962).

Earenfight, T., *Catherine of Aragon: Infanta of Spain, Queen of England* (Pennsylvania, 2021).

Ellis, R., 'The Juvenile Translations of Elizabeth Tudor', *Translation and Literature*, 18:2 (2009), pp. 157–80.

Emmerson, O. and Ridgway, C., *The Boleyns of Hever Castle* (Lucar, 2021).

Erickson, C., *Bloody Mary* (London, 1978).

Fenno Hoffman, Jr, C., 'Catherine Parr as a Woman of Letters', *Huntingdon Library Quarterly*, 23:4 (1960), pp. 349–67.

Forse, J.H., 'Advertising Status and Legitimacy: or, Why Did Henry VIII's Queens and Children Patronize Travelling Performers?', *Early Theatre*, 16:2 (2013), pp. 59–90.

Gairdner, J., 'The Age of Anne Boleyn', *English Historical Review*, 10:37 (1895), p. 104.

Gairdner, J., 'Mary and Anne Boleyn', *English Historical Review*, 8:29 (1893), pp. 53–60.

Gairdner, J. and Motta, B., 'The Draft Dispensation for Henry VIII's Marriage with Anne Boleyn', *English Historical Review*, 5:19 (1890), pp. 544–50.

Garrett, C., *The Marian Exiles* (London, 1966).

Gater, G.H. and Wheeler, E.P. (eds), 'Durham Place', in *Survey of London: Volume 18, St Martin-in-The-Fields II: the Strand* (London, 1937), pp. 84–98. *British History*

Online, http://www.british-history.ac.uk/survey-london/vol18/pt2/pp84-98 [accessed 1 August 2022].

Girouard, M., *Elizabethan Architecture: Its Rise and Fall, 1540–1640* (New Haven and London, 2009).

Goldring, E., *Robert Dudley, Earl of Leicester, and the World of Elizabethan Art* (New Haven and London, 2014).

Graham-Matheson, H., 'Elisabeth Parr's Renaissance at the Mid-Tudor Court', *Early Modern Women*, 8 (2013), pp. 289–99.

Graham-Matheson, H.J., 'All wemen in thar degree shuld to thar men subiectit be': The Controversial Court Career of Elisabeth Parr, Marchioness of Northampton, *c.* 1547–1565', unpublished PhD thesis (University College London, 2015).

Graves, J., *A Brief Memoir of the Lady Elizabeth Fitzgerald* (Dublin, 1874).

Gristwood, S., *Game of Queens: The Women Who Made Sixteenth-Century Europe* (London, 2016).

Gunn, S.J., 'A Letter of Jane, Duchess of Northumberland, in 1553', *English Historical Review*, 114:459 (1999).

Guy, J., *The Children of Henry VIII* (Oxford, 2013).

Harbison, E.H., 'French Intrigue at the Court of Queen Mary', *American Historical Review*, 45:3 (1940), pp. 533–51.

Harbison, E.H., *Rival Ambassadors at the Court of Queen Mary* (London, 1940).

Harris, B.J., 'Power, Profit, and Passion: Mary Tudor, Charles Brandon, and the Arranged Marriage in Early Tudor England', *Feminist Studies*, 15:1 (1989), pp. 59–88.

Harris, B.J., 'Women and Politics in Early Tudor England', *Historical Journal*, 33:2 (1990), pp. 259–81.

Harris, B.J., 'The View from My Lady's Chamber: New Perspectives on the Early Tudor Monarchy', *Huntingdon Library Quarterly*, 60:3 (1997), pp. 215–47.

Harrison, B.A., *The Tower of London Prisoner Book* (Leeds, 2004).

Hart, K., *The Mistresses of Henry VIII* (Stroud, 2009).

Hatfield House, *Hatfield House* (Norwich, 2007).

Hayward, M., *Dress at the Court of King Henry VIII* (Leeds, 2007).

Hibbert, C., *Elizabeth I: A Personal History of the Virgin Queen* (London, 1992).

Hoak, D.E., *The King's Council in the Reign of Edward VI* (Cambridge, 1976).

Hosington, B.M., '"How we ovght to knowe God": Princess Elizabeth's Presentation of her Calvin Translation to Katherine Parr' (Université de Montréal/University of Warwick, 2018).

Howard, M., *The Tudor Image* (London, 1995).

Howey, C.L., 'Dressing a Virgin Queen: Court Women, Dress, and Fashioning the Image of England's Queen Elizabeth I', *Early Modern Women*, 4 (2009), pp. 201–8.

Hughes, P.L. and Larkin, J.F. (eds), *Tudor Royal Proclamations*, 3 vols (London, 1964–9).

Hughey, R., *John Harington of Stepney: Tudor Gentleman* (Ohio, 1971).

Hunt, A., 'The Monarchical Republic of Mary I', *Historical Journal*, 52:3 (2009), pp. 557–72.

Hunt, A. and Whitelock, A. (eds), *Tudor Queenship: The Reigns of Mary and Elizabeth* (Basingstoke, 2010).

Hutchinson, R., *Young Henry: The Rise of Henry VIII* (London, 2011).

Impey, E. and Parnell, G., *The Tower of London: The Official Illustrated History* (London, 2000).

Ives, E., *The Life and Death of Anne Boleyn* (Oxford, 2004).

Ives, E.W., 'Faction at the Court of Henry VIII: The Fall of Anne Boleyn', *History*, 57:190 (1972), pp. 169–88.

Ives, E.W., 'The Fall of Anne Boleyn Reconsidered', *English Historical Review*, 107:424 (1992), pp. 651–64.

Ives, E.W., 'Henry VIII's Will – A Forensic Conundrum', *Historical Journal*, 35:4 (1992), pp. 779–804.

Ives, E.W., 'Henry VIII's Will: The Protectorate Provisions of 1546–7', *Historical Journal*, 37:4 (1994), pp. 901–14.

James, S., *Catherine Parr: Henry VIII's Last Love* (Stroud, 2008).

James, S.E., 'Lady Jane Grey or Queen Kateryn Parr?' *Burlington Magazine*, 138 (1996), pp. 20–4.

Jones, M.K. and Underwood, M.G., *The King's Mother: Lady Margaret Beaufort, Countess of Richmond and Derby* (Cambridge, 1992).

Jones, N., *The Birth of the Elizabethan Age: England in the 1560s* (Oxford, 1993).

Jordan, W.K., *Edward VI: The Threshold of Power* (London, 1970).

Keay, A., *The Crown Jewels: The Official Illustrated History* (London, 2012).

King, J.N., 'Queen Elizabeth I: Representations of the Virgin Queen', *Renaissance Quarterly*, 43:1 (1990), pp. 30–74.

Kirby, J.W., 'Building Works at Placentia 1532–1533', *Transactions of the Greenwich and Lewisham Antiquarian Society*, 5:1 (1957).

Lacey, R., *The Life and Times of Henry VIII* (London, 1972).

Lawson, S. (ed.), *Eltham Palace* (London, 2011).

Lerer, S., *Courtly Letters in the Age of Henry VIII: Literary Culture and the Arts of Deceit* (Cambridge, 1997).

Lipscomb, S., *The King is Dead: The Last Will and Testament of Henry VIII* (London, 2015).

Lloyd, C., *The Royal Collection* (London, 1992).

Loach, J., 'The Function of Ceremonial in the Reign of Henry VIII', *Past and Present*, 142 (1994), pp. 43–68.

Loades, D., *Two Tudor Conspiracies* (Cambridge, 1965).

Loades, D., 'The Reign of Mary Tudor: Historiography and Research', *Albion: A Quarterly Journal Concerned with British Studies*, 21:4 (1989), pp. 547–58.

Loades, D., *The Tudor Court* (Bangor, 1992).

Loades, D., *Elizabeth I: The Golden Reign of Gloriana* (London, 2003).

Loades, D., *The Six Wives of Henry VIII* (Stroud, 2010).

Loades, D., *Mary Tudor* (Stroud, 2012).

Loades, D. (ed.), *Chronicles of the Tudor Kings* (Godalming, 1996).

Lovell, M.S., *Bess of Hardwick: First Lady of Chatsworth* (London, 2005).

MacCulloch, D., *Reformation: Europe's House Divided 1490–1700* (London, 2003).

Mazzola, E., 'Something Old, Something New, Something Borrowed, Something Ermine: Elizabeth I's Coronation Robes and Mothers' Legacies in Early Modern England', *Early Modern Women*, 1 (2006), pp. 115–36.

McIntosh, J.L., *From Heads of Household to Heads of State: The Preaccession Households of Mary and Elizabeth Tudor, 1516–1558* (New York, 2009).

Mears, K., *The Crown Jewels* (London, 1986).

Mears, N., 'Court, Courtiers, and Culture in Tudor England', *Historical Journal*, 46:3 (2003), pp. 703–22.

Merton, C.I., 'The Women Who Served Queen Mary and Queen Elizabeth: Ladies, Gentlewomen and Maids of the Privy Chamber, 1553–1603', unpublished PhD thesis (University of Cambridge, 1992).

Moorhouse, G., *The Pilgrimage of Grace: The Rebellion that Shook Henry VIII's Throne* (London, 2002).

Moyle, F., *The King's Painter: The Life and Times of Hans Holbein* (London, 2021).

Norton, E., *The Temptation of Elizabeth Tudor* (London, 2015).

Norton, E., *The Lives of Tudor Women* (London, 2016).

Orme, N., *Tudor Children* (New Haven and London, 2023).

Paul, J., *The House of Dudley: A New History of Tudor England* (London, 2022).

Perry, M., *The Word of a Prince: A Life of Elizabeth I from Contemporary Documents* (Woodbridge, 1990).

Pollnitz, A., *Princely Education in Early Modern Britain* (Cambridge, 2015).

Porter, L., *Mary Tudor: The First Queen* (London, 2007).

Porter, L., *Katherine the Queen: The Remarkable Life of Katherine Parr* (London, 2010).

Porter, R., *London: A Social History* (London, 1994).

Poulton, R. and Pattison, G., *Woking Palace* (Woking, 2017).

Read, C., 'Lord Burghley's Household Accounts', *Economic History Review*, 9:2 (1956), pp. 343–8.

Reynolds, A., *In Fine Style: The Art of Tudor and Stuart Fashion* (London, 2013).

Richards, J.M., 'Mary Tudor as "Sole Quene"?: Gendering Tudor Monarchy', *Historical Journal*, 40:4 (1997), pp. 895–924.

Richards, J.M., '"To Promote a Woman to Beare Rule": Talking of Queens in Mid-Tudor England, *Sixteenth Century Journal*, 28:1 (1997), pp. 101–21.

Richardson, A., *Famous Ladies of the English Court* (London, 1899).

Richardson, R.E., *Mistress Blanche: Queen Elizabeth I's Confidante* (Eardisley, 2018).

Ridley, J., *Bloody Mary's Martyrs: The Story of England's Terror* (London, 2001).

Robinson, J.M., *The Dukes of Norfolk* (Chichester, 1995).

Rowlands, J. and Starkey, D., 'An Old Tradition Reasserted: Holbein's Portrait of Queen Anne Boleyn', *Burlington Magazine*, 125 (1983), pp. 88–92.

Rowley-Williams, J.A., 'Image and Reality: The Lives of Aristocratic Women in Early Tudor England', unpublished PhD thesis (University of Wales, 1998).

Rowse, A.L., *The England of Elizabeth* (London, 1951).

Rowse, A.L., 'The Coronation of Queen Elizabeth', *History Today*, 3:5 (1953).

Russell, G., *Young and Damned and Fair: The Life and Tragedy of Catherine Howard at the Court of Henry VIII* (London, 2017).

Scarisbrick, D., *Tudor and Jacobean Jewellery* (London, 1995).

Scarisbrick, J.J., *Henry VIII* (London, 1968).

Schutte, V., 'Royal Tudor Women as Patrons and Curators', *Early Modern Women*, 9:1 (2014), pp. 79–88.

Schutte, V., *Princesses Mary and Elizabeth Tudor and the Gift Book Exchange* (Leeds, 2021).

Schutte, V. and Hower, J.S. (eds), *Writing Mary I: History, Historiography, and Fiction* (Basingstoke, 2022).

Scott, J., *The Royal Portrait: Image and Impact* (London, 2010).

Scott, K., *St James's Palace: A History* (London, 2010).

Shulman, N., *Graven with Diamonds: The Many Lives of Thomas Wyatt* (London, 2011).

Sim, A., *Food and Feast in Tudor England* (Stroud, 2011).

Skidmore, C., *Edward VI: The Lost King of England* (London, 2007).

Soberton, S.B., *Rival Sisters: Mary and Elizabeth Tudor* (Amazon, 2019).

Soberton, S.B., *Ladies-in-Waiting: Women Who Served Anne Boleyn* (Amazon, 2022).

Somerset, A., *Elizabeth I* (London, 1991).

Starkey, D., *Elizabeth: Apprenticeship* (London, 2001).

Starkey, D., *Six Wives: The Queens of Henry VIII* (London, 2003).

Starkey, D., *Henry: Virtuous Prince* (London, 2008).

Strickland, A., *Lives of the Queens of England, from the Norman Conquest*, 12 vols (London, 1840–8).

Strickland, A., *The Life of Queen Elizabeth* (London, 1906).

Strong, R., 'The Popular Celebration of the Accession Day of Queen Elizabeth I', *Journal of the Warburg and Courtauld Institutes*, 21:1/2 (1958), pp. 86–103.

Strong, R., *Portraits of Queen Elizabeth* (Oxford, 1963).

Strong, R., *Splendour at Court: Renaissance Spectacle and Illusion* (London, 1973).

Strong, R., *The Cult of Elizabeth: Elizabethan Portraiture and Pageantry* (London, 1977).

Strong, R., *Lost Treasures of Britain* (London, 1990).

Struthers, J., *Royal Palaces of Britain* (London, 2004).

Tait, H., 'The "tablet" and the girdle-prayerbook at the Renaissance court of Henry VIII', *Jewellery Studies*, 2 (1985), pp. 29-57.

Tallis, N., *Crown of Blood: The Deadly Inheritance of Lady Jane Grey* (London, 2016).

Tallis, N., *Elizabeth's Rival: The Tumultuous Tale of Lettice Knollys, Countess of Leicester* (London, 2017).

Tallis, N., *All the Queen's Jewels, 1545–1548: Power, Majesty and Display* (Abingdon, 2023).

Taylor-Smither, L.J., 'Elizabeth I: A Pathological Profile', *Sixteenth Century Journal*, 15:1 (1984), pp. 47–72.

Thorp, R.M., 'Religion and the Wyatt Rebellion of 1554', *Church History*, 47:4 (1978), pp. 363–80.

Thurley, S., *The Royal Palaces of Tudor England: Architecture and Court Life 1460–1547* (New Haven and London, 1993).

Thurley, S., *Hampton Court: A Social and Architectural History* (New Haven and London, 2003).

Thurley, S., *Whitehall Palace: The Official Illustrated History* (London, 2008).

Van der Merwe, P., *Royal Greenwich: A History in Kings and Queens* (London, 2020).

Victoria County History, *A History of the County of Middlesex*, xii (London, 2004), pp. 108–115. Available at British History Online, https://www.britishhistory.ac.uk/vch/middx/vol12/xii.

Von Raumer, F., *The Political History of England, During the 16th, 17th and 18th Centuries*, i (London, 1837).

Walker, G., 'Rethinking the Fall of Anne Boleyn', *Historical Journal*, 45:1 (2002), pp. 1–29.

Walpole, H. (trans.), *Paul Hentzner's Travels in England During the Reign of Queen Elizabeth* (London, 1797).

Warnicke, R., 'Anne Boleyn Revisited', *Historical Journal*, 34:4 (1991), pp. 953–4.

Warnicke, R.M., 'Anne Boleyn's Childhood and Adolescence', *Historical Journal*, 28:4 (1985), pp. 939–52.

Warnicke, R.M., *The Rise and Fall of Anne Boleyn* (Cambridge, 1989).

Warnicke, R.M., 'The Fall of Anne Boleyn Revisited', *English Historical Review*, 108:428 (1993), pp. 653–65.

Warnicke, R.M., *The Marrying of Anne of Cleves: Royal Protocol in Tudor England* (Cambridge, 2000).

Warnicke, R.M., *Wicked Women of Tudor England: Queens, Aristocrats, Commoners* (New York, 2012).

Warton, T., *The Life of Sir Thomas Pope* (London, 1772).

Watkins, S., *In Public and in Private: Elizabeth I and Her World* (London, 1998).

Weir, A., *Britain's Royal Families* (London, 1989).

Weir, A., *The Six Wives of Henry VIII* (London, 1991).

Weir, A., *Children of England: The Heirs of King Henry VIII* (London, 1996).

Weir, A., *Elizabeth the Queen* (London, 1998).

Weir, A., *Henry VIII: King and Court* (London, 2001).

Weir, A., *The Lady in the Tower: The Fall of Anne Boleyn* (London, 2009).

Weir, A., *Mary Boleyn: 'The Great and Infamous Whore'* (London, 2011).

Weir, A., *Elizabeth of York: The First Tudor Queen* (London, 2013).

Weir, A., *Jane Seymour: The Haunted Queen* (London, 2018).

Westfall, S., 'The Boy Who Would Be King: Court Revels of King Edward VI, 1547–1553', *Comparative Drama*, 35:3/4 (2001/2), pp. 271–90.

Whitelock, A. and MacCulloch, D., 'Princess Mary's Household and the Succession Crisis, July 1553', *Historical Journal*, 50:2 (2007), pp. 265–87.

Wiesener, L., *The Youth of Queen Elizabeth*, 2 vols (London, 1879).

Wilkinson, J., *Henry VII's Lady Chapel in Westminster Abbey* (London, 2007).

Wilson, D., *Sweet Robin: Robert Dudley, Earl of Leicester 1533–1588* (London, 1981).

Wilson, D., *Elizabethan Society: High and Low Life 1558–1603* (London, 2014).

Wilson, V.A., *Queen Elizabeth's Maids of Honour and Ladies of the Privy Chamber* (London, 1922).

Worsley, L. and Souden, D., *Hampton Court Palace: The Official Illustrated History* (London, 2005).

ACKNOWLEDGEMENTS

'YOU CAN MAKE anything by writing', wrote C.S. Lewis. That may be true, but writing this book has reinforced my belief that you cannot do so alone. Crafting *Young Elizabeth* has taken me on an extraordinary journey, and it has been one that I would have been unable to complete without the generosity and assistance of many. First and foremost, I would like to pay tribute to my late dear friend, Christopher Warwick, who supported me with every aspect of the book from its conception to reading early chapter drafts. It saddens me deeply that he will not be able to read the final product, but I hope that he would have been proud. Thank you, Chris, for being the most selfless and kindest of friends, and for continuing to inspire me each day.

I am fortunate to have a very loyal and supportive readership, and to them I offer my heartfelt thanks for reading my books and for the endless support. I could not be more grateful, and I very much hope that you will enjoy reading *Young Elizabeth* as much as I've enjoyed writing it.

I owe the team at Michael O'Mara Books a wealth of gratitude, but most especially Mike O'Mara and Louise Dixon, who commissioned this book in the first place. Louise's patience, insights and careful editing have been invaluable, and I am also grateful to Lucy Stewardson for reading and commenting on the early drafts. Thanks to Nick Fawcett for his meticulous copyediting, and Ed Pickford for typesetting the book. Also, to Judith Palmer for her careful picture research, and to Ana Bjezancevic for designing the beautiful jacket. I'd also like to thank the publicity team for all their hard work in championing both me and the book.

My agent, Donald Winchester, deserves immense thanks for his exhaustive patience, sound advice, and for reading and commenting on parts of the book. Similarly, I owe a huge debt of gratitude to Joanne Paul and Elizabeth Norton, who both took time out of their own busy schedules to read drafts. Their feedback has, without doubt, enhanced the book's quality. The same is true of John Cooper, whose expertise I've been fortunate enough to benefit from with all my books.

Thanks are also due to Sarah Whale, archive assistant at Hatfield House, who sent me copies of the Cecil Papers, and I am also very grateful to the staff at the British Library, National Archives, and IHR who are always exceptionally helpful. Most especially, I wish to thank Karen Limper-Herz, Lead Curator of Incunabula and Sixteenth Century Printed Books at the British Library, for allowing me to see the New Testament inscribed by Elizabeth and sharing her expertise. Without doubt, this was one of the highlights of my research.

Huge thanks to my brother-in-law, Stephen Peters, for encouraging me to look at Elizabeth's health issues through another lens, and for putting me in touch with Seb Kane, whose insights into the brain were both fascinating and enlightening.

I am immensely grateful to three special friends who have been fountains of knowledge while working on the book. Kate McCaffrey, who kindly shared some of her MA research with me, and Owen Emmerson for helping me with transcriptions and being a sounding board for some of my theories. I would also like to thank Alfred Hawkins, who on more than one occasion has taken me (and Kate and Owen) behind the scenes at the Tower of London – his knowledge of the fortress is second to none. Thanks to all three for their unwavering support, love, and friendship.

There are three other special ladies who I'd also like to thank. Alison Weir, Tracy Borman, and Sarah Gristwood have all been by my side since the beginning of my writing career, and I could not be more fortunate in having them as both friends and mentors. Thanks are due to each of them for their insights, their expertise, and their generosity, all of which have been immeasurable.

I am also extremely grateful to the following friends and historians for their support, and for sharing their knowledge and research with me: Gareth Russell, Melita Thomas, Ellie Woodacre, Nikki Clarke, Valerie Schutte, and Estelle Paranque.

Likewise, my friends and family have, as always, been the most amazing champions. Thank you so much to all, and special thanks to Fiona Slater,

Brian Auld, Julian Humphrys, Mike Jones, James Peacock and Jay and Faye Taylor. Thanks to my Dad for continuing to join me on my research trips, and for driving me wherever they may lead! Thank you, Mum, for inspiring my love of Elizabeth in the first place (and for making the divine Elizabeth cake!). Finally, *Young Elizabeth* is dedicated to my husband, Matthew. I began this book on the brink of the pandemic a year before our wedding, and it is true to say that without Matt's unending patience (there was a lot of that!), faith, and love, the book would never have made it over the finish line. Matt, you are my greatest joy, love of my life, and the most inspirational person I know.